CHINA BETWEEN EMPIRES

THE NORTHERN AND SOUTHERN DYNASTIES

Mark Edward Lewis

THE BELKNAP PRESS OF
HARVARD UNIVERSITY PRESS
Cambridge, Massachusetts
London, England
2009

Library of Congress Cataloging-in-Publication Data

Lewis, Mark Edward, 1954–

China between empires : the northern and southern dynasties / Mark Edward Lewis.

p. cm.

Includes bibliographical references.

ISBN-13: 978-0-674-02605-6 (alk. paper)

ISBN-10: 0-674-02605-5 (alk. paper)

1. China—History—220-589.   I. Title.   II. Title: Northern and southern dynasties.

DS748.17.L49 2008

931'.04—dc22   2007002457

CONTENTS

Introduction   1

1   The Geography of North and South China   6

2   The Rise of the Great Families   28

3   Military Dynasticism   54

4   Urban Transformation   86

5   Rural Life   118

6   China and the Outer World   144

7   Redefining Kinship   170

8   Daoism and Buddhism   196

9   Writing   221

Conclusion   248

Dates and Dynasties   261

Pronunciation Guide   265

Notes   267

Bibliography   299

Acknowledgments   325

Index   327

MAPS

1. Landscape of Contemporary China 8

2. Provinces of Contemporary China 9

3. Major Buddhist Temples outside Cities 24

4. Three Kingdoms, ca. A.D. 250 34

5. Western Jin Dynasty, ca. A.D. 300 76

6. Sixteen Kingdoms, A.D. 330 77

7. Sixteen Kingdoms, A.D. 366 78

8. Sixteen Kingdoms, A.D. 395 80

9. Northern Wei's Unification of North China 82

10. Rebel Garrisons and the Division of North China ... 83

11. Ye in the Three Kingdoms 93

12. Luoyang under the Northern Wei 103

13. Korean Peninsula, Sixth Century 153

14. Trade Routes between China and the Western World ... 165

15. Daxingcheng (Chang'an) under the Sui 251

16. Luoyang under the Sui 253

17. Grand Canal 255

FIGURES

1. Xi Kang Seated in the Woods   50

2. Cavalry Escort   52

3. Armored Warrior on an Armored Horse   59

4. Military Horses and Grooms   60

5. Military Pack Horse with Grooms   61

6. Battle Scene   62

7. Xianbei Figurines, Civil and Military   75

8. Infantry with Swords, Shields, Bows, and Arrows   81

9. Scenes at a Rural Estate   97

10. Cai Shun's Filial Piety, Set in a Mountain Forest   99

11. Great Buddha at the Yungang Caves   104

12. Songyue Pagoda at Dengfeng   106

13. Drawing and Bird's-Eye View of the Songyue Pagoda   107

14. Drawing and Cross-Section of the Yongning Temple Pagoda   111

15. Plowing, Sowing, and Harrowing   122

16. Harrowing with Seated Driver   123

17. Walled Compound with Moat in the Countryside   132

18. Steke Depicting a Boat   157

19. Votive Stone Stupa with Trigrams and Deities   186

20. Story of Guo Ju and His Wife   191

21. Great Buddha at the Longmen Caves   209

CHINA BETWEEN EMPIRES

The Northern and Southern Dynasties

INTRODUCTION

NATIVE accounts of Chinese history prefer to focus on times of unity and military power, and as a consequence they slight the four centuries after the Han state collapsed at the hands of religious rebels and regional warlords. The relegation of this period to secondary status is reflected in the absence of any conventionally agreed upon name. Following the traditional practice of periodization by dynasties, modern Chinese scholars call this the Wei, Jin, and Northern and Southern Dynasties. Western scholars have suggested alternatives such as the Age of Disunion or the Early Medieval period—but the former assumes that Chinese unity under a single regime was the normal state of affairs, which it was not, and the latter imposes a Western template on Chinese history.

While acknowledging its limits, I have adopted a modified Chinese name—the Northern and Southern Dynasties—for two reasons. First, this designation simplifies the native terminology by recognizing that the political world during these four centuries was defined by a split between the drainage basins of China's two major rivers. During the so-called Wei period—better known as the Three Kingdoms—China was divided between one state that ruled the Yellow River valley in the North and two that partitioned the Yangzi valley in the south. The subsequent Jin period united China for only three decades, followed by a century of renewed division between the Yellow River and the Yangzi.

But a second and more important reason for preferring the rubric of "north and south" is that major changes associated with this geographical division in many ways define the historical significance of this period. The southward migration of a large percentage of the Han population,

and the cultural innovations elicited by their encounter with an unfamil-
iar landscape and distinct peoples, led to a divergence of the south from
the culture of the north. While the name "Northern and Southern Dynasties" acknowledges that fact of political division, it also suggests the
expansion and diversification of the Chinese cultural sphere during this
seminal epoch in the history of imperial China.

Five central themes of diversification are interwoven in the chapters
that follow:

(1) the geographic redefinition of China, both its internal structure
    and its relations with the outer world;
(2) the emergence of a new social elite distinguished by a novel set of
    cultural and literary practices;
(3) the appearance of a discrete, often hereditary, military popula-
    tion and new military institutions;
(4) the progressive detachment from society of an imperial govern-
    ment underpinned by this military power; and
(5) the rise of major religions no longer strictly mapped onto the
    dominant social and political groupings.

As its position on this list suggests, the single most important development in the four centuries between the Han and Tang dynasties was the
geographic redefinition of China. This had at least four aspects. First and
most significant was the full-scale colonization and settling of the Yangzi
valley to the south. While this river had been part of a broadly defined
Chinese cultural sphere since prehistoric times and part of its political
sphere since the Warring States period, it had nevertheless remained a
secondary geographic zone. At the end of the Western Han (202 B.C.–
A.D. 8), less than a quarter of the registered population lived in the Yangzi
River valley, and these people were regarded as having a distinct and
somewhat alien regional culture.[1] But under the pressure of invasion and
flood, a significant southward migration of the Chinese population began
in the Eastern Han (A.D. 25–220) and reached its full force in the early
fourth century. In their steady occupation of the south, the Han Chinese
cleared hillsides and drained marshes in order to expand their agricultural activities, displacing or absorbing native peoples in their wake.
They also began to move higher into previously unoccupied reaches of
hills and mountains. This process of filling up unoccupied land that had
been incorporated into the Chinese realm was the second major geographic change during the Northern and Southern Dynasties.

The third aspect of geographic redefinition entailed an extension of China's knowledge of the outside world and a revised understanding of its place in that larger sphere. The arrival of Buddhism brought with it regular trade with Central Asia and the Indian subcontinent. In China's worldview, Japan moved from the realm of myth to reality during this period. Although the far south remained largely alien territory, the city that evolved into modern Guangzhou (Canton) emerged as a vibrant trade center, and it brought parts of the Chinese population into contact with Southeast Asia as well as India and points west through sea trade.

A final geographic redefinition occurred within Chinese culture itself: the creation of intermediate social spaces between the household and the state. Whereas Han literature had focused on the court and the capital, subsequent centuries witnessed the rise of a literature devoted to discrete regions and local cultures. The ambit of literature came to include rural villages, mountain landscapes, and desolate frontier zones. This extension of the range and themes of literature and high culture transformed China's social elites. They developed a new set of physical spaces—the garden, the temple, the mansion salon, the country villa—in which to assemble and engage in cultural and religious activities.

The second central theme of the Northern and Southern Dynasties was the emergence of this new elite. The great Han families had distinguished themselves largely by their material wealth—especially land—their networks of social connections, and their domination of court offices. Wealth and political power were the hallmarks of status in early imperial China. Elites of the Northern and Southern Dynasties, by contrast, divided themselves more finely, through the range of cultural and literary activities they pursued. Verse composition, calligraphy, philosophical conversation, distinctive costume, and refined bearing were all cultivated and invoked to distinguish a self-defined group of genteel families from those who were merely wealthy or powerful. These status-generating activities gradually became conflated with new methods of recruiting men for official positions—methods which allowed a hereditary claim to entry-level government posts. The Northern and Southern Dynasties was also the period when elites began to define their kin groups through the composition of detailed, written genealogies.

A third major force of diversification was the rise of armies drawn primarily from hereditary military households. After the abolition of universal military service in A.D. 32, the Han court relied primarily on non-Chinese horsemen, convicts, and volunteers. The warlords who arose at the end of the Han manned their armies with servile tenants, nomadic warriors, and defeated religious rebels. In the decades and centuries that followed, these tenant soldiers and refugees formed a largely hereditary pool of soldiers, while non-Chinese horsemen formed another. These two bodies of soldiers eventually dwarfed the military power of individual landlords and lineage coalitions. From the early decades of the fifth century, the shift of military power away from elite families and back to the court allowed the reassertion of imperial authority.

The dependence of imperial power on this military base led to a fourth theme of the Northern and Southern Dynasties, the separation of imperial government from society as a whole. This process had begun during the Han empire, which created a pan-imperial culture based on a non-phonetic script and a ritually-constructed capital that transcended the ties to region and place that had marked the earlier Warring States. In the Northern and Southern Dynasties, the grounding of imperial authority in military power derived from populations outside the conventional civil order removed the court even further from the concerns of daily life. In these four centuries, for the first time in Chinese history, alien rulers invaded and occupied China and took control of its bureaucratic machinery. The fact that the Yellow River valley, the traditional heartland of the Chinese empire, was ruled by foreign emperors for essentially nine of the eighteen centuries after the fall of the Han dynasty in 220 (and three more centuries, if the Tang ruling house is considered "alien") dramatically demonstrates the degree to which the government of China became detached from its people and society.

The final major source of diversification during the Northern and Southern Dynasties consisted of religious movements not tied to established political or social units. During the Qin and Han empires, the state had practiced its cults, with the ruler as chief sacrificer or high priest and his kinsmen or officials as secondary priests. The household or lineage was defined through sacrifices to ancestors conducted by their leaders. Cults not sanctioned by the state—such as those dedicated to mountains, immortals, or animal spirits—were practiced by regional coalitions of leading families and sometimes low-level officials. But with the rise of the great millenarian rebel movements that toppled the Han, religions drew together individuals whose only social or political ties were their shared faith. Daoism and Buddhism provided new modes of social organization as well as new models of the worlds occupied by the living and the dead. These two religious institutions altered every aspect of life in China.

The cumulative impact of these inter-related changes in the north and the south, and not the mere fact of protracted division, earns these centuries a major place in Chinese history. By the time China was reunited by the Sui Dynasty in 589, it was a different world. The once-peripheral Yangzi had become the breadbasket (or rice basket) of China, a fact marked by the Sui's construction of the first Grand Canal to provision the northern capitals from the produce of southern provinces. The intellectual universe of Chinese elites—and the very language with which they articulated it—had changed as well. That elite, defining itself through both genealogy and new literary practices, was incorporated into the state order through its hereditary claims to entry-level posts. At the opposite end of the social spectrum, the hereditary status of tenants and soldiers was also written into the legal order that the Sui and Tang inherited from preceding centuries. The imperial government, underpinned by a military system derived from a modified "tribal" structure, asserted its transcendence of the mundane civil order, while Buddhism and Daoism, as well as the social spaces created by their temples and shrines, transformed both the state system of which they were now part and the kin structures in which they played a major role. This new China found itself incorporated into a greater world, where it exchanged goods and ideas with states that shared a common Buddhist religion and in some cases a common writing system. In all these ways, the neglected centuries between the Han and the Tang left a profound, permanent impression on Chinese history.

I

THE GEOGRAPHY OF
NORTH AND SOUTH CHINA

DURING the early Qin and Han empires, the most important geographical division was between the loess highlands of the upper Yellow River
and the flood plain of the lower Yellow River. The entire history of the
Han dynasty could be described in terms of the shifting balance between
these two regions (Map 1).[1] But as voluntary or forced migration moved
increasing numbers of Chinese southward over the course of the centuries, this division within the Yellow River basin progressively yielded in
importance to another—the division between the Yellow River valley and
the Yangzi River valley to the south.

The Han policy of resettling nomadic tribes inside the borders of China
in order to incorporate them into its expeditionary armies led to an increasing intermixture of Chinese with non-Chinese cultures in the Yellow
River basin. It also set off the first wave of southward flight. Several million Chinese, mostly peasants, moved south during the last century of the
Han, and this migration accelerated after the dynasty fell in A.D. 220. By
320 several million more Chinese had settled in the lower Yangzi River
valley. The Yellow River basin became the scene of constant warfare between states founded by rulers from non-Han tribes, culminating in the
sacking of the old imperial capitals of Luoyang in 311 and Chang'an in
317. Between 280 and 464, the registered population of the Yangzi valley and points south increased five-fold, largely due to migration, and
Jiangnan—the area "south of the Yangzi"—became a major center of
Chinese culture.[2]

Throughout the period of division, until China was reunited under the
Sui at the end of the sixth century, the northern half was ruled by non-

Chinese peoples whose actions pushed more of the Han population out of the Yellow River basin and toward the Yangzi. That push was complemented by the pull of regular rainfall and fertile soils in the south.[3] At reunification in 589, roughly 40 percent of the registered population of China lived in the Yangzi valley. The newly united empire sought to bind together the north and south through the creation of the greatest artificial waterway in the history of mankind, the Grand Canal, but the two regions nevertheless remained distinct. During the Tang dynasty in the seventh, eighth, and ninth centuries, the former southern frontier zone became the demographic, economic, and cultural center of China.

As late as the mid-eighth century more than half of the population still lived in the north, but by the end of the thirteenth century only about 15 percent did so. This was not due to a decline in the northern population, which increased during this period, but to a dramatic rise in the population of the south. For the second half of China's imperial history, the great geographic and cultural divide was between north and south, between the Yellow River basin and the Yangzi—a division that emerged in the four centuries between the Han and the Tang.[4]

Agriculture and Water Control

Throughout Chinese history, agriculture in the north has been carried out primarily on small-scale family farms, often no more than a few acres in size. Landlords owned only a small proportion of the available farmland, and large lineages holding vast estates were nonexistent in this part of the empire, even in late imperial China. For most of this history, north China's dry-land agriculture produced primarily wheat, millet, sorghum, and soybeans (an important supplement and a source of nitrogen for the soil), though in the eighteenth and nineteenth centuries cotton and tobacco were introduced from the Americas as commercial crops.[5] These major grains were often interplanted with vegetables. Because rainfall in the north was uneven, floods, salinization of the soil, locusts, and droughts were frequent calamities—and any one of these could reduce annual yields. Consequently, famine was a constant threat.

The southern countryside, on the other hand, was devoted primarily to growing rice as a food crop and producing silk, tea, and various oils as commercial crops. As in the north, farms were extremely small and intensively worked, but land ownership was concentrated in the hands of great lineages that rented farmland to peasant tenants. Although individ-

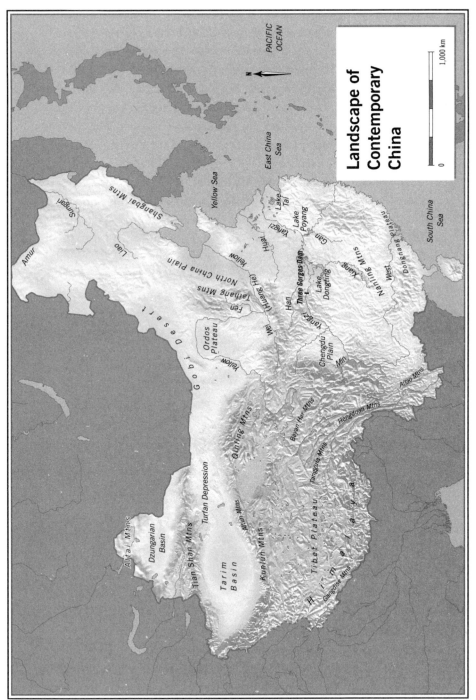

MAP I

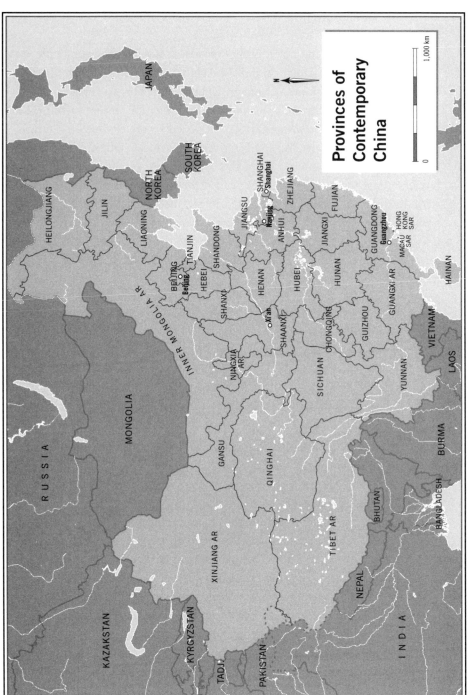

Provinces of
Contemporary
China

MAP 2

ual tenant families lived in poverty, water was abundant and regional famines were rare.

Because rainfall in the north occurs mostly in the late summer (with about 70 percent of annual rainfall in August), the Yellow River runs low during the peak months of the growing season. This pattern means that river water was virtually unavailable for irrigation during most of China's history. State-sponsored irrigation systems were confined to major tributaries such as the Wei and Fen rivers or to the Dujiangyan project in central Sichuan (Map 2). From the beginning of the early empires, farmers along the Yellow River depended for their water primarily on stone-lined wells, usually seven to ten meters deep. They were dug by groups of five or six peasants and privately owned by prosperous individual households. The difficulties of irrigation and the scarcity of rainfall in the north China plain made the conservation and economical use of water crucial.

But the greatest danger in the Yellow River basin was flooding. The river's color came from the enormous amount of silt it carried as it made its way from the central highlands to the sea. After passing the last great tributary, the river slowed, and silt was deposited on its floor, causing the river to overflow its banks and making ever-higher dikes essential. But no matter how high the dikes rose, the silting continued, so that the risk of flooding always returned, and each time more dangerously than before. According to available records, the Yellow River has burst its dikes on 1,593 occasions. In many places the race between silting and dikes raised the river above the surrounding countryside. Today, it crosses a lengthy stretch of Henan more than ten meters higher than the adjacent land. Such huge dikes could be maintained only by the imperial state. This combination of large-scale, government-built water control based on dikes with small-scale, family-built irrigation based on wells suggests an important feature of north China's political structure: a centralized imperial state apparatus erected on a small-scale peasant economy.

The torrential downpours of August also raised the subsurface water level, causing salt accumulation in the soil serious enough to reduce or even eliminate yields. Under the People's Republic, for which we have adequate records, roughly 10 percent of the north China plain has been affected in this manner each year. The worst-hit areas became marshy breeding grounds for locusts—a third major natural calamity to plague the area.

Some evidence suggests that, despite these natural disasters, farmers at the beginning of the Han may have produced five crops every four years—that is, one crop in most years, and two crops in the best years. Texts describing the most advanced techniques in use in the Yellow River basin one century later, at the end of the first century B.C., indicate that farmers often attained even higher yields. They typically raised spring crops of sorghum or millet and a winter crop of wheat. Since winter wheat was harvested in July, too late to plant another crop of millet, the wheat was usually followed by a summer-sown crop such as soybeans.[6] Under the best circumstances, this allowed for three crops in two years (that is, six crops, rather than five, in four years). Since the frost-free period ranged from six to seven months a year, a farmer had to harvest the spring crop and plant winter wheat within six weeks, before the frost set in.

The duel threat of floods and water-logging shaped the residential patterns of villages in the north. In the early imperial period, villagers followed the Paleolithic pattern of building their homes in a cluster on high ground. This contrasts with, for example, the Chengdu plain in the drainage system of the Yangzi River, where the great Dujiangyan water-control project in the second century B.C. eliminated flooding and permitted houses to be widely scattered over the countryside. The nucleated, tightly knit, inward-turning villages of north China had a higher degree of intravillage solidarity than those farther south but were less integrated with neighboring villages in market networks and in the broader regional economy.

When floods and water-logging did not endanger their crops, peasants in the north had to worry about drought. Total annual rainfall in the north China plain fluctuates greatly: a dry year may have only 12–14 percent of the rainfall of a wet one. But even in a good year, only 10–15 percent of the rainfall comes in the spring—the most important period for the millet crop. In the 1,800 years from the first empires to the early Qing, the north China plain suffered 1,078 recorded droughts, and in the first 28 years of the People's Republic there were seven major droughts. Water requirements have risen dramatically in recent times because of increased population, new industrial processes, flush toilets and washing machines in households, and increased alfalfa production for livestock, to meet the rising demand for meat. Ground water is now more than a hundred feet below the surface, making most wells no longer usable.

In contrast with the low, flat north China plain, the landscape south of the Yangzi River is dominated by mountains and hills. Southern China can be divided into three zones: the south (consisting of the Yangzi River basin), the southeast littoral or coastal region (roughly equivalent to modern Fujian province), and the southwest region (embracing the provinces of Yunnan and Guizhou). The southeast coast is very hilly but highly productive along its river valleys. This area first came under Chinese influence during the southward migrations that followed the collapse of the Han dynasty, but it remained lightly settled until well into the Tang dynasty and was not represented at the imperial court until the eighth century. With its abundance of natural harbors, it relied more on fishing and international trade (particularly important after the tenth century) than did any other region of China. The southeast coast ultimately developed strong ties with Taiwan, Japan, and Southeast Asia and thus came to play a key role in Chinese trade with the outer world. The frontier region to the southwest was settled by the Chinese only in the course of the eighteenth and nineteenth centuries, and so does not figure significantly in the history of the Northern and Southern Dynasties. This area is mountainous and covered with jungles in the lowlands and is still occupied by dozens of different tribal peoples.

South China proper consists of the basins of the Yangzi and its major tributaries: the Han, Gan, and Xiang rivers. It is divided into three macroregions: central Yangzi, lower Yangzi, and Sichuan. Southern China enjoys regular rainfall and an abundance of lakes, rivers, and streams, but because of its rough terrain, extensive agriculture was possible only in the river valleys, the delta of the lower Yangzi, and the marshy lands around the great lakes of the central Yangzi (though in later periods corn and potatoes introduced from the Americas were grown on the lower hills). Terracing of hillsides became significant only in late imperial China.

Rivalry between the lower and central Yangzi macroregions defined the political history of the southern dynasties, just as competition between Guanzhong and Guandong defined the history of the Han. The central Yangzi region encompasses two great lakes, Dongting and Poyang, and a system of lesser lakes and marshes that collect the runoff of excess rain in the spring and summer. These lakes are fed by three great tributaries: the Han River, flowing in from the northwest, which provided one of the major routes for southern migration; the Xiang River, flowing in from the south and draining modern Hunan province; and the Gan River, also flowing in from the south but farther east, and draining modern Jiangxi. Once past the Gan River and into its lower reaches (the second macroregion), the Yangzi has no other major tributaries. It slows down and spreads so wide that the opposite bank cannot be seen. The sediment it drops as it approaches the sea has built up a great delta that advances at a rate of one mile every seventy years.[7]

The Min River basin in Sichuan forms the third major macroregion of the Yangzi valley. Because of extensive irrigation works, the lowlands of this region became highly productive during the early empires, but a ring of mountains set the region apart from the rest of China.[8] The Yangzi itself left Sichuan through the celebrated Three Gorges region, which offered a dangerous passage by water. The difficulty of access meant that Sichuan seldom provided a base for a larger state, though it served as a refuge for the founder of the Shu state in the Three Kingdoms period and later as a sanctuary for the Tang emperor during the An Lushan rebellion in the middle of the eighth century. After the Han dynasty fell, Sichuan's isolation also facilitated the establishment of an independent theocratic state that played a crucial role in the history of Daoism.

The chief environmental threat in south China was not flood or drought, as in the north, but excessive rainfall, which often made the lowlands too swampy for cultivation but a fertile breeding ground for malaria. In the literature of the Han through the Tang periods (from 200 B.C. to A.D. 900), the south was depicted as a land of swamps and jungles, diseases and poisonous plants, savage animals and even more savage tattooed tribesmen. It was a place of exile, from which many disgraced officials never returned.[9] The indigenous peoples spoke languages that were unintelligible to people from the Yellow River basin, probably related to modern Thai, Vietnamese, and Khmer. In prehistoric times, those living south of the Yangzi were culturally affiliated with Southeast Asia, both continental and oceanic.[10]

As more Chinese moved south over the centuries, their drainage projects, large and small, turned expanses of lakes, ponds, and marshes into cultivated fields. Great landlords rather than the state took primary responsibility for drainage and irrigation works, and small farmers relied on their patronage. The government sometimes provided advice on water control and remitted taxes for those who were willing to settle in marshy areas, though often this policy simply subsidized the economic activities of families who were influential at court. By playing a key role in the technologies of land reclamation and agriculture, southern landlords built up more extensive estates and dominated local society to a higher degree than did great families in the north. This regional difference continued to the very end of imperial China.

As China's population shifted southward, rice became its major food crop. Although it can be grown on dry land and in the north, rice grows best in the wet paddy fields of the south. Because water is the major carrier of nutrients to the young plants, cultivation depends less on the quality of the soil than on control of the quantity and quality of the water, along with the timing of its application. Consequently, even in areas with high rainfall, the construction of elaborate irrigation systems requiring frequent maintenance and large-scale organization at the local level was essential. Water management was one of the basic functions of the great families of the south.

However, the provision of water was only one step in wet rice cultivation. In all other activities, the individual farmer's effort determined the final yield. Careful preparation of the field so that the water's depth was uniform, repeated plowings to prepare the soil, and maintenance of the banks to hold the water required constant labor. Most demanding of all was transplanting the small rice plants into the main field from seed beds. This process must take place at precisely the right time and be accomplished within a week. The correct spacing of plants—critical to the crop's yield—depended on an intimate knowledge of the characteristics of the soil. Thus, the industry and skill of the individual farmer was crucial in rice production, and a "good" peasant could increase yields several fold simply through the quality of his labor. The earliest evidence of rice transplantation dates from the end of the Han empire, and the spread of technical expertise was key to the growth of south China as a major grain-producing region.[11]

South China's productive and well-watered terrain allowed the region to benefit from the commercialization of agriculture, urbanization, long-distance bulk trade, and regional specialization—much more than in the north China plain. With its numerous lakes and rivers, supplemented by millions of miles of canals (by the mid-twentieth century there were 150,000 miles of canals in the Shanghai delta alone), south China eventually developed the finest water-based transportation network in the preindustrial world. However, this culminated well after the Northern and Southern Dynasties.

Mountains and Migration

Movement through mountain passes and along waterways facilitated the shift of population between the Yellow River and the Yangzi. There were three major migration routes—one each for the Yangzi's three macroregions. The easiest route started from the flood plain of the Yellow River and proceeded southeast across the almost imperceptible divide between the lower Yellow River and the Huai River basin in central China. There were no topographic obstacles to restrict movement other than the numerous marshes that lined the Huai. This indeterminate river had no clear channel but drained into several large marshes and lakes that waxed and waned with rainfall, following a changing course to the sea. At certain times it emptied into the Yangzi itself.

As this migration route approached the Yangzi, it split into an inverted Y, with the eastern branch leading to the mouth of the Yangzi and on to Hangzhou, while the western branch proceeded up the Yangzi to Poyang Lake. From there, refugees could travel down the Gan River and over the Meiling Pass to the Bei Jiang River and on to what is now Guangdong. Migrants following this southeast migration route tended to concentrate in the lower Yangzi region, where they provided laborers for estates and soldiers for the army around the southern capital of Jiankang (earlier Jianye; modern Nanjing).[12]

The second migration route began from either of the old Han capitals, Chang'an within the passes or Luoyang on the central plain. The route from Chang'an crossed the Qinling Mountains at Wuling Pass, a difficult climb to over 7,000 feet that traversed a plank road built along cliff walls. It proceeded down the Han to the important river-junction city of Xiangyang. There it joined with the route that started from Luoyang and crossed the Funiu Mountains. The combined route proceeded south along the Han River to the Dongting Lake region.[13] Following this itinerary, refugees from the old Han capitals concentrated in the central Yangzi region, where they provided recruits for the Western Military Command. Some continued south along the Gan River and beyond to Guangdong, or southwest along the Xiang River to Changsha and then down to what is now Vietnam.

The third and most westerly route presented the greatest difficulty and consequently was of the least historical importance. It led from Chang'an west to Baoji, then southwest over twisting mountain roads to the Min River basin in the heart of modern Sichuan. Fully one third of the 270-mile route employed trestle roads built into the sides of cliffs. A celebrated poem by the Tang poet Li Bo (Li Bai) sang of the extraordinary difficulties of following this treacherous path:

> Yi-yu-xi!! Perilous!! High!!
> The road to Shu is hard,

Harder than scaling the sky.
...

Above, lofty peaks that turn back the sun's flight,
Below, crashing waves of rivers reversed in their course.
Yellow cranes in flight still cannot cross it,
Apes hoping to get over, laboriously they climb.
How twisting the path of Mount Qingni,
Nine turns every hundred paces,
Winding through the precipitous cliffs.
A traveler there could touch the stars, gasping for breath,
Hands rubbing his chest, he sits down and sighs
When could you expect to return from this journey to the west?
The treacherous path and precipitous crags cannot be climbed.
You only see mournful birds, wailing on ancient trees.
...

The road to Shu is hard,
Harder than scaling the sky.
When people hear these words, youthful features grow old.
The linked peaks less than a foot from Heaven,
The dried pines hanging down from vertical cliff walls.
The clamor of the rapids echo through the canyons,
The rumble of the falling boulders thunder through the ravines.
The road as perilous as this,
Alas, you poor traveler from a distant land,
Why on earth have you come?[14]

The contrast between lowlands and highlands featured prominently in the history of rural China. North China's lowlands were settled well before the Warring States and early imperial periods, but the mountains were largely unexploited except for timber and an occasional mine or salt well. Early migrants to the south continued this pattern, forcing indigenous peoples to find refuge on higher ground. But with the coming of Daoism and Buddhism, monasteries and temples were established outside the cities in the hills and were provisioned from previously untilled hillsides and mountainsides. These highlands became the "kernel" of the monastery's holdings.[15]

Basing the monastic economy in the highlands had several attractions apart from avoiding conflicts with established proprietors. First, the Buddhists, like the Daoists, followed a Chinese tradition that associated spiritual activities with mountains, both as religious retreats and as the dwelling places of spirits with whom one might seek contact. Second, these marginal lands required capital inputs and organized labor for development, which the monasteries could supply and which the state and wealthy families had little interest in providing. Third, the monasteries became pioneers in new forms of industrial production, notably water-powered mills and oil presses, which required rapidly moving water— abundant on hillsides and along the upper reaches of rivers.[16]

While these developments were most prominent in the south, with its hilly landscapes in close proximity to lakes and rivers, they also took place in the north. Thus at the same time that Chinese civilization began its long southward shift, it also started to colonize hills and mountains throughout the country.

Writing the Periphery

With the shift of population southward and upward into the hills, China's rural landscapes, mountain scenes, and frontier regions all entered the realm of literary culture. This new interest of the literati contrasted strongly with the court-dominated high culture of the Qin and Han empires, which had gone to great lengths to negate the regional particularities of the old multistate world they had unified and replaced.[17] The Han literati had concentrated attention on the capital and away from the periphery through the development of world models that either denied regional cultures or reduced them to appendages of the capital.

For example, in the "nine regions/nine heavens" model (or the related "magic square" model) and the "five zones of submission" model, the world was structured as a geometric grid or a series of zones in which the level of civilization declined as one moved away from the capital. In another approach, Han literati characterized regions according to the types of exotica that moved to the center as tribute from tribes or kingdoms on the periphery. As one moved farther away from the capital, cultural variations became more pronounced, and this increasing exoticism served as a spatial marker of barbarism that delimited and defined the civilized center. Thus, Han texts spoke of northern nomads who had no cities but lived on horseback and moved with their herds; of southern Yue people who wore their hair untied and tattooed their bodies; and of peoples in the southwest who slept with their mothers and ate their eldest sons.

The negation of regional culture in these early world models was echoed in administrative geography. In Warring States administrative theory, a fixed number of households constituted a first-level unit, a fixed number of first-level units constituted a second level unit, and so on up to the level of the state. The structure was purely formal. Han administration lacked this recurring numerical character, but it was still detached, as a matter of policy, from the natural units of local society such as villages and regions. In the administrative geography of the *Book of the Han* (*Han shu*), the state consisted of a hierarchical network of cities where government offices were located. The villages where the majority of the population actually lived fell below the level of these urban centers but were undifferentiated in nomenclature from the local capital; they were effectively hidden from official view. And like the "natural" villages, the "natural" regions—which corresponded to the old Warring States and were thus considered a threat—had no place in Han administrative geography.

Like the world models and administrative systems of the Qin and Han, the literature of the early empires was also a product of the court, both sociologically and thematically. The most prestigious literary genre was the epideictic rhapsody, which developed in the Warring States as a device to seek service with kings or, later, with the emperor. Its major topics were veiled criticism of the ruler for his failure to employ the poet, and celebration of the glories of imperial hunts and capitals. These poems treated the capital as a replica of the cosmos and the definition of civilization, and reduced all regional centers to deficient versions of the central metropolis. Sima Xiangru's "Rhapsody on the Imperial Hunting Park" is a good example of this. Histories written during the Han dynasty were also centered on the ruler and his court. Finally, the Han court claimed authority to stipulate the canonical texts that were held to provide exemplary models for all writing. Court-based writing as embodied in this official canon was studied in the Grand Academy in the capital.[18]

As Han literati gradually became alienated from an imperial court dominated by eunuchs and the emperor's relatives by marriage, the capital's claims to centrality and its denial of value to regional cultures began to weaken. New local networks based on ties between teacher and student or patron and client articulated regional interests at the expense of the center. Commemorative inscriptions, shrine art, and collective biographies of worthies from specific regions testify to a new sense of local place as being fundamental to the identities of literati and artists. Commentaries on the canon that the Grand Academy had rejected were honored and elaborated in regional centers. The emphasis on regional

cultures intensified after the breakup of the Han empire into Three Kingdoms (Wei, Shu, and Wu). Many of the great families of the Northern
and Southern Dynasties made a point to preserve within their families regional variants of the canonical ritual expertise that distinguished them
from *arrivistes* and from the imperial militarists in the capital.[19]

A major literary revolution marked the fall of the Han—the full-blown
development of the lyric poem. The Cao family that rose to power in
north China and their followers produced the first significant body of
Chinese lyric verses by named authors.[20] Unlike the rhapsody, which
served to criticize, persuade, or praise the ruler, the new lyric presented
the experiences and emotional responses of the poet—the limited, frag-
mentary impressions of an individual mind that were inevitably rooted in
a sense of place.[21] The lyric's topics were no longer imperial parks, capitals, and rituals but the banquets of peers, moments of parting, or the
sight of mountains at dusk.

This new, intimate world of lyric poetry, focused on the social discourse of a small group of like-minded friends, was described in a letter
to Wu Zhi from Cao Pi (A.D. 187–226), who ruled as the first emperor of
the Wei dynasty. Following the death of several of his poet friends in a
plague, Cao Pi wrote: "In bygone days, when traveling we drove our carriages side by side, and when we halted we placed our mats together.
When were we ever apart? Whenever the wine was passed round, accompanied by the music of pipes and strings, our ears reddening in intoxica-
tion, we would lift up our eyes and chant lyrics, not even aware of our
own happiness."[22] Here are the major elements that would define the social life of the literati throughout the Northern and Southern Dynasties
and beyond: collective excursions, banquets, wine, and music.[23]

The sociable world of lyric verse also had its dark side, however. Liu
Yiqing's *New Account of the Tales of the World* (ca. 430) records a story
about the tense adversarial relationship between Cao Pi and his brother
Cao Zhi, who had earlier been a political challenger and remained a poetic rival:

Emperor Wen of Wei [Cao Pi] once ordered the Prince of Dong'e
[Cao Zhi] to compose a poem in the time of walking seven paces, or
suffer the supreme penalty. No sooner had the emperor spoken than
Cao Zhi had completed his poem.

Boil beans to make a soup;
Strain lentils for the stock.

Stalks burn beneath the pot
While beans shed tears within.
Originally from a common root,
Why such haste to burn the other?

The emperor looked deeply embarrassed.[24]

This story, like the poem that it frames, is apocryphal, steeped in a myth of political, romantic, and artistic rivalry between the Cao brothers that has shaped the reading of their lives and poems across the centuries.[25] However, like so many invented tales that become canonical, it dramatizes in its excesses a fundamental truth of the period. While the new modes of poetry were devoted to sociability, they included performances in the court that—if not usually a matter of life and death—could be crucial to a man's self-respect, his role in the world, and any hopes he might have for a successful career. Many leading poets of the period were executed for political missteps.

The links of political power and poetic activity extended down through the elite via poetic circles tied to princely courts. Other circles, formed around leading members of the great families, held themselves apart from the immediate context of politics. Biographies in the dynastic histories portray literary gatherings in city mansions (for example, the great houses along the celebrated Black Clothing Street in Jiankang) and in the country estates of the Xies, the Wangs, and other leading families. Stories of these gatherings collected in the *New Account of Tales of the World*— an anthology of the "pure conversation" of the Jiangnan elite—leave a vivid impression of the social exchanges in which notables of Jiangnan constituted themselves as a self-conscious elite.

In these "pure conversations," poetry and other literature played a crucial role.[26] Verse, along with music and calligraphy (including the famous gathering around the great calligraphers Wang Xizhi and Wang Xianzhi at the Orchid Pavilion), became the *lingua franca* with which the leading families communicated.[27] Through these artistic and social performances, they announced themselves to be the lofty figures captured by that most coveted of epithets, *fengliu* (literally "wind type"). As exemplars of *fengliu*, they held themselves above those who were merely rich or militarily powerful. This aesthetic definition of authority became so influential that the military dynasts who ruled in the south after 420 devoted themselves to artistic and literary pursuits in an attempt to match the attainments of their courtiers.

The southern landscape and its varied vegetation became subjects not just for poetry but also for scholarly study. The best-known books written about the Jiangnan countryside were *Record of Dwelling in Famous Mountains* (*Ju ming shan zhi*, written before 433) in which the celebrated poet of mountain landscapes Xie Lingyun gave detailed geographic information about scenic mountain sites, and a record by the famous Buddhist monk Huiyuan (334–416) of his own mountain journeys. A substantial literature on the exotic vegetation of the south included Xi Han's *The Appearance of Southern Grasses and Trees* (*Nan fang cao mu zhuang*, dated 304), Wan Zhen's *A Record of the Remarkable Objects of the Southern Provinces* (*Nan zhou yi wu zhi*), and Shen Ying's *A Record of the Remarkable Objects of the Waters and Soils in the Coastal Regions* (*Lin hai shui tu yi wu zhi*, ca. 275). Closely related to these works were anthologies of accounts of strange or marvelous phenomena, such as Zhang Hua's *A Treatise on Curiosities* (*Bo wu zhi*, before 300).[28] Some of these collections mixed tales of the miraculous with accounts of regional flora and fauna.

This period also provides the first evidence of the writing of "records of localities," though little of this genre survives apart from titles.[29] However, fragments preserved in encyclopedias and the examples offered by Chang Qu's local history of Sichuan, *Record of the States South of Mount Hua* (*Huayang guo zhi*, before 355), and by Li Daoyuan's compendium of local lore arranged by waterways, *Commentary to the Classic of Waterways* (*Shui jing zhu*, before 527), suggest something of the elaborate accounts of local geography, cults, and folkways that were composed in this period.[30] In contrast with the abstract administrative geographies and tribute lists in the Han, these works represent a total revalorization of peripheral regions and the countryside. Variations and eccentricities that were previously ignored or cited as proof of barbarism became objects of enthusiastic study and a form of self-definition.

Painters, Hermits, and Sacred Places

This new attention to localities also found expression in the visual arts. The emergence of landscape as a subject of painting is most closely associated with Gu Kaizhi, who in addition to being a celebrated portrait painter in the fourth century was the first named landscape painter in China. He was also a participant in the pure conversation salons, a noted wit and buffoon, and an aspiring poet who claimed to be a match for the great Xi Kang.[31] Some fragments of early writings on painting are attributed to him as well, and in the most extended of these the early Daoist master Zhang Daoling instructs his disciples on how to depict a mountain landscape:

> On the east side of the middle section, a steep cliff of cinnabar shale, partially shaded, should be made to tower in lofty darkness, with a lone pine planted on it. It is placed opposite the cliff near the Heavenly Master to form a gorge. The gorge should be extremely narrow. I would like this closeness to cause [all space] between the two walls to be remote and pure, which must help to establish it as the dwelling place of the divinities . . . To the west, a rocky torrent appears. However, as it adapts to its steep confines, I will cause it to flow down through the ridge as an underground stream that emerges after a while to the east. It descends down the gorge as a stony brook that sinks into a deep pool. The reason for its falling now to the west and now to the east is that I wish to make the painting seem natural.[32]

These passages, along with the rest of the fragment, treat the mountain scene as an object of fascination in itself, as a setting for human activities, as an expression of the lofty character of the people found there, and also as the home of wild and magical creatures such as a white tiger drinking from the stream and an auspicious phoenix dancing above the gorge. Placing a phoenix in a mountainscape was significant, because in Han art this bird stood on city gates and the roofs and walls of elite housing compounds. The magical attributes of what had been the highest forms of human habitation were here transferred to the mountains. In an anecdote retold in *New Account of Tales of the World*, Gu Kaizhi also discusses how to place people within a mountain landscape in order to depict their character.[33]

The rise of countryside excursions, with their poetry writing and landscape painting, was linked to the emergence of an aesthetic eremitism that redefined the relation of city and countryside and provided yet another means to articulate the distinctive features of locality. In the pre-Qin through the Han periods, retirement from the world as a hermit was a moral or political act—taken either because the age was decadent or because state service was fundamentally destructive and corrupting. In contrast with the sparse and formulaic Han records of these exemplars of personal integrity, during the Northern and Southern Dynasties detailed

accounts of hermits as distinct individuals with their own artistic and religious commitments appeared in profusion. Scholars collected these accounts and wrote introductions to them that gradually developed into an
elaborate discourse on eremitism.[34] Withdrawing from the human world
because of political principles was only one behavior in a spectrum that
ranged from living in mountain caves with animal companions to claiming to live as a "recluse in the court" by composing verses about mountains and affecting lofty disdain for worldly affairs.

To some degree, all elites of the southern dynasties incorporated elements of aesthetic reclusion into their lives. As gardens, villages, and
mountains replaced the hunting park and the capital as the centers of
Chinese literary geography, the countryside was brought into the city—
both in reality and in literature—and knowledge of local landscape and
regional characteristics became a requirement of elite status. Gardens,
in particular, were considered an essential setting for aesthetic eremitism, and many were built inside the southern capital at Jiankang, in its
immediate suburbs, and amid the estates in the hills of Kuaiji (modern
Shaoxing). Some painters of landscapes became specialists in garden design, and it is likely that the laying out of gardens borrowed aesthetic
standards developed in the appreciation and depiction of mountain scenery. Walking alone or with a companion in an urban or suburban garden
became, for some, the equivalent of a retreat into nature.[35]

Many Buddhist recluses (both lay practitioners and monks) and Daoists
withdrew from society for religious rather than aesthetic reasons. The supreme exemplar of the religious mountain hermit was the celebrated Tao
Hongjing, who retired to Mount Mao not far from Jiankang in 492.
There, he brewed elixirs and served as confidant and adviser to Emperor
Wu of the Liang. For his efforts he enjoyed the title of "chief minister in
the mountains" and received regular financial support from the imperial
court to pursue his scholastic and alchemical research.[36] Among the recluses who created new sacred sites open for the occasional spiritual retreat, the most famous was Huiyuan, who founded a lay Buddhist community at Mount Lu that was frequented by several notables. Huiyuan
discovered the Mount Lu site while traveling to a hermitage on another
mountain, so clearly a network of Buddhist sites on southern mountains
was in place by the end of the fourth century.[37]

Over time, Buddhism and Daoism created a new sacred geography that
paralleled and reinforced the literary and political geography of excursions, suburban gardens, and mountain estates.[38] In the Northern and

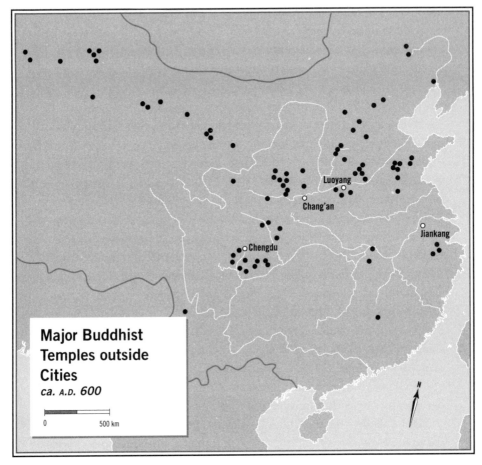

Major Buddhist Temples outside Cities
ca. A.D. 600

MAP 3

Southern Dynasties, mountains became not only retreats where the great families gathered to compose poetry and forge their elite lifestyle but also sacred ground from which leading families and dynasts drew spiritual strength. Closely linked to these sites were new scriptures, most notably the Shangqing and Lingbao Daoist revelations that emerged from the old families of Jiangnan.[39] The derivation of sacred texts from recluses— or at any rate from people outside the court—and the dependence of the court on regionally based religious authorities as sources of cosmic power again reversed the old hierarchy that favored the urban center over the rural periphery.

An even more radical geographic transformation came about with Buddhism's sacralization of India, a distant and alien land that Faxian (who made a pilgrimage there from 399 to 414) referred to as a "Middle Kingdom." Over the centuries China itself would be transformed into a sacred Buddhist land, as the new religion created an ever-expanding range of regional sacred places at the sites of Buddhist monasteries or retreats.[40] The imperial authorities attempted to bring these new belief systems within the imperial sphere by sponsoring the publication of religious canons and building great monasteries in Luoyang or Jiankang, but they could not control the newfound spiritual power emanating from sites scattered across the hills and mountains of China (Map 3). In the same way, poetry created a new cultural landscape beyond the control of the court.[41] Once a given site had been commemorated in verse or story, it took on a cultural life of its own. Later poets revived it through their own visits, or cited it as precedent and model for their personal experiences.

The north participated in all of these developments, to a degree, but one geographic feature distinctive to it was the nomadic frontier, with its stark landscapes, cruel climate, and alien customs. Although the best-known examples of "frontier" verse date from the Tang and recount experiences in military campaigns, the tradition was already taking shape under the dynasties that ruled north China between the Han and Tang empires.[42]

The Birth of Elite Regionalism

The centuries after the fall of the Han witnessed new forms of literary practice and new genres, corresponding ideals of cultural excellence and political authority, a reevaluation of village, countryside, and mountains, a new sacred landscape, and new sources of textual authority. These cumulative changes validated local and regional traditions at the expense of the monolithic claims of the imperial center and found their classic expression in the Jiangnan region in south China, where they defined the leading families.

Even the southern capital itself was drawn into this altered political geography. Although Jiankang had served briefly as the capital of Wu state immediately after the fall of the Han empire, it remained a frontier city. China's legitimate historical capitals were Chang'an and Luoyang, sanctified by the Zhou and the Han. In seeking legitimation of their new capital in this remote frontier of the Chinese world, the Jin court made two arguments. First, they cited the testimony of the celebrated Three Kingdoms political strategist Zhuge Liang, who, upon visiting Jiankang, announced that its landscape was a "coiled dragon and crouching tiger" and that this was suitable for a capital city. Second, they recounted the story of Qin Shihuang, China's first emperor, who, upon visiting the city during one of his tours of the empire, was told by a local diviner that the site of Jiankang had the "colored vapors" (*qi*) of an imperial capital. In five hundred years, the diviner concluded, an emperor would appear there.[43]

As these stories indicate, Jiankang, bereft of the classical authority of the northern capitals, turned to the marginal arts of geomancy and the reading of *qi,* and drew its sacred power entirely from the surrounding landscape. Even in the story of the First Emperor, insight into the future was attributed to a local diviner and elders, who sanctified the site in a local tradition. In one version of the story, the diviner who predicted the imperial future for Jiankang was described as a Daoist "perfected" man, a hermit from the hills who made his prophecy and then vanished.

Of course reverence for Han classicism and longing for the north did not die out in the southern dynasties. Early in the Eastern Jin, during a celebrated excursion to Xinting, Zhou Yi and his friends wept over the lost mountains and rivers of the north, and Chancellor Wang Dao swore to recover these sacred provinces for China. A generation later the great military man Huan Wen would proclaim his ambition to retake the north, only to meet with the opposition of Sun Zhuo and others who now were content with the natural beauties of the south. For military men like Huan Wen and Liu Yu, the dream of recapturing the north remained a gnawing ambition, and a necessary prelude to claiming the imperial title.

This aspiration for reconquest, and the northern expeditions that put it into effect, marked a line of tension between the military men on the one hand and the chief exemplars of the Jiangnan cultural elite on the other. The complex web of literary and religious practices that had come to define Jiangnan's distinctive elite culture was tied to local powers and traditions that had no place in the classical culture of north China. This tension also helps to explain the military weakness of the southern dynasties, where power at court was based more on the flowering of poetry and garden design than on the cultivation of military virtues. The new southern culture invented in Jiangnan was ultimately unable to secure itself against the militarized civilization of the north, and in the early Tang the families of the region would be reduced to a secondary role.

But the nurturing of the *literatus* ideal, the formation of poetic societies, the affirmation of local traditions through verse and local histories, and the cultural construction of a sacred and literary geography independent of, although not uninfluenced by, the imperial system—all of these traditions, pioneered in Jiangnan during the southern dynasties, survived as the classical forms for the articulation of elite regionalism in the later history of China.

ㄹ

THE RISE OF THE
GREAT FAMILIES

THE FALL of the Han led to what is often described as the aristocratic era of imperial China's history, in which a relatively small number of great families dominated the social and political spheres. While this description is not entirely accurate, it is true that relative imperial weakness during this period helped some families to gain disproportionate influence at court and in the countryside. Although no family was able to dominate the court for more than a few generations, some families maintained a significant degree of influence for centuries and were recognized as social elites. More important than their own fate, however, these families transformed the definition of high status in China, and in so doing they changed forever the relations between social elites and the court.

The Pursuit of Status among the Great Families

By the middle of the second century A.D., the Han upper class consisted of families of wealthy large-scale landlords who generally espoused—with greater or lesser sincerity—Confucian values and learning and considered themselves gentlemen. The individual with scholarly or literary attainments garnered prestige in his local community and might earn income as a teacher or a government official, and in some cases an appointment to the Grand Academy. However, several obstacles confronted men aspiring to these careers.

First, access to office relied on a system of recommendations, and as a result it tended to be more a function of family wealth and prestige than of ability. Writing in the late first century A.D., the scholar Wang Chong complained that people honored wealth and office rather than moral or intellectual attainments, and that wealthy families secured office for generations by recommending one another, while poor scholars were passed over. Hundreds of biographies preserved in the histories confirm that actual cases of upward social mobility were extremely rare, while important families were able to produce high officeholders for six or seven generations. Over time, as the prestige of scholarly attainments increased and as more and more would-be scholars competed with one another for a fixed number of positions, the chances for any given individual—especially one without family influence—fell even further.[1]

Another obstacle to high office was the changing nature of the court itself. The imperial system had been built around the semidivine ruler who served as the fount of all authority. Consequently, power in the Han court shifted steadily from the official bureaucracy to those individuals who immediately surrounded the person of the emperor—those who could control what he heard or saw and who could speak in his name. Emperor Wu had made a point of weakening his chief ministers by regularly changing them, while transferring the actual conduct of court business to the secretaries who attended him in his private chambers. Though formally low in rank, these secretaries supplanted the official cabinet as the primary shapers of policy, and they became what the Chinese described as an "inner court." Emperor Wu also abolished the supreme military official in the outer court and created a new supreme commander, the marshal of state, within the inner court. After Emperor Wu's death in 87, the marshal of state, Huo Guang, became regent for the young Emperor Zhao and defeated the most powerful officials in a struggle for control of the court.

The inner court ultimately came to be dominated by eunuchs and imperial affines (the emperor's relations by marriage). In the last decades of the Western Han, several eunuchs took control of many aspects of the court, while the Wang family attained power through successive marriages to emperors. These patterns continued under the Eastern Han. The first three emperors, who came to the throne as adults, were effective leaders, but thereafter the Eastern Han court was dominated, in bloody alternation, by eunuchs and imperial affines who routinely held the post of marshal of state and commanded the capital army.

The domination of the court by women and feminized men contradicted the values of scholars and the landed elite, and the court's political emasculation of the official bureaucracy threatened their power. After

A.D. 150 a series of triangular struggles among eunuchs, imperial affines, and an increasingly organized partisan movement representing the converging claims of high officials at court and the landed elite in the provinces resulted in the triumph of the eunuchs over the imperial affines, who were driven into an alliance with the partisans. This new alliance took political action through networks based on education and patronage: teachers and former students, recommenders and those they recommended, or tutors and clerks who had been in the service of great families. These networks, denounced by their opponents as "factions," engaged in an ever more savage campaign of criticism against the eunuch party and their allies, a campaign which they described as "pure critique."[2]

The pure critique movement was notable in that it provided the earliest organized form for an empire-wide elite resistance to the power of the court. Moreover, in its denunciation of the character of the eunuchs and the emperor, it established the assessment of personality as a central component of politics. This became especially important in the wake of the collapse of the Han. The movement also pushed many high literati officials, who had previously based their claims to superiority on advocacy of universal values over mere local concerns, to increasingly identify themselves with the regional interests of influential landed families. All of these late-Han developments were crucial in shaping the definition of elites that would predominate during the Northern and Southern Dynasties.

In the short term, however, the partisan pure critique movement met disaster when the eunuch party triumphed at court in 166. The death of Emperor Huan in 167 led to a brief resurgence of the anti-eunuch party, who had secured the regency, but a eunuch *coup d'état* in 168 led to the execution of the regent and the imprisonment of large numbers of the anti-eunuch party, more than a hundred of whom died in prison. A "proscription of factions" banning anti-eunuch partisans from holding office lasted until the Yellow Turban rebellion in 184.

Their decades in the political wilderness—which roughly corresponded to the reign of Emperor Ling (r. 168–189), who allied with the eunuchs—nevertheless served to strengthen the alliance of the now powerless official bureaucracy and the influential landed families. New patterns of social organization at the local level flourished, and an increasingly self-conscious elite began to describe itself as the "pure stream" and the defender of Confucian civilization against a corrupted court and a benighted ruler. By asserting their superiority over the emperor himself in this way, the elite families of the late Eastern Han progressively separated the idea of authority from the fact of wealth or office, and in so doing created an ideological basis for the later claims to authority made by the great families of the Northern and Southern Dynasties.[3]

This new self-consciousness of the elite as a distinct group manifested itself in several forms. First, its members increasingly arrogated to themselves the right to praise and blame members of society, which in theory was the sole prerogative of the ruler. Groups of county-level officials with no imperial standing joined together to set up engraved steles (upright commemorative stones) honoring local worthies for their scholarly attainments or their moral conduct. These inscriptions reveal how the local elite internalized the ideal of the Confucian gentleman in their self-image.[4] Important also were funerary shrines, exemplified by the offering shrines of Wu Liang. As the cardinal Confucian virtue of filiality assumed crucial importance in the Eastern Han, the staging of lavish funerals and the erection of elaborate mortuary shrines for continued offerings became a major mechanism for asserting one's gentlemanly qualities before one's peers. Extensive wall art in them depicted the culture-hero sages of antiquity, the great rulers of China's past, exemplars of filiality or other moral conduct, and the heaven or paradise that was the goal of the spirit of the departed. These late-Han shrines were miniature models of the universe that gave pride of place to the values and idealized self-portraits of the deceased.[5]

The compilation of private, collective biographies of worthy men from various regions in China was another sign of the new self-consciousness of landed elites. These books assessed strong and weak points and made comparisons with men from other localities with respect to scholarship and moral integrity. The biographers' concern with comparative assessments was a harbinger of the fascination with judging men's talents and characters that would figure so prominently in the centuries of political disorder following the fall of the Eastern Han.[6]

The Han Collapse and the Rise of the Three Kingdoms

The Eastern Han empire collapsed for several reasons. In the countryside, a rising population and the increasing concentration of land in the hands of powerful families led to widespread misery, social breakdown, and banditry. The capital-based army was too small and too remote for police action, even if it had not become a sinecure for the sons of wealthy families and thereby lost its military effectiveness. As for the standing armies at the frontier, after universal military service was abolished they had become private commands of the generals who recruited them and in whose service they were permanently bound. Tensions on the frontier were exacerbated by the Eastern Han policy of "using barbarians to fight barbarians," which led the court to resettle supposedly allied tribes inside China, where they continued to pillage Han villages.

As the countryside grew increasingly disordered and violent due to wandering peasant bands and nomad forces, the court lacked both the ties to local families to maintain peace and the military power to forcibly restore it. Each local community had to protect itself, which led to the creation of additional armed groups beyond imperial control. More backward areas organized their defense around the kin ties that had defined the early Chinese village. In economically prosperous regions, defense forces took the form of tenants or dependents led by their landlords. And in certain areas, notably Sichuan and Shandong, peasants led by local eminences formed militarized religious societies that promised relief from famine, the healing of diseases, and a millennium of "Great Peace" that would either reform the Han or sweep it away.

The rebellion in 184 of one of these movements, the Yellow Turbans, and the series of local uprisings that followed did not directly topple the Han dynasty, but they did reveal its bankruptcy.[7] When an informant disclosed the imminent uprising, it was discovered that local officials had known about the movement but had chosen not to expose it. Adherents of the Yellow Turbans were found even within the palace guard and among the eunuchs. When armed rebellion finally broke out in sixteen commanderies to the south, east, and northeast of the capital, the imperial forces that tried to quell it were defeated, and several princes were killed or captured. Ultimately, armies recruited and led by supporters of the anti-eunuch partisans, many of them drawing their forces from the peasants associated with the great families, put down the Yellow Turban rebellion.[8]

The generals who led the decisive victory against the Yellow Turbans just east of Luoyang were immediately removed from their posts by eunuchs whom Emperor Ling had put in command of a newly restructured capital army. However, the death of the emperor on May 15, 186, led to the appointment of a regent who secretly summoned the frontier general Dong Zhuo to the capital from the northwest and put out political feelers to the anti-eunuch faction. When the eunuchs discovered these clandestine moves, they murdered the regent, which in turn provoked junior officers of the new capital army, notably the cousins Yuan Shao and Yuan Shu, to seize Luoyang and massacre the eunuchs.

This triumph was short-lived, however. Having seized control of a court from which they had been excluded for two decades, the anti-eunuch partisans found that political power now resided not in office but in military force. Once Dong Zhuo arrived in the capital, he established himself as a military dictator, which led the officers of the armed forces that had destroyed the eunuchs to flee east to recruit new troops from their local bases. Concerned about this impending threat, Dong Zhuo took the boy emperor Xian and his court back to Dong's home base, Chang'an. His soldiers burned Luoyang to the ground.[9]

Although the last Han emperor was not formally deposed until 220, the burning of the capital and abduction of the court in 190 effectively ended the Han dynasty. The decades of warlordism leading up to the empire's short-lived reunification under the Jin dynasty in 280 was known as the Three Kingdoms (Map 4). The states of Wei, Wu, and Shu were dominated by militarists and to a lesser extent by great families based in landed estates. In some cases these two groups overlapped, but the key distinction was between those who merely wielded local influence and those who, by accumulating military forces, could act at the regional or imperial level. In the chaos of the period, the former were limited in scope and prey to marauding armies, while the latter exercised political power by amassing substantial forces from the ranks of defeated rebels, non-Chinese soldiers, and bandit gangs.[10] This divergence of military power from social authority became a defining feature of the political history of the Northern and Southern Dynasties.

The most important of the warlords during the last decades of the Han was Cao Cao, a leading militarist, poet, and institutional reformer whose policies remained influential long after his death.[11] The adopted grandson of a eunuch, he rose to prominence as one of the officers in the palace army that crushed the eunuchs and then raised forces against Dong Zhuo. After Dong Zhuo's assassination by Lü Bu on May 22, 193, his feuding subordinates allowed the young emperor and his court to return to Luoyang. When Cao Cao's more powerful rival, Yuan Shao, attempted to set up a new puppet emperor, Cao Cao escorted Emperor Xian into de facto captivity at his base in Xu. Prior to this dramatic move, Cao Cao had been only one of many military adventurers on the

MAP 4

north China plain. But with the emperor as a symbol and "restoration" as a slogan, he attracted many talented young men into his service. With their advice and administrative support, he built up his military power and defeated each of his rivals in turn. In 205 he eliminated his archrival Yuan Shao and reunited the flood plain of the Yellow River, which was still the demographic and economic heartland of China.

In his earliest days Cao Cao had relied heavily on violence and authoritarian policies that alienated much of the Han local elite. As protector of the Han court, however, he followed the advice of Xun Yu and others to act as a Han loyalist and moral exemplar. But when his position grew more secure after the defeat of Yuan Shao in 205, he began to revert to more authoritarian policies. His tendency to fiercely punish those who remonstrated against him intensified after his 208 conquest of the northern part of Jing province in the central Yangzi region. After seizing its capital town of Xiangyang in the middle reaches of the Han River, he brought into his court many literati who had been assembled by a rival warlord, Liu Biao. These writers had fled south to avoid political hazards in the north, and they filled Cao Cao's court with talented men who eschewed political or moral criticism.[12]

The conquest of Xiangyang in 208 marked the high point of Cao Cao's military ventures. His campaign continued southward to Jiangling on the Yangzi, where he assembled a large fleet to proceed downriver and complete his conquest of China. But his ships were destroyed at Red Cliff by the forces of Sun Quan, the warlord who controlled the lower Yangzi region, assisted by troops that another military adventurer, Liu Bei, had led south after the defeat of Jing province. The details of the engagement at Red Cliff—a turning point in Chinese political history—have been thoroughly occluded by early partisan accounts and later mythology.[13] Whatever actually occurred, the battle demonstrated for the first time, though far from the last, the difficulties faced by northern armies that attempted to occupy the south—not least of which were the distances that had to be covered and the necessity of fighting on water rather than land. Cao Cao's retreat north ended any hope for the rapid reunification of China.

Cao Cao's position in the north was more secure after victories over the non-Chinese Wuhuan in 207 and, four years later, over warlords who controlled the Fen River valley and the region of the old Han capital, Chang'an. The victors at Red Cliff, for their part, fell out in a struggle to secure the central Yangzi region. Liu Bei initially held a dominant position in the region, from which he expanded into southern Sichuan at the invitation of another local potentate. Sun Quan was at first unable to oppose this rising power because he had to defend against Cao Cao's armies, which had occupied the area south of the Huai River. But in 215 Sun defeated some of Liu's commanders and pushed back into Jing province, a move that was assisted by Cao Cao's victory that year over the Daoist state of Zhang Lu in Hanzhong (northern Sichuan). This success did little, however, to alter the balance of power or to check the emerging tripartite division of the old Han realm.[14]

Liu Bei's rise resumed in 219 when he won a decisive victory over Cao Cao's commander in northern Sichuan and brought the entire region under his rule. From this base he launched an offensive under his general Guan Yu down the Han River against Cao Cao's forces in Xiangyang, who suffered severe reverses. Alarmed by the rise of Liu Bei and still resentful over his loss of Jing province, Sun Quan abandoned his former ally and united with Cao Cao to defeat Liu and kill Guan Yu. Hostilities were briefly halted by the death of Cao Cao in 220. His son Cao Pi claimed the imperial title in the name of a new Wei dynasty, marking the official end of the Han. Liu Bei made a counter-claim to the same title for his state of Shu. In 222 he also attempted to revenge Sun Quan's earlier betrayal, but the campaign ended in a disastrous defeat and the loss of Jing province. Now sealed up in his Sichuan base, Liu Bei died the next year.[15] Thus, by 223 China was formally divided into three states, although Sun Quan's Wu state did not claim imperial status until 229.

Most accounts of the Three Kingdoms focus on the state of Wei, where the Sima family seized power in a *coup d'état* in 249, progressively eliminated the Caos' allies, and formally established their own Jin dynasty in 265. Chinese historians have argued that the Cao family lay outside the network of great families that emerged in the late Han, that Cao Cao initiated policies to exclude these families from his government by bringing in "new men," and that his son Cao Pi carried forward this suspicion of powerful families and added to it a suspicion of his own brothers. Cao Pi failed twice in attempts to conquer Wu state and died young in 226, but his successor Cao Rui kept the family paranoia and isolation alive.

In contrast with the self-destructive behavior of the Caos, according to this view, the Sima family established ties of marriage and political alliance with major families, cultivated the leading military men, and thus established themselves as leaders of a diffuse social elite set against the isolated, authoritarian Caos. In Marxist analyses elaborated under the People's Republic of China, this interpretation was translated into the argument that the Cao family represented the interests of small-scale "gentry" landlords, while the Sima represented the great landed families. The triumph of the latter in their coup, followed by a massacre of the family of the regent Cao Shuang and his allies, was thus the result of either the strategic and moral failings of the Caos or their inability to correctly analyze the class structure of their day.[16]

While arguments based on details of property relations and class structure in this period founder for lack of evidence, one can roughly discern the relations of the Caos to the leading families on the basis of the policies that Cao Cao introduced to secure his power. First, however, one should note that the difficulties and fate of the Cao family were not unique and thus not an expression of their specific character failings or strategic short-comings. They directly resulted from the contradictions inherent in establishing a political regime on a foundation of military power, and they were enacted with minor variants in the other two states of the period.

The political history of the last decades of the Han and of the early decades of the Three Kingdoms was defined by a split between locally powerful landed families and military men acting at the regional or imperial level. Some military men were offspring of leading families who recruited large armies, while others were adventurers without family background. But in all cases those who rose above the local level to establish statewide regimes relied on military power. Thus it is not surprising that the successors of the warlords who founded states in the 220s were unable to maintain authority.[17] Without the prestige of military success won by a charismatic strongman who carved out a realm and would become a hero of later fiction, heirs had only three ways to secure their position: by administering through the armies that had established their power, by building up a civil bureaucracy, or by relying on locally powerful families to impose order in their localities.

That the failure of the Caos was inherent in the military origins of their state can be demonstrated by the parallel evolution of Wu state.[18] The Sun family emerged as rulers of the lower Yangzi from an alliance of powerful families containing both recent northern émigrés and families that had established regional bases during the Han. The northern émigrés were all military adventurers whose family backgrounds had at best provided them with a first step in recruiting soldiers. By the 250s only the southern families remained in power. Thus the evolution of Wu was in fact a shift from a government dominated by military men to one dominated by established families. The Liu state in Sichuan followed a similar path.

In all three cases, the military power and prestige that created the state largely ended with the founder, and the attempt to establish an enduring state resulted in the shift of authority to locally powerful families. When the court was strong, it established an accommodation with the local powers, but when it became weak, the great families asserted their independence from the center. The political history of the Northern and Southern Dynasties was dominated by this tug of war between military dynasts and locally powerful families.

Character Evaluation and Claims to Office

The difficulty of translating a purely military power into a stable regime is demonstrated by recruitment practices in the Three Kingdoms and later under the reunited Jin empire. The key institution in this history is conventionally called the system of Nine Ranks and Impartial Judges (also known as Nine Rank [Method for Designating] Men to Office), and it became the basis for hereditary claims to entry-level government posts.[19] Though not formally established until the beginning of the Wei dynasty in 220, the system was initiated by Cao Cao around 208 in order to change himself from a military strongman into an imperial administrator.

Cao Cao needed to recruit talented men to staff his government, but he was contemptuous of the Han elite's moral pretensions and posturing, and of the system of recommendations that had allowed them to monopolize offices. He needed to purge staunch Han loyalists while recruiting ambitious local leaders in order to avert their resistance or rebellion. These recruited "new men" had to be fused with his original followers and with the competent Han officials who remained in his service. Adding to these difficulties, Cao Cao had to pursue these policies when much of the population, both elite and peasant, had been driven from its place of residence, so that appeals to local recommendations as practiced under the Han no longer made sense. Cao Cao devised the Nine-Rank system of appointments to deal with these problems.

Under this law, the official bureaucracy was divided into nine ranks, with rank one highest and rank nine lowest. Trusted agents of the court were appointed as impartial judges and sent to their home commanderies to recruit officials and assign ranks to them. The impartial judges themselves were selected by the minister of finance, at the recommendation of the governor of a given judge's home commandery. The judges received dossiers and recommendations from local people and then briefly met the candidates, whom they ranked in nine local grades. These grades were distinct from the rankings of offices at court, but the two were mapped onto each other, so that a given local rank led to a given level of appointment at court. Since the impartial judges were familiar with the area to which they were sent but—owing to their loyalty to the court—were motivated to avoid favoritism, the Personnel Board of the Secretariat was bound by their rankings in making entry-level court appointments.

Cao Cao decreed that men should be promoted to a higher rank solely on the basis of talent—not filial piety, nor uprightness, nor incorruptibility. As he himself made clear, this was a conscious attack on the claims for moral authority made by the late-Han elite in their resistance against the eunuchs and the court:

> Assist me in bringing to light and promoting the unorthodox and the lowly. As long as a man is talented, he should be recommended. When I obtain him, I will employ him. A man of virtue is not necessarily to be advanced in office, and a man to be advanced in office is not necessarily virtuous . . . Even if a man has some small failings, why should he be rejected? Now the empire must obtain those men among the commoners who, whether or not they possess ultimate virtue, will fight courageously and intrepidly against the enemy . . . Among those who bear disgraced names or are mocked by the world, some still, inhumane and unfilial though they may be, possess the arts of ordering a state or using troops. Let each of these who is known be recommended; let none be neglected.[20]

However, the definition and evaluation of talent was no simple matter. By the time Cao Cao began his talent search, the criteria for making such judgments had for decades been a subject of study and debate. The collective biographies of the late Han had taken as their major theme the assessment of worthy men, and out of this context emerged an entire genre devoted to judging men's abilities and characters. The earliest such texts were produced by leading participants in the pure critique movement that opposed the eunuchs.[21] The sole surviving example is Liu Shao's *Study of Human Abilities* (*Ren wu zhi*, dated 240–250), which discusses the nature of human character and abilities and the methods for detecting them. Liu Shao makes several arguments that came to typify ideas about human talents, their perception, and their use in recruitment.

First, he argues that talents and propensities are hidden and can only be discerned by men of extraordinary perception. "The principles of innate endowment are subtle and mysterious. Without the perceptiveness of the sage, who can completely penetrate them?"[22] This meant that character evaluation was as much about the judger as the judged, and from the late Han dynasty men were praised or rated in terms of their ability to judge others.[23] This talent also underpinned the self-recruitment of an elite that renewed itself from generation to generation.

Second, he insisted that although character was internal and hidden, it necessarily manifested itself in external signs, above all the face and the voice. "The signs of firmness, pliability, illumination, vitality, purity, and fixity are all visible in bodily form and facial features. They become manifest in voice and expression, and emerge in the emotions and tastes."

Third, he asserted that talents and character were fundamentally inborn and thus hereditary. "Abilities come from innate talents, which differ in their capacities and take on different responsibilities in government. Thus the ability to take full responsibility upon oneself comes from the innate talent of purest integrity. Such a person in the court will serve as chief minister, and his administration will be a government of rectitude that improves and corrects." Education could intensify innate tendencies or gifts but could not reverse or fundamentally alter them.

Fourth, he argued that hidden character and dispositions would inevitably manifest themselves in moments of change. "What is meant by watching a man's feelings at the moment of change in order to discern his constant standards? People have thick faces [a 'poker face'] and deeply hidden feelings. In order to seek them out, you must observe the true sense of their words, and minutely examine what they spontaneously approve of in their responses. Observing the true sense of their words is like hearing the beauty or ugliness of music. Examining the spontaneous approval in their responses is like seeing that which their wisdom can and cannot do. To do these two together, each is sufficient to check the other." In this he carried forward early Chinese ideas about the importance of detecting any process at its moment of origin. This idea had developed in the intellectual traditions associated with the *Canon of Change* (*Yi jing*) and the military texts, and Liu Shao made it central to the reading of human character.[24]

Liu Shao's *Study of Human Abilities* suggests how Cao Cao's program of recruiting talented men would be subverted in subsequent decades as men of lofty ancestry claimed not only hereditary access to offices but also a right to hold them by virtue of innate, inherited abilities. By the time Cao Cao's son Pi established the Wei dynasty and officially put the Nine-Rank system into effect, recruitment had already shifted away from Cao Cao's program of seeking effective military men and administrators. The first Wei ruler espoused instead an aesthetic vision of excellence that would underpin the hereditary claims of the great families in subsequent centuries.

Cao Pi wrote a book entitled *The Qualities of the Gentleman* that did not survive, but from another essay we know of his theory that character is revealed in literary writing. Thus it comes as no surprise that he made poetic composition a standard for recruitment to office. While his brother Cao Zhi did not write about the aesthetic grounds of character assessment, an anecdote portrays him displaying all of his talents in order to elicit recognition of his superior character from a visiting scholar. These talents included an astonishing hodgepodge—dancing, juggling, fencing, reciting humorous fiction, discoursing on the origins of the universe, classifying and ranking people through history down to the present day by their talents, and composing and criticizing verse. At the very end he even threw in discourses on political affairs and the military arts.[25]

Cao Pi and Cao Zhi were leaders of a lyrical poetry circle, and Pi is recognized today as the father of literary critical theory in China. The criteria by which he judged poetry were the same as those he applied to the judgment of human character and the assessment of pure conversation.[26] The second Wei emperor, Cao Rui, in his own decree on recruitment, added that those selected for office should possess "wisdom, literary distinction . . . purity, cultivation, refinement, and tranquility."[27] While the exact meaning of all these terms is not clear, the clustering of literary distinction, purity, cultivation, and refinement clearly goes well beyond the scholarship and morality demanded in the late Eastern Han, or the "talent alone" requirement of Cao Cao. Thus, within the first decades of Wei rule the skillful manipulation of language, as associated with lyric verse and pure conversation, had become the criterion for judging talent and consequently the key to government office.[28] Outsiders with military or administrative skills but none of the cultural sophistication enjoyed by offspring of established families found any hope of advancement blocked.

This pattern was reinforced when the Sima family rose to dominance in 249 and reasserted the power of China's landed families. The seventeen years between the Sima coup and the establishment of their dynasty saw a number of rebellions reportedly plotted by partisans of the Caos and retaliatory massacres carried out by the Simas. In addition to suppressing four rebellions, one of which lasted for almost a year, the Simas had to murder the Caos' boy emperor in 260 before the uprisings could be brought to an end.[29] Three years later, immediately following their conquest of the Shu-Han state in Sichuan, the Sima put down a rebellion by the victorious general Zhong Hui, who had been one of their fiercest loyalists. Thus the ability to detect character—especially the elusive trait of loyalty—became a matter of life and death.

Torn between the need to reward allies and the danger of granting them too much power, the Sima rulers modified the Nine-Rank system and allowed it to be gradually modified by others. The cumulative result allowed the great families to co-opt the system for their own benefit but also in the short term for the benefit of the Sima family. The process began sometime after 240 when Sima Yi established a new layer of grand impartial judges above the provincial level. These judges were appointed directly by the minister of finance without reference to local recommendations and were responsible for appointing the impartial judges who traveled to the commanderies. This eliminated the role of local governors in the selection process and may have been intended to strengthen the position of the imperial court. However, since commandery governors were appointed by the Secretariat, this reorganization also removed the highest bureaucrats of the court from the process of selection. And since impartial judges were now required to be of local rank two (the highest rank given to non-nobles), the actual result was that the people in the highest levels of local society defined the pool of candidates from their area.

The second step in modifying the Nine-Rank system was the Sima rulers' decision to restore hereditary titles of nobility. The recipients of these titles were members of the imperial family enfeoffed as princes, as well as leading allies from the great families who were designated as "founding" nobles. The hereditary titles given to imperial kin entitled them to honorary entry-level posts in the central bureaucracy at rank three or four, whereas the "founding" nobles—even those with a local rank of one—could receive an entry-level post no higher than rank five. Hereditary titles passed to the eldest son only. Thus the descendants of these families gained a hereditary rank, and those with the higher ranks gained a hereditary claim to an initial appointment.

More important than these exceptional hereditary titles, however, was the practice of fixing initial rank solely on the basis of a father's office at the time of his son's entry into imperial service. In the early stages, family background and individual talent had both supposedly figured in the dossiers that were gathered on candidates, but by the time the Jin reunified China in 280 it appears that the father's official rank at the time of his son's entry into office at the age of twenty had become the sole criterion for fixing the son's local rank. This principle even overrode hereditary rank—that is, the eldest son of a founding noble entered the court at a rank fixed by his father's office rather than his father's title.

The net result of these changes was to establish a qualified hereditary principle for access to office. In practice, only members of the imperial family were guaranteed rank on a hereditary basis, and these were largely honorific. For all others, access to the nine ranks in the bureaucracy was hereditary only if the father had achieved an office of rank five or above by the time his son was ready to start a career. In the Western Jin, men still wrote essays and memorials criticizing the hereditary monopoly of a small number of families at court, but such complaints disappeared in subsequent dynasties when the principle of inheriting entry-level rank was more firmly established.[30]

Special procedures were put in place to allow exceptional individuals without the necessary family background to enter the court. Local governments continued to make annual recommendations of individuals in the established Han categories of "filially pious and incorrupt" and "flourishing talent." In addition, the Jin court sometimes sent down special decrees requesting the recommendation of individuals, who were given examinations in the capital and might be appointed to a probationary position as a palace gentleman (rank eight) awaiting appointment or, in extraordinary cases, directly to office at rank six. Another avenue of admission for men from lesser families was to secure a position on the staff of a high official, often by presenting examples of literary work or demonstrating brilliance in conversation. Officials such as governors, regional inspectors, or ministers in the central court were entitled to appoint their own staff, so ambitious men of talent could try to earn their patronage and thereby enter the court as clerks. Clerks of the highest officials obtained a rank of seven, while those of lesser officials were correspondingly reduced.[31]

But these relics of earlier modes of selection did not alter the fact that by the end of the third century, heredity not only guided initial appointment to official service but also altered the very structure of government. Office holding, and the hierarchy of offices, had become more and more a matter of status and a demonstration of social rank, and less and less a marker of actual power—for several reasons.

First, the nonhereditary modes of access allowed entry only at the bottom of the hierarchy. Even after a lifetime of hard work and outstanding performance a person who began in the lowest rank could advance only to a rank of four or five, the same level as colleagues who had just arrived at court and whose sole claim to office was a lofty pedigree, not experience or skill. So limited were the prospects of those who entered by recommendation and examination that these avenues were rejected by men who had any other possibility of securing a post. By the end of the Western Jin, entrance to the court by means of recommendation and examination had become a stain on one's record that a man of birth would avoid at any cost. What had been the high road to office in the Han—talent and character—had become a means of recruiting desperate members of undistinguished families for inconspicuous clerical careers.[32]

Second, the whole panoply of offices was increasingly divided into those that were "pure" and therefore suitable for men of high birth and those that were "sullied." In addition, some offices were substantive, entailing real responsibilities, and others were insignificant.[33] Some posts—such as those close to the emperor or crown prince, or those in the Personnel Department—were both pure and substantive. Others, such as appointments to the Imperial Library, were pure but insignificant. Some, such as censor, were sullied by the nature of the work but highly substantive. Finally, some posts were both sullied and insignificant. For the established families, among whom "purity" was the hallmark of their character and conversation, only pure offices would do. The issue of whether those offices carried substantive authority was secondary.

Consequently, while older families held most of the nominally high offices as signs of their status, no family remained truly powerful at court for more than a few generations. Key bureaucratic posts could be held by "new men" with no base of independent power—men who were dependent on the ruler and thus more apt to do his bidding. The focus among men of breeding on the status of offices even led them to eschew career moves that would have augmented their political power. This tendency—along with the fact that hereditary claims applied only to entry-level rank, that subsequently improving one's position still depended on performance, and that only the top rungs guaranteed one's offspring a good start in life—limited the development of anything that could truly be called an aristocracy, that is, a hereditary class that dominated or monopolized political power.

Pure Conversation and Eremitism among Elites

While a hereditary claim to initial office was fundamental to the growing status of certain families even though their actual political power was constrained, the emerging elite did not confine their ambitions to the political realm. This is perhaps the most significant change in the centuries between the Han and the Tang, and it figured in every aspect of life: the city, the countryside, family, religion, and the intellectual sphere. The Northern and Southern Dynasties witnessed a proliferation of new social spaces and of groups acting in those spaces—new "intermediate" organizations and activities that lay between the family and the state. Although these developments were not limited to established great families, nor even to a more broadly defined elite, such people were the primary actors for the simple reason that they had the time and self-confidence to cultivate new roles. Consequently, novel activities, rather than conservatism, came to define elite membership. Although it sounds paradoxical, elite status was defined by a hereditary claim to entry into state service and, simultaneously, by the refusal of such service in order to cultivate a life outside the state bureaucracy.

This contradicts a Western stereotype of China that still informs much scholarship: the Hegelian notion that the Chinese state "swallowed civil society" so that government service was the only career that was truly honored. While recent scholarship has increasingly entertained the idea that forms of civil society developed in late imperial China (that is, from the establishment of the Song dynasty in the eleventh century), there has been no fundamental challenge to the cliché that in earlier periods the state was all-encompassing. Even in the study of later periods it continues to pervade much argument without being explicitly articulated.[34] Consequently, both Chinese and Western scholars often treat the emergence of a limited nonstate "public" realm not as a positive or even an interesting development but as proof of decay or corruption. The most extreme expression of this tendency characterized the intellectual history of third-century China as divided between "nihilistic revolt" and "intellectual escapism," but other charges of decadence, escapism, and bad faith on the part of the elite of the period abound.[35]

While nonstate spaces figure throughout this book, here we will examine two of the most important ones that defined the new elite: conversation and eremitism. The linked hierarchies of the Nine-Rank system tied advancement at court to position in a local society integrated under its leading families, and the connection between the two was "pure conversation."[36] The pivotal importance of conversation in the Nine-Rank system lay in its use as a tool for judging character, as demonstrated in the *Study of Human Abilities*. An early synoptic chapter, "The Structural Principles of Innate Talents," inventories types of human talent, each exemplified by its manifestations in conversation and debate. In the later chapter "Meeting and Recognizing," Liu Shao argues: "A single morning would suffice to recognize one aspect of a man, but to fully examine every aspect you will need three days. Why do I say three days are necessary? A man who would be crucial to the state has three innate talents, so without three days of conversation you cannot fully know him. One day you will talk about morality, one day about legal institutions, and one day about policies and strategies. Only after this can you fully know his talents and recommend him without doubts."[37] Liu Shao's link of conversation with recommendation figured in actual practice in his own day (ca. 190–248), as shown in Xiahou Hui's recommendation of Liu for office, "I have heard his pure conversation and thus learned his sincere opinions."

The phrase "pure conversation" (qing tan) alludes back to the late Han elite who emerged as a politically self-conscious group in the partisan struggles against the eunuch-dominated court. The political discourse of this group, called "pure critique" (qing yi), focused on the assessment of character through conversation; leaders of this movement, especially Guo Tai, were celebrated for their skills in this area. Thus the late Han elite had already fused conversation, character evaluation, and claims to office. At the end of the Han and in the early decades of the Wei the terms qing yi and qing tan were interchangeable, and even in later centuries when the range of the latter term had broadened, it still occasionally retained a narrower meaning of "character evaluation."[38] Thus both theory and usage show that the emphasis on conversation among the Chinese elite emerged in association with new patterns of political action and recruitment for office.

From the beginning, however, conversation figured as prominently in elite social discourse as in political usage. The clearest demonstration of this is the New Account of Tales of the World (Shishuo xinyu). This work, compiled in the first half of the fifth century under the imperial prince Liu Yiqing, contains anecdotes about 626 individuals, virtually all attested in historical sources, from the leaders of the late Han partisan movement to the poet Xie Lingyun (d. 433). Best described as fictionalized history, it is devoted largely to stories of conversations and character assessments that take place at banquets, on excursions, and in country villas—the new social spaces of a local society that was as important as the court in defining elite membership and social rank.

Anecdotes in the New Account reveal several basic points about elite families in the post-Han period. First, literary style and personal bearing were central to elite membership. In many of the stories, a short *bon mot* or witty observation based on puns or recondite allusions gives the speaker a reputation for brilliance. Indeed, a single phrase of a few words is sometimes enough to attain social celebrity or political office. Second, character assessment is the predominant theme of the book, and the ability to evaluate the character of others was taken as a key aspect of one's own character. The sort of assessment that had been primarily political at the end of the Han had evolved into a wide-ranging analysis of human nature in which every aspect of elite life was framed in the matrix of social conversation and debate.[39]

Third, and most important, character assessment in the *New Account* is primarily a form of competition. At the simplest level, many anecdotes compare two or more individuals, asserting the superiority of one or the other. Indeed, whole chapters of the book are devoted to "appreciation and praise" or "classification according to excellence." Other anecdotes dramatize competition in the form of brief exchanges of dialogue: "When Huan Wen was young, he and Yin Hao were of equal reputation, and they constantly felt a spirit of mutual rivalry. Huan once asked Yin, 'How do you compare with me?' Yin replied, 'I have been keeping company with myself a long time; I would rather just be me.'"[40] Such anecdotes show how members of the Wei-Jin elite fashioned themselves through a constant process of identification and differentiation, in which men who were potentially alike or on the same level differentiated themselves through competitive comparisons. In other anecdotes, members of the elite stage debates or competitive expostulations on a chosen theme, declaring the most eloquent as victor.[41]

Sometimes this social competition turned savage:

Whenever Shi Chong invited guests to a banquet, he always had beautiful women serve the wine. If a guest failed to drain his cup, Shi would have a servant decapitate the woman who served him. Once Chancellor Wang Dao and his cousin Generalissimo Wang Dun visited Shi Chong. The chancellor was not much of a drinker, but he forced himself to drain every toast until he was dead drunk. However, each time it came to the generalissimo he deliberately refused to drink in order to observe what happened. Even after three women had been beheaded his expression remained unchanged and he still refused to drink. When the chancellor chided him, he said, "If he wants to kill people from his own household, what is that to you?"[42]

This gruesome potlatch is a test of wills in which the two men struggle to demonstrate who truly possesses the ultimate virtue of "cultivated tolerance," a refined detachment and impassivity in the face of provocation. But here cultivated tolerance has been pushed to such a degree that it threatens the human community.[43]

At the highest level, the entire *New Account* can be read as a competitive struggle for glory and mastery that climaxes in the triumph of its "hero," Xie An, over his militarist counterpart, Huan Wen. Xie An is celebrated in anecdote after anecdote as the great exemplar of cultivated tolerance, the supreme expositor of verse and philosophy, and the possessor of a charismatic, inner power that ultimately vanquishes his archrival.

> Huan Wen held a feast and concealed armed men on the premises. He invited many gentlemen of the court, with the intention of killing Xie and Wang Tanzhi. Wang was fearful and asked Xie, "What can we do?" Xie, with no change of expression, said to Wang, "The survival of the Jin dynasty depends upon our conduct now." The two of them then entered together. Wang's fear grew ever more apparent on his face, while Xie's cultivated tolerance made him ever calmer. Going up the stairs to his seat, he began to chant in the Luoyang manner a poem by Xi Kang: "Flowing, flowing mighty streams." Huan was intimidated by his calm and distant manner, and hastily dismissed the soldiers. Hitherto Xie and Wang had been of equal reputation. It was only after this that they were distinguished as superior and inferior.[44]

This tale, dramatizing the victory of the hero of the *New Account* over his chief rival, also demonstrates his superiority to his friend Wang Tanzhi. While pure conversation was the defining mode of sociability of the Wei-Jin elite, it was a form of social exchange that denied the possibility of equality. Like the state, the elite used conversation above all for ranking.

The first evidence of an elite society defined by conversation comes from the final decade of Wei power, which ended with the Sima coup of 249. The regent Cao Shuang had gathered at his court a group of brilliant men who excelled in conversation. They devoted their discourse to "Dark Studies," the revived use of the *Classic of the Way and Its Power* (*Dao de jing*), the *Master Zhuang* (*Zhuangzi*), and the *Canon of Change* to ground political or social thought in cosmic philosophy. These men, several of whom became celebrated in the history of Chinese thought, included He Yan, Wang Bi, Xiahou Xuan, Xun Can, Pei Hui, and Zhong Hui. While their character and activities are radically distorted by the pro-Sima bias of our records, it is clear that as talented conversationalists they secured high posts at court and became the center of social circles including not only Cao Shuang and his allies but even members of the Sima family.[45]

After the massacre of 249 and other purges of Cao supporters, the practices of public conversation and Dark Studies temporarily fell into abeyance. This led to the emergence of new forms of eremitism. Confronting the dangers of the court, many men asserted the possibility, and even superiority, of a life outside of political service. However, the places of retreat were no longer the "cliffs and caves" of Han hermits but rather mansions, villas, or gardens. Men gained social prestige by refusing office and staying on their estates, or taking up service and then withdrawing, or claiming an air of lofty detachment while remaining in office.[46] This vogue for eremitism shaped career patterns, social life, political activity, and writing. Indeed, a new literary genre developed around the theme of declining service.[47]

Most important, however, was the role that it played in redefining the social order. From the late Warring States through the Han, Chinese scholars and political actors had defined the career options of the "man of service" (*shi*) as a choice between state service and withdrawal from the public realm. However, in the eremitism of the third and fourth centuries, the elite sanctioned, and even celebrated, new forms of public life outside the state sphere. In praising their marginalization or even refusal of state service, members of the great families justified independence from the court on the basis of their inherent nobility.

The emergence of eremitism after the Sima coup is identified with the so-called Seven Worthies of the Bamboo Grove—Xi Kang, Ruan Ji, Xiang Xiu, Liu Ling, Shan Tao, Ruan Xian, and Wang Rong.[48] The first two were celebrated poets, while the rest are little known. The men were not linked as a group in life, but shortly after their deaths they became the mythic prototype for poetry circles, as well as emblems of the life of cultivated nonconformity and withdrawal from society. Depicted as devoting themselves to a life outside the confines of the city and its conventional morality, a life devoted to friendship, poetry, music, drinking, and drugs, they became the model of elite reclusion, a model emulated not only by elite families but even by members of the imperial ruling houses (Fig. 1).

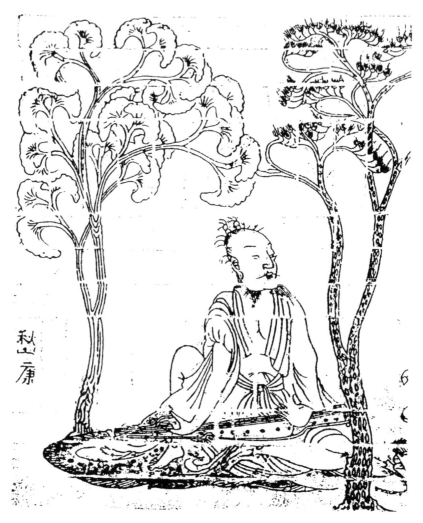

Fig. 1   Drawing of Xi Kang seated in the woods, playing a lute (*qin*), from a brick mural of the Seven Worthies of the Bamboo Grove. Xishanqiao, Nanjing, late fourth to early fifth century.

Once the Cao regime was supplanted in 265 and China was reunited under the Jin dynasty in 280, the dangers of politics receded. Decades of relative peace and the increasing security of the great families' position under the Jin government facilitated a revival of public conversation and the reappearance of Dark Studies as an intellectual fashion. Although the succession of a feeble-minded heir in 290 led to a brief and bloody battle between the family of the new emperor's mother and that of his consort, the decisive victory of the latter in 291 restored political order. Indeed, the head of the consort's family, Jia Mi, became the center of a literary group known as the Twenty-Four Friends. They ushered in a poetic renaissance, featuring such major figures as Zuo Si, Pan Yue, Lu Ji, his younger brother Lu Yun, and the early literary critic Zhi Yu.[49]

The Golden Age of the Great Families

In 300 the epoch of peace abruptly ended in what came to be called the Rebellions of the Eight Princes. An imperial prince who had been an ally of the empress used his position as commander of the imperial guard to massacre the empress's family and seize control of the court. This aroused the opposition of other princes, who had been appointed local military governors in an attempt to secure the Sima family's position. During the next decade one prince after another rose to dominance, only to be destroyed in turn by a coalition of rivals.[50] This process discredited the court and devolved into warlordism, destroying the military resources of those committed to the Jin regime.

The end of peace brought into play a new group of actors, the nomads who had been resettled in China since the Eastern Han. Warring princes increasingly availed themselves of alliances with the chiefs of these tribes, who soon developed their own ambitions (Fig. 2). A coalition of tribesmen formed around a sinicized Xiongnu chieftain, Liu Yuan, who claimed descent from the Han ruling house and in 304 declared himself king of Han. In 311 he sacked the eastern capital, Luoyang; by 316 he had occupied the north China plain; and in 317 he captured the western capital, Chang'an. The Jin court fled south and established a new capital at Jiankang, initiating a centuries-long division between north and south. No Chinese ruler controlled the Yellow River basin until 581, and China was not reunited until 589.

The southward flight of the Jin court ushered in the golden age of the great families, but not the same families as before. Probably more than a million people fled south with the Jin. The earlier émigré families in the south (the Gu, Lu, Zhu, and Zhang families), who had grown rich and powerful under the Wu state, were hostile to the newcomers, but an accommodation was reached. Under the leadership of Wang Dao, the new arrivals from the north set up a puppet Sima court at Jiankang, wooing the southerners into a tenuous alliance through gifts of honors and appointments. The northern families regained their privileges and received

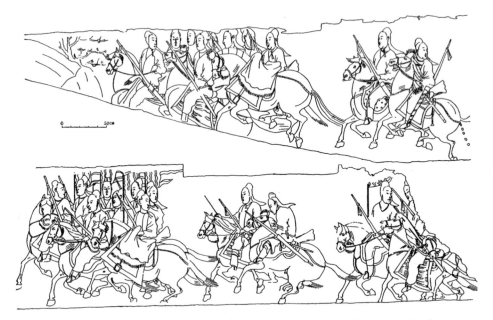

Fig. 2   Drawing of a cavalry escort, from a passageway mural in the tomb of
Lou Rui. Taiyuan, Shanxi, 570.

court recognition for the estates they carved out to replace their lost lands
in the Yellow River basin.[51] Some newcomers secured their social position by marrying into older families.

With a powerless imperial line, this new southern dynasty, the Eastern
Jin, was dominated for almost a century by several newly risen families
who developed rich estates worked by serfs in the area of Jiankang. Rival
ministers, supported by their own and allied families, fought to secure influence at court and thereby control the patronage and prestige that only
the court could bestow. They constantly maneuvered to outwit their opponents and attain political power, or perhaps the throne itself. The only
threat to their ascendancy came from other newly risen families with
strong military proclivities who had settled in the central Yangzi region
and built up strong armies composed of refugees.

In this world of deadly rivalry for prestige that could be converted into
the wealth and power of court appointments, the aesthetic definition of
status that had developed under the Wei took on new importance. Com-
peting with the established southern families and military *arrivistes*, the
northern émigrés adopted the badges of pure conversation, poetry, and
music as the definition of true nobility, wrapping themselves in a refined

style of philosophical quietude, nominal eremitism, and literary attainments that set them apart from the vulgarity of mere money or force. This vision of elitism based on style informs the anecdotes of the *New Account of Tales of the World,* with its emphasis on comparing and judging people for their literary graces, linguistic skills, philosophical balance, and affected withdrawal into nature.

While the great families of the south battled for prestige and patronage at court, a different form of elite survived in the north. Throughout the fourth century both Guanzhong and the north China plain suffered wars between barbarian states that rose and fell with confusing rapidity. Although the proto-Tibetan ruler Fu Jian briefly united the Yellow River basin, the disastrous failure of his southern expedition in 383 led to renewed fragmentation that ended some sixty years later with reunification under the Northern Wei state founded by the Tuoba (Tabgatch) tribe.

The powerful families in north China during this period differed from their peers in the south. Largely excluded from the courts of alien chieftains, they preserved themselves as leaders in their localities, maintaining Confucian values and literary traditions while also directing the communal self-defense forces that were essential in the north. They thereby preserved greater family unity and, perhaps, moral seriousness than the southern elite, but they lacked the court life, poetic circles, and cultivated airs of those who had followed the court south. Only with the Northern Wei reunification in the early fifth century would the families of the north again have an occasion to pursue office at court and a life of literary refinement in the capital.[52]

3

MILITARY DYNASTICISM

THE FOURTH century was the nadir of imperial power in China. In the north, militarized villages and powerful families clung to their bases, while a succession of short-lived, non-Chinese dynasties wielded limited authority over certain regions. In the south, an impotent court was the arena of a struggle for power and honor among wealthy aristocrats who carved out estates in the vicinity of the capital or in the central Yangzi valley. But unlike the European world at the fall of the Roman empire, transitory barbarian kingdoms were not followed by a general collapse into the militarized local powers of feudalism.

There were at least two reasons for this difference. First, the most eminent families remained committed to the empire as a source of wealth and status that distinguished them from thuggish military men, greedy merchants, and boorish landlords. Second, the early decades of the fifth century were a turning point when wielders of substantial independent military power established dynasties in both the north and the south. Through the control of armies that dwarfed the forces of local magnates, the military dynasts revived the emperor's power and achieved a local demilitarization that significantly weakened the great families. Although both the northern and the southern dynasties failed to transform armies into a foundation for a stable polity, they reversed the trend of devolving power. And the last of them was able, through force of arms, to reunite China at the end of the sixth century.

Origins of Military Dynasticism

Two decades of civil war between the Yellow Turban uprising in 184 and Cao Cao's rise to supremacy had provoked large-scale peasant flight.

Consequently, substantial tracts of land in the fertile flood plain of the Yellow River and Guanzhong were abandoned, and large numbers of peasants were homeless. Seeking to transcend the private bases of his own power, Cao Cao seized this land, along with tools and flocks of defeated Yellow Turbans, and distributed them to his armies and to peasant refugees who would pay a percentage of their crops in taxes and, in some cases, provide military service. In addition to providing income, these new colonies kept peasants out of the hands of warlord rivals.[1]

The first colonies, peopled by captured Yellow Turbans, were established in 196 in the vicinity of Cao Cao's headquarters. They followed the pattern of frontier military colonies under the Han but were now spread across the lower Yellow River basin. Another precedent was the use of state lands by Han local officials to defray government expenses. Colonies were divided into military and agricultural: the latter provided only taxes, while the former provided military service and a share of provisions for troops. The rate of taxation varied from 40 to 60 percent, depending on whether peasants provided their own oxen or relied on oxen loaned by the state.

Inhabitants of the two types of colonies were listed on separate population registers, and they were legally tied to their place of residence. Bound to service for life, soldiers could marry only into other families on the military registers, and they had to provide a son or other relative to inherit their position.[2] Consequently, inhabitants of military colonies (which the majority of Wei soldiers were) became a hereditary service group in which sons succeeded fathers. This shift toward a hereditary army was reinforced by the prevalent idea in the late Han that talents and characters were fixed at birth and thus crucial in determining a man's role. The hereditary army was a mirror image of the increasingly hereditary political elite.

Indeed, in establishing colonies with hereditary tenants and soldiers, Cao Cao followed the pattern set by powerful families. The Wei ruling house became the largest landlord, with its state-owned colonies corresponding to the great families' estates, and the colonies' tenants and soldiers serving the same function as estate dependents. These Wei innovations—a hereditary soldiery and substantial state-owned lands worked by tax-paying tenants—were the pillars of military dynasticism in the Northern and Southern Dynasties. All subsequent regimes of the period relied on some form of these institutions to maintain their power against armed local magnates.

After the Han collapse, many communities—usually led by a major local family—withdrew into hills or wastelands where they constructed forts for protection from marauders. Some communities also moved south in the third and fourth centuries and set up forts in the hills above the Yangzi River.[3] While these armed groups could not act at the regional or imperial level, they shaped the actions of the warlords and dynasts who could. In challenging the court's control of the countryside, they provoked attacks from any dynast seeking to expand beyond the immediate vicinity of the capital. At the same time, they included experienced fighters who could be recruited into state armies, and the forts' chieftains developed military skills that made them good candidates to be officers or commanders of the court's armies. For ambitious and energetic rulers, these forts provided a "free" version of a military colony.

While the Wei dynasty in the north used military colonies to restore imperial authority, the Wu state in the lower Yangzi pioneered another variant of military dynasticism. In the Eastern Han the appointment of generals to standing commands had forged strong ties of dependence between soldiers and their commanders. The Wu state was founded by military adventurers of this type, whose soldiers, as in the north, developed into a hereditary class bound to their generals by ties of obedience similar to serfdom. The generals were likewise bound by loyalty to their commander-in-chief, Sun Quan. Once the Wu dynasty was established at Jiankang, it incorporated the armed lineages of the Yangzi valley and recognized their private armies as armies of the state. Lineage heads received titles as generals and officials at court, and, unlike the north, a general's son inherited his troops upon the father's death.

The émigré generals received fiefs in the form of tax income from specified areas, where they became de facto rulers. Their soldiers were employed as labor teams to clear forests, drain marshes, and do all the work necessary to open up the southern wilderness to agriculture. Lands cleared by armies were then converted into military colonies like those in the north, and in times of peace the soldiers provided for their own sustenance. A supplemental pool of laborers and soldiers came from indigenous inhabitants, the "mountain Yue" who were impressed into the service of their conquerors.[4] This opening of the lower Yangzi basin through military colonization and settlement by powerful families concentrated land ownership to a much greater degree than in the north, where numerous peasants maintained small farms outside the control of the great families. In the Yangzi valley, there were only great estates.

After the Sima coup in 249, military colonies declined in the north. To cultivate the support of established families that had felt threatened by

the Cao regime, the new Jin dynasty rulers allowed their allies to disman-
tle the agricultural colonies and claim the land and labor as their own:
"The Wei house gave their nobles and officials 'ox-renting client households' [in agricultural colonies], with the number of households in ratio
to their ranks. From that time on peasant households that dreaded state
service were happy to be awarded to officials. Honored and powerful
households were able to mobilize hundreds of workers."[5]

These households, which had paid a tax/rent to the state in lieu of labor service, now transferred their payments to leading families while re-
taining the privilege of not providing service to the state. Thus, an institution that was intended to strengthen the state was co-opted by the great
families. However, this was not a simple privatization. Instead, families
that were themselves tied to the state through receiving a title or office legally obtained tenants who provided service and payment only to their
new lord. In 264, a decree abolished the agricultural and military colonies but left in place the practice of awarding tenants and, later, land to
privileged families.

The south followed a similar pattern. Shortly after Cao Cao established military and agricultural colonies, the state of Wu did likewise. Before long Wu also began to award obligation-free tenants (known as "redeemed clients") to meritorious subjects. Even before this, it seems that
the heritable troops served their commanders in times of peace as dependent tenants. Early in the regime a decree proclaimed, "The former commanders Zhou Yu and Cheng Pu have clients. In all cases no enquiry will
be made into them." This suggests both that no one would investigate the
origins of these tenants, who may have fled from another landlord or
state land, and that the state would make no census in order to claim labor services or tax.

Shortly afterward the commander Lu Meng received six hundred households from Wu's military colony at Xunyang. After his death his heir received three hundred households and 50 *qing* (about 580 acres, if Han
measures were still in force) for the maintenance of Lu Meng's tomb. There
are many records of state awards of clients to leading military figures, so
that the Daoist text, *The Master Who Embraces Simplicity* (dated before
343), by Ge Hong, in a chapter entitled "The Failings of Wu," said, "The
bound servants were legion."[6] Thus in both north and south the state
tried to secure its position by creating colonies on state-owned land with
dependent tenants, only to ultimately disperse both land and tenants as
serfs to leading officials. This shows that both the attempt and its failure
were intrinsic to the states that emerged in the Three Kingdoms period.

While the legal dependency of tenants was not yet universally recognized, it was clearly developing. This process can be traced through the evolution of the term *buqu*.[7] It had emerged in the Han as a compound formed from names for two levels of military unit, and had come to mean "army" or "troops." In the Eastern Han, when both generals and landed magnates developed close ties with their soldiers, *buqu* came to mean "private troops." As applied to families in military colonies and those awarded to leading officials (families who also worked at agriculture), the term came to mean more generally "dependent" or "client." By the Tang, it had become a legal category indicating a dependent client who held an intermediate position between a slave and a free man.

Using dependents for both agriculture and warfare created a tension between the need to increase wealth by growing crops and the necessity of augmenting power by mobilizing troops. If the state and landlords sought to maximize their income, they reduced the level of training of their soldiery. On the other hand, if they wanted to maintain skilled warriors, they needed to find other people to work their land. The use of agriculturalists as soldiers moved away from the professional military that had developed in the Eastern Han. This tension was particularly striking among the landed families, who during the centuries of division failed to develop or progressively lost military capacities beyond those of emergency self-defense. States, on the other hand, found new pools of soldiers among the non-Han tribesmen and refugees, and this divergence in the capacity to recruit and train soldiers facilitated the resurgence of imperial power.

The first attempt to develop such power and thereby reunite China occurred in the decades between the establishment of the Jin dynasty in 265 and its collapse in the first decade of the fourth century. Both Wei and Wu states had begun to award dependent clients to leading officials, while preventing families from actively recruiting followers from the numerous refugees and fugitives in the countryside. Under Cao Cao, a general from the Sima family had forced a local magnate to allow a tenant to be recruited into the army, on the grounds that the magnate had no right to extend shelter to peasants on his own accord. In 269 Emperor Wu of the Jin (Sima Yan), attempting to accumulate grain to prepare for the reconquest of the south, decreed, "Powerful local interests cannot encroach on the isolated and weak and subject them to service, privately placing them on their household registers." Officials in the mid-270s still enforced laws against privately recruiting clients, and in 280 after the reunification Jin carried out a census to officially fix the number of clients at a low level.[8] Jin wanted to reward its followers with private clients, but to restrict that number in order to develop its own military population.

This military population came from several sources. Even though the Wei colonies had been abolished, Jin continued to separately register military households, thus preserving a hereditary soldiery. More important, the use of non-Chinese soldiers continued in the Three Kingdoms and under the Jin. Cao Cao, for example, defeated Wuhuan forces in 207, resettled them inside China, and made them the core of the finest cavalry in China.[9] He recruited other non-Chinese troops, and Jin continued this policy of resettling surrendered nomads in the interior and employing them as soldiers.

Cavalry had earlier served for reconnaissance, pursuit, and archery, but technological innovations that came into widespread use in the early fourth century transformed horsemen into a powerful strike force. Han cavalrymen had worn simple lamellar armor composed of squares of iron or leather corded together on the front and back of the torso. By contrast, pictorial representations as early as the fourth century show the body of riders and horses almost completely covered with armor (Figs. 3, 4,

Fig. 3   Drawing of a Northern Wei armored warrior on an armored horse (including face armor). Guyuan, Ningxia.

Fig. 4   Rubbing of military horses, one in armor, and grooms. Dengxian, southern Henan, late fifth to early sixth centuries.

and 5), and textual sources speak of capturing thousands of "armored horses" in a single battle.[10]

A new style of saddle combined with the use of stirrups provided riders with a much more secure seat. The terracotta cavalry of the First Emperor's tomb had been mounted on what appears to have been small leather pads secured with straps, and Han sources refer to riding on "pads of hide." The Three Kingdoms period provides evidence of a military saddle shaped to fit the hips and upper legs, presumably so the rider could maintain his seat while striking with a spear or sword.[11] The earliest figurine equipped with two stirrups dates from about 322, while the earliest datable example of an actual stirrup comes from a burial in 415. Stirrups have also been found in undated tombs that appear to be from the fourth century. Heavily armored cavalry thus seems to have appeared well before the stirrup, which was probably introduced to help stabilize armored horsemen while they were fighting.[12]

The fighting power of the armored warrior was also significantly increased by the introduction of the *dao* as a standard side weapon during the four centuries of Han rule. This was a strong, single-edged sword with a slight curve like a saber. With its chopping action it could be forcefully swung against infantry or cavalry and was thus more effective than the thin, straight, two-edged *jian* sword that it replaced. In the same pe-

Fig. 5   Rubbing of military pack horse and grooms. Dengxian, southern Henan, late fifth to early sixth centuries.

riod the multibladed *ji* lance, which could be used to either spear or hook, was replaced by simpler and stronger lances that were thrust or held level (Fig. 6).[13] The cumulative impact of these innovations made the cavalry of the third and fourth centuries much more formidable than its Han predecessors.

The Jin armies of hereditary soldiers and non-Chinese cavalry consisted of an inner army and provincial garrisons. The first comprised about one hundred thousand men based at the capital Luoyang and controlled by the court. The second, commanded by regional military governors, was considerably larger. In addition, provincial governors raised small numbers of local militia, but they were generally disbanded after unity was restored in 282. The most important military policy of the Jin was to place armed forces under imperial princes. Anxious to avoid the sort of coup that had brought his family to power, the Sima founder emulated early Han practice by enfeoffing twenty-seven imperial princes in 265. These fiefs were usually not large—from five thousand to twenty thousand households—and the private armies they were permitted to raise did not exceed five thousand men. However, by 290 six truly powerful princes had also been appointed military governors in the most populous provincial centers, commanding armies numbered in the tens of thousands. After 290 the state allowed military governors to concur-

Fig. 6   Drawing of armored warriors and horses, sword, lance, and shield from a battle scene mural. Dunhuang.

rently hold office as provincial governors, thereby combining civil and military authority in what became virtual small kingdoms.[14]

This policy ended in disaster. It led to an internecine war between the princes that drained the military resources of the Jin dynasty and allowed non-Chinese forces serving the Jin to found their own dynasties. While the Jin gave agents of the state authority over most of its military resources, this did not solve the problem of controlling those agents. The rise of hereditary claims to entry-level posts had reduced the capacity of the emperor to control his officials, and the attempt to rely on ties of kinship to replace those of appointment signally failed as well.

Military Dynasticism in the South

Following the southward flight of the Jin court, the military struggle between the government and local powers replayed what had taken place in the north. However, whereas the northern state's superior military power had depended on nomadic troops, in the south it relied on refugees. But in both cases, political power flowed into the hands of the chiefs and generals who commanded these warriors.

As refugees became the ultimate source of power, political rivalry in the south took the form of a struggle between the two macroregions into which the majority of refugees flowed—the lower Yangzi River basin around the capital Jiankang, and the central Yangzi River basin around its confluence with the Han River. The new government's attempts to secure the lower Yangzi began immediately after the founding of the Eastern Jin dynasty. When Sima Rui declared himself emperor in 317, he was supported by a coalition of northern émigrés with private armies of clients and poor neighbors who had accompanied them on the flight south. The initial response of the established great southern families was hostile. In the decade when the Rebellions of the Eight Princes had ravaged the north, the lower Yangzi had also witnessed several major rebellions, as well as two attempts by Jin commanders to set up independent states. The established families had mustered their private forces to suppress these threats, and the Eastern Jin emperor looked to them like another northern usurper attempting to establish himself as their ruler.

However, a mission led by the northern émigré Wang Dao persuaded the most influential families to support the new regime, and the rest of the southern elite followed suit. The reasons for the decision were probably a combination of the northerners' style, the perceived benefits of the offices and titles that an imperial court could bestow, the promise of assistance in restoring order to a region in turmoil, and security against semi-independent émigré bands led by middling landlords.[15]

A few years later, the first struggle between central and local powers turned into a battle between the lower and central Yangzi regions. In 321 the founding emperor of the Eastern Jin decreed a general registration of those who had fled south, prior to restoring the northern practice of limiting the number of court-recognized clients. The court also freed many servants and slaves who had fought as soldiers for émigré families, and formed these men into a court-controlled army. Wang Dao's cousin Wang Dun, who in 319 had been charged to occupy the central Yangzi region, perceived this military expansion as a threat. He led his army down the Yangzi in 322, entered the capital, and purged those responsible for restricting the number of clients and building up the court's army. Wang Dun effectively took control of the Jin court, and only his illness and death in 324 allowed the Sima family to restore its position.[16]

The Eastern Jin dynasty's situation did not improve, however. One opponent of Wang Dun had been a fortress chief named Su Jun, who was rewarded with an appointment as commander of the defense line along the Huai River. He soon came into conflict with leading officials at court who were suspicious of local military powers, and in 327 he in turn rebelled and occupied the capital. The court was rescued only by appealing for aid from Wang Dun's successor, Tao Kan. A native southerner of humble origins (and great-grandfather of the poet Tao Qian), Tao established a semi-independent state in the central Yangzi.

The tension between the two regions and the importance of military power increased when the central Yangzi fell under the control of Huan Wen in 345. Like his rival Xie An, Huan Wen came from a low-level military family that rose to power and influence after the Jin dynasty moved south.[17] Immediately upon taking control of Jing province, he led an expedition up the Yangzi River to occupy Sichuan. Leaving his baggage train at the river, he rapidly marched to the capital, Chengdu, where he defeated the army of the Daoist Cheng-Han state. This victory gave him extraordinary prestige, and for the next quarter of a century he dominated southern politics.

In the years immediately after the Jin court and the great northern families moved south, they treated their situation as an exile and spoke of returning north, as in this anecdote dated to 311: "Whenever the weather was clear, all those who had crossed the Yangzi would gather at Xinting [a suburb of Jiankang] to eat and drink on the grass. Zhou Yi in the midst of the company sighed and said, 'The scenery is not really inferior, but when you lift up your eyes there is that difference between the Yellow River and the Yangzi.' Everyone looked at each other and wept. Only Wang Dao took on a serious expression and with deep feeling said, 'We should unite our strength for the ruling house to reconquer China. How can we sit here like Chu captives facing one another and weeping?'"[18] Despite these noble sentiments, a decade later when a military man of humble origins assembled an expedition to retake the north, Wang Dao stopped him so that the court could divert his troops and supplies to a battle with Wang Dun.

With Huan Wen's rise, the reconquest of the north became even more controversial. Emigré families were now comfortably settled in estates in Guiji and had sinecures at court. A second generation had grown up in the south and become habituated to the southern climate and customs. For them, the lost north was an alien land. More important, the prestige of reconquering the Yellow River basin would enable victorious generals to make claims to the emperorship. In subsequent decades the tension grew ever stronger between ambitious military men who hoped to use a successful northern expedition as a prelude to establishing a dynasty, and an anxious court for whom reunification now meant disaster.[19]

Huan Wen suggested a northern expedition immediately after his victory in Sichuan, but the court, wary of the recurring menace from the central Yangzi, stalled. However, as the Former Zhao state that had occupied the core of the Yellow River basin disintegrated, the pressure to act became intense. In 349 the imperial affine Chu Pou was sent north with an army from the capital region, but after an initial success he was defeated and abandoned his gains. In 353, in response to threats from Huan Wen, another army was sent out under the celebrated hermit and conversationalist Yin Hao, but this expedition was betrayed by its Qiang allies. More than ten thousand men were slain when Yin Hao fled in panic. At Huan Wen's insistence, Yin Hao was dismissed from office and spent the rest of his life in retirement studying Buddhist scriptures.

The celebrated calligrapher Wang Xizhi, nephew of Wang Dao, spoke for much of the court when he wrote:

> When we learned of Yin Hao's defeat, those in and out of office were desolate. We could not even for a moment dispel our worries. With our little territory south of the river to have assembled and lost so much, the whole world is trembling with fear . . . Now with our army destroyed, and all our resources exhausted, we cannot even fix our resolve so high as to defend the line of the Huai River. It would be best to withdraw our defense to the Yangzi, and have all the military governors and generals return to their old bases. As for everything north of the Yangzi, we should just keep it on a "loose rein."[20]

Since a "loose rein" referred to allowing barbarians to manage their own affairs, this memorial dismissed the Yellow River basin as an undesirable country inhabited by barbarians.

The court's failure opened the door for Huan Wen. In 354 he invaded Guanzhong and fought his way to the gates of Chang'an, but the enemy's scorched-earth tactics forced him to withdraw for lack of supplies. In 356, however, he conquered Luoyang and called upon the court to move back to the Eastern Han capital. This proposal met with general opposition. In 359 another court army was sent out under Xie Wan (An's younger brother), and like all previous forces from the capital region it suffered a grievous defeat and lost most of the territory in the north to the advancing forces of the Murong Xianbei state. In 365 Luoyang was again lost.

Huan Wen gradually took control of the highest offices at the Eastern Jin court. In 363 he was appointed grand marshal in charge of all military affairs, and the next year governor of Yang province (the capital region), thus combining command of all the strategic areas of the Eastern Jin. The empire was in effect ruled by a military dictator who was on the point of establishing his own dynasty. In 369 he began the final stage of his usurpation with the largest of the northern expeditions, sending fifty thousand men along the Huai River and its tributaries and even excavating a north-south canal to allow his troops to be provisioned by boats. Unfortunately, the year had been dry and the rivers were low, making boat transport impossible. Risking everything on a bold advance, he was checked by the Murong troops and again ran out of supplies. Forced to burn his boats and his baggage train, he retreated south on foot but was overtaken by the Murong cavalry and crushed in battle. This disaster seems to have had little effect on his political position, and he even sponsored the composition and public performances of a rhapsody celebrating the expedition.[21]

Huan Wen's dominance was marked by the first clear evidence of a significant decline in the number of families whose members held military posts. This demilitarization of the southern elite is suggested in the *New Account of Tales of the World,* which contrasts the martial Huan Wen to Xie An, who embodied the moral and aesthetic virtues of the cultivated elite. Huan Wen's militarist character was criticized in a frequently cited anecdote:

> After Huan Wen had conquered Sichuan, he assembled all his officers for a banquet at the Lishi Hall. The local eminences of Sichuan without exception flocked to the assembly. Huan had always had a stalwart disposition and bold, straightforward character, and on this day the tone of his voice rang out heroically as he told how throughout history success had always proceeded from human effort and survival had been tied to talent. He was extraordinarily rugged and flint-like, so the entire company incessantly praised him. When the group had dispersed, and everyone was savoring the lingering flavor of his words, Zhou Fu of Xunyang said, "It is too bad that all of you never saw Generalissimo Wang Dun [the first central Yangzi rebel]."[22]

The celebration of his heroic, martial character at the moment of his first triumph leads to a prophecy of his future usurpation. In other anecdotes Huan denounces the pure conversation and eremitism that defined the elite, preferring instead to sponsor poetry that celebrated his military achievements.[23] Nevertheless, in his admiration for Xie An, his appreciation of scholarly expositions, and his insistence on socializing with his peers, Huan Wen was a lover of civil culture as well as the military arts.[24] In contrast, his son Xuan, who led military forces in an attempt to fulfill his father's ambitions, is depicted entirely as a devotee of the arts and never described as "martial" or "flint-like." Thus the demilitarization of the elite extended even to Huan Wen's own family.[25]

Huan Wen attempted to strengthen the state in relation to the great families. First, he tried to restrict the numbers of private clients in order to reduce the possibility of revolt.[26] He opposed separate registers for the northern émigré population (white registers) and the established southern population (yellow registers), and he also opposed the "lodged" administrative units that preserved the names of the northern prefectures and commanderies from which the refugees had fled. This bookkeeping system seemed to affirm the goal of returning to the north, though in actuality the court wished to stay in the south. To offer émigrés a respite and encourage them to register, the court had reduced the tax and corvée demands on those listed on the white registers. Several attempts, called "residence determinations," had been made to register refugees in the southern administrative units where they actually resided. In 364 Huan Wen carried out the most thorough and far-reaching of the residence determinations, which was said to have greatly enriched the state and no doubt weakened the leading families who opposed his policies.[27] This shows the close ties between the interests of the military men—often of lower status—and the state, and their shared difficulties with the leading émigré families.

Huan Wen's standardization of census registration facilitated the next major step in the rise of military dynasticism in the south, the establishment of the Northern Headquarters Troops. In 376 Xie An, now controlling the court, placed his nephew Xie Xuan in charge of defending the region north of the capital. To man the new army, Xuan apparently recruited leaders of militarized émigré settlements in the region, who perhaps were responding to the rising threat of the Former Qin state led by Fu Jian. Such men would have enlisted as middle-level officers who brought along their own subordinates and hereditary troops.[28] This army of one hundred thousand men underwent considerable training to provide a professional core for the Jin army, and in 383 they demonstrated their worth by blocking Fu Jian's invasion.

The emergence of the Northern Headquarters Troops was both a continuation of earlier developments and a turning point in southern history. The great families' withdrawal from military service accelerated as the middle and even upper ranks of the army were filled by men of humble origin. Military service became identified with low status, unworthy of men of learning and pedigree. Under the southern dynasties this went so far that in the sixth century Yan Zhitui wrote:

> I constantly observe literary scholars who have read a few military books, but lack all experience of command or strategic planning . . .
> In times of war they foment rebellions, persuading and deceiving others into factional alliances. With no idea of which side will survive and which perish, they insist on supporting one or the other. This is the root of destroying self and family. Beware! Beware! Those who have mastered all the weapons and are skilled at riding can truly be called warriors. Now officials from leading families who without any study call themselves warriors are nothing but rice sacks and wine jars.[29]

The Xie family, like the Huans, were not rice sacks and wine jars. They combined extensive military activity with their cultural pursuits. While Xie An's military career is suppressed in the *New Account* due to its suspicion of martial heroism, his biography in the *Book of the Jin* records considerable military accomplishments. Kinsmen such as Xie Wan and Xie Xuan were also active in military commands.[30]

Although hereditary troops entered the Northern Headquarters Troops with their commanders, volunteers from among refugees and militarized communities formed its core, supplemented by vagrants, convicts, and aboriginal peoples pressed into service.[31] These sources are identical with those that the Eastern Han had used to replace peasant levies with a more professional standing army. Similarly, the Northern Headquarters Troops represented a form of professionalization.

In 399 leading officials at court decided that the Northern Headquarters Troops were not reliable, so they again tried to fashion an army from liberated slaves and dependents of powerful families. But in the same year the government executed a Daoist leader from an established southern family, whose son Sun En then offered peasants the chance to avoid conscription by joining him in rebellion and escaping to the Isle of the Immortals. The rebellion swept through the Guiji region, where most of the émigrés' families' estates were located, and down into the lake region inhabited by the earlier southern families. It took three years of savage, seesaw combat, including major naval campaigns, for the Northern Headquarters Troops to suppress the rebellion.[32]

This pivotal campaign, during which Sun En's forces devastated the economic base of the leading court families, highlighted the government's dependence on its new professional forces. It was the first major campaign led by a general of humble origins, Liu Laozhi, who a year before had conspired with the court to eliminate Wang Gong, the last man of pedigree to lead the Northern Headquarters Troops. The campaign also witnessed the emergence of the unrelated Liu Yu, who rose through the ranks to become Liu Laozhi's right-hand man.

In 402 Huan Wen's son Xuan, having inherited his father's command of the central Yangzi, took advantage of the chaos in the east to blockade shipments of grain down the river and lead his forces against the capital. Liu Laozhi accepted a bribe from Huan Xuan to change sides, thus leaving Jiankang defenseless. Once Huan Xuan occupied the capital, however, he purged the commanders of the Northern Headquarters Troops as a prelude to declaring himself emperor. At this point, an event occurred that altered the political and social balance of power in the south. Junior officers of the Northern Headquarters under Liu Yu, who had feigned support of Huan Xuan to secure his own position, staged a *coup d'état,* drove Huan Xuan from the capital, and then defeated his forces in the central Yangzi region. Liu Yu restored the Jin dynasty, but he had become the real leader of the state. After a northern expedition in 409, the defeat of a revived Daoist rebellion under Sun En's successor Lu Xun, and the recapture of Luoyang and Chang'an in 417, Liu Yu assumed the imperial mantle in 420.

The establishment of the Liu Song dynasty in 420 marked a pivotal point in the history of the southern dynasties and of China. Since the fall of the Han dynasty, the imperial court had declined for two centuries. Although supported by influential families who needed a court to preserve their own privileges and prestige, centralized power had waned, giving way to the fragmented power of eminent families in the south and short-lived barbarian states in the north. Professional armies—fashioned from volunteer refugees, conscripts, and hereditary troops to augment the powers of ambitious lineages—seized power in the coup of 403.

When the commoner Liu Yu became emperor in 420 the balance between the imperial line and the great families radically shifted. For the next two centuries, the southern dynasties (Lui Song, Qi, Liang, Chen) were ruled by military men of humble origins, who increasingly asserted their authority at the expense of the great families. These dynasts could not challenge the magnates in their localities, and they continued to recognize their claims to hereditary entry-level offices. The court even copied their deportment and artistic activities—an acknowledgment of the families' social preeminence. But the dynasts stripped the great lineages of the three bases of their political power: military force, administrative authority, and wealth.

The southern dynasts maintained their authority by distributing troops throughout the key regions of the empire and placing each regional command under a member of the imperial family. The single largest command was left at the capital under the emperor, but his brothers and nephews held smaller military posts in the central Yangzi region, Sichuan, or the far south. These regional troops replaced the coalitions of private, landlord-led armies that had dominated most localities during the third and fourth centuries. Military commanders continued to be recruited from non-elite families, and the military became a primary route to power for ambitious commoners.[33]

The southern dynasts also transferred decision-making and administrative power to nominally low offices filled by commoners, while the high offices dominated by elite families were stripped of real authority. Just as the personal secretaries of Han emperors had supplanted the formal bureaucracy, so power to make policy and draft decrees was transferred from the formal bureaucracy to the Secretariat, and the key posts became the Secretariat Receptionist or the Secretariat Drafter. The top posts in the Secretariat itself were likewise transformed into empty sinecures, and actual authority was placed in the hands of men of humble background who were completely dependent on the emperor. In the provinces, power resided with the imperial princes who commanded the military forces. But to reduce the threat they posed to the central court, southern emperors appointed low-level document clerks who were charged with observing the princes and reporting to the emperor. These clerks dominated local administration, and the constant surveillance led one imperial prince to complain to his mother, "I cannot even take five steps without permission. How am I different from a prisoner?"[34]

Most of the newly influential commoners in the central court and local administrations for whom we have records were merchants who had grown wealthy in the booming economy of the Yangzi region. They brought to the court many trappings of the urban life of the period, most notably the erotic songs and poetry that had flourished in the pleasure quarters of the major cities and came to dominate the poetic circles of the Qi and Liang courts.[35] These ambitious commoners at court were also quick to translate their new political power into economic influence throughout the region. Officials of merchant background sent out as inspectors to control the imperial princes availed themselves of commercial privileges and networks that came with their court connections to accumulate large fortunes, which they used to buy both land and political influence in the countryside. In addition to such legal opportunities, the document clerks and inspectors supplemented their wealth with bribes and gifts from those who needed to cultivate their support.[36]

The efflorescence of trade in the fifth century led to the revival of a money-based economy, particularly in the regions around the capital. Like the landed nobility in early modern Europe, many members of old families found it difficult to translate landed wealth into the cash that was now necessary to maintain an elite lifestyle as well as to pay taxes. They consequently had to pawn or sell estates piecemeal to uphold their prestige at court or in local society. As the economy boomed and as wealth from merchants continued to move into the court in the late fifth and early sixth centuries, the capital witnessed a frenzy of conspicuous consumption in which rich commoners, scions of great lineages, and members of the imperial family competed in building lavish palaces, staging banquets, and making donations to the Buddhist church, which had become a de facto state religion. Many old, established country estates broke apart under the economic strain.[37]

While the military dynasts succeeded in weakening the great families, the court failed to maintain a stable political order. The military monopolies of the imperial princes weakened their local rivals but led to constant tensions and warfare among the princes themselves. This first appeared after thirty years of tranquility following the foundation of the Liu Song. In 453 the emperor was murdered by an heir whom he was about to depose. This triggered a battle between the princes that was won by Liu Jin, who ruled for a decade as Emperor Xiaowu. However, he killed several brothers to maintain his authority, and his own death gave rise to a War of Uncles and Nephews. The death of his successor in 472 led to another armed rebellion by an imperial prince from the central Yangzi. Although this was put down, the commander who led the defense, Xiao Daocheng, took control of the court and in 479 established the Qi dynasty. Continuing the policies of its predecessor, this dynasty lasted for only twenty-two years of conspiracy and strife before being supplanted by a rebel imperial prince, Xiao Yan, who established the Liang dynasty in 502.

During this period, the underlying dynamics of the repeated civil wars remained constant. Prodded by ambitious generals and commoner followers who would gain great wealth and power if their patron seized the throne or dominated the court, imperial princes battled to secure the succession for themselves or for some child ruler whom they could control. To improve their chances, the princes recruited ever larger armies, and in response ambitious men formed private armed bands of hundreds or even thousands of followers to seek service with the princes. The formation of these bands was facilitated by the fact that many peasants had been ruined by inflation and the state's revived demands for taxes in cash.

But like the mercenary companies in European armies of the late medieval and early modern periods, these armed bands remained independent under their original commanders, who sometimes switched sides if the balance of power changed. Rather than settling on state-owned lands and becoming farmers, the soldiers wandered the countryside like bandit gangs, living off what they could extract from the peasants in state-sanctioned pillaging. In the late sixth century, the historian He Zhiyuan wrote: "The Later Liang state is smaller than a single Han commandery. Nevertheless, half of the people are private troops who eat without plowing and wear clothes without raising silkworms. Some serve the nobility, and some their own commanders. They bring their families with them as they move about from east to west. Under the provincial commanders they pillage, and act as bandits for the local officials." While this was an extreme case, the depredations of princely armies on peasant populations figure elsewhere in the historical record. As conflict between imperial princes intensified, the size of these roving armies increased, and any controls on their behavior vanished. Private estates also fell prey to these bandit gangs, except for families who armed themselves, built forts, and became militarized local bullies in their own right.[38]

The militarization of the princes and local society culminated in 547 when a general who had defected from the north, Hou Jing, besieged the capital with a few thousand men. Several imperial princes chose not to intervene, instead waiting for the emperor to fall so that they could take his place. Others sent troops, but these independent companies found it

more profitable to pillage the capital region than to risk their lives breaking the siege. The city itself, filled with profligate, fashion-conscious dan-
dies, proved unable to mount a defense. After a protracted blockage and
assault, the capital fell, the emperor died in his palace, and the Liang dynasty disintegrated in a civil war between rival imperial princes.[39]

This conflict devastated the capital region and shifted power away
from the central and lower Yangzi to the newly opened territories of the
far south (modern Fujian, Jiangxi, Guangdong, Guangxi). Here, leaders
of semi-bandit military gangs carved out private bases in a new, more
brutal form of military dynasticism. The war was won in 557 by Chen
Baxian, commander of an armed gang of a thousand men who rose to
eminence by suppressing peasant revolts in the far south. His short-lived
Chen dynasty never recovered from the devastation of the civil war, however, and from the loss of Sichuan, the Han River valley, and everything
north of the Huai River. A few decades later the Chen state fell to northern armies.[40]

Military Dynasticism in the North

One might say, oversimply, that in the fourth century south China had a
dynasty with no army, while north China had armies with no dynasty.
The barbarian states—called the Sixteen Kingdoms—that ruled different
regions in the north were established on the principle of the tribal confederation, in which a supreme chief exerted authority through success in
battle and the booty that he distributed to his followers. Members of diverse tribes or lineages followed whoever was militarily successful, so
that while the states are identified by the ethnic group of their rulers, their
makeup was quite heterogeneous.[41]

Since these states were formed on the basis of the supreme chief's military successes, any serious defeat led to a rapid collapse. The death of an
individual chief also dissolved the personal bonds between ruler and subordinates that created the state, so these kingdoms were endangered at
each succession. This instability was exacerbated by the fact that the
early states that occupied the regions of the two former capitals and tried
to reunite the north were founded by nomads who had been resettled inside China, grown up there, and either served the Jin court or been Jin
conscripts. In contrast with the earlier Xiongnu and some later confeder-
ations, they had no base outside of China and no distinct political tradition. They were little more than temporary assemblages of fighting men.

The military states that arose in the central and western regions of the Yellow River basin differed from the states of the northeast. The former were fundamentally nomadic armies that survived by pillage, whereas the Murong Xianbei tribes of the northeast were a semi-sedentary people who lived in a mixture of forest villages, agricultural communities, and nomadic camps. They benefited from possession of a relatively stable geographic base, and due to the mixed nature of their economy and regular trade relations with the Chinese, they proved adept at combining nomadic armies with a Chinese administration (Fig. 7). Thus in the confused history of the period, the northeast (what is now southern Manchuria and northern Hebei) remained a world apart that was ruled by a series of four Xianbei states, all named Yan (Former, Later, Southern, and Northern).[42] Equally stable in nomenclature but of little political consequence was the Gansu corridor in the far northwest that initially survived as a Jin province and was ruled sequentially by five mixed Chinese-barbarian states all called Liang (Former, Later, Southern, Western, and Northern).

In contrast with these states in the far west and far east, which enjoyed a certain stability due to geographic isolation, those in the center were little more than armed bands that swelled to great size as their leaders won victories, only to disintegrate when he suffered a defeat, or died and left the state to an unproven successor. This chaos was exacerbated by the fact that each state absorbed with their forces intact the subordinate chiefs or generals of defeated enemies. These commanders again would shift their loyalties as soon as the ruler was defeated.[43]

The rapid succession of rising and falling states in north China began even before the Jin fled south (Map 5). The designated heirs of the Xiongnu Han state that drove the Jin out of the north were murdered in 310 (one year before occupying Luoyang) and again in 318. The second murder led to a massacre of much of the ruling family, which ended when the survivor, Liu Yao, moved the capital to Chang'an and changed the name of his state from Han to Zhao. This led a bandit-turned-general named Shi Le to break with the Lius and establish his own Zhao state (called Later Zhao by historians) in the flood plain of the Yellow River (Map 6). Shi Le defeated Liu Yao in 328 to reunite much of the north, but when he died in 333 his son and heir was murdered by a cousin, Shi Hu. Dominating his state through violence and terror, Shi Hu even murdered his own heir, the heir's wife, and twenty-six of his children. Nevertheless,

Fig. 7   Drawings of figurines depicting Xianbei, mostly military men, from Eastern Wei and Northern Qi tombs.

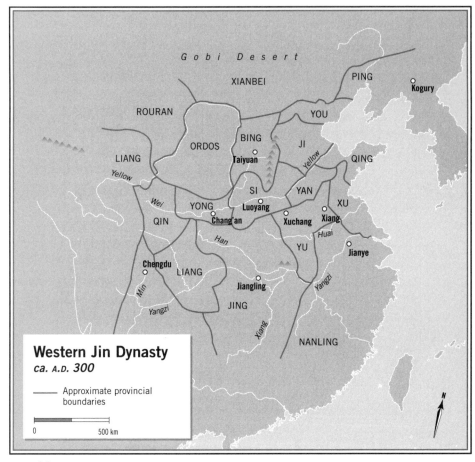

MAP 5

when he died in 349 the state fell apart, with three successive heirs being killed and replaced in less than a year. The process culminated in the seizure of power by an adopted son of Shi Hu, Ran Min, who was ethnically Chinese and who led a general massacre of the non-Chinese in the capital region in 350.[44]

This Han Chinese revival was cut short in 352 by the Murong state, which expanded from its base in the northeast to defeat Ran Min and occupy the flood plain. However, the Murong in turn were defeated by a state dominated by Di and Qiang tribesmen founded in 351 in Guanzhong. This state, named the Former Qin to recall the empire that had emerged from the same region, reached its apogee under Fu Jian,

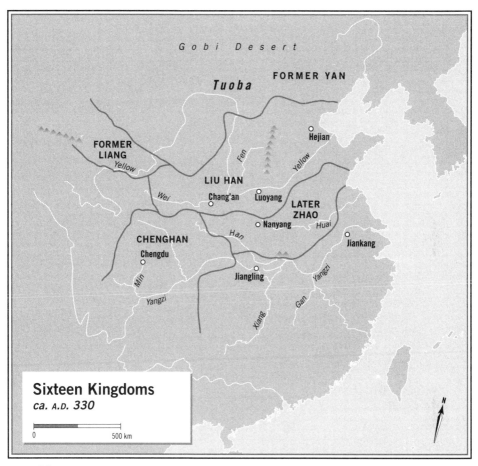

MAP 6

who between 357 and 381 reunited all of north China (Map 7). In 383 he assembled a substantial army to invade the south, but a check by the Northern Headquarters Troops at the Fei River, a tributary of the Huai, led to a hasty retreat followed by the complete collapse of his empire.[45]

Apart from the structural instability of these states, several points of general significance emerge from this confusing political narrative.[46] First, despite blurring between the two groups, all the northern states administratively distinguished Chinese from non-Chinese subjects.[47] The nomadic warriors who formed the armies were controlled by their own rulers and often given distinct titles such as "compatriots" to distinguish them from the Chinese subjects who provided grain and service. This

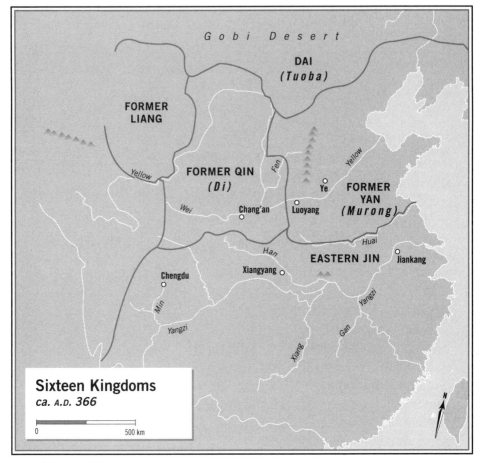

MAP 7

distinction—apparently intended to prevent the outnumbered nomads from being submerged by the masses they ruled—provided the basis for a dual administrative system that characterized the hybrid nomad-Chinese states.

Second, in a pattern that can be traced back to Cao Cao, the depopulation of the north meant that vast expanses of land were untilled and the limiting factor on agricultural production was labor. Consequently, the northern states aimed for the control of people rather than the occupation of territory. Virtually all the "barbarian" states in north China forcibly moved tens or hundreds of thousands of captured people to the areas around their newly established capitals to take advantage of their labor. Thus Liu Cong reportedly moved 80,000 people from Chang'an to

Pingyang after he conquered the Guanzhong region in 316, and Shi Le was said to have moved 150,000 Di and Qiang peoples from Guanzhong to his capital in Hebei in 329. When the Former Qin state arose after 351, these movements were reversed. However, throughout this period the forcible movement of population invariably followed the establishment of a state.

Finally, the armies of these states moved across a landscape dotted with forts where armed communities led by local families had taken refuge in defensible terrain. As the Jin state collapsed, these communities, with provisioned fortifications and, often, the rudiments of a local law, became the basis of order in the fourth century throughout the north and much of the south. Leagues of forts sometimes formed to extend power across entire regions. The nomadic conquerors alternately fought them or sought to co-opt them through the gift of titles and government recognition of their status.

While some states (notably the Yan states founded by the Murong tribe in the northeast) endured by incorporating elements of Chinese political practice, only the Tuoba (Tabgatch) tribe at the end of the fourth century was able to transform loyalty to a leader into loyalty to a dynasty. The Tuoba emerged as a significant power to the west of the Murong following the collapse of Fu Jian's state after 383. The Tuoba state had been conquered by Fu Jian in 376 but was restored by Tuoba Gui in 386. Their "backwardness" compared to the Murong proved a blessing, because contacts with the steppe regions enabled them to obtain large numbers of horses and allies. Tuoba Gui also benefited from the timely death of the Murong chief in 396, after which the Murong armies rapidly deteriorated. Within two years the Tuoba had swallowed up the Murong realm, and Tuoba Gui ruled north China east of the bend in the Yellow River (Map 8).[48]

This dynamic leader undertook innovations that allowed his dynasty to reunify north China for more than the lifetime of a single ruler.[49] Chief among them was breaking up the semi-independent tribes that had remained the basic unit of earlier states. After completing the conquest of the more sinicized Murong tribe in 398, Tuoba Gui—inspired by their capital at Ye—decided to build a Chinese-style capital at Pingcheng (near modern Datong). He reorganized the people into eight artificial tribes in permanent settlements around the new capital. These artificial tribes, structured as military units, received provisions from resettled herdsmen and agriculturalists. By removing their traditional leaders, forcing them

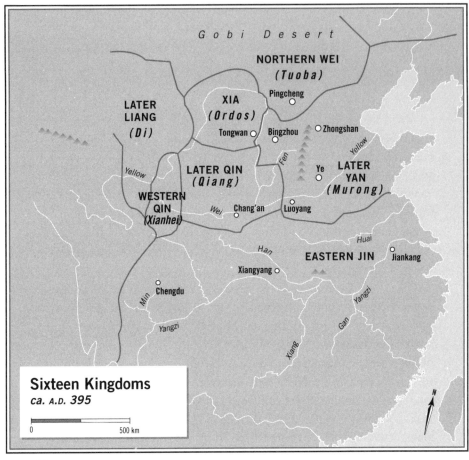

Gobi Desert

NORTHERN WEI
(Tuoba)

Pingcheng ○

LATER
LIANG
(Di)

XIA
(Ordos)

Tongwan ○ Bingzhou ○   ○ Zhongshan

Yellow

LATER QIN
(Qiang)

Fen

Ye ○ LATER
YAN
(Murong)

WESTERN
QIN
(Xianhei)

Yellow

Wei Chang'an ○ ○ Luoyang

Huai

○ Chengdu

Min

Xiangyang ○

Han

EASTERN JIN   ○ Jiankang

Yangzi

Yangzi

Gan

Xiang

Sixteen Kingdoms
ca. A.D. 395

0   500 km

N

MAP 8

to abandon nomadism, and making them dependent on the state for income, Tuoba Gui converted the nomadic tribal armies into a hereditary military-service class bound to the state. He thus transferred loyalty from the person of the chief to the institution of the dynasty, thereby allowing the Northern Wei to perpetuate itself across successions. This professional, hereditary capital army became the largest single force in the state, and its primary striking arm. Commanded by the emperor and his immediate followers, it assured their superiority over any potential opposing force (Fig. 8).

Between 400 and 440 the Northern Wei conquered the entire Yellow River basin (Map 9), and in 450 an expedition reached the north bank of the Yangzi. At this point the Tuoba still exercised a purely military con-

Fig. 8   Rubbing of infantry with swords and shields, or bows and arrows.
Dengxian, southern Henan, late fifth to early sixth centuries.

trol over northern China. Lacking ties with the indigenous Chinese elite,
the Northern Wei ruled through military garrisons dispersed across their
territories in walled towns that served as the capitals of new administrative districts. Units were also distributed in smaller camps throughout
each district. For most of the fifth century, garrison commanders and
their troops were members of the Tuoba confederacy. Chinese were excluded from these military posts, which also constituted the administrative structure of the empire.[50]

In 493 the emperor Xiaowen decided to transform the Northern Wei
into a classical Chinese state by moving the capital to Luoyang, requiring
Chinese costume and language at court, and fusing the Xianbei and Chinese elites through arranged intermarriage and shared rankings.[51] Most
military districts with Chinese populations were converted into civil provinces administered by Chinese governors. Chinese militias began serving
in rotation for local self-defense, and the original Tuoba garrisons were
either shifted to the new capital armies at Luoyang, moved to camps at
the northern frontier, or absorbed into the local population.

This change from the military administration of the early Tuoba state
to more traditional Chinese forms ended in disaster. As the court became
sinicized, army garrisons at the frontier that preserved the values, language, and costume of their forebears steadily declined in status. This

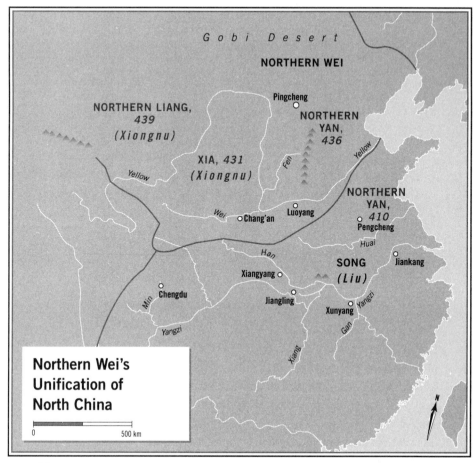

MAP 9

was exacerbated by the policy of replenishing garrisons with reprieved convicts. In the early decades of the sixth century, agents of the court ruthlessly exploited the frontier garrisons, selling their food, horses, and even weapons for personal gain. The refusal of one governor to issue grain to a starving garrison in 524 triggered mutinies that spread along the frontier (Map 10). To appease the garrisons, the court shifted many of them south to regions where food was available, but the rebellion resumed, and within a year most of the countryside north of the Yellow River was in rebel hands.

The court defeated the rebel armies only with the assistance of an allied tribal group of Indo-European (probably Iranian) origin that dominated central Shanxi. These people, known as Jie or Jie Hu, were distinguished

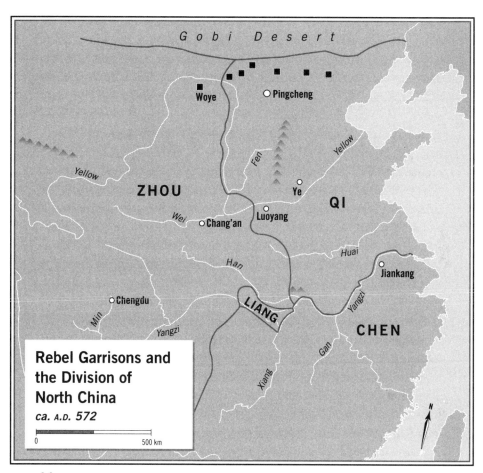

Rebel Garrisons and
the Division of
North China
ca. A.D. 572

MAP 10

by deep-set eyes, high noses, and bearded faces, features that had identified them when they were the targets of a massacre at the fall of the Later
Zhao state in 349.[52] They were one of several tribal groups who, under
traditional leaders, were resettled as allied states within the Tuoba realm.
Their leader, Erzhu Rong, led his armies to Luoyang in 528, massacred
most of the court, and then defeated the rebel forces. He established a
puppet Wei emperor who turned on Erzhu Rong in a carefully arranged
palace ambush and assassinated him with his own hands.

Erzhu Rong's death did not save the dynasty. His heir reoccupied Luoyang and established a new emperor, but the Erzhu family in turn was defeated by a coalition of second-level leaders who had taken command of
the garrison rebels. Chief among these was Gao Huan, supposedly a Han

Chinese raised among the Xianbei. He conquered the flood plain of the Yellow River, while the Guanzhong region was occupied by forces under a commander of Xiongnu descent, Yuwen Tai. In 534 the Northern Wei emperor and his court fled from Luoyang to take refuge with Yuwen Tai in Chang'an, a move that marked the division of north China into two states, the Eastern and Western Wei. These two warring states were both nominally ruled by Wei dynasty puppets until 550, when Gao Huan's heirs established the Northern Qi dynasty. Seven years later the Yuwen regime established the Northern Zhou dynasty in Guanzhong.[53]

The Zhou and Qi states both exemplified military dynasticism. Their rulers had risen through military service and based their power on a central army composed of former members of the garrisons or the Wei capital armies, supplemented by military followers of local elites. They also followed the Wei in that officers, largely drawn from the garrisons or non-Han tribes, did not have their own personal troops but relied on forces mobilized by the state and thus under the control of the ruler.[54]

The western state, the Zhou, was at first at a serious disadvantage in terms of the numbers of tribesmen and horses at its disposal, which forced it to recruit from the local population of Guanzhong. The Zhou recognized the militias of local strongmen and grouped them under the command of court appointees. The local strongmen received military titles and were given Xianbei surnames.[55] While the number of men thus recruited was not large, probably only a few thousand, this institutional innovation helped to establish strong links between the Zhou imperial court and local society.

More important to Zhou's strength and the ultimate reunification of China were the Twenty-Four Armies. Wei soldiers, non-Chinese tribesmen in Guanzhong, and members of Chinese families with military proclivities were placed under twenty-four divisional commands. Apparently, most soldiers were recruited individually, rather than entering under their commanders or the local elite. Some texts suggest that the soldiers themselves tilled fields, while others indicate that they lived off land and labor provided by the state and were exempted from taxes and corvée. It is possible that the armies combined Han peasant recruits who worked the land with non-Han soldiers based in walled communities who were awarded land worked by servile populations.[56]

Freed from the burden of agriculture and thus able to train full time, this Zhou army of crack troops from the elite of Guanzhong, both Chinese and barbarian, became the finest fighting force of its day. It mobilized to the full the resources of its region, drew in the leading Chinese families to provide administration, and was securely located in Guanzhong, which had been the base for all previous Chinese empires. In 577, after half a century of warfare, it conquered the rival Qi to reunite north China. Four years later, in 581, a Zhou general named Yang Jian seized the throne and established the Sui dynasty, and eight years after that, in 589, Sui forces overwhelmed the southern Chen, bringing all of China under a single ruler for the first time in almost four centuries.

However, just as the fact of conquest had not been sufficient to guarantee a lasting empire for the Qin, so the triumph of the Northern Zhou military system was not enough to secure an empire for the Sui. As repeated failures in the fifth and sixth centuries had shown, control of armed forces was necessary but not sufficient to rule in China. Many institutional changes were needed to secure the economic, social, and intellectual bases of empire in a world that had changed considerably since the Han had last ruled a unitary Chinese state.

4

URBAN TRANSFORMATION

FROM THE Warring States through the Han empire the notion of a capital evolved from a city with an ancestral temple to one distinguished by a palace and towers, and later to a ritual center conforming to the ideal articulated in the *Rituals of Zhou* and the presence of buildings sanctioned by the Confucian canon. This reflected the evolution of the state from an archaic theocracy ruled by nobles based on ancestor worship to territorial states centered on an absolute ruler to a world empire grounded in a text-based canon.

The transformation of urban life continued under the Northern and Southern Dynasties, with three primary developments. First, the division of China and its expansion southward into the Yangzi valley created regional capitals tied to distinctive local geography and cultures, which in the south radically differed from those of the north. Second, the emergence of new literary and cultural forms defining the elite required new physical spaces in the city for these activities. Most notable, particularly in the south but also in northern cities, were semi-public gardens, which arose along with the rural villa. Third, the rise of the institutional religions, notably Buddhism, led to new forms of architecture and city planning, most significantly the temple as a new kind of public space.

Regional Cities and Customs

The major Han writings about cities were court-based rhapsodies praising the capital. In the late Han period a small body of poems developed a new approach to the urban environment, treating the city as a frame for individual experience. These lyrics differed from Han rhapsodies in that cities, even capitals, were viewed in bits and pieces—a household here, a street scene there, or the spectacle of rural life just beyond the city gate. Some poems also depicted the city from the point of view of ordinary people, or even the miserable and impoverished.

A typical example is this excerpt from a song of blighted love:

> I hear you have a new love
> And so have come to say farewell.
> Our whole life in the city
> Did we ever party with measures of wine?
> Today we party with measures of wine,
> But tomorrow dawn I will stand at the head of the canal.
> I trudge along the imperial canal,
> With the water flowing east and west.
> West of the city wall there is a wood gatherer.
> East of the city wall there is a wood gatherer.
> They both urge me on,
> But without a family, for whom can one be proud?[1]

The poet manipulates elements of city life to tell of a woman's despair. The drinking party, later a standard feature of urban poetry, marks a parting; but here the departing person is an abandoned lover rather than a traveler. The woman's pacing along the waterway suggests both the possibility of suicide and her inability to decide. The city wall marks the edge of the ordered world, and in these poems going beyond the gates often leads to scenes of despair and death. The fuel gatherers are the poorest denizens of the outer reaches of the human world, but with families even they are happier than the abandoned woman.

Themes of abandonment and life's evanescence crystallized in the celebrated *Nineteen Ancient Poems*. This collection of songs, conventionally dated to the late Eastern Han, dwells on separation and the brevity of life—"the sorrow of impermanence."[2] While there is nothing specifically urban in these themes, urban elements as experienced by ordinary people are crucial to the poems' effectiveness. The second poem concludes with a woman proclaiming her past as a singing girl in a bar, a role conventionally equated with prostitution in the city's pleasure quarters.[3] The mournful singing of a woman also appears in the fifth poem, where it descends from a lofty tower "level with the clouds," with fine lattice windows—the sort of building typical of a Chinese city. The twelfth poem announces, "The eastern city wall is high and long, winding and twisting back on itself," and after couplets on the rapid passage of time and the seasons it continues:

> In Yan and Zhao there are many beauties,
> But the loveliest has a face of jade.
> She wears fine silk
> And at her door rehearses a clear melody.
> How utterly sad it is!
> With strings taut, one senses how she presses on the bridge.
> Letting her feelings gallop, yet she draws tight her belt.
> Murmuring low, she hesitates a moment.
> "I long to be a pair of swallows,
> Carrying mud in my beak to nest beneath my lord's roof."[4]

Throughout the songs, the sorrows of life take on a distinctive urban flavor, as in this figure of a girl singing at the door to display her wares. Her "galloping" feelings echo a recurring image in these poems: a team of horses racing through the city. In poem thirteen (and perhaps fourteen, which seems to be a pendant or continuation) the speaker drives a carriage through the city's Upper Eastern Gate, only to confront the town's cemetery with its message of mortality. This linking of the chariot and death figures again in poem three:

> Green, green the cypresses on the ridge,
> Heaped, heaped, the stones in the stream.
> Man's life between Heaven and Earth,
> Rushes like a traveler with far to go.
> Find joy in measures of wine,
> For the moment be generous, not stingy.
> Drive our carriages, whip our nags,
> To wander for pleasure through Nanyang and Luoyang.
> What a hurly-burly is Luoyang!
> With courtiers one after the other.
> The alley-fringed great boulevards,
> With the mansions of princes and peers.
> The two palaces distantly face one another
> With their gate-towers more than a hundred feet tall.

> Feast without limit to delight the heart,
> Why be oppressed by sorrows and cares?[5]

The next poem echoes the theme of life's brevity and urges the reader to "whip his high-stepping horses" and be the first to "occupy the road to power." Here the capital, celebrated by the rhapsodies, appears to outsiders as at best an entertaining spectacle, at worst a taunting display of what they lack, and—like everything else in these poems—an image of the transience of worldly pleasure and glory. Even the chariots that the poet summons to pursue pleasures or power echo images of life's brevity and the traveler's sufferings.[6] These literati lyrics portray the city as a world of sorrows, arousing feelings of grief or isolation in the sensitive reader through their depictions of unhappy women and unattainable power.

The shift away from the city as an idealized, ritualized capital figures not just in lyrical poetry but also in three rhapsodies on regional capitals written by Zuo Si between A.D. 280 and 300, during the brief reunification under the Jin.[7] Zuo Si patterned his "Three Capitals" on the rhapsodies of Ban Gu, which had defined the ideal of the capital that emerged under the Eastern Han, as well as on a second set of rhapsodies on capitals by Zhang Heng. But Zuo Si introduced new ideas about the nature of a capital or a city. First, by depicting the capitals of the Three Kingdoms and omitting the capital of his own day, Luoyang, Zuo's rhapsodies suppressed the theme that had structured its predecessors: the evolution and perfection of rites in the one true imperial capital. In effect, he wrote a capital rhapsody without a capital. Second, by creating a dramatic sense of place and of local culture through depictions of landscape, society, and folkways in Sichuan, Jiangnan, and the Yellow River basin, the "Three Capitals" rhapsodies more closely resembled a proto-ethnography and a celebration of regional culture than the old poetics of empire.

Zuo Si drew the rhetoric and standards for his masterpiece from lyric verse, "songs on objects" such as the ocean, rivers, wind, clouds, and trees, and "excursion rhapsodies," which told of ascending a high place or taking a journey. He insisted on the new ideal of verse as a depiction of actual experience, describing what the poet saw.[8] His intended audience was the cultivated elite who lived in the new world of verse exchange and pure conversation—men who cultivated a shared sense of attachment to specific places with their regional customs and character. The cities of his poems were the worlds where these people lived. This new audience, and new aesthetic, explain not only Zuo Si's decision to write rhapsodies about regional capitals but also his claim to be superior to earlier writers through his accurate rendition of local landscapes and customs.

In his preface, Zuo Si argues that the primary failing of Han rhapsodies was to ignore reality. Fascinated by obscure language and dramatic effect, the Han poets composed rhapsodies lacking substance and truth. Zuo argued: "One who expresses himself in verse should sing his true feelings. One who climbs to a height and composes a rhapsody should celebrate what he has seen. One who praises an object considers first and foremost its true nature, and one who honors a deed should base himself on the facts. Without truth and facts what can the reader believe?" The poet must also consult maps and gazetteers to verify the accuracy of his poems, as Zuo celebrates himself for doing.

His "Shu Capital Rhapsody," describing Chengdu in Sichuan, begins with an account of mountains that offers not a generic invocation of their twisting forms, as in the Han rhapsodies, but rather the names, locations, and shapes of actual peaks. Zuo culls local features from textual accounts of Chengdu, and he fills the markets with goods appearing in lists of regional products from the *Records of the Historian/Astrologer* (*Shi ji*) and from records of Sichuan's tribute to the court. The poem also refers to eminent local families and famous literary figures from the region—ironically including the famous Han rhapsodists Sima Xiangru and Yang Xiong. Rather than recounting an imperial hunt—a central feature of Han rhapsodies—Zuo Si narrates an expedition by Chengdu's local grandees.

The rhapsody on the capital of Wu, Jiankang, follows convention in beginning with mockery of the previous speaker. The critic—a fictive prince of Wu—focuses on the limited, regional scope of the first poem. After describing the all-encompassing learning of the ancient sages, the prince continues:

> On their jade tablets and stone records,
> What does one hear of touring lodges and traveling palaces
> In the Min Mountains of Shu?
> But you speak of Shu's wealth and possessions,
> Praising this petty region for its forests and preserves.
> You brag of its geographic barriers,
> Thinking these the greatest of natural defenses.

You boast of the fertility of its taro fields,
Thinking they will save Shu from natural cataclysms.
Only a provincial pedant would sigh in admiration
At the trifling enumeration of such things.
To assess your local capital in such grandiose terms
Is not the bold vision of the Great Man.[9]

Despite the prince's denunciation of regionalism, the rhapsody on Wu's capital simply provides even longer lists of local products paid as "tribute" to the central court, drawn from records of remote regions such as the *Mountain Classic*. Like the poem on Chengdu, the rhapsody on Jiankang celebrates the region's great families, but it also describes exotic local peoples with strange customs—such as tattooed bodies—and their distinctive music and dances. The poem explicitly contrasts these marvels with the possessions of the "central states."[10] Thus, although the Wu capital rhapsody begins with the conventional rhetoric of the superiority of the center to the periphery, its contents again celebrate local history, nature, and custom.

The final poem reprises the critique of the earlier cities as limited, provincial centers, and celebrates the Northern Wei capital of Ye, in modern Hebei, as an imperial city. Nevertheless, it too radically differs from the Han examples. Whereas imperial rites had defined the Han capital, marking the culmination of history and the dramatic climax in the poems of Ban Gu and Zhang Heng, they scarcely figure in Zuo's work. The section on rituals recounts only a feast for the barbarians who submitted to the Northern Wei, followed by a list of other rites and a panegyric (poem of praise) for the Wei's modesty in yielding the throne to Jin.[11] This focus on the submission of barbarians invokes the theme of periphery versus center, reducing the earlier poems to praise for barbarian customs. However, celebration of the center is undercut by the fact that this discussion of rites is not the climax of the poem. Instead, it leads to a lengthy account of the rare natural products of the capital region and the eminent worthies in its history.[12] The poem thus culminates in an account of local products, customs, and great families, with rites serving only to point to the future Jin.

While Zuo Si's rhapsodies are the most elaborate descriptions of cities defined by their customs, later works touched on this theme. As the north-south divide became more fixed by the fifth century, many anecdotes or speeches discussed what distinguished the northern heartland of

Chinese culture, now the realm of "barbarians," from the wild southern lands where the true "Chinese" regime had taken refuge. These works occasionally touched on the distinctive cultures of the cities in the two zones.

One striking north-south urban contrast was an account by Yan Zhitui (531–591) of the distinctive roles of women. He focused specifically on the behavior of women in the city of Ye. A regional town near Anyang in modern Henan, it had become prominent under Cao Cao, who made it his capital. It was subsequently the capital for several Jin princes, for the Later Zhao state founded by the Shi family, and finally for the Eastern Wei and Northern Qi states that emerged from the civil war that destroyed the Northern Wei in the 530s.[13] Thus, when Yan Zhitui fled to Ye as a refugee and subsequently became a courtier of the Northern Qi, the city was one of the two northern capitals.

In his account Yan wrote:

> The women east [south] of the Yangzi have almost no social dealings. Even families related by marriage might go a dozen years with no contact except expressing goodwill through letters or gifts. But in Ye by custom it is entirely the responsibility of women to maintain their family's status, to handle legal disputes, make formal calls, and receive the powerful. The women's carriages fill the streets, and their fine silks fill the government offices, where they seek offices for their sons and make complaints about injustices suffered by their husbands.[14]

Here the public spaces of Ye are marked by a substantial female presence. Women in the south, by contrast, were largely excluded from the public realm and even from the semi-public spaces of social exchanges. Yan attributes this difference to the non-Chinese, nomadic societies of the steppe, where the elite of the Northern Wei and their successor states originated, and where men and women enjoyed relative equality. In one story from the *History of the Northern Dynasties*, fashions among the women of Ye determined the city's fate. In this story a new hairstyle that emerged among the women at the Qi court and then spread throughout the realm was in fact an omen presaging the dynasty's fall.[15]

While repeated occupations and rebuilding limit what can be learned from archaeological excavations at other capitals of the period such as Luoyang, Jiankang, and Chang'an, Ye as it existed from the third to the

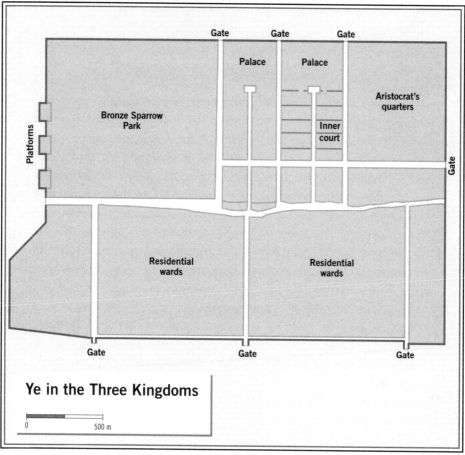

Gate   Gate   Gate

Palace   Palace

Aristocrat's
quarters

Bronze Sparrow
Park

Platforms

Inner
court

Gate

Residential
wards

Residential
wards

Gate   Gate   Gate

Ye in the Three Kingdoms

0   500 m

MAP 11

sixth centuries has been much better preserved and studied (Map 11).[16] This Ye was a rectangle bisected by a major east-west road. The area north of the road contained palace complexes, aristocratic residences, and an imperial park. The south was a grid of residential wards. The central palace complex in the northern part of the city was aligned on a north-south axis and approached by a major thoroughfare from the central southern gate. A second complex to the east contained the major government offices, as well as the residences of imperial kin and leading officials. The western third of the northern section was a large imperial retreat, the Bronze Sparrow Park, which contained an arsenal and other facilities. This plan provided the immediate model for the capitals of the subsequent Sui and Tang dynasties, as well as for early capitals in the Korean peninsula, Palhae (Bohai) in the far northeast, and Nara Japan.

Cityscapes, Villas, and Gardens

The southern capital Jiankang exemplifies the emergence of new semi-public spaces as settings for the activities that constituted cultural power, above all the urban garden and country estate. These artificial replicas of nature transferred the newly significant mountainscapes into the city and, conversely, extended the civilized realm into the mountains or foothills. Because these spaces were distinctive possessions of the great families who dominated society, they also provided new arenas for display. Gardens and nearby estates served as urban markers of status in the same way that towers, walls, and offices had spatially delineated Han social hierarchy. Significantly, these spaces were also settings where verses were written and exchanged. As poetry and conversation became hallmarks of the elite, gardens and estates defined a new geography of power.

Southern gardens and villas emerged from the encounter of northern émigrés with the vegetation and topography of the Yangzi basin, whose abundant rainfall and hilly terrain differed dramatically from the northern plains. Whereas much of the north was already deforested, many southern hills remained untouched and featured distinctive vegetation. As refugees traveled south, the dispersed temperate forests of the Yellow River basin, consisting of evergreen and deciduous trees, gave way to subtropical broadleaf evergreen vegetation along the hilly regions of the Yangzi valley. As the great families cut wood for building cities and cleared land for their estates, the southern lowlands too were gradually deforested. However, as the preface and poems of the *Orchid Tower* collection of 353 shows, the hills remained covered with trees and other indigenous plant life.[17] These vegetation-covered mountains—an alien world of animals and spirits—provided a model for the villa and garden, and these three linked sites came to define the cultural geography of the Yangzi during the southern dynasties.[18] They replaced the hunting park and capital as the thematic focus of Chinese cultural geography. This spatial inversion of power brought the countryside into the city—in actuality and in literature—and made knowledge of local landscape a prerequisite of elite status and power.

Since pre-Han times, mountains had been thought of as the negation of the social world, a counter-realm of both savagery and divine liberation.

The southern hermit who came to culturally embody both these attributes of mountain life was the recluse Guo Wen (d. 334), who wore the skins of animals that he found dead, tamed a wild tiger who became his companion, and ate only crops that he grew himself or fruits that he gathered from the forest. To demonstrate the folly of withdrawal, Confucius had noted that he could not "form a group with birds and beasts as companions." Eschewing civilization and human companionship, Guo Wen fulfilled precisely these conditions.[19] Yet he was celebrated during his lifetime and later incorporated into the Daoist pantheon.

However, Guo Wen accepted the invitation of the chief minister Wang Dao to move into his newly constructed West Garden at Wang's residence in Jiankang, whose orchards, strange rocks, birds, and wildlife artificially reconstructed Guo Wen's habitat in the mountains. This was one of the earliest of the great gardens built in the capital—the urban equivalent of a country estate, and, like it, modeled on the southern mountainscape. Guo Wen ignored the social eminences who came to gawk at him, and during his seven years in the capital never once left the West Garden. Though living in the city, he remained a hermit. When finally he attempted to escape back to the mountains and was captured, he resolved to fast to death and accurately predicted the exact day of his demise.

A less radical southern eremitism entailed living in the mountains but in a comfortable residence. This was the practice of Xie Lingyun (385–433), the father of poetry on mountain scenery. His program for living in the hills is the subject of his rhapsody "On Dwelling in the Mountains."[20] But as his preface makes clear, there were several ways in which men could dwell in nature: "The residing in nests and lodging in caves of antiquity may be called 'cliff-resting.' Living in the mountains under ridgepole and roof [in a house] I call 'dwelling in the mountains.' Residence in the wooded wilderness we may term 'hills and gardens,' and in the suburbs 'beside the city wall.'"[21] Xie's first category corresponds to the classic, political eremitism of earlier ages or of Guo Wen, the second refers to Xie Lingyun's own pattern celebrated in the poem, the third to a country villa, and the fourth to an urban garden. The preface also contrasts this poem with earlier ones on capitals, palaces, towers, and imperial hunts. He thus identifies his world as an alternative to the traditional capital.

After recounting the mountains and rivers that surround his lodge, Xie Lingyun describes the actual dwelling, which includes a garden, orchards, and groves of bamboo. He explains how he landscaped the surrounding hillsides and how his workers exploited the mountains' resources.[22] Despite insisting on withdrawal from the world of men, he also discusses how his lodge became a gathering place where Buddhist monks and to a lesser extent Daoist adepts engaged in study and writing.[23] Such activities are the religious counterparts of the poetic circles that defined the social elite. Thus, despite clearly distinguishing mountain lodges, country villas, and urban mansions with gardens, in practice and in writing Xie conflated the diverse forms of "natural" settings, as did most men in the period.

The country estates of the established southern families were located to the southeast of Jiankang, in the region around Lake Tai. The northern émigrés who arrived later with the Jin court developed estates to the east of the capital in Guiji. These rural villas served not only as settings for literary activities but also as the theme for both verse and landscape painting, identified above all with Gu Kaizhi. A literary vision of the country estate was first sketched in the late Eastern Han, notably in an account of an idealized estate written by Zhongchang Tong. His vision of a residence ringed by mountains and water, with orchards, bamboo groves, gardens, and a threshing ground, is cited by Xie Lingyun as a classical model of "dwelling in the mountains."[24] By the third century, great estates had become a conventional site for the literary and social activities of elites (Fig. 9).

The clearest early description of a country estate is in the preface to a collection of poems that describes Shi Chong's villa a few miles from the capital of the province he administered. For a farewell party for a friend returning to the capital, he held a banquet with musical performances and poetic compositions. The poems were gathered in an anthology, the preface to which described the estate and its social uses:

Both high and low ground had clear springs, and an abundance of fruit trees, bamboo, and pines. There were medical herbs, ten *qing* of cultivated land, two hundred head of sheep, as well as chickens, pigs, geese, and ducks. There were also water mills, fish ponds, and caves; indeed there was everything to delight the eye and satisfy the mind . . . Day and night we roamed and feasted, regularly changing our seats. We climbed up hills to gaze down, or sat in rows along the banks of the streams. Lutes, zithers, and mouth organs were placed on chariots to form an orchestra. When they stopped, drums and wind instruments alternated with them. Then everybody composed a poem to express his innermost feelings.

Fig. 9 Drawing from a rubbing depicting domestic scenes at a rural estate.
Sixth century. Museum of Fine Arts, Boston.

This preface and anthology provided the model for the more famous *Songs of the Orchid Tower* collection that was written in 353 and immortalized in Wang Xizhi's calligraphy.[25]

In addition to their role in literary production and forming social circles, country estates also shaped political careers. Ambitious literati routinely declined office or resigned from posts to establish a reputation as a writer or seek social advancement. This is exemplified by Xie An, hero of the *New Account of Tales of the World,* who dominated the southern court in the late fourth century. In his youth he rejected all offices and lived on his family's estate in the foothills of Guiji. An adept of pure conversation, lyric poetry, and calligraphy, he engaged in social outings with peers such as Wang Xizhi and Zhi Dun, forming a clique that controlled both the imperial court and Guiji society. He also educated the talented youths in his family and visited local temples. Only when his brother died did he take up service at court and rise to unparalleled prominence by defeating Fu Jian's invading army in 383.[26] Such practices became widespread in the period, leading to many attacks on hypocritical eremitism.

Wang Dao's West Garden was only one of many gardens inside the Eastern Jin capital, its suburbs, and the mountainside estates of the elite (Fig. 10). One of the most important was the Hualin Garden at the northeast corner of the city, a royal park that was begun in the Three Kingdoms period.[27] Numerous gardens were built in the Dongtian district, including those of Shen Yue and his contemporary Wei An. The biography of Xu Mian recounts how he devoted two decades of his life to improving his garden. The Western Residence on Mount Jilong in the northwest corner of Jiankang, where Xiao Ziliang assembled a celebrated poetry salon and political faction, included an elaborate garden whose artificial mountains were said to surpass the natural ones in the region.[28] Together with the Hualin garden, it flanked both sides of the imperial palace with artificial mountainscapes.

Gardens were so important in the life of the southern literati that Xie Lingyun, Shen Yue, and Yu Xin wrote canons of appreciation into their poems, based on aesthetic and cosmological principles of "garden criticism." Garden appreciation also figures in anecdotes on leading literati: "When Wang Xianzhi was passing through Wu on his way from Guiji, he heard that Gu Bijiang had a celebrated garden there. Although he had no previous acquaintance with the owner, he went straight to his home. At that time Gu was entertaining guests at a drinking banquet in the garden, but Wang wandered freely about, pointing out what he liked or dis-

Fig. 10   Rubbing of the story of Cai Shun's filial piety, set in dwellings in the mountain forests, Luoyang region, Northern Wei.

liked, acting as though there was no one else around."[29] The fact that Wang Xianzhi would make a significant detour simply to view a garden, and become so obsessed with its features that he perceived nothing else around him, suggests the fascination with garden aesthetics that had emerged by the fourth century.

Evolving principles of garden appreciation went hand in hand with the rise of specialists in garden design. Zhang Yong, a noted painter, calligrapher, and writer, was charged by Emperor Wen of the Song to rebuild the Hualin Park in 446. Another painter, Jiang Shaoyu, restored the imperial garden of the Northern Wei between 493 and 495. Dai Yong—a recluse, Buddhist layman, and, like his father Kui, a painter and maker of Buddhist images—was praised by Emperor Wen as one who knew gardens. When Dai Yong died, the emperor lamented that he did not have the chance to show him the Hualin garden then under construction.[30] Emperor Wen also praised Dai's contemporary, Zong Bing, author of

Introduction to Landscape Painting. A disciple of the Buddhist monk Huiyuan, Zong loved mountains and waterways and delighted in excursions to distant places such as Mount Lu. According to his biography, he decided to become a hermit and built himself a hut on Mount Heng, but he fell ill and returned to Jiangling. He drew images of the mountains he had visited on his walls and played his zither so loudly that the painted mountains resounded with the simulated sound of the wind.[31]

Gardens not only transformed the city and suburbs into "mountain and water" landscapes and provided a convenient setting for literary gatherings but also served as a reservoir of images for poetry. Vegetal imagery—the names and attributes of rare flowers—pervades accounts of feminine beauty that define the palace poetry sponsored by the imperial princes Xiao Gang and Xiao Yi in the Liang dynasty. This shared imagery suggests a parallel between garden and boudoir as enclosed realms of delight.

Gardens and mountain landscapes could define the capital at Jiankang in part because at first there were no city walls. The earlier Wu rulers and the first Eastern Jin emperors were satisfied with the natural defenses provided by the "coiled dragon" and "crouching tiger" topography, later reinforced by a bamboo stockade that emphasized even more the links of the capital to the natural setting. When the stockade was enlarged in 332, orange trees were planted just outside, and no brick wall was built until around 480. In place of a clear break between urban capital and surrounding countryside, Jiankang blurred one into the other. Gardens built throughout the capital and its surroundings contributed to this blurring. The gardens of Mount Jilong and the Hualin Park abutted directly on the wall, with hills immediately beyond, so that from the gardens the break between capital and landscape was invisible.

This absence of physical boundaries was reproduced socially in the excursions of literary salons into the countryside for parties devoted to drinking, calligraphy, and composition. It also figured in the movements of leading figures from court to suburban mansion to garden in the hills to estate in the mountains and then back again. Being a member of the social elite in the southern dynasties meant moving between city and nature—carrying the significance and power of the capital into the countryside in the form of estates, poetry, and painting, and also carrying nature into the city through the creation of gardens and the cultivation of the spirit of the "recluse in the court."

While aspects of garden culture were unique to the south, gardens also became a major feature of cities in the north. The *Record of the Buddhist Temples of Luoyang (Luoyang qielan ji)*, written in 547 by Yang Xuanzhi, describes gardens in many of the Buddhist temples constructed in Luoyang between Emperor Xiaowen's relocation of the Wei capital there in 493 and its burning in 534. Some gardens were built by members of the imperial family, others by wealthy commoners, and still others by unspecified members of the Buddhist order. Some of these used rare plants and artificial hills to construct on earth the garden scenes depicted in Buddhist visions of paradise, as shown in the cave paintings at Dunhuang.[32]

Yang's book describes the most beautiful of these gardens, employing classic themes of garden appreciation: "To the west of the [Great Forest] Monastery was a garden with abundant exotic fruit trees where there was continuous birdsong in the spring and chirping of cicadas in the fall. In the garden was a meditation building containing monastic cells, which were small but exquisitely built. The stillness of the meditation building, the calm of the cells, the splendid trees framing the windows, and the fragrant azaleas around the steps gave the feeling of being in a mountain valley rather than a noisy city."[33] As this short passage shows, a garden was intended not merely for viewing but was economically productive, with its harvest of exotic fruit. It recreated a mountain scene, and was arranged with framed windows and strategically placed views to direct the vision and thoughts of those who entered. Finally, it was conducive to tranquil contemplation, which in this case took the form of Buddhist meditation.

In all, the *Record of the Buddhist Temples of Luoyang* describes more than twenty gardens and refers to others. It says that around Longevity Hill, where the imperial princes had their residences, not only the princes but also their wives, the princesses, and their affines competed in building ever more elaborate gardens.[34] The garden at the residence of the minister of agriculture, Zhang Lun, was particularly notable: "The splendor of his garden with trees, hills, and ponds could not be matched by any of the princes. He had a Jinyang Mountain built that looked completely natural. There was range upon range of cliffs with towering summits, and the deep chasms and cavernous ravines all linked together. High forests of towering trees blotted out the sun and moon, while the wind blew mists through the hanging creepers and dangling vines. Rough stone paths that seemed impassable would suddenly allow a way through, while deep creeks were twisting at first and then straight. Lovers of mountains and the wilds would wander there, forgetting to return."[35] Like the literati garden builders of the south, Zhang Lun composed a rhapsody describing his garden.

Private gardens also figure in tomb art from the Luoyang region beginning in the early sixth century, as scenes for the shared pleasures of married couples.[36] Thus the northern capital Luoyang, along with Jiankang and the major southern cities, was also a city of gardens. To be a member of the elite meant to frequent these urban re-creations of mountainscapes or paradises.

Buddhist Temples as Semi-Public Spaces

While the *Record of the Buddhist Temples of Luoyang* contains abundant documentation on gardens, its primary theme is, of course, temples. In addition to gardens and places of meditation, these structures contained housing for monks or nuns and religious halls with statues and paintings, where monks and laymen listened to preaching or engaged in contemplation. Such buildings were constructed in every city in China, and others dotted the countryside. Many temples had halls that were open to the public at large and thus marked a major innovation in the spatial structure of the Chinese city.

In the major features of its physical layout—a rectangular shape, a city wall, a large palace district in the center or north of the town, a grid of streets, a division into wards—the rebuilt Northern Wei capital, Luoyang, carried forward later Han traditions (Map 12). The city was composed of a political district restricted to officials and a residential district made up of state-regulated markets and private dwellings. What made the new capital different from the old was the large number of Buddhist temples. Some were open to the public, who crowded in to witness preaching and spectacles and to engage in relatively free association. In addition, temples were the sites of mass public festivals that allowed open mingling of crowds. Lay associations linked to temples became a new form of voluntary association. In later imperial China similar roles would be played by guild halls, tea houses, or theaters, but the temple was the first major form of semi-public space between the political realm and the private household.[37]

Buddhist architecture in China had developed gradually. Only a single temple is known to have existed in Luoyang at the end of the Han dynasty, and by the late third century A.D. there were still only three. By 316, however, the number had increased to forty-two. After the fall of the

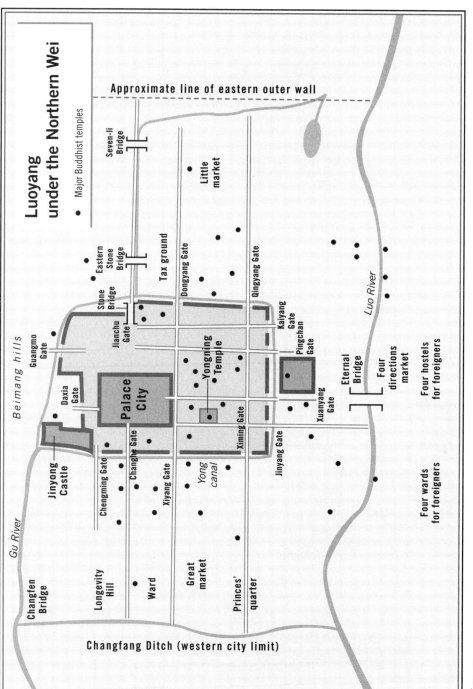

Luoyang under the Northern Wei

• Major Buddhist temples

Beimang hills

Gu River

Changfen Bridge

Longevity Hill

Ward

Great market

Princes' quarter

Changfang Ditch (western city limit)

Jinyong Castle

Chengming Gate

Xiyang Gate

Yong canal

Jinyang Gate

Daxia Gate

Palace City

Changhe Gate

Ximing Gate

Xuanyang Gate

Guangmo Gate

Stone Bridge

Jianchu Gate

Yongning Temple

Kaiyang Gate

Pingchan Gate

Eternal Bridge

Four directions market

Four hostels for foreigners

Four wards for foreigners

Luo River

Eastern Stone Bridge

Tax ground

Dongyang Gate

Qingyang Gate

Stone Bridge

Seven-li Bridge

Approximate line of eastern outer wall

Little market

MAP 12

Western Jin, the monk Fotudeng, who accompanied Shi Le as an adviser during his military campaigns, reported that during his travels he had seen or established 893 temples.[38]

Nevertheless, few religious images survive from the period, and it seems that temples open for the public worship of images were still rare. This was in part because there were still few large-scale Buddhist images that could be viewed from a distance, and in part because the emphasis on devotion to images was only fully introduced by Daoan, and later his disciple Huiyuan, from around 360. There are almost no records of wonder-working images in the north from this period, in contrast with the south where texts refer to large audiences adoring images.[39] Not until the Northern Wei emperor Taiwu conquered Liangzhou (modern Dunhuang) in 439 did substantial numbers of images and artists from Central Asia enter north China, and large-scale public image worship become prevalent.

The first major sign of this was the carving of the caves at Yungang, which probably began shortly after 460.[40] One of the earliest surviving examples of cave temple sculptures, the Yungang statues are an important landmark in the history of Buddhist art (Fig. 11). However, they

Fig. 11   The great Buddha at the Yungang caves. Near Datong, northern Shanxi, fifth century.

were a considerable distance from the capital. Buddhist art and architecture did not become features of urban life until the introduction of the multistoried pagoda (Figs. 12 and 13). This style of building, now a major element in our image of China, was inspired by an account in the *Lotus Sutra* of a great, bejeweled, seven-story tower. The text became widely known only with the translation by Kumarijiva in the early fifth century, which soon led Central Asian artisans to build a pagoda in the early Northern Wei capital of Pingcheng (northern Shanxi). Early depictions of this story are particularly abundant at Yungang.

The early pagodas in Pingcheng and its vicinity, like earlier ones built in the south, were usually three stories high and built of stone, although there is one reference to a pagoda of five stories. Craftsmen captured in military campaigns in the south introduced construction methods for erecting more substantial Buddhist monuments in Pingcheng. The chief example was the first Yongning Temple built in 467. It included three large halls and a seven-story pagoda that was the highest construction in China at the time, towering over both the earlier pagodas and the royal palace.[41] Buddhist pagodas assumed the role that towers had played in the Warring States, visibly demonstrating the majesty and power of the ruling house.

Pingcheng was originally a tent city at the Chinese frontier, however, and even after an elaborate palace complex was built there it remained remote from trade routes and of little importance as a pilgrimage center. Only when the Northern Wei moved their capital to Luoyang in 493 did the Buddhist temple become a dominant feature of the urban landscape, serving both as the focus of lay piety and a demonstration of elite status. According to a hostile account in the *Book of the Wei*, one third of the surface area of the Wei capital, whose walled area matched its Han predecessor but which included large suburbs, was occupied by temple complexes. Yang Xuanzhi states that the city contained 1,367 temples. His work describes fifty-five examples, concentrating on the largest and most splendid, and it is his account that gives us some sense of this first truly Buddhist capital in China.

> After the august Wei came to power and established its capital by Mount Song and the Luo River, Buddhist faith and teaching both flourished. Aristocrats and high officials parted with their horses and elephants as if they were kicking off their sandals. Commoners and great families gave away their wealth with the ease of leaving behind one's footprints. As a result monasteries and pagodas were packed

Fig. 12   The Songyue Pagoda. Dengfeng, Henan, 523.

Fig. 13   Drawing and bird's-eye
view of the Songyue Pagoda.
Dengfeng, Henan, 523.

0 1   6 M

closely together. Men competed in drawing the heavenly beauty of
the Buddha and copying the image he left behind in the mountains.
Temple spires were as high as the Spirit Mound [an ancient symbol
of Chinese emperorship], and the preaching halls were as grand as
the Afang Palace [the great palace complex of Qin Shihuang].

Bodhidharma, founder of the Chan (Zen) school in China, is supposed to
have said that the Yongning Temple, the greatest in Luoyang, surpassed
the temples in the Buddha's own realm.[42]

This highlights important features of Buddhism in the Northern Wei
capital. First, almost all the temples described by Yang were lay foundations. Of the fifty-five temples he recorded, thirty-four were sponsored by
members of the ruling elite—twenty by the imperial clan, eight by officials, and six by eunuchs. Only one temple was founded under the guid-
ance of monks, in contrast with the more than eight hundred supposedly
founded by Fotudeng in the fourth century. A dozen recorded temples
were sponsored by wealthy commoners who imitated the pattern of their
political lords.[43] Thus, building temples, or the conversion of private
mansions into places of worship, had become an essential attribute of political power or social prestige.

Lay donations focused on the forms of Buddhist devotion that most
welcomed lay participation and deemphasized the intercession of monks,
that is, to temples and images. This focus on lay piety in the fifth and
sixth centuries, characteristic of both the north and the south, marked a
turning point in Buddhist history.[44] Apart from a few nunneries that were
open only to privileged guests, due to the gender of their inhabitants
rather than their sacred character, Buddhist temples in Luoyang had public halls where the common people gathered to make offerings to images.
Thus, while these temples were founded by wealthy people, their patrons
consisted of crowds of the populace who daily gathered in the temples to
worship or converse. Although Luoyang, like earlier capitals, had zoning
regulations on residence wards and controls on popular gatherings, its
temples, which according to Buddhist doctrine were open to people from
"all four directions," allowed the mingling of Chinese and "barbarian,"
men and women, rich and poor, monks and laymen. Indeed, the grander
the temple the greater the pressure to open it to the people, as imperial
kin and wealthy families competed in conspicuous displays of public gen-
erosity in the form of Buddhist images and festivals for the benefit of the
populace.[45]

As devotion to images became the standard form of lay piety, both the south and the north produced "miracle tales"—often from Indian prototypes—of statues that wept, sweated, or walked and of magical trees distinguished by their remarkable shapes. Yang Xuanzhi records cases in which such miracles were witnessed by large crowds in the temples, as in the following account of the Pingdeng monastery, also noted for its superb mountain views and shade-providing trees:

> Outside the monastery gate was a golden statue twenty-eight Chinese feet high with a solemn visage. It regularly proved its spiritual power, in that whenever the state was to have good or bad fortune it would first display an omen. In the first month of 528 its face had a sorrowful expression. Both eyes shed tears, and its whole body was damp. People called it "Buddha sweat." All the men and women in the capital emptied out the markets and wards to go look at it. A monk took a piece of clean silk floss to wipe its tears, but in an instant the floss was completely soaked. He took another piece, but it too was instantly soaked. The weeping and sweating lasted three days. The next year in the fourth month Erzhu Rong entered the capital and many officials were executed so that the dead covered the ground . . . In August 530 the statue again wept bitterly. Since its omens had always been proven true, court and countryside were all terrified, and the government banned people's looking at or listening to the statue.[46]

Other stories tell of statues that summoned help when thieves attempted to steal them, statues hidden in the ground that produced miraculous light to signal their presence and indicate that the site should become a temple, and even a statue that killed a man's child when he failed to honor a pledge to cover the image with gold. Such tales of wonder-working statues were also common in the south, and they featured many of the same themes: miraculous origins, ability to speak or weep, and the power to manifest prophetic signs.[47]

The temples were also the centers of regular festivals and public performances that gathered large crowds from all ethnicities and all walks of life:

> [The Changqiu Temple] had a three-story pagoda the gleam of whose golden basin and sacred pole shone throughout the city. There was

also a statue of a six-tusked elephant bearing Sakyamuni Buddha up into the sky. The ornaments and Buddha statue were made entirely of gold and jewels, and its unique workmanship beggared description. On the fourth day of the fourth month [the Buddha's birthday] it was taken out in procession with lions and gryphons leading the way. Sword-swallowers and fire-belchers pranced on either side of the procession. There were men who climbed flagpoles, rope-walkers, and every kind of amazing trick. Their skill was greater and their clothes stranger than anywhere else in the capital, and wherever the statue rested spectators would pack round in a solid crowd in which people were often trampled to death.[48]

The celebration of the Buddha's birthday was even more spectacular at the Jingming Temple, which boasted a seven-story pagoda and spectacular gardens. All the Buddhist statues of the capital, more than one thousand in number, were assembled and then wheeled in front of the imperial palace where the emperor scattered flowers on them. The lay faithful and monks packed the sides of the road, holding flowers, listening to Indian music, and witnessing performances like those described above.[49]

The greatest temple, and the one that most clearly linked political power to Buddhist temple complexes, was the second Yongning Temple. This great complex was constructed by the Dowager Empress Ling in 516 after she seized power. Its surrounding walls were pierced by four gates that led into a large courtyard containing twin towers, a Buddha hall with jeweled statues, a lecture hall, a library, and rows of multistory cloisters housing both native monks and visiting dignitaries. Its crowning glory, however, was its nine-story pagoda that was implausibly said to soar 900 Chinese feet high (Fig. 14). A golden pole on top rose another 100 feet, and it could be seen at a great distance from the capital. The pole itself was topped by a golden basin for collecting dew.

In addition, a large golden bell was hung from each corner of each of the nine stories. "North of the pagoda was a Buddha-hall, modeled on the Supreme Ultimate Hall [the main ceremonial building] of the imperial palace. It contained an eighteen-foot-high gold statue, ten man-sized gold statues, three statues studded with pearls, five statues woven from gold thread, and two jade statues. They were all of brilliant, unmatched workmanship." The author also notes that sutras and images presented by foreign countries were stored in this temple. Since these were the highest forms of tribute, and tribute was crucial to imperial power, the temple

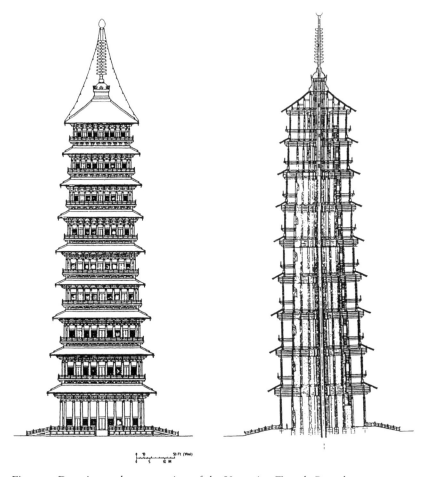

Fig. 14   Drawing and cross section of the Yongning Temple Pagoda.

was clearly a central, if not *the* central, locus of imperial authority. This is dramatized in a story that when the pagoda was finished, the dowager empress and her son ascended to its pinnacle and gazed down at the imperial palace which "appeared to be no larger than the palms of their hands" and the capital seemed "no bigger than a courtyard." This Buddhist temple complex, towering above the imperial palace, was the greatest visible manifestation of imperial power.[50]

When Erzhu Rong occupied the capital in 528, he stationed his army in the Yongning Temple. Similarly, when loyalist forces gathered under Yuan Hao, they also based themselves there. The young puppet emperor Zhuang was held prisoner in the temple in 530 prior to his execution. The temple was destroyed by a great fire in 534, and within the year

Luoyang was abandoned. In a final epiphany, however, that suggests the ability of the Buddha's *dharma* to survive the dynasty, travelers from Shandong reported having seen the pagoda "bright and luminous and looking like new," hovering over the ocean. After a moment it was lost in the mist.[51]

Although the *Record of the Buddhist Temples of Luoyang* shows how Buddhist temple halls, gardens, and towers transformed the Chinese cityscape and how Buddhist festivals altered its calendar, it reveals nothing of what the religion meant to its devotees.[52] Evidence on such matters is sparse, consisting mostly of inscriptions from the Buddhist caves at Yungang and Longmen and on free-standing steles. Most of these contain dedications to the imperial family and the state, often followed by prayers for the happy rebirth of deceased family members or the safety of those still living.[53] Along with the anecdotes telling of strange stories that swept Luoyang, many of them pertaining to divine retribution or inspired conversions, these inscriptions provide what little we know of the mental world of those who participated in the urban mass Buddhism of the sixth century.

Lacking any text dealing with the south comparable to the *Record of the Buddhist Temples of Luoyang,* we cannot reconstruct the Buddhist transformation of Jiankang and other cities in the Yangzi valley. However, there are accounts of individual temples, often with anecdotes indicating the role they played in elite life. Thus the *New Account of Tales of the World* mentions temples in the capital or Guiji visited by members of the elite who beheld sacred images, engaged in debates, or worshipped. Another entry refers to exchanges between a local official and the numerous monasteries in Yuzhang commandery in Jiangxi on the Buddha's birthday.[54]

More important evidence for the large number of southern temples, and for their role as sites of public gatherings, comes from numerous references to crowds that, like those in Luoyang, assembled to witness wonder-working images. These show that the imperial house and great families established many major Buddhist temples in the capital and in Guiji. One passage in the *Book of the Liang Dynasty* tells of crowds of "tens of thousands" assembling to behold relics of the Buddha's body that glowed of their own accord, and to contribute huge amounts of gold and silver to the temple that contained the relics. Others tell of miraculous statues, as in the following case from the *Biographies of Eminent Monks* (written by Huijiao, 497–554): "Everybody wholeheartedly supported making the Buddha image. With its halo it stood sixteen feet high and was truly remarkable. Every evening the image emitted light that shone through the halls, and even behind the image. Then by itself it walked to Mt. Wan. All the town's [Xiangyang, in the middle Yangzi] people worshipped it. Then it turned around and came back to the temple."[55] In the first half of the sixth century, Jiankang was said to have more than 700 Buddhist temples, out of a total of 2,816 for the entire Liang realm. This indicates that the situation in southern cities was comparable to the better-documented north.

A final piece of evidence for the rise of urban piety in the south comes from attempts by Emperor Wu of the Liang to revive imperial power and assert his authority over the monastic order by, among other policies, becoming a bodhisattva through offering vows and staging mass assemblies.[56] At irregular intervals the emperor held Universal Assemblies or Assemblies Open to Everyone at monasteries in the capital, featuring lectures, confessions, ceremonial banquets, and vows. The participants were gathered from all walks of life, including monks, officials, and commoners. Seating was arranged in order of the dates on which participants had first taken vows. Thus the unique event of the bodhisattva vow was periodically renewed through mass assemblies with people from every social stratum in the capital. While total numbers of participants in these rituals are not recorded, they clearly provided an unprecedented occasion for ordinary people to come into the presence of the emperor, who normally was hidden behind the walls of his palace. This again demonstrates how the new intermediate space provided by the temples transformed spatial relations within the Chinese realm.

Urban Economies

In addition to the development of new cultural spaces, the economic role of cities in the Northern and Southern Dynasties also changed. Most important was the decline of urban areas and trade in the north, and the emergence in the south of a more dynamic urban commercial network based on river trade, coastal and oceanic commerce, and the opening of unexploited hinterlands.

The limited data on northern cities suggests that constant warfare, minimal security, and the absence of any enduring government led to a general decline of trade, a sharp decrease in the use of money, and a consequent reduction in the scale and diversity of urban populations.

While periods of reunification allowed for sporadic recoveries of commerce, particularly long-distance exchange with Central Asia, such intervals were brief. Most regimes established their own capitals, many of which were built or rebuilt as capitals in a very short span of time. To provision these cities, captive populations were forcibly resettled in their vicinity. These populations included both Han Chinese, who generally engaged in agriculture, and nomadic peoples who pursued animal husbandry.

The fiscal foundation of the state was land that the state seized or confiscated and then redistributed to this servile population. The practice adapted the pattern of relying on internal "military colonies" established by the Cao Wei and Wu states during the Three Kingdoms period, which became a defining feature of Chinese society between the Han and the Song empires.[57] However, reliance on state-owned land was not a measure of the northern dynasties' power or the expansion of their governments' range but rather demonstrated weakness and retraction. The inability to register population and politically mobilize the elite led the state to act simply as a great landlord in a sea of smaller landowners. The northern states' administrations in the fourth century seem to have extended little beyond the immediate hinterland of the capital, with the rest of the countryside controlled by coalitions of armed landlords. The Northern Wei's reliance on military garrisons for local administration again demonstrates this state of affairs, with garrisons replicating the capital at the local level. The situation was similar in the south, where the imperial princes' armies dominated local administration, and the court functioned primarily to transfer funds to local families in the form of salaries.[58]

The best-documented northern urban economies are those of the Tuoba Wei capitals of Pingcheng and Luoyang.[59] Pingcheng was established as a formal capital in 398, when Tuoba Gui forcibly resettled half a million people, including a large number of artisans, in the city and its vicinity. The same year he initiated the construction of a large Buddhist building complex, including a five-story pagoda, lecture hall, meditation hall, and monks' quarters. Accounts of visitors from southern China say that the city was dominated by its huge palace complex, where slaves in associated workshops produced the government's material needs, including cloth, alcohol, metal goods, wooden objects, and pottery. Dependents also kept the ruler's herds, and the palace functioned as a massive granary and arsenal. The residential districts seem to have largely housed servants, stewards, guards, and hangers-on to the palaces and monasteries. Resident merchants likewise apparently were palace dependents. The government does not seem to have issued any currency until its move to Luoyang. Maintaining this command economy was difficult, and repeated droughts in the region made matters worse. Large-scale abandonment of land and food shortages were two reasons for moving the capital to Luoyang.

While more economically diverse, Luoyang remained an artificial creature of the imperial court and its associated monasteries. The city was filled with people (about half a million) resettled from Pingcheng and smaller population centers, and its walls, roads, and neighborhoods were reconstructed under imperial direction. The walled inner city was given over primarily to palaces, government buildings, and monasteries, while the rest of the city was divided into walled wards. The eastern suburb was primarily residential, with a small market for consumer needs; the northern one was kept largely empty for military training grounds. Commerce and industry were concentrated in the south and the west (see Map 12).

A large foreign community was housed in a special district in the southern part of the city, located between the Luo and the Yi rivers. Four hostels served foreign visitors and new immigrants from each of the "four directions," while four wards housed permanent foreign residents, numbering between forty thousand and fifty thousand people. These communities, largely merchants, had a special market known either as the Four Directions Market or the Eternal Bridge Market. Rare animals sent as tribute were also kept there. Foreigners could move north of the Luo River into the city proper only as a special imperial favor largely reserved for aristocratic refugees from the south and eminent Buddhist monks.

The western district was dominated by residences of the imperial family and their affines, as well as the numerous monasteries they founded. It was also the location of the Great Market and the main commercial district. Many wards in this district were occupied by tradespeople such as butchers or craftsmen. Others were reserved for musicians and singers, two primarily for brewers, and two for coffin-sellers and undertakers. Economic activity, except for the highly profitable trade in luxury and exotic goods from foreign lands, remained at a low level, largely focused on consumer goods and services. Cash, which the state did not issue until 485 and then immediately debased, was generally scarce.

Like other northern capitals, Luoyang under the Wei seems to have been largely provisioned from its hinterland and populated by resettled people. Most leading monasteries were provisioned by specially designated captive households settled around the capital, and it is likely that the imperial government relied on a similar system. Many leading families relied on slaves to work their fields, which resulted in a popular saying, "If you want to know about agriculture ask a male slave; if you want to know about weaving, ask a female one." The great agricultural manual written in this period, *Essential Methods of the Common People (Qi min yao shu)*, mentions both slaves and hired labor, and sometimes it uses slaves as a measure of value. Officials and generals were rewarded with grants of land and dependents, and military garrisons also lived off their own allotted land. This indicates that the capital, and the government as a whole, still relied on a dependent population working state-held land, with tax revenue as a secondary source.

The economic situation in the south was different.[60] Due to less frequent warfare and an abundance of rivers, local and inter-regional trade flourished under the southern dynasties. Consequently, the *Book of the Sui* noted that in Jiankang "most of the commoners were merchants and traders." Because the city was not divided into wards, markets arose in many locations, often next to temples. Urban merchants brought in products from nearby regions such as Guiji and Lake Tai, where the estates of the great families produced abundant crops of grain and fruit, as well as timber from the hills. They also received goods shipped along the Yangzi as well as coastal trade. Like the cities of early imperial China, Jiankang also had an underworld of gamblers, burglars, thieves, and gangsters; collaboration between officials or imperial clansmen and these criminals was not uncommon.

Jiankang's key role was as a trade entrepot. Because bulk commodities could be transported efficiently on the region's river system, estates could sell surpluses to the capital to be consumed or trans-shipped to other cities. Rice was already double-cropped in some areas, but the most important commercial crops were fruits, vegetables, and timber. Fish from lakes and the ocean was dried and shipped long distances. Large-scale handicraft production of ceramics, lacquer, bronze mirrors, textiles, and paper also flourished. Archaeological excavations indicate a dramatic increase in the number of kilns, and pottery was sold in a growing market. Bronze mirrors were a major export, some making their way as far as Japan. But as Buddhism increased in importance, bronze was increasingly diverted to the production of statues. Sea-based foreign trade to Japan, Korea, and Southeast Asia expanded to become a major feature of the southern economy.

One consequence was the re-monetization of the south. The Liu Song dynasty at first issued large amounts of reliable currency, but in the internecine wars of the late Song and the Qi the currency was debased, leading to general immiseration. The Liang founder managed to restore the currency, and in 523 went so far as to pay all officials entirely in cash. Later records indicate that in this period most of the urbanized regions of the south used cash, except for the ports of Guangzhou and Jiaozhou in the far south, which used gold and silver accumulated in foreign trade.

The rise of a cash economy often had a devastating effect on families whose wealth was tied up in country estates. To cut a figure or play any social role in the capital required large amounts of cash to purchase luxury goods. Charitable contributions to the Buddhist order, which became highly competitive during this period, also required cash. In times of relative tranquility, large harvests depressed prices, which meant that the necessary funds could be raised only by selling land or taking up posts away from the capital. Positions in the hinterland produced fortunes in the form of bribes and departure gifts but were commonly regarded as little short of exile. Yet the attempt to monetize land holdings was often ruinous. Offspring of formerly humble families gained considerable wealth through trade, the army, and government service, often receiving tax exemptions with their appointments as imperial legates. They were thus well-positioned to buy up land on terms unfavorable to the sellers. Like the peasants in Han times, great families gradually whittled away their estates until they faced total ruin. To survive, many families, including the imperial clan, had to engage in trade, usury, or the operation of pawn shops. Although a booming urban economy in the south was turning the region into the economic center of China, it helped destroy the families who had dominated local society in the area for centuries.

5

RURAL LIFE

LIKE the urban world, rural society during the Northern and Southern Dynasties carried forward major features from the Han, but also underwent significant changes. First, the era witnessed several innovations (or the first written evidence of older practices) in the crops and technologies that sustained Chinese society. Most but not all of these crops were linked to the southward expansion of Chinese civilization and the consequent introduction or increased production of southern plants.

Second, new forms of social organization arose in rural areas during the period. Country estates controlled by powerful families continued to predominate as they had in the late Han, but abandoned lands, especially in the north, came under the direct ownership and administration of the state. These lands, and their tenants, were not only exploited by the state for its own needs but were awarded to high officials and to the rising Buddhist monastic order. In the north, the breakdown of order and the constant necessity of self-defense also produced a new form of village society that altered relations between local communities and the state, while south of the Yangzi literati retired to the countryside and produced the first writings about rural and agricultural life in the imperial period.

New Crops and Agricultural Techniques

Most of our knowledge about the new forms of agricultural practice in the centuries between the Han and the Tang comes from the *Essential Methods of the Common People (Qi min yao shu)*. Jia Sixie wrote this text between 533 and 534, during the civil war that destroyed the Northern Wei but prior to the establishment of the Northern Qi in the east. Little is known of the author's life, except that he served as grand commandant of Gaoyang commandery, near the border of modern Shandong and Hebei. He also refers to his own agricultural experiences, including once owning a herd of two hundred sheep. Although he was a literati official, his language throughout the text is simple and straightforward, devoted to technical matters based on personal observation and a close reading of earlier manuals.

This reliance on personal experience produces a bias toward northern agriculture and a relative neglect of animal husbandry and irrigation, which were crucial in the northwest. However, the author's gathering of material from all of China and from the entirety of prior writings on agriculture makes this the earliest surviving summation of Chinese agriculture and the sole source for much of our knowledge of earlier texts, of which more than 160 are quoted. In addition to describing the cultivation and processing of crops throughout China, this manual—written in the heyday of northern Chinese agriculture—provided the prototype for all later comprehensive accounts. And because it was the last all-inclusive manual that did not take agriculture in the south as its model, *Essential Methods* provides a significant indicator of the timing of the southward shift of Chinese civilization.[1]

In his introduction the author discusses the aims and contents of his book:

> I have collected material from classics and commentaries, and even from proverbs and folksongs, checked these with experienced farmers, and verified them in my own practice. Beginning with plowing and cultivation, down to the processing of vinegar and meat pastes, I have completely recorded everything that can provision life . . . The worthy and wise criticize abandoning agriculture to pursue secondary occupations which make you rich in the short term but poor in the long run, as starvation and cold gradually develop. Therefore I have omitted all matters pertaining to trade. Flowers and wild grasses can delight the eye, but they only have blossoms in the spring with no fruit in the fall. Consequently they are empty and artificial, and do not merit being preserved here.[2]

This introduction suggests that the book is aimed at ordinary farmers and not the large landowners who produced crops for market. Similarly, the dismissal of flowers and ornamental grasses indicates hostility toward the gardening craze among elites in the period, although in fact these gardens played a significant economic role in the production of fruits.

However, a thorough examination of the book itself presents a different picture. First, it is unlikely that heads of small peasant households could read such a book. Owners of more substantial estates were the primary literate audience. Moreover, many of the crops described in the book were clearly grown for market as well as household consumption, and references to the use of tenants and even slave labor suggests that these products were cultivated on a large scale. In one case Jia measures the costs of a process in terms of the price of purchasing a slave, which was not an option on small farms. Thus, the book is clearly aimed at a landlord audience and not individual peasant households.

The book first discusses the proper size of a farm, and it suggests three hundred *mu*—in this period, between forty and fifty acres—as reasonable.[3] While this is far larger than a typical peasant holding during the Han, which was just over ten acres, it is only 15–20 percent of the size of a major Han estate, which could reach three to four thousand acres. A decree of the Northern Wei Emperor Xiaowen in 477 specified that a household of two adult males, i.e., a father and one unmarried son, should have sixty *mu* so that there would be no unused labor or unexploited land. The earliest form of the state-allocated equal-field system, initiated by the same emperor in 485, gave similar amounts of highest-quality land for individual peasant farms.[4] Thus the typical holding suggested by Jia Sixie is about five times larger than what a well-off individual peasant household of the period would own. This suggests that his intended audience is middling landlords with a handful of tenants or slaves. References in the book to the number of animals, trees, and various tools on the farm support this conclusion. This targeted readership suggests something of the range of literacy in the period. It also indicates that estates in north China were smaller than in the Han, an idea supported by other evidence.

The book describes a system of farming that required intensive use of both land and labor and was highly productive, given the absence of mechanization. The emphasis on the intelligent and disciplined application of human labor found in Han manuals was developed by Jia Sixie to a much higher degree. This was particularly true of rice production in the south. Intensive agriculture of this sort did not require truly large estates, as found in the West, but rather the thorough exploitation of relatively small areas.

The *Essential Methods* begins with an account of clearing "land in mountains or marshes."[5] This emphasis on opening new land, rather than clearing shrubs and trees from abandoned fields, reflects historical circumstances. Faced with constant marauding armies and bandits, many villages had moved to hilly or marshy land more distant from cities and major roads and hence more defensible and less subject to attack. Consequently, agriculture in the north increasingly required exploiting hillsides that had once been considered wasteland. The same was true in the south, where the prime land of the river valleys and lakes was already occupied by established families when the émigré clans arrived. As a result, they established estates in the hills of Guiji and in similar locations in the central Yangzi. The rise of Buddhism and Daoism encouraged this movement of Chinese civilization into the hills and mountains. *Essential Methods* thus explains how to clear land, plant crops, and make a living in rough, hilly terrain.

Essential Methods does not discuss the introduction of the single-ox plow, but it is depicted in some tomb art from the third century. Han plows had required at least a pair of oxen, which few peasant households could afford (Fig. 15). The single-ox plow, with a short, curved beam, significantly reduced the capital required for animal labor in agricultural production. A single-ox mould-board plow that turned the earth over as it turned it up was also introduced in the north. In the fifth century the Northern Wei state even distributed oxen to peasants in certain regions and organized systems allowing peasants to hire other people's oxen in return for labor such as hoeing fields.[6] These developments suggest that animal power became much more prominent in north Chinese agriculture in the centuries following the Han.

Land turned by a plow is frequently left in large lumps, particularly in the case of the heavier alluvial soil in the flood plain of the Yellow River or the valley of the Huai. Up through the Han, clods were broken up with a hand-held maul or rake. In more advanced agriculture, these lumps are broken up by harrowing. Animal-drawn harrows with fork-like tines are depicted in murals from a third-century Jiayuguan tomb in Gansu and in a pottery model from an early fourth-century tomb in Guangdong, but *Essential Methods* is the first Chinese text to discuss harrowing techniques (Fig. 16). It describes an animal-drawn harrow with iron tines, and a flat bush-harrow that was dragged at least twice across plowed fields to create a layer of finer soil that served as dust-mulch. In southern rice paddies, a similar harrowing was achieved with rollers, but these apparently were not used in north China.[7]

Fig. 15   Drawing of plowing, sowing, and harrowing. Jiayuguan, Gansu, third century.

Jia Sixie devotes a chapter to selecting seeds. All major crops grown in this period—wheat, barley, millet, and rice—produce shoots of uneven lengths and ripening periods. To reduce this problem, Jia advocates methods for selecting and setting aside the best heads of grain for use as seeds: "For foxtail and panicled millet, whether glutinous or nonglutinous, the seed-grain should be collected separately every year. Select the finest heads of even color, cut them with a harvesting knife, and hang them in a high place. In the spring prepare the grains and sow them separately to provide the seed-grain for the next year." The abundance of seeds produced by these cereals meant that, compared with the West, a smaller percentage of the harvest had to be set aside as seeds. Jia recommends that seeds should be selected for different ripening times and resistance to drought, which both reduces losses due to weather and allows planting and harvesting to be spread over longer periods so that more grain could be produced by the same number of workers. In a self-described "selective" list, Jia names ninety-eight varieties of millet and (despite his northern bias) thirty-seven varieties of rice, a considerable advance over what was known in the Han.[8]

Another innovation, also linked to the south, was pre-germinating seeds by soaking them before planting. This was especially important in rice farming. Germination before planting greatly accelerates growth, and it is particularly helpful for wet rice, which has difficulty sprouting in water that is too deep or muddy. *Essential Methods* describes at length

Fig. 16   Drawing of harrowing. Note the technique of sitting on the harrow, rather than just pressing down with the foot, as in Fig. 15. Jiayuguan, Gansu, third century.

how different seeds should be soaked in various decoctions, often involving processed animal parts serving as fertilizers and pesticides. Others, such as mallow, were to be dried in the sun before planting. Such methods had been described in the Han, but not to this extent.[9]

The next task was to sow the prepared seeds. From the Warring States period we have records of sowing by hand along straight ridges turned up by the plow. Seeds were scattered at intervals, or inserted with a dibble (digging-stick). In Han times the most advanced way of sowing was with a seed-drill. In this method, oxen drew an implement carrying a seed-box that was shaken by a man so that the seeds dropped at regular intervals. This tool was attributed by a late Han text to the agricultural innovator Zhao Kuo, but the earliest surviving detailed description is in *Essential Methods*. Jia carefully distinguishes those crops that are suitable for sowing with the drill from those whose shapes or other characteristics require using the older method of dibbling. He recommends the dibble for wheat, barley, dry rice, ginger, and roots and tubers.[10]

The most important form of sowing described in *Essential Methods* is the transplantation of wet rice. In this method, which came to dominate East Asian agriculture, pre-germinated rice seeds are sown in seed beds; after two to eight weeks, depending on the variety, they are transplanted into the main field. Rice transplantation is first mentioned in the *Monthly Ordinances of the Four Classes of People* (*Simin yueling*), written in the late Eastern Han. However, models of rice fields from tombs probably dating from the early Eastern Han show well-spaced rice seedlings arranged in straight rows, indicating transplantation. Moreover, a later Han model found in a Sichuan tomb is inscribed with the phrase "holes for transplanting rice seedlings." However, *Essential Methods* is the first surviving text to give a detailed account of the procedure, including the specification that the seedlings should be trimmed and planted in a shallow manner to encourage the production of more shoots. While the origins of the technique are uncertain, it probably emerged in Southeast Asia, where irrigation and wet rice cultivation developed at an early stage, and was gradually transferred to south China and on into the north.[11]

In the drier north, the goal at sowing time was to ensure the maximum amount of moisture in the soil. Soil was turned to trap any snowfall in the ground, and plants were placed at regular intervals in straight rows with the seed-drill. In the south, where moisture was not an issue, dryland cereals such as millet or wheat were often simply broadcast. However, the chief staple, rice, was grown in seed boxes and transplanted in order to accelerate growth and produce a high density of shoots and grains. Straight-row planting also facilitated weeding. In both north and south, the techniques in use were far more labor-intensive than those employed in Europe, and produced much higher yields.

Chinese agriculture was further distinguished from Western farming by the early use of fertilizer. Pre-Han and Han texts describe the use of animal manures and silkworm droppings, as well as the fertilizing value of rotting weeds. *Essential Methods,* however, provides the first account of the use of green manures: plants grown solely for the purpose of improving the soil. It advocates plowing young aduki beans into the soil before planting melons, mallow, or other vegetables. While many plants could be used as green manure, the most valuable were beans, which fixed nitrogen in the soil.[12]

Essential Methods is also the earliest surviving Chinese text to elaborate a theory of crop rotation to keep land in continuous use. Jia Sixie carefully describes which crops should precede or follow others. Combined with the systematic selection of earlier-ripening varieties, crop rotation allowed multicropping, particularly in the south, where the abundance of water and milder climate produced two or three main crops in a year. Even for the north Jia describes how alternating barley, winter wheat, and an intermediate planting of beans or turnips could produce three crops in two years. This is the first description of inter-planting different crops or varieties to secure maximum use of land without crowding and to allow one specie's actions to benefit others.[13]

While the state and wealthy landlords built granaries, the most common method of grain storage for peasants since the Neolithic period was to bury grain in airtight earthen pits, sometimes lined with matting or grasses to keep out water. As late as the Tang dynasty, the imperial granary still used pits for storage. Jia Sixie argues that storage in pits rather than jars is better for all seed grains except rice. He recommends that millet should be parboiled before storage to prevent mildew, while wheat should be burned in the husk to improve resistance to insects. Rice was to be husked and polished, because parboiling altered the flavor in a way that the Chinese did not like. In addition to methods of storage, Jia Sixie also describes how different food crops can be preserved through salting, pickling, or rendering into pastes.[14]

Jia Sixie lists thirty-one species of vegetables grown in the north of China, of which twenty are still grown today, along with large numbers of fruit trees, including both those known for centuries in the north or introduced during the Han from Central Asia, and those more recently encountered in the south such as lichees, loquats, bananas, and coconuts. He cites early regional accounts of distinctive flora and fauna in the south, and as with other crops he lists numerous varieties of fruit—forty-five of jujubes, twelve of peaches, twelve of pears—and describes diverse methods of propagation, including seedlings, cutting, and grafting. He also discusses cultivating trees both for gardens and for lumber. While production of vegetables and fruits for sale in markets was already a common practice in the Han dynasty, Jia advocates a more radical turn to market farming, with hundreds of *mu* being devoted to a single commercial crop.[15]

The southward shift of the Chinese population meant that in the long run the wet region south of the Yangzi, with its massive rice production, became the food basket and demographic center of China.[16] Rice seems to have originated in the piedmont wetlands of Southeast Asia, where it became best adapted to growth in water. It has been grown extensively in south China since the Neolithic, and as a dry-land crop in parts of the north. Because the productivity of rice farming is largely proportional to the labor invested—the quality of water and timing of its application, the pre-germination of the seeds, the preparation of the field, the spacing and speed of transplantation, and the intensity of hoeing and weeding—rice encouraged the already prominent Chinese tendency toward intensive cultivation.[17] Small highly productive plots worked by skillful peasants militated against the replacement of human labor with capital-intensive machinery. This continued reliance on a skilled peasantry shaped the social structure of China's rural society.[18]

Mechanization *did* enrich both north and south in the form of water-driven machinery, used primarily on the estates of Buddhist monasteries and laity, to mill grain and press oils. Small water-driven pounding pestles were used by the time of Cao Cao, and Shi Chong had more than thirty such devices at the end of the third century. Truly large-scale milling installations with more elaborate machinery appeared around the beginning of the sixth century. Because these required rapid water flow, they were often built on hillsides. These powerful mills ground much larger amounts of flour to a higher degree of fineness, while other water-driven machinery pressed oil for cooking and lighting. These installations became major sources of income for their owners, and they opened up new economic niches for professional operators.[19]

Another major change in agriculture in this period was the development of tea culture in the south. Tea requires well-drained soil and substantial rainfall distributed fairly evenly over the year, which makes it well suited to the hillsides of south China. Growing tea allowed southern farmers to exploit terrain that was not suitable for rice or other available crops. The first clear reference to drinking tea is in the biography of an official who died in 273, although it might earlier have been used medicinally. However, in the Northern and Southern Dynasties the drink was confined to elements of the southern elite. Tea drinking became closely associated with Buddhism, as a means both of staying alert in meditation and avoiding solid food in the afternoon, but evidence on this dates largely from the Tang dynasty.[20] Because of its cultivation on hillsides, combined with its still-limited demand, tea was largely produced by individual peasant households or monasteries.

An anecdote from the *Record of Buddhist Temples in Luoyang* points to a major contrast between north and south in terms of diet:

When Wang Su first came to Wei [from the south], he did not consume mutton, yoghurt-drinks, or such northern fare. Instead he regularly ate carp stew, and when thirsty he drank tea . . . Several years later he attended a banquet hosted by Emperor Gaozu, where he consumed a great deal of mutton and yoghurt. The emperor was startled and said, "Of the flavors of China, how does mutton compare with carp stew, and tea with yoghurt?" Su replied, "Lamb is the finest produce of the land, while fish are the best of water creatures.

While preferences vary [between regions], they can both be called delicacies. However, there is a great gap between their flavors. Mutton is like such great states as Qi and Lu, while fish is like such little states as Zhu and Ju. Only tea completely misses the mark, and is the true slave of yoghurt."[21]

The *New Account of Tales of the World,* written in the south, features stories that go in the opposite direction, with southerners challenging northerners' taste for milk products, a southerner who claims to have nearly died because he ate some yoghurt, and a northerner who makes a fool of himself at a banquet because he does not recognize tea.[22] These and related anecdotes in the commentaries and dynastic histories show how the great north-south divide that had developed in China included a distinction in cuisine in which the north was marked by "barbarous" products of animal husbandry, such as lamb and dairy, while the south was distinguished by its taste for the produce of rivers and oceans, as well as newly fashionable tea.

The north-south distinction between a rice-based diet and a millet-based one does not figure in these debates. Probably cereal grains were too basic, and hence too low in prestige, to merit discussion among elites. Debated foods were both regionally distinctive and characteristic of an upper-class diet. The southerner who claimed to have nearly died from eating yoghurt received it from chancellor Wang Dao, a member of an émigré family who had fled south in 307 and the leader in establishing the Jin court at Jiankang. The fact that a prominent émigré entertained a guest with milk products indicates that this was no longer strictly "barbarian" fare, but at least by the third century (and perhaps even in the Han) was fashionable among the northern elite. Moreover, the fact that the "poisoned" man describes himself as a "native of Wu" who almost became a "northern ghost" suggests that the tension between the recent émigré families and established southerners could be articulated through the same dietary contrasts as those between the "barbarian" north and the south.[23]

Social Organization of Families in the North and South

The Northern and Southern Dynasties were also distinguished in their familial structures. First, they differed in the role played by women in the household economy, as noted by the sixth-century scholar Yan Zhitui:

In the south even those who are poor devote themselves to outer appearances. Their carriages and clothing have to be costly and spot-
less, even if their wives and children starve. But household affairs
in the north are largely controlled by women. They never do without fine silk, gold thread, and kingfisher feathers, but they use lean
horses and decrepit servants as long as these fulfill their roles . . .
Women north of the Yellow River are vastly superior to southerners
in the work of weaving and sewing, and the arts of embroidering
patterns on fine silk.[24]

This is the domestic equivalent of Yan's account of the public role played
by women in the city of Ye. Women in the north were far more powerful
than those in the south, and they did not deprive themselves or their children in order to keep up appearances. Since these appearances are defined through the appurtenances of office-holders, Yan suggests that in
the south, unlike the north, the demands of public careers came before
household needs. Northern women's greater concern for the household
manifests itself also in their superior skill in every aspect of cloth production, classically women's work, from plain fabrics to embroidery.

Another contrast between north and south described by Yan Zhitui is
the use of speech as a social marker:

In the south the natural environment is mild and agreeable, so people's pronunciation is clear, high, and precise. Their failing is that
they are shallow and superficial, and their words are often unrefined.
In the north the landscape has deep mountains and valleys, so people's pronunciation is sinking, muddy, and blunt. They benefit in being simple and straightforward, with many ancient verbal expressions. However, the speech of southern gentlemen is superior to that
of those in the north, while the speech of northern commoners is
better than that of those in the south. Even if you switched their
clothing, you could distinguish a southern gentleman from a commoner after hearing a few words, but if you listened to a northern
courtier and commoner speaking behind a wall, even after an entire
day it would be hard to distinguish them.[25]

This passage combines explanations based on natural environment and
history. The moist and balmy southern climate manifests itself in speech
that is like clear liquid, with sharp definition, while northern pronuncia-

tion expresses the rustic simplicity and lack of definition of its earthy, undulating landscape. For the same reasons, northerners are straightforward and honest, in contrast with the superficiality of the more refined southerners.

Yan follows this with a class-based analysis of speech in which the differences between the north and south result not from environment but from their different histories. In the south the émigré elite, the majority of the old Han ruling class, had the finest pronunciation, while commoners speaking the local Wu dialect had the poorest. The elite's linguistic conservatism exacerbated this class distinction in pronunciation.[26] In the north, on the other hand, the elite of the period were great families who remained behind when the court fled south. Because they were lower on the social scale than the émigrés and in regular contact with their tenants, their pronunciation was inferior to the former, and closer to that of peasant neighbors. The language at all levels of the old northern heartland, however, preserved more elements of the classical language of China than did that of the south.

From this, Yan concludes that locally powerful families in the north were socially closer to those whom they dominated than were great families in the south.[27] The émigrés' flight southward to found a new court, in contrast with the immobility of the remaining northern elite who lacked ties to the short-lived non-Chinese courts, produced sharp differences in kin structures and relations to local, rural society. The émigré families entered a realm where developed land was already in the hands of established southern families. Newcomers who built substantial estates had to expand into hilly or marshy marginal land that had not been exploited for agriculture. They relied on the labor of local Chinese peasants, from whom they differed in customs and language, or on that of local non-Han "Yue" peoples, who were even more culturally distinct from their masters.

When ambitious members of these southern families moved to the capital to seek a court career, they frequently dissociated themselves from their less successful relatives in the countryside. Sometimes cousins fought one another for office and power at court. The rise of a monetized urban economy in the fifth and sixth centuries also impoverished branches of leading families and reduced their rural base. New employment opportunities drew peasants off estates and into the cities. These developments loosened the structure of southern families even more, both in their ties to kin and in their relation to the local population that surrounded them.

In the north, by contrast, the chaotic political situation encouraged kin to remain together in the countryside, and village communities to adhere closely to their leading families in forming local self-defense organizations. Security depended on social adhesion, the economy tended toward local autarky, and for decades at a time no imperial court lured away ambitious individuals. Rural society was characterized by strong kin ties among many families sharing a common surname, who acted as the nucleus of more integrated village communities.

Evidence for these developments scattered through the surviving records shows a consistent contrast between north and south. Several authors, for example, note the greater emphasis in the north on loyalty and cooperation within larger kin groupings, such as those with a common surname: "The northern lands emphasize sharing a surname, and call all such people 'blood kin.' If people of the same surname come from far away to seek refuge, without exception they use every ounce of their strength to assist them. If they did not exert themselves to the fullest, they would be rejected by their village community. In contrast, when Wang Yi heard that Wang Yu, also of the Wang family of Taiyuan, had settled south of the river, he sought refuge with him. Wang Yu treated him rudely, so Yi excused himself and departed."[28]

This contrast between the north, where community mores enforced the obligation to treat anyone with the same surname as close kin and provide assistance, and the south, where a common surname sanctioned no claims whatsoever, was even more striking in the case of Wang Dao and Wang Dun. These cousins conspired to kill a northern kinsman who sought to join them in the south, and shortly thereafter they went to war with each other. Weak bonds figure in accounts of other leading southern families, such as the Xie.[29] By contrast, in several cases members of great families in the north expended their property to rescue distant kin of the same surname, and even kin by marriage.[30]

Dynastic histories also contain stories indicating that northerners not only insisted on obligations to more distant kin, but also preserved closer relations and shared more common property within individual households. The practice was widespread in the north of registering many households, in some cases dozens, as a single family.[31] Southern families, on the other hand, were inclined to divide property and thus households. A classic example is the story of the family of Pei Zhi, who began life in the service of the Southern Qi state but went over to the Northern Wei. His mother donated herself as a slave to a Buddhist monastery, was redeemed by her sons, became a nun, and finally returned home. The account continues: "Although Zhi sent the salary from his provincial office to provide for his mother and younger brothers, each kept their separate personal property. They dwelt together, but each had their own cooking pot, and in the one household there were several stoves. This was probably because they had been influenced by customs south of the river."[32]

The reference to separate pots and multiple stoves apparently became a hostile stereotype of southerners, for a story preserved in the Song dynasty (960–1279) *Broad Records of the Taiping Reign Period* (*Taiping guangji*) tells of a Wei official sent on a mission to the southern Chen. He responded to mockery of the north with a poem telling how if southerners "share a pot, they each boil their own rice" and if they "share a pan, they each cook their own fish."[33] Thus, even eating together, the most basic measure of a shared life, was supposedly abandoned in the south. Other texts offer more conventional observations on the division of property, such as a memorial written around 454 in the south which states that fathers and sons divided property in "seven out of ten" elite households and "five out eight" commoner households, and that families would not even rescue kin who were starving or freezing.[34]

The collapse of administration in the north had undercut the legal foundation of land ownership. While abandoned land could be seized by the state for "military colonies," anyone able to open untilled land in the hills (which had officially belonged to the state since Han times) or resettle abandoned agricultural land became the de facto owner. Consequently, the armed communities based around forts were de facto owners of the land they held, which in practice meant that the dominant local family or families effectively owned the land, and all peasant plots were held through them (Fig. 17). These peasants were thus equivalent to tenants or serfs. Such ties of dependency between armed landholders and peasants had emerged throughout rural China from the late Han, but they were particularly strong in the north.[35]

Given their role in local defense, both great families and village society in the north were far more militarized than those in the south. This is shown in records of military activities during the two great dynastic disasters of the mid-sixth century, the civil war following the Hou Jing rebellion in the south (548–557) and that following the Revolt of the Six Garrisons in the north (523–534). In the latter many powerful families led military forces to defend their localities, sometimes in alliance with the imperial court and sometimes with the rebels. In the south, no estab-

Fig. 17   Drawing of a walled compound with moat in the countryside. Western Wei sketch of a detail, Cave 127, Maijishan, near Tianshui, Gansu.

lished family played a military role in the battle against Hou Jing or the subsequent civil war. Instead, local military power devolved into the hands of "new men" who gathered private military forces whose services they sold to the highest bidder.[36]

The cohesion of northern households often led to their opposition to court service. This figures in the dying words of a local magnate to his sons and nephews: "It suffices if you can obey your elders in the household, be affectionate to your neighbors in the village, and take up a post in the local commandery, perhaps rising as high as a scribe in the Bureau of Merit, in all cases serving with loyalty and purity. Do not undertake long journeys to serve in the capital, where I fear you will gain neither wealth nor honor, but simply call down troubles upon your family. If you forget these words, then you have no father, and if ghosts have consciousness, I will not return to eat your sacrifices."[37] Here the father sets loyalty to the family and village in opposition to service at court, and he makes the former the basis of father-son ties.

A handful of northern families had traditions of state service, but between the fall of the Western Jin in the early 300s and the reunification of the north by the Wei in the mid-fifth century, even these families largely eschewed office and devoted themselves to their local base. This is exemplified by the Cui family of Boling. Despite a history of state service dating back to the Han, throughout the fourth century no member of the family did anything except keep the family's reputation and local power intact by defending themselves, their neighbors, and their clients.[38] They accumulated land, intermarried with leading neighbors, above all the Lis of Zhaojun, and supported their community. Both histories and stone inscriptions indicate that they spent most of their time in the vicinity of Boling. Around 475 between ten and twenty adult male Cuis lived in a single household, which probably had more than thirty members. At one point, when two adult sons died, the head of the household was one of their widows, Madam Li. "Family affairs, large and small, were all decided in consultation with her. When the brothers went out, if they obtained even a slight bit of wealth, it was all put in Madam Li's storehouse. Each season when it was divided she would supervise."[39] More distant Cui kin gathered for major festivals, as did members of the Li family. Distant kin were appealed to for material help. The Cuis also relied on one another for education, as there were no schools during this turbulent period.[40]

The Northern Wei court began trying to recruit Cui men along with representatives of other leading families in 431, without success. Only after the Wei moved the capital to Luoyang in 493 and adopted a policy of sinicization did Cui family members begin to leave their local base to take up official posts, first military and then civil. With the Rebellion of the Six Garrisons in 523, they reverted to a military role, but different branches of the Cui family aligned with different political actors. Thus, in decades of state service, the Cuis began to break up as a coherent family unit, in many cases loyalty to political superiors supplanting loyalty to kin. The split of the Wei into warring Western and Eastern halves accelerated this tendency. Certain lines of the family settled in the Western Wei capital of Chang'an, cutting physical ties with their kin. Family members had to choose between local position and a commitment to office, and those who chose office had to choose yet again between a high but dangerous one and a low but secure one. As a result of such individual decisions, by the late sixth century the Cui family had lost its local character. All politically active members had left the family base, which ceased to serve as either a focus for the family or a refuge in times of trouble.

Other leading northeastern families abandoned their local bases and dispersed at this time. The "pull" was the attraction to ambitious individuals of a resurgent court in a new capital after the Sui reunification of China in 589. The "push" was the equal-field system first introduced in

485. This allowed peasants to secure land without patronage from a great family, who thus lost their dominance of local society. In addition, the Sui encouraged local officials to restrain the powerful families, abolished the Nine-Rank system of appointment to office, and eliminated local patronage positions. These policies further reduced the local influence of northern families and prevented their members from securing a post without leaving their place of residence.[41]

Consequently all the Cuis of whom we have any record in the subsequent Tang dynasty descended from those men who abandoned their local base to serve in the court, and the same seems to have been true of other families. In this way the leading families of the north, hitherto associations of kinsmen and dependents organized to secure local power through mobilizing their community, became exclusive lineages constituted through common descent established in written genealogies, who defended their position through privileged access to office. Most kin no longer lived together or provided mutual assistance, and any line that failed to produce officials for a couple of generations was dropped from the genealogy that defined the family. With this increasing focus on the central court and bureaucratic office, the practices and values of northern families converged with those of southerners, who for centuries had focused on service at court rather than their local bases, and had sacrificed the claims of kin ties to those of political office.[42]

Although the conduct and values of major families in the north and south converged, they remained distinct well into the Tang dynasty. Writing in the mid-eighth century on families and genealogies, Liu Fang remarked:

The families of Shandong are simple and sincere, so they value relations by marriage . . . The families of the south are refined, so they value the exceptional individual . . . The families of Guanzhong are heroic, so they value offices . . . The families of the far north are martial, so they value noble kin . . . As for their flaws, those who value relations by marriage give affines priority over their own lineage. Those who value exceptional individuals advance talented children of secondary marriages at the expense of those of the official wife. Those who value offices slight the married couple to emulate the splendid and glorious. Those who value noble kin pursue power and neglect the rites and teachings.[43]

The enduring influence of the north-south distinction can be seen in this passage: the northern regions share relative simplicity and military traditions, while the south is distinguished by its emphasis on culture and the talented individual.

State-Owned Lands

The centuries after the Han dynasty witnessed a reliance, unique in Chinese history, on direct state ownership of land, especially in the north. The earlier Qin and Han empires had left the largest possible amounts of land in the hands of peasant freeholders from whom they extracted taxes and service. Agricultural land owned by the state and worked by slaves or sharecroppers had played a secondary fiscal role, providing money to defray expenses of local government offices. However, the emergence of significant landlordism during the Han had already challenged this system, and the civil war following the Han's collapse forced ever more peasants to seek refuge with powerful clans who offered them refuge as tenant-serfs on their estates. These estates became economic and military hubs, whose owners offered both potential support and a constant threat to any central government.

From the third century on, no government was able to challenge the power of these landed magnates. Instead, the Three Kingdoms all mimicked them by distributing abandoned fields to refugees who paid taxes in exchange for protection and in some cases gave military service. While the Han had set up agricultural colonies to populate frontier zones and thereby facilitate defense, under the Cao-Wei these land grants took the form of internal colonies.[44]

The first record of such agricultural colonies dates to A.D. 196, when land around Cao Cao's capital at Xu that had been confiscated from Yellow Turban rebels or abandoned by fleeing peasants was awarded to surrendered rebels or refugees. In the general chaos, becoming a colonist could have been an appealing prospect and thus a voluntary choice. But as the system expanded in subsequent decades to virtually all commanderies in Wei state, the colonies came to rely on conscription, and people sometimes fled. Agricultural colonies were placed under an administration distinct from both the military colonies and regular local government. They were also physically separate, with parts of regular commanderies being hived off as colonies under a separate administration, or an entire commandery converted into a colony. Chief administrators of colonies seem to have been placed at the same level as heads of commanderies, as indicated by salaries and the fact that when the colonies were abolished their administrators became commandery officials.

Colonists initially paid a fixed amount on plow oxen rented to them by the government, but this was gradually converted into a sharecropping system in which the colonist paid 50 percent of the harvest if he provided his own ox, or 60 percent if he used a government ox. These rates were probably comparable to those levied by landlords on tenants. In addition to providing oxen, the state in some places improved irrigation and introduced new agricultural techniques, for which the colonies were particularly suited because labor was closely supervised. The payment of rent seems to have been their sole obligation.

The military colonies were apparently established somewhat later, largely to provision Wei armies with grain as they attempted to reconquer the south. Best documented are the colonies in the Huai River valley that provisioned the armies confronting Wu state. These colonies, placed under the bureau of revenue founded in 223, were organized into military units grouped into regularly spaced encampments of about sixty men. Laborers were sharecroppers and paid the same percentages as in the agricultural colonies. The only difference was that these colonists provided military service as well as grain, whereas the agricultural colonists did not. Each soldier received about three acres, and after payment of rent he had enough left over to support a small nuclear family. These "military households" were a significant element in the hereditary Wei soldiery.

The Cao-Wei regime also had a regular civilian administration for the peasant population. It abandoned the Han practice of imposing a head tax on individuals and a household grain tax based on expected yields, levying instead a single household tax paid in cloth and a flat grain tax based on acreage. These shifts, which required less gathering of information, reflected the state's inability to maintain an adequate census or to rate the quality of parcels of land. These changes may have been possible because the colonies provided a significant supplement to the state's income.

Our limited documentation indicates that the colonies initially provided sufficient grain for the armies, and their extension across the realm supports this conclusion. However, in 264, shortly before the Sima ended the Wei, a decree abolished the offices in charge of the agricultural colonies "in order to equalize government service," that is, to place the colonists on the same footing as other peasants. There were several reasons for this. Ever since the founding of the Wei in 220, Cao rulers had sought to secure support from high officials by granting them the use of rental oxen and putting them in charge of agricultural colonies. The officials were granted the right to employ households under their control in commercial activities. These legal grants encouraged officials to arrogate land and households for their own use, and the colonies gradually reverted to the status of the estates on which they were patterned.

Another reason for the abolition was the conquest of Shu in 263, which reduced the urgent needs the colonies had met. The abolition of agricultural colonies signaled a return to a more classic form of government, although the military colonies facing Wu continued to function. The abolition of agricultural colonies almost certainly pleased the powerful families whose support the Sima had cultivated in order to secure their own position prior to formally supplanting the Cao family.

The reunification of China in 280 under the Jin dynasty led to a general, if short-lived, restructuring of government land policy. Neither the details of the policy nor the extent to which it was implemented can be reconstructed from surviving sources.[45] In any case, the outbreak of the Rebellions of the Eight Princes and the subsequent southward flight of the court dramatically reduced the already limited power of the Jin court. Although on paper the Eastern Jin government limited the numbers of tenants and retainers the great landed families could hold, and although it occasionally attempted to rationalize population registration and landholding through "determinations of residency," the Jiankang regime held no land of its own and lacked the power to regulate ownership by others.[46]

Even the old Han claim (reiterated by a Jin decree in 336) that all nonagricultural land—the "mountains and marshes"—belonged to the state became an empty letter as northern émigré families developed villas and gardens in the foothills and recently drained lowlands. The few decrees that tried to block this development were ineffective, and although the state occasionally founded colonies to open up the resources of mountains and marshes, these largely fell into the hands of powerful families. Irrigation and drainage projects were also crucial for the opening of the south, but again leading families were more important actors than the state.[47]

Strikingly, there were no decrees to limit the accumulation of agricultural land. Southern governments attempted to found military colonies along their northern frontier, generally without success, as proposals to establish agricultural colonies were either not implemented or were rapidly co-opted by local officials to enrich themselves. One of the few forms of state-owned land that developed in the south was "emolument lands" whose income paid official salaries that the central court, lacking monetary resources, could not cover. As this policy largely benefited the leading families, its success is not surprising. But by the Liang dynasty even these fields had been taken over by powerful families.

While state-owned lands played a minor role in the south, they continued to be crucial in the north. Virtually all the non-Chinese dynasties, except for the Yan states founded by the Murong tribes, forcibly resettled tens of thousands of people around their capitals to engage in animal husbandry and agriculture to provision the state and its armies. Such policies were little different from the Cao-Wei policy of establishing agricultural colonies around their temporary capital at Xu, although the histories provide almost no information on these later practices.

The one exception to this lack of detail is the Northern Wei decision to convert forcibly resettled populations into "samgha households" (households belonging to the Buddhist monastic order).[48] In the year 469 the controller of Buddhist clergy Tanyao memorialized: "[I] request that the households of Pingqi [a commandery founded with war captives] and those able to provide sixty *hu* of grain each year to the Office of Buddhist Clergy be designated 'samgha households' and the grain 'samgha millet.' This grain will be distributed to the starving in years of famine. I further request that those guilty of major crimes and state slaves be classed as 'Buddha households' and charged with maintaining monasteries, working in their fields, and bringing in the harvest."[49] This proposal was accepted, and the *Book of the Wei* (*Wei shu*) states that these institutions, along with "monastic households" of hereditary serfs attached to individual monasteries, soon spread throughout the commanderies and garrisons. A second memorial from Tanyao in 476 led to the establishment of further samgha households from prisoners-of-war taken at Liangzhou (modern Gansu).

The locations cited in Tanyao's memorial, along with the emphasis on growing more drought-resistant millet, indicate that these colonies were often founded in drier or more marginal regions that were newly opened to agriculture. The figure of sixty *hu* suggests that about half of the harvest was routinely paid as rent. Other memorials indicate that the monastic order or the state provided tenants with oxen, again following the pattern established on earlier state-owned lands. Monastic provision of tools and assistance with irrigation is also likely. The establishment of such colonies was preceded by a survey and evaluation of the land.

While the practices of the samgha households resembled those of earlier state agricultural colonies, their ties to Buddhism entailed modifications. Because the Buddha households attached to monasteries as laborers and slaves consisted of people who had been sentenced to hard labor or reprieved from death sentences, this institution reflects a new practice of sparing the lives of people in order to present them to the church whose doctrine of forgiveness had rescued them. The specification that the millet produced was to be used for famine relief shows the court's willingness to exploit Buddhism's emphasis on charity in order to transfer the traditional functions of the Chinese state to the new faith. Like other forms of gifted land and property, the samgha households were probably a permanent and inalienable good attached to the monastic order as a whole and as such represented a new mode of corporate ownership that developed in China with the rise of Buddhism.[50]

The major system of state-owned land in the north was the equal-field system (*jun tian*). In 486 Emperor Xiaowen of the Northern Wei adopted a modified form of an earlier Jin institution. State-owned lands were divided into family-sized plots and given to peasants in exchange for the payment of taxes and the provision of labor service on imperial construction projects. With modifications, this policy continued under the subsequent Qi and Zhou dynasties and into the Tang. It stipulated that each married couple was entitled to a grant of land from the state for the duration of their working, or rather taxpaying, lives. The land remained the property of the state and was returned when the couple no longer paid taxes or provided labor service.

If there was more than one adult male in a household, the size of the grant would, in theory, be doubled, and households that had slaves also received a small allotment of land for each adult male slave. In the northwest, but not elsewhere, land was also allotted for keeping herds of cattle. In areas where land was left fallow for a year to improve its future yield, the allotment of land could in theory be doubled or tripled, depending on the frequency of fallowing. A separate category of hereditary land was instituted for land used to grow the mulberry trees needed to produce the silk in which certain taxes were paid. Since such land needed decades before it became productive, it was passed on from generation to generation within the family, subject in theory to legal limits on the size of total holdings.

Because the purpose of the equal-field system was to bring under cultivation as much abandoned land as possible, the original legal grants of land were substantial. But in places where land was scarce, most families received less than the legally stipulated amount. The law was also intended to limit the accumulation of larger estates by officials and the great families, but such limits worked no better than similar attempts under the Han dynasty.[51]

Writing about Village Life

Rural China changed significantly in the centuries following the collapse of the Han, not just in life but in literature. In the writings of Tao Qian (365–427) we find some of the earliest poetic accounts of agricultural work written in the voice of a named individual.[52] Described by Zhong Rong in his *Rankings of Poetry* (*Shi pin*, dated before 517) as the "patriarch of the poets of reclusion," Tao gave up his official career in midlife, retired to a village, and wrote poetry about sleeping in his hut, toiling in the fields, suffering poverty, and escaping into the pleasures of drink. Although the relatively prosperous Tao has been mocked for hypocrisy in writing in the voice of a poor farmer, his verses describe the vicissitudes of a country life which he witnessed firsthand, and to a degree experienced.

Tao's work defined a genre now conventionally known as "farmstead poetry"—verses written about country scenes and the life of rustics as understood by poets. While this poetry is sometimes equated with Western pastoral, the writings of Tao and the handful of major writers who followed his lead are characterized by a degree of realism and detail completely absent from the Western genre.[53] In addition to poetry describing his rural retreat, Tao also composed the prose narrative "Peach Blossom Spring," which in Chinese literary history became the definitive arcadian dream of an isolated rural life free from the poisons of urban existence and entanglement with the state. Despite its idyllic setting, this work remains realistic in that the physical elements of the hidden village and its livelihood were commonplace features of actual rural life. The poem is idealizing only in its elimination of class relations and the ravages of nature. In this way, Tao's life and writings defined yet another form of eremitism, associated with the farming village rather than the mountain landscape.⁵⁴

Tao's attempt to capture the experience of farming life can be seen in these couplets about the wild unpredictability of the weather, plagues of insects, and natural disasters:

> Capped, I met the troubles of the age;
> First married, I lost my wife.
> Fiery droughts repeatedly ablaze;
> Insects rampant struck my fields.
> Storms came from every side;
> So the harvest did not meet one man's needs.⁵⁵

Other accounts are less cataclysmic but nonetheless speak of the troubles of farming, as in this couplet adapted from a Han poem, but not unrelated to farming experience: "I planted beans below the southern hill; weeds flourish, bean sprouts are few."⁵⁶ In such observations, for the first time in Chinese literature, we encounter the mundane frustrations along with the repeated catastrophes that so regularly accompany a life totally subject to the unpredictability of nature.

Tao's poetry also touches on the constant labor of a peasant's life, as in the couplet "At dawn I rise to clear away the weeds; bringing along the moon, I return shouldering my hoe."⁵⁷ Here the image of the moon as companion marks not solitary drinking or the bonds tying the poet to an absent lover but rather how the full day's labor drags on into the night. The moon that the peasant "brings" along with his hoe is just another tool, a portable light that allows him to extend an already lengthy day of toil.

At a couple of points the sheer burden of work and its tenuous rewards threaten to drag the poet down:

> Never setting work aside;
> Yet cold and hungry, I always eat chaff.
> How could I hope for a full belly;
> I only want a sufficiency of rice.
> Against winter, just enough rough cloth
> And coarse linen to cope with the heat.
> But I cannot get them;

Pitiable and grievous, indeed.
On summer days I bear a constant hunger;
On winter nights I sleep without a cover.
Toward dusk I long for the cock to crow;
At dawn I wish the sun would go away.[58]

In contrast with the idyll of Western pastoral verse, or accounts of the delights of gardens and nature in the poetry of his contemporaries, these verses by Tao recognize the countryside as a place where even constant toil often could not secure a modest existence.

The farmstead poems introduced the practice of regularly incorporating what Zhong Rong called "farmer's words." Tao's verse is strewn with references to "hamlet lanes," "level fields," "dogs' barking," "cocks' crowing," "fine shoots," "beans and millet," "frost and hail," "clearing fields," and assorted farming implements.[59] The language of villagers provides not only occasional vocabulary for his verse but even the topic:

At times with the men of the villages and wastes,
Parting the grasses, I share friendly intercourse.
When we meet there is no idle chatter;
We only speak of the growth of mulberry and hemp.[60]

Here the growth of crops defines both the labor of the peasant and the limits of his language and social interactions.

In what is perhaps their best-known feature, the poems of Tao Qian also describe the joys of farming life. Yet here again, he focuses on the narrow limits of pleasure and its immediate links to the body. In contrast with the delights of the city, which Tao eschews, the gratifications of the countryside are marked by simplicity. They are the immediate complements of the toils and dangers of the peasants' life, for in a world of such grinding labor the mere fact of rest, along with enjoyment of the crudest wine and humblest fare, becomes the ultimate pleasure. Among the clearest celebrations of these limited rewards are the couplets: "For seating, nothing better than lofty shade; for walking, nothing better than entering my thorn gate. For food, nothing better than garden mallows; for delight nothing better than my young sons." Other poems mention the plain covering of the bed, the rustic clothing, or the coarse grain that just fills the belly, while another describes a rustic banquet in which he entertains neighbors with newly-strained wine and a single chicken, illuminated by a fire of thorns.[61]

A notable feature of Tao's accounts of rural life are repeated references to his homemade wine, which sometimes seems to form the chief consolation of his existence.[62] These visions of rural pleasures, haunted by lingering intimations of the abandoned urban world, are summarized in a poem Tao addressed to an otherwise anonymous Registrar Guo:

> Thick, thick, the woods before the hall;
> In midsummer storing the cool shade.
> The south wind comes with the season;
> Its swirling gusts blow open my gown.
> Abandoning society, I enjoy retired pursuits;
> Rising from sleep, I play with books and lute.
> Garden vegetables still grow in excess;
> Last year's grain still unfinished today.
> Providing for oneself has proper limits;
> More than enough is not my desire.
> I pound sorghum to brew good wine;
> When the wine matures, I pour it out myself.
> My young son plays at my side;
> Learning to speak, but cannot yet form sounds.
> I truly delight in these things;
> And for a moment forget the ornate hairpin [of office].
> Far, far, I watch the white clouds;
> How deep my longing for the past![63]

Even for this most rural of Chinese poets, the joys of country life remained a form of exile.

6

CHINA AND THE OUTER WORLD

THE QIN conquests that created the first Chinese empire in 221 B.C. roughly defined the borders of the Chinese people and their culture. Post-Han attempts to extend the empire into the northern steppes, central Asia, southern Manchuria, Korea, and continental southeast Asia were generally short-lived, and the peoples of these regions remained beyond Chinese control. Nevertheless, the surrounding non-Chinese cultures played a crucial role in Chinese civilization. Their states shaped the Chinese empire, and their peoples ruled the Yellow River basin, the traditional Chinese heartland, for about half of Chinese imperial history after the Han dynasty's collapse. Conversely, neighboring peoples not ruled by China adopted many features of Chinese culture and politics, and by the reunification of China in 589 they formed part of a larger East Asian, or perhaps a pan-Asian, world system.

For purposes of analysis, the people surrounding China can be divided into three groups. To the north and northwest lay nomads who created polities radically different from the Chinese model, but which nevertheless formed a symbiotic relation with the Chinese state.[1] In the near northeast were semi-nomadic peoples, including the Tuoba, who established hybrid states combining nomad armies with Chinese administration. Finally, to the northeast, southeast, southwest, and west were sedentary peoples who formed either trade-based city-states or agrarian states which, by the Tang dynasty, formed an elaborate trading system united by a common Chinese script and statecraft, and a common religion, Buddhism.

The Northern Nomads in China

The first two categories are variant forms of nomadic states: the purely nomadic states to the north and northwest, which stayed outside of China, engaged in trade, demanded tribute, and regularly pillaged; and the dual states of the northeast, which combined nomad armies dependent on the court with a Chinese-style bureaucracy to extract income from the peasantry.[2] The first pattern is exemplified by the Xiongnu, who controlled the region north of China through most of the Han dynasty, the latter by the Tuoba people, whose Wei state reunited the Yellow River drainage basin in the fifth century.

When the Han state collapsed, the behavior of the northern nomads demonstrated how, in the process of resettling inside China and serving in the Han armies, a symbiosis had emerged between them and the Han empire. Rather than attempting to conquer territory or establish their own dynasties, they first sought out new patrons among the warlords. The subsequent Cao-Wei and Jin dynasties continued to offer payments and trading rights to nomad rulers in exchange for military service, and nomadic horsemen were essential to their armies.[3] However, as the Jin disintegrated in the Rebellions of the Eight Princes, this patronage disappeared, and the nomadic chiefs had to seek new bases of power.

The first to try was a Xiongnu chieftain, Liu Yuan (r. 304–310), who had grown up as a hostage at the Jin court and was consequently steeped in Chinese culture. He sought to establish a Chinese style court with literati bureaucrats for his Former Zhao (or Han Zhao) dynasty. Indeed, as his family had earlier been adopted by the Han ruling house, he even claimed to be reviving the old Han empire. However, he and his sons succeeded only in alienating their tribal followers, who remained the true basis of state power, without gaining support from the Chinese, who still viewed the Liu rulers as barbarians.

A second chieftain, Shi Le, who began as a general for Liu Yuan, adopted the policy of directly obtaining wealth through large-scale pillaging of the Chinese populace. The appeal of tribal traditions and the distribution of booty attracted numerous defectors from the Xiongnu Liu house. In 319 Shi Le declared his own Later Zhao dynasty, and in 329 destroyed the last remnants of his rivals. However, their reconquest of north China reduced the occasions for combat and thus gradually reduced the dynasty's income from booty. Attempts to recruit Chinese officials also met with limited success. Shi Le's son and successor, Shi Hu, maintained the state through a combination of pillaging villages and hiring foreign administrators, but after his death in 349 the regime was destroyed by Ran Min, an adopted Chinese son of Shi Hu, who led a general massacre of non-Chinese at the capital city Ye.[4] The Former Qin state that briefly united northern China followed a similar pattern of military success that attracted allies, failure to establish a regular administration, and finally collapse following a military setback.

Ultimately, nomad polities in China required a literati bureaucracy that could perform routine administration and extract regular taxes for transfer to the nomads. The successful alternative to the Xiongnu model of a state based on trade, tribute from a Chinese empire, and pillage arose in the northeast. This region was inhabited by sedentary agriculturalists, steppe pastoralists, and forest villagers who combined hunting, fishing, and food-gathering with agriculture. This diverse economic base, along with the inhabitants' protracted contacts with Chinese who had settled in the region, facilitated the establishment of a state combining armies of nomad horsemen with bureaucratic administration of the peasantry. Emperor Wu Han established Han commanderies in the northeast in 108 B.C., but it remained a frontier region far from the economic and demographic centers of China and remote from the wars those centers attracted. During the collapse of the Han, this region, ruled by the Gongsun warlord family, enjoyed peace and stability, so many Chinese from the Yellow River plain sought refuge there.

The tribes of the region, known as the Xianbei, consisted of many independent peoples with no overarching organization. The most successful group was the Murong, who first gained notice by assisting the Cao-Wei state in eliminating the Gongsun warlords.[5] In 281 the Jin court bestowed the old Xiongnu title of *chanyu* on the Murong ruler, indicating both the lingering prestige of the title and the rising importance of the Murong. This ruler was the first Murong chief to give his sons a Chinese education and to adopt some Chinese customs, but, unlike the contemporary Xiongnu Liu family, he and his descendants did not establish a full-blown Han-style court. Instead, they gradually developed a mixed state, a process made easier by the fact that they enjoyed fifty years of capable government under a single ruler, Murong Hui (r. 283–333).

The first decade of Murong Hui's reign consisted largely of attacks on the neighboring Puyo kingdom in what is now the Chinese province of Liaodong and North Korea. These campaigns provided large numbers of captives who were either sold to the Chinese as slaves or settled as agriculturists under Murong control. In 294 Hui established a new capital and began to formally encourage farming in his realm. He even requested mulberry bushes and silk worms from the Jin court. These policies were successful enough that in 301 the Murong could send grain for the relief of neighboring Jin provinces ruined by flooding. This grain was collected by Chinese administrators recruited to supervise the agricultural foundations of the Murong state.

Chinese advisers were also imported to help strengthen the Murong armies through incorporating Han Chinese infantrymen and siege-craft specialists. These new forces allowed the Murong to defeat their former superiors, the Yuwen tribe, in 302 and secure a stable base to which many Chinese fled during the Rebellions of the Eight Princes. In 308 Murong Hui declared himself "great *chanyu*," but soon thereafter he also accepted a title bestowed by the collapsing Jin court, which helped to attract Chinese officials. These dual titles symbolized the hybrid character of the Murong state, which from 322 began to swallow up neighboring tribes. The state also adopted a strategy of building and stocking walled settlements to protect villagers from the attacks of nomadic forces from the central plains. This strategy proved its effectiveness in 338 when an invasion by Shi Hu's army suffered a major defeat, allowing the Murong to expand south and west.

The Xianbei tribes, like many nomads, practiced fraternal succession, which had led several non-Chinese states both inside and outside China to internal strife and collapse. To minimize succession disputes, the Murong adopted the Chinese practice of father-son succession, with the ruler's brothers and uncles receiving major appointments as generals or officials. This policy attempted to make the dynasty a collective good belonging to the entire ruling house, and to reduce (though not eliminate) struggles among brothers.

Through such reforms, the Murong built a large state stretching from the northeast as far south as the Huai River. Refugee Chinese literati served as bureaucrats while nomad tribesmen formed the core of an army that also included Chinese infantry and siege equipment. Income extracted from the peasantry played the same role as tribute and pillage in the old Xiongnu state, that is, it gave the ruler an unmatched source of revenue to buy support from tribal followers, who, as paid soldiers or officials, became dependent on and subject to the court. Reliance on pastoralism gradually gave way to more intensive agriculture that channeled wealth into the state's coffers. In 337 the Murong ruler founded a new state of Yan, a name with an ancient Chinese pedigree in the region, and in 353 declared himself emperor.

Although this state (Former Yan) was short-lived, at least one of its achievements was significant. In 357 a Yan army crushed the forces of the nomadic Chile, a tribe that had risen to power on the steppes as the Xianbei center of gravity shifted southward. This victory was so impressive that the Xiongnu *chanyu* shifted his allegiance to the Murong Yan state. This was the first time in China's history that a dynasty of foreign origin, ruling over the traditional Chinese heartland, defeated the kind of nomadic coalition on the frontier that had baffled Han rulers for centuries. The Murong owed this success not just to their more effective use of nomadic cavalry forces and military skills, but to their understanding of how nomadic coalitions were constructed and where their weak points lay. Successful rulers like the Murong played the game of tribal politics by manipulating marriage alliances and encouraging rivalries within the tribes, and they incorporated defeated tribesmen into their own state more easily than could the Han Chinese. The success of dynasts of nomadic origins against the steppe became a recurrent feature in later Chinese history, until the Manchu Qing finally defeated and absorbed the Mongols and the peoples of what is now Xinjiang.[6]

The Murong state's expansion was halted by Fu Jian, who availed himself of factional splits at the Yan court to conquer the state in 370. When Fu Jian's own Former Qin state collapsed after his southern defeat in 383, the Murong's western neighbors, the Tuoba, emerged and by 396 had secured control of the northeast. The Tuoba inherited the dual state fashioned by the Murong, adopting the Yan model and largely staffing their bureaucracy with former Yan officials. With the restructuring of the military forces by Tuoba Gui, the new Northern Wei state successfully combined a functioning administration with an army of nomadic warriors whose loyalties had been transferred from the earlier tribes to the dynasty. This combination allowed the Tuoba to occupy Luoyang in 423, reassert control over the steppes with campaigns in 425 and 429, and in 430 to reconquer the Guanzhong region that had been occupied by the last descendants of the old Xiongnu ruling house. In 439 the Tuoba Wei dynasty completed the reunification of north China by conquering the Liang state that ruled the Gansu corridor.

The Tuoba inherited not only Murong institutions but also their policies for controlling the steppe. In 399 they repeated the Murong's success in defeating the Chile tribes, which allowed the rise of a new steppe power, the Rouran. Tuoba knowledge of life on the steppe allowed the Wei court to understand the weaknesses of their rivals, as shown in a court debate over the advisability of an offensive against the Rouran:

> The Rouran rely on the fact that they are far away, and think that our power cannot reach them, so they have taken no precautions for a long time. In the summer they disperse their men and livestock, and in the autumn when the latter have grown fat they reassemble to escape the cold by moving south to plunder us. Now if we take them by surprise in the spring, they will be unprepared. When our great army suddenly arrives, they will certainly panic and flee. The stallions will be guarding their herds, and the mares looking after their newborn foals, so it will be difficult to keep them in order when fleeing. Having abandoned their grass and water, then within a few days they will be in desperate straits, and we can annihilate them with one attack.[7]

Following these principles, the Tuoba Wei made at least one major attack on the Rouran per generation, carrying off such large numbers of people and livestock that it took the tribe decades to recover. These men and livestock served to replenish the garrisons along the Northern Wei frontier. For a century this policy kept the Rouran in a state of relative weakness and division, up through the last Wei campaign in 492. Only with the shift of the capital to Luoyang and the gradual alienation of the frontier garrisons from the court did the Rouran reemerge as a major threat.

Nevertheless, throughout the Northern and Southern Dynasties no nomadic state was able to copy the Xiongnu in extracting from China the wealth necessary to forge a steppe empire. Only when the Sui reunited China in 589 did the Turks take control of the north and west and begin, on the Xiongnu model, to demand payment from the Chinese in exchange for peaceful relations and service as auxiliary armies. The subsequent Tang ruling house, which emerged from the Chinese clans of the northwest and assimilated the martial values and practices of the steppe nomads with whom they intermarried, were at first, like the Northern Wei, adept at exploiting the organizational weaknesses of nomadic states. The second Tang emperor was able to split the Turkic confederation, defeat them in great battles in 630 and 647, and be recognized as the Heavenly Khaghan, thus ruling both China and the Turks. This success, however, did not outlive him, and his court-reared successors soon lost control of the Turks, who resumed their old pattern of alternating war and demands for tribute.[8]

These evolving relations with the nomadic peoples of the north had a major impact on the nature of the Chinese imperial system. One of the key features of the early Qin and Han empires was the creation of an imperial realm that self-consciously transcended ties to the local topographies and customs that had defined the earlier Warring States. The state featured a high cult focused on the sacred person of the emperor (son of transcendent Heaven), was centered in an artificial capital erected by imperial fiat, used a written language based on archaic canonical texts that was detached from all speech, and required officials to leave their families and communities to become the emperor's servants. The spatial range of this early imperial system was roughly defined by the range of Chinese culture. This overlay of polity on culture was reinforced by the simultaneous emergence of the Xiongnu empire to the north, creating a bipolar world divided between the "civilized" agricultural people ruled by the Chinese state and the nomadic "barbarians" ruled by the *chanyu*.

The large-scale settlement of nomads inside China, their recruitment into military or political service, and the destruction of the Xiongnu empire ended the clear political distinction between sedentary and nomadic peoples. This made possible a broader, encompassing world order including both sides of the old ecological divide. The second ruler, Taizong (r. 626–649), justified his combined role as emperor of the Chinese and khan of the Turks by stating, "Since antiquity everyone has honored the Chinese and looked down on barbarians; I alone love them as one. Therefore their tribes follow me like a father or mother."[9] More broadly, in the first century of the dynasty, some 1.7 million foreigners became Tang subjects. These Japanese, Koreans, Sogdians, and others played a crucial role in government, receiving the highest military and civilian posts.

However, power ran in the opposite direction: nomadic chiefs ruled over both Chinese and nomads within an empire. This first happened under the Northern Wei, and it recurred throughout later Chinese history. Although some literati through the centuries argued that Han Chinese should not serve "barbarian" rulers, in practice most Chinese elites proved willing to accept any conqueror who built a proper capital, sacrificed to Heaven, served as patron of the state canon, and provided offices and salaries. Sometimes condemned as opportunism, this behavior accepted the full implications of claims to universal empire, which measured the ruler's legitimacy by his ability to include distant peoples within his realm.

In this way, the Northern Wei and subsequent nomadic dynasties simply extended the transcendence of local ties and loyalties that allowed the creation of a Chinese empire from the fractious Warring States. The later notion of an overriding loyalty to a Han Chinese people and their culture marked a shift away from the imperial model, toward the modern idea of a nation-state. The pivotal role in Chinese history of "conquest dynasties" and their legitimacy within the imperial model has been the topic of considerable study by Japanese scholars. While the term has questionable political overtones, given that it justified Japanese rule of China, it provides a useful reminder that all Chinese dynasties were established by military power, that from the Eastern Han onward foreign troops and culture were fundamental to that power, and that the "Chinese" empire was thus never Chinese in the manner of a modern nation-state.[10]

Sedentary Neighboring States

While the nomads to the north related to China through pillage, extraction of tribute, or conquest, peoples to the northeast (modern-day Korea and Japan), southeast (modern Vietnam), and southwest (modern Yunnan and Guizhou) were sedentary populations whose relations with China tended toward imitation. Like the term China, the terms Korea, Japan, and Vietnam are anachronisms, but the political entities that ultimately formed these states came into existence during the Northern and Southern Dynasties, and their emergence was closely linked to relations with China.

Independent states surrounding China were routinely founded through an investiture process in which certain local chieftains sent gifts to the Chinese court and received titles as kings or dukes and the appropriate seals of office. In the northern part of what became Korea, the early state of Koguryo sent tribute to the Han in A.D. 32 and then adopted the title of king. A later state in the south of the peninsula, Paekche, established relations with the Jin court in 372, and by 386 its ruler had received titles from the Chinese court as a general and deputy king. In the third century, Himiko, a priestess-chieftain in the Japanese islands, sought titles from the Northern Wei court, and in the fifth century more than a dozen tribute missions were sent from the would-be Japanese court in hopes of receiving titles and support from the dynasts of south China. Such titles were valuable because they set ambitious local chiefs apart from their rivals, and the prestige and influence of the reflected splendor of the Chinese empire enhanced their ability to create states.[11] While this submission was purely formal, and those who received titles might actively combat Chinese influence and armies, the language and practices of statecraft in East Asia formed around the Chinese model.

The rise of states in Korea and Japan was also facilitated by the increasingly frequent travels of Buddhist monks. As Korea and Japan converted to Buddhism, China became a major pilgrimage destination for men seeking education and texts. They returned home bearing not only the doctrines of Buddhism but also accounts of China and examples of Chinese material culture, most notably writing. Similarly, the goods and technologies introduced to surrounding states by merchants and traders facilitated the adoption of a Chinese model.

The political emergence of the Korean peninsula demonstrates this process. The Han dynasty's founder established a client state east of the province of Liaodong, and after the third-generation king of this state killed the Han governor in 109 B.C., Chinese armies occupied the area and set up four commanderies. During the next century, the common people in the Korean peninsula and the Chinese provinces probably shared a similar culture. While tribal peoples possibly related to the Xianbei continued to practice their traditional modes of life, elite culture from the Chinese central plains came into what is now North Korea through large-scale immigration. But after A.D. 106 the Koguryo state in the Yalu River valley pushed the Han westward toward Liaodong, becoming the first Chinese-influenced sedentary state to successfully assert its independence from China.[12]

In 244 Koguryo was conquered by a Cao-Wei army, but it reasserted its independence when the Jin collapsed, occupied the old Han commanderies, and by 334 had secured control of what is now North Korea and southern Manchuria. At the same time the Murong Xianbei occupied much of the old Puyo state, and in 342 they inflicted a crushing defeat on Koguryo. Koguryo soon recovered, and in 373 (when the Murong state was destroyed by Fu Jian) it established a Chinese-style Grand Academy, adopted a legal code based on that of the Jin, and began to convert to Buddhism. In the next century Koguryo brought much of Korea under its control and emerged as a major regional power.[13]

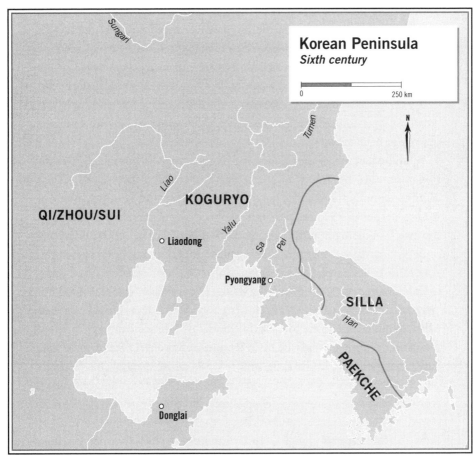

Map 13

In the second half of the fourth century, while Koguryo was expanding from the north, the small city-state of Paekche emerged in the southwestern corner of the Korean peninsula (Map 13). In 369 it defeated its former overlord and soon received recognition and titles from the Jin court at Jiankang. In 415 these titles were elevated to the rank of full king. Scattered evidence indicates that Paekche's ties to the Jin court went far beyond titles. The names of emissaries from Paekche indicate possible Chinese origins, and bricks in early sixth-century Paekche tombs follow models from the south of China. Paekche chronicles also depict a court that had adopted architectural, musical, and poetic styles from the Chinese. Paekche became the primary center from which some of these practices, along with the Buddhist religion, were transmitted to Japan.[14]

While the Northern and Southern Dynasties recognized the Korean states as independent clients, the reunited Chinese empire at the end of the sixth century felt emboldened to reassert direct rule. It was the failure of a series of campaigns intended to reconquer Korea that led to the fall of the Sui; the second Tang emperor failed as well. Only with the aid of a second Chinese-derived Korean state, Silla, formed in the southeast, did the Chinese finally defeat Koguryo. Afterward, Silla—not China—occupied the peninsula.

Japan's emergence resembled that of Korea, but at a later date. In addition to sending missions to China in the third century, the priestess-queen Himiko manufactured Chinese-style bronze mirrors and military banners to display her ties to the Northern Wei court and thereby augment her prestige. Following Himiko's death, ties between China and Japan lapsed until 413, after which more than a dozen Japanese missions visited the southern dynasties to request titles, seals of office, bronze mirrors, and military banners. After 502 these visits ceased. When they resumed between 600 and 614, the ambassadors to the Sui court no longer desired titles, rendered useless by the establishment of a single dynasty in Japan, but rather sought to study Chinese institutions and strengthen trade ties. The Japanese court in the sixth and seventh centuries was able to channel most trade with China through its hands, and the prestige derived from these imported luxury goods assisted the rise of centralized political power. Sixteen Japanese ambassadors came during the three centuries of Tang rule, and the timing of their arrival seems to have been determined solely by the interests of the Japanese court.[15]

But the most important Chinese cultural imports into Japan came via Korea. In addition to new styles of armor and iron metallurgy for prestige goods, these imports included the Chinese textual canon and practices of statecraft as taught by Korean teachers. Buddhism and its temple architecture were also introduced by Koreans. The Japanese state developed in close association with the Paekche state in southwest Korea, and throughout these centuries ties between southern coastal Japan and Korea were closer than those between the Japanese southern coast and parts of Japan not easily reached from the sea. Immigrant communities from Korea that were administered by the central court maintained a near monopoly of literacy in this period.[16]

The rise of a Japanese, or more accurately a Yamato, state in association with China climaxed in the early seventh century with the wholesale adoption of the Chinese style of government. Over several decades the Japanese introduced the Chinese writing system, established a legal code on the Chinese model, built a Chinese-style capital, and imposed population registration and land allocation inspired by China but adjusted to Japanese practices.[17] The Japanese even began to refer to their ruler as emperor and to describe themselves as the center of a world, in the Chinese manner. They established tribute relations with their own "barbarians" and in some communications placed their ruler on a level with the Chinese emperor. The idea of a distinctive "Japanese spirit" first began to appear in Japanese writings against this backdrop of Chinese learning and institutions.[18]

What is now Vietnam never developed an independent state during the Northern and Southern Dynasties, but it did evolve politically under the impact of periodic Chinese occupation.[19] At least half a millennium before the formation of the first Chinese empire, this region, including modern North Vietnam, Guangxi, and Guangdong provinces, was defined by the Dongso'n culture. When conquered by the Qin, it became known as Lingnan. After the fall of the Qin, the area maintained independence for a century as the Southern Yue state, owing nominal loyalty to the Han court until it was absorbed into the Han empire in 110 B.C. Tombs from the area mix Chinese-style and local Yue-style grave goods. The defeat of a rebellion under the Trung sisters in A.D. 40–42 led to large-scale Han immigration, but the rebellion has become a centerpiece in modern Vietnamese accounts of the emergence of their nation. During this century the towns of Jiaozhi (near modern Hanoi) and Panyu (modern Guangzhou) emerged as the two great trans-shipment centers for expanding Chinese sea trade with Southeast Asia. Outside the cities, where Chinese and foreign traders lived, the land was inhabited largely by indigenous tribal peoples.

When the Han collapsed, Lingnan briefly emerged as an independent state, until it was occupied by Wu in 226 and divided into two regions, Jiaozhou and Guangzhou. This division, made permanent in 264, was the first move toward splitting off the south, ultimately to become a separate state. At this time Jiaozhou was dominated by several major families who distanced themselves from Wu by allying with the Cao-Wei state in the Yellow River basin. In subsequent centuries these magnates, led by the Ly family, controlled the region. Although their first open rebellion in 541 ended in disaster, the Hou Jing rebellion forced the withdrawal of

Liang imperial forces in 550, which left Jiaozhou independent until the reunified Sui state occupied the area in 602. In the early decades of the Tang, Jiaozhou and indeed all of Lingnan was ruled by great families whom the central court allowed to handle all local affairs.

Just as inside China proper educated people speaking mutually unintelligible languages communicated in the nonalphabetic Chinese script, so these politically and linguistically divided areas of East Asia came to share this tool of written communication. This is important because Chinese graphs not only represented sounds but also carried certain meanings that implanted a body of roughly shared ideas across the East Asian world. These included not only basic political concepts such as rule by a "pole-star" emperor and his officials but also ideas about the family and social hierarchy that are often lumped together under the rubric of Confucianism or "East Asian values." Although Chinese graphs were ultimately modified or abandoned outside of China, the ideas they embodied informed intellectual conversation for literate elites across all of East Asia.[20]

The newly emergent East Asian world was linked not only by state structures and writing systems but also by trade. As states emerged to China's east and south, tribute missions were regularly sent to Chinese capitals. These were always accompanied by traders, and as trade flourished in the southern dynasties, the Yangzi valley was drawn into an international trading network with Korea, Japan, and Southeast Asia. In this way, sea-based trade for the first time became a major element of the Chinese economy (Fig. 18).

In the web of sedentary neighbors surrounding China, Central Asia—including what is now Xinjiang, Afghanistan, northern Pakistan, and parts of the former Soviet Union—had been occupied prior to contact with China by city-states formed around oases. The Chinese had explored and then occupied the eastern part of this region during its war against the Xiongnu, but after the fall of the Jin all regular relations between the Chinese courts and the city-states ceased. The leading centers—Kucha, Karashahr, Gaochang, and Kroraina—continued to serve as major conduits of trade and Buddhist influence. Major translation projects were conducted in these city-states, and eminent monks traveled from there to India and China.[21] Between the Han and the Tang, Chinese people became familiar with western Central Asia and India through the writings of a small number of Buddhist pilgrims who recorded their trav-

Fig. 18   Detail of a rubbing of a stele depicting a boat. Chengdu, Sichuan, fifth to sixth centuries.

els, above all Faxian.[22] Texts from India also played a major role in the development of Chinese theories of painting and poetry, and certain Indian literary genres and practices provided models for new forms of Chinese writing.

Trade and Buddhism

The most important forms of exchange between China and the outer world remained trade. China's foreign trade had begun as an adjunct to government policy, and because of government suspicion of merchants it was dominated by foreigners. During the early Chinese empires, merchants from the oasis towns of Central Asia obtained Chinese silk through purchase in frontier markets or tribute, traded the fabric to merchants in nearby towns, who in turn traded it farther west. After passing through many hands along these "silk roads," it arrived in India, Persia, and ultimately Rome. Wherever it was traded, silk was a precious commodity that often figured in religious rituals.[23]

Most of the goods that flowed in the opposite direction from the west into China were exotic curiosities or rare items that contributed to the self-aggrandizement of the ruling elite: precious metals, glass, slaves and entertainers, animals both wild and domestic, furs and feathers, rare plants and woods, exotic foods, perfumes and drugs, textiles and dyes, secular and sacred art objects, as well as books and maps telling of foreign places.[24] When brought as tribute, these rare goods testified to the power and prestige of a Chinese ruler who could summon offerings from across the world. When purchased by the elite, these items demonstrated the wealth and taste of their purchaser, who participated in the passion for things foreign that characterized the Chinese elite from the Han through the Tang. These exotica included innovations in costume, white face powder, new musical instruments and songs, foreign fruits, and new styles and techniques in the arts, all of which became defining elements of Chinese civilization.

Arriving along with goods and fashions were cultural elements that had a deeper impact. The most important was Buddhism, but merchants also brought in other religions such as Manichaeism, Zoroastrianism, Nestorian Christianity, and Islam. These religions not only offered new visions of the cosmos and new means of organizing human society but also created a demand for new types of goods, or new uses for older goods that suddenly became more precious. Both tea and sugar were associated with the rise of Buddhism; the chair was likewise introduced into China from western regions through Buddhism, through its role in the iconography of the Future Buddha Maitreya, its role in meditation, and its use in monasteries.[25] Even the development of writing paper and printing received a major stimulus from the Buddhist belief in reproducing sacred texts as a meritorious act.[26]

More important in the development of trade were rare, precious commodities used in Buddhist ritual that could not be obtained in China.[27] The first few centuries of the common era witnessed the production of many of the key early scriptures of Mahayana Buddhism, which emphasized lay piety, a divinized Buddha, the universal salvation of all beings, and the pivotal role of bodhisattvas who chose to remain in the world even after attaining enlightenment in order to complete the work of universal redemption. These texts emphasized lay charity as a form of virtue and extended that charity from providing food and housing for monks to providing decorations and images for stupas (domed funerary monuments) in which relics of the Buddha were stored, and later for temples in which images of the Buddha were placed. While all these practices had a long pedigree in Indian Buddhism and emerged within the monastic community, in China they appeared in the context of an emphasis on lay piety. They made it important for believers to acquire certain types of rare commodities that could be presented to Buddhist images and temples, or in other cases collected at home for the prestige of displaying them.[28]

Chief among these were the "seven treasures." In the earliest texts this term referred to the major items that a king had to possess, and in other early texts they refer to unspecified precious objects. However, in *The Great Event,* the key Mahayana text introducing a divine and eternal Buddha, the treasures are specifically gold, silver, lapis lazuli, crystal or quartz, pearl, red coral, and agate or coral. Subsequent texts substituted red precious stones such as rubies, and others cited diamonds. These treasures figured in numerous Buddhist contexts. The palace of a king destined to become a Buddha due to his charitable donations is made of the seven treasures, as are monasteries in a Buddha land. Buddhist heavens are often decorated with these substances, and they even became constituent elements of the immortal trees found in Daoist paradises. In some texts the symbolic vehicle that carries the worshipper to enlightenment is a bullock cart made of the seven treasures. In real life, the Sui founder in 582 placed the relics he had received from a monk in a container made from the seven treasures, from which they were divided into thirty red glass bottles to be distributed throughout the empire. Thus these seven objects came to symbolize the finest that the world has to offer, and they defined the physical aspects of Buddhist worship.[29]

The association of these substances with distant paradises is not accidental, for they came into China from the far west. This is clearest in the case of red coral. Coral had figured as a precious item in Han poetry describing the dwellings of immortals or the emperor, and the Cao-Wei and Jin dynasties put pieces of coral in the imperial crown. It became a display item in the life of the southern elite, as in the following anecdote:

> Shi Chong and Wang Kai competed for supremacy, exhausting every refinement in decorating their carriages and clothing . . . [Emperor Wu] once gave Kai a coral tree more then two *chi* high. Its branches and twigs spread luxuriantly, in a manner rarely matched. He showed it to Chong, who after looking at it shattered it with a single blow of an iron baton. Devastated and thinking that Chong had been jealous of his treasure, his tone and expression grew severe. Chong said, "It

is not worth this resentment; I will repay you at once." He then ordered his attendants to bring out some seven coral trees of three or four *chi,* with branches and trunks surpassing anything in the human world, and lustrous colors that overwhelmed the eye . . . Kai was speechless and completely at a loss.[30]

An avid collector of red coral, Shi Chong was reported to have been a devout follower of Buddhism. Histories of the period indicate that coral was a product of the Roman empire. Indian texts confirm that coral from the Mediterranean and the Red Sea was a major trade item, and some Chinese sources describe its purchase in Central Asia.[31]

Others of the seven treasures also reached China through long-distance trade from the west. The highest quality pearls came from India and Ceylon, and inferior ones were obtained from Persia. Such pearls have been recovered from the foundations of several Northern Wei temples. The sources of the finest lapis lazuli were in western Central Asia. While glass by this period was manufactured in China, glass vessels found in an early fifth-century tomb in association with a golden Buddha were produced by glass-blowing technologies not yet known in China. In addition to these "seven treasures" of foreign origin, such items as incense and various perfumes that were used in Buddhist worship were also imported from India.[32]

Long-distance trade in precious commodities associated with Buddhism also moved in the other direction. While the Chinese export of silk long antedated the rise of Buddhism, silk banners had become indispensable to Buddhist ceremonies throughout Central Asia by the fourth century, according to the pilgrim Faxian. They were hung over monks' seats in ritual gatherings and carried in processions of Buddhist images. The pilgrim Song Yun carried large numbers of banners with him and donated them to monasteries through which he passed. Rulers in north China in the fourth through the sixth centuries often granted silk to monks, both Chinese and foreign, in recognition of their religious services. In the subsequent Tang and Song dynasties it became routine for emperors to reward particularly eminent monks with robes of purple silk embroidered with gold, and such robes were also presented to Buddhist images.

Even after the Byzantine and Sassanian empires began to produce their own silk in the sixth century, superior Chinese silk floss, which was rewoven into silk, remained a valuable trade commodity. As Persian and Byzantine designs gradually began to appeal more to their own tastes, these silks also penetrated into eastern Central Asia and reduced the market for Chinese fabrics. In the late fourth century the king of Kucha, in what is now Xinjiang, supposedly rewarded the great translator Kumarajiva with a seat made from Byzantine silk. Although silk was the primary fabric involved in international trade, the spread of Buddhism also encouraged a long-distance trade in Indian cotton, valued by ordinary Buddhists because it did not entail killing silkworms.[33]

Buddhist monasteries were major consumers of luxury goods in their own right. Temples and stupas were decorated with gold, silver, silks, and beads of coral, glass, or semi-precious stones. As described by Xuanzang in the seventh century, the rivalry between Buddhism and the reviving Brahmanic faith led to competitions in the rich decoration of their respective temples.[34] Buddhist pilgrims or other monks traveling from temple to temple often had to spend or donate large quantities of gold or silk. Although food and lodging were provided by temples along the route, travel whether by land or sea had to be paid for, and relics also required offerings. Xuanzang donated fifty gold coins, one thousand silver coins, four silk banners, two pieces of brocade, and two sets of ritual robes to a Buddha bone at Nagarahara. He also received silks from the king of Turfan, which he distributed to each of the stupas that he passed on the way. The later pilgrim Yijing carried silk with him from China, which he had made into a ritual robe for a statue of the Buddha at Bodhgaya.[35] Thus the movement of Buddhist people also had a significant impact on the economy of the emerging Asian world system.

The period also saw an explicitly religious trade in relics similar to the one found in medieval Europe. Wang Xuance, the leader of several Tang diplomatic missions to northern India, spent more than four thousand bolts of silk to purchase a parietal (skull) bone of the Buddha at a monastery in northwestern India. The tremendous value placed on relics in Tang China is indicated by an anecdote told by Duan Chengshi (d. 863) of a monk who received a "rotten [finger]nail" as a donation. He decided to sell it to a foreign merchant:

"Where did you obtain this object, High One? If you must make a commodity of it, I won't stint on the price." The monk made a trial of asking for a hundred thousand. The Westerner gave a great laugh and said, "You haven't reached it! Go as far as you will, and then speak again!" He kept adding, up to five hundred thousand, and even then the Westerner said, "This is worth a thousand myriads!"

So he gave it to him for that. The monk inquired after its name and he said, "This is the Precious Bone."[36]

Actual relics could also be replaced by objects made from one of the seven treasures, and several "finger bone" relics found buried under stupas or temples were actually made of glass or crystal. Such substitution was linked to the belief that the cremated bodies of the Buddha and of particularly pious monks produced hard, crystalline pellets known as *sarira,* which could be simulated with precious substances. As in medieval Europe, the value of relics sometimes led to cases of theft.[37]

Foreigners in China

In addition to the goods and faiths that they carried into China, the monks and merchants themselves gradually became a large, permanent foreign presence in China that altered urban life during the Northern and Southern Dynasties. The earliest record of a Buddhist community in China does not specify whether the monks were Chinese or foreigners, but they were almost certainly the latter. The first clear record of foreign monks refers to translators who settled in the Eastern Han capital in the middle of the second century. Among these were foreign merchants who had joined the monastic order, so the two groups were clearly closely connected. Foreign monks also figure in accounts of the third- and fourth-century "pure conversation" circles of the great southern families.

The rising importance of Buddhism in the fourth century and the eminence of some foreign monks called into question the superiority of being Chinese. When the Sogdian Kang Sengyuan built himself a meditation hall in the mountains with a fragrant garden, so many leading figures of the capital flocked there to admire his bearing that he was ultimately forced to abandon his retreat. More explicit was the eulogy written for the Kuchean monk Srimitra by Wang Ming (351–398): "So the outstanding people of a generation may be born among the barbarians, while there are also those of exceptional talents among us here. Therefore we know that eminence and greatness are granted by Heaven. How could this depend on being Chinese or 'barbarian'?"[38] This eulogy is particularly noteworthy because Srimitra never learned to speak Chinese, although he was celebrated for reciting magical spells.

The potential equality of barbarian and Chinese in this period, and the possibility that the former might be superior, was applied not only to individuals but also to whole nations. As India became a holy land for Chinese Buddhists, its identification as the "Middle Kingdom" reduced China to a peripheral position.[39] Conversely, those who rejected Buddhism regularly used the fact of its foreignness to denounce its validity.[40] Whichever position was taken, Buddhism had become a conduit for rethinking the relation between China and the outside world, as well as between Chinese and foreigners.

By the sixth century some foreign pilgrims and students were beginning to think of China itself as a sacred Buddhist realm. *The Record of the Buddhist Temples of Luoyang* tells of a foreign monk describing Luoyang as a true Buddha realm on earth, and of Bodhidharma saying that the Yongning Temples surpassed even the buildings in the Buddha's own paradise. The same text describes a monastery devoted to housing the foreign monks of Luoyang: "At this time Buddhist scriptures and images were all flourishing in Luoyang, so foreign monks converged on this happy land like spokes on a wheel . . . so Emperor Xuanwu built this temple to accommodate them. The complex of cells and covered cloisters numbered more than one thousand rooms. Graceful bamboo lined the courtyards, lofty pines brushed the eaves, while rare, exotic flowers and grasses clustered around the steps. There were more than 3,000 monks from a hundred lands."[41] Significantly, this monastery was located near the great market of the city, which was also full of foreigners.

Subsequent texts relate that foreign monks came to China to participate in campaigns of relic distribution held by the founder of the Sui dynasty between 601 and 604. By the Tang dynasty several sites in China, notably Mount Wutai, which had become world-renowned as the abode of the bodhisattva Manjusri, became the goal of pilgrims from India, Central Asia, Korea, and Japan. In the same period China also became a center of the cult of the future Buddha Maitreya, which likewise attracted foreign devotees.

Foreigners came to play a prominent role in the religious imagination of the medieval Chinese world. As strange, exotic figures tied to religious activities, they became linked with Chinese images of ghosts and spirits. When ghosts took possession of kinsmen or professional mediums and tried to transmit messages in writing, these "ghost writings" were often identified as horizontal scripts resembling the "western barbarian" scripts of India and Central Asia rather than the vertical script of Chinese.[42] Not only was the written script of the dead linked to foreigners, but the language of magical spells that played a central role in Buddhism also remained closely identified with foreign tongues. Thus texts speak of the "art of Indian spells" and identify monks skilled in magic as men from outside of China. Moreover, Buddhist icons still identified the highest religious figures of that faith as "foreign" well after its beliefs and practices had been naturalized in China.[43]

Apart from those who came to teach or study Buddhist law, most foreigners in China were merchants. Depending on the routes they took to enter China, they were distributed in different cities and played a distinct role in the local economy of each region. The same "silk roads" along which Buddhists came into China from India and Central Asia were crucial for Chinese foreign trade. The routes ran from Syria, Persia, and Samarkand, as well as India, through eastern Central Asia and the northwestern frontier zone of China to the capital at Chang'an (Map 14). They had all been used in the Han dynasty, but the scale of trade had increased several fold. An alternative land route, of minor importance, passed from Sichuan through modern Yunnan, down the Irrawaddy River in Burma and across to Bengal. A route across Tibet used by some Buddhist pilgrims was too hazardous and slow to be of use for trade.[44]

Because the primary trade routes passed through Central Asia, the largest concentrations of foreign merchants from lands to the west were in the capitals Chang'an and Luoyang. After the Sui reunification, Chang'an was the end point not just for the silk roads but also for the Grand Canal. Chang'an had two great markets, one in the east and one in the west, with foreign traders concentrated in the western market. Cities to the west of Chang'an all had large foreign communities, and in Dunhuang and Liangzhou in the Gansu corridor foreigners far outnumbered native Chinese. The population of foreign traders in these regions consisted of Persians, Syrians, Turks, Indians, and above all Sogdians.[45]

The Sogdians were an Iranian people who originally inhabited Transoxiana, in modern Uzbekistan and Tajikistan. The core of this region lay between the rivers Amu Darya and Syr Darya and was dominated by the city of Samarkand, but it stretched west to Bukhara, east to the Ferghana valley, and north to Shash (modern Tashkent). The Sogdians lived in numerous independent city-states, and consequently often fell under the domination of foreign powers.[46] Although the cities were occasionally drawn into warfare, they continued to flourish throughout the period.

While the Sogdian towns practiced an irrigation-based agriculture, the key to their prosperity was trade. From at least the third century they regularly traveled to the upper Indus valley, where they traded with Indian

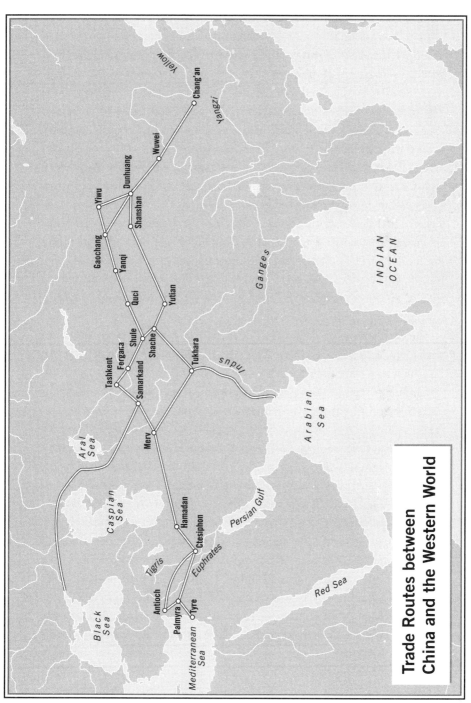

Trade Routes between China and the Western World

MAP 14

merchants coming from Kashmir and other regions. Their trade with the oasis towns of what is now Xinjiang and with China had been established by the early fourth century, as evidenced by the so-called ancient letters discovered at Dunhuang which date to 311 and by remarks in Chinese records. By the middle of the sixth century they had established direct trade relations with Constantinople. They thus came to dominate trade along the silk roads stretching from China to Byzantium, and their Indo-European language became its *lingua franca*. The Chinese told stories that identified the Sogdians as the trading people par excellence: "Mothers give their infants sugar to eat and put paste on the palms of their hands in the hope that when they are grown, they will talk sweetly and that precious objects stick [to their hands]. They are skillful merchants; when a boy reaches the age of five he is put to studying books; when he begins to understand them, he is sent to study commerce. They excel at commerce and love profits; from the time a man is twenty, he goes to neighboring kingdoms; wherever one can make money they go."[47]

The Sogdians were controlled by their own headmen and subject to their own laws. The northern Chinese governments appointed Sogdian headmen to office with the title *sabao,* an official who controlled the community's civic and religious affairs.[48] They practiced a form of Zoroastrianism, but they developed a pantheon and rituals from several Mesopotamian and Indian cults. Although the Sogdians never adopted Buddhism in their homeland, several of them became celebrated for their work translating Buddhist scriptures into Chinese. The Sogdians also introduced other cultural innovations into China, including new forms of metal work and ceramics, as well as popular forms of music and dance.

Unlike the Buddhists and traders who came into China from the west, the southern Yue or Man peoples became "foreign" because China's southward expansion made them outsiders in what had been their own lands. As early as the Three Kingdoms period, "mountain Yue" were driven into the hills by Chinese occupation of the lowlands and press-ganged into labor or military service. Scattered records throughout the southern dynasties describe them both as objects of exploitation by southern rulers and the great families and as occasional rebels who militarily resisted the new powers.

Like the earlier Han dynasty, the southern dynasties established military commanderies to control the Yue in specified regions. While the records left by the southerners reflect primarily Yue relations to the governments and leading families, scattered accounts tell of Yue and Han people engaging in trade in local markets, Han merchants venturing into regions still inhabited by the Yue, the Yue working as seasonal laborers for Han enterprises, Han households fleeing their landlords by escaping to the Yue, intermarriage between the Han and the Yue, the emergence of Han settlers who came to dwell among the Yue as landlords and powerful families, and even Yue conversion to the Daoist faith.[49]

Tomb art supplements these scattered textual references. The most important finds come from what had been the province of Yongzhou in the Han River valley near the modern Dengxian and Hanzhong in Henan. The evidence includes a statue of a civil official with an unusual hairdo—the front of the head shaved and the hair tied back in a pointed knot—that matches accounts of the Man people in this region, and another of a man with an unusual duck-shaped hat that is unique to the area. Bricks depict *buqu* (serfs serving as private armies) parading with arms, leading horses, and playing military music. It is possible that these men were originally Man, but there is nothing in the images to demonstrate this.[50]

Some evidence indicates that by the late Northern and Southern Dynasties and under the Sui the southern natives were largely assimilated in the basin of the Yangzi River and its tributaries. By this time many Man people were legally categorized as "good" (free) subjects, and, according to one Sui account, it had become illegal to enslave the Man. Enjoying the status of ordinary Han peasants, the Man were allowed to hold taxable land. Despite scattered records of Man uprisings in remote or isolated regions, the military commands devoted to controlling the indigenous peoples in the Han, Huai, and Yangzi River basins had ceased to exist.

The most noteworthy aspect of relations between "foreigners" and "Chinese" is the fluidity of these two categories. The earliest "foreign" dynasty, the Former Zhao founded by Liu Yuan, featured a ruler raised in a Chinese court who was well-versed in Chinese language and culture and committed to creating a Chinese-style state. He claimed descent from the Han ruling house and presented himself as a Han restorationist. Similarly, when Emperor Xiaowen of the Northern Wei moved his capital to Luoyang, he had the court adopt Chinese language and costumes, gave all courtiers Chinese names, and imposed intermarriage between the Chinese and Tuoba elites. In this period we find instances in the *Book of the Wei* where men whose grandparents were Xianbei are described by their fellows as being "Han," sometimes as an insult.

The Northern Zhou and Qi regimes that emerged from the rebellion of the garrisons in part reversed this trend. The Qi court routinely used the Xianbei language, and ambitious Han parents instructed their children in this tongue to advance their careers. The Zhou court, for its part, bestowed Xianbei surnames on its Han followers, while at the same time self-consciously modeling its government on (and taking its name from) the Han classic *Rituals of Zhou,* thus being more canonically "Chinese" than the great families who dominated contemporary society.[51]

Further evidence for the permeability of boundaries comes from tomb art and Buddhist images. Several members of non-Chinese families closely connected with the ruling house of the Northern Qi had Chinese-style tombs that contained ceramics decorated with distinctive Central Asian motifs. Many tombs through the north of China feature images of people in Xianbei attire (men in caftans with tight sleeves and wide lapels, trousers tucked into boots, and a high cap with a neck cloth in the back; women in the same style of caftan but with a skirt and hair in braids or buns). Such figures appear in tomb murals, ceramic figurines (especially as armed attendants), and images of Buddhist worshippers. A notable example of such cross-cultural fusion is a lacquer coffin found in a tomb at Guyuan. It includes classic figures from Chinese Daoist iconography, such as the Queen Mother of the West and her consort and a set of scenes depicting classic exemplars of filial piety dating back to such legendary figures of antiquity as Cai Shun, all labeled with cartouches. All of these figures are depicted in Xianbei attire, thus inventing a Chinese history and cosmos in which everyone was Xianbei, or a Xianbei world that embodied Chinese history and values.[52]

A final example of this blurring of boundaries between the Chinese and the foreign is a Buddhist stele dating to around 471 produced in Chang'an.[53] The back depicts the story of how Sumedha, an earlier incarnation of the historical Buddha, through several rebirths became a universal, wheel-turning king and finally was born as the historical Buddha, Sakyamuni. The scenes that make up this story have several unusual features. First, the final birth as Sakyamuni is clearly set in China. When the central figure of the story appears as Sumedha, he is dressed in Xianbei attire; when he becomes a *cakravartin* king, his robe becomes Chinese; but when he dwells in the Tusita Heaven awaiting his final rebirth as Sakyamuni, he reverts to his Xianbei attire. In contrast, the two females in the story, a woman who sells flowers to Sumedha and the mother of the Buddha, are depicted in Chinese robes. Similarly, in the images of the donors at the base of the stele, most of the men wear Xianbei garb while the women are dressed as Chinese.

This visual narrative is thus set in an India that is transposed into China, where the hero alternates between a Xianbei identity and a Chinese one, and gender roles are framed in terms of Chinese and "foreign." This indicates an aspiration to inclusiveness within a universal state to which all peoples belonged, and also depicts the values of a people for whom ethnicity as proclaimed in clothing and conduct had become more a matter of choice than genealogy.

7

REDEFINING KINSHIP

WHILE the fundamental structures of family organization did not change during the Northern and Southern Dynasties, several major new elements appeared. The basic unit at all levels of society remained the individual nuclear family living as a household and dividing property among all the sons, although larger lineages might have hundreds or thousands of households living in close proximity. As in the Eastern Han, some wealthy households consisted of three generations, but this pattern was not common.[1] However, new practices permitted those households to link up with related families and to redefine their own structure.

Lineage cemeteries and new festivals allowed families to join more distant kin and thereby seek cooperation or assistance. New forms of writing, or extended use of old forms, altered how larger kin groups conceived of their own membership. The rise of institutional religions provided a path for women to leave the household and take on a more active, public role, including the role of author. Finally, the Buddhist religion changed the relation of the living to the dead by providing rituals that could secure a better rebirth or afterlife. Some changes also placed a new emphasis on the relation of mothers and sons, modifying the exclusive father-son tie that defined the earlier lineage structure.

Cemeteries and Festivals

Two important changes in the relations of families to their ancestors between the late Han dynasty and the Tang were the construction of family cemeteries and the regular gatherings of scattered members of a lineage at tombs associated with the Qingming Festival, also known as the Cold Food Festival. Both these developments were important because they bound together larger groups of people as kin.

The systematic laying out of cemeteries where members of different households of the same lineage would be buried dates back to the last century of the Han.[2] In the Western Han, shrines had been associated with the graves of single individuals and thus served as personal monuments. During the Eastern Han, however, people began to build offering shrines in front of multichambered family tombs. These shrines were at first still dedicated to individuals, but with the later burials of kin in the other chambers of the tomb, the shrine became a family or lineage memorial where descendants made offerings to the oldest common ancestor and those buried in association with him. Examples from the Han seem to have extended across no more than four generations and did not necessarily include all members of a given generation.

In addition to multichambered graves for a single household, Han Chinese also extended the practice of burying in a single graveyard kin who had not shared a household while alive. This pattern of placing tombs together had begun with the "mountain tombs" of the Western Han imperial line. Eastern Han emperors were no longer buried under artificial mountains, but their mausoleums were placed in a designated area outside the walls of the capital, Luoyang. In the later Eastern Han, the practice of arranging kin burials in a single cemetery spread more widely among elite families. The excavated Yang family graveyard in Hongnong near the Tong Pass in Shaanxi includes seven simple single-family graves lined up from east to west. Inscriptions identify six of the occupants and date four of the tombs. The farthest east tomb belonged to Yang Zhen, who was buried in 126, while the next to the last tomb belonged to a grandson buried in 173. The last tomb may have contained a great grandson. Since only two of Yang Zhen's five sons are buried there, it seems that the cemetery was reserved for the senior branch and excluded collateral lines.

Another, looser structure is exemplified by the cemetery of the Cao family, which supplanted the Han dynasty. This late second-century graveyard was described in the early sixth century by Li Daoyuan in his *Commentary to the Classic of the Waterways* (*Shui jing zhu*), a comprehensive guide to the cultural geography of China. He described four tombs. Three of them, belonging to a father and two sons, formed a cluster, while another tomb for a member of a different line was set off as an independent burial unit in the same locality. Excavations begun in 1974 have found five large, multichambered tombs spread over an area of a mile and a quarter; the only ones that are close together belonged to a father and son. Within this large area are several smaller clusters of graves or large tomb mounds that local people have always called the "mounds of the Cao family." The tombs of this lineage cemetery vary considerably in the presence or absence of shrines and other stone memorials, and the looseness of the arrangement probably reflects the physical dispersal of the lineage in life.

From inscriptions we know that the Wu family graveyard in modern Shandong contained at least five tombs belonging to members of three generations. A pillar gate and stone sculptures marked the entrance to the cemetery, where tombs were dispersed into several units. None of the tombs has been excavated, but since multichambered tombs housing members of more than one generation were common among the elite in this region—the Cao family cemetery is not too distant—it is likely that the Wu family followed this practice. Two such tombs have been found, although their relation to the Wu family remains unclear. The inscriptions indicate that more than one line was buried in the cemetery, demonstrating a broader genealogical range than that of the Yang family in the west. Women may have been buried in the cemetery.

The construction of family graveyards developed in several regions during the Northern and Southern Dynasties.[3] In the south, archaeologists have excavated a cluster of six graves containing members of the Zhou family of Yixing who were buried in the late third and early fourth century in what came to be called the "mound of the Zhou tombs." The people buried here belonged to an eminent southern family that provided crucial support for Wu state and the subsequent Western Jin dynasty but ultimately were destroyed in a rebellion against northern émigrés in the early decades of the fourth century. The six tombs are lined up on a north-south axis, with their entrance passages facing east-southeast.

Seven tombs representing three generations of the Wang family, who dominated the Eastern Jin court throughout the first half of the fourth century, have been excavated in the northern outskirts of Jianyang. These single-chambered, barrel-vaulted tombs, all facing south, are lined up in two rows. They do not contain any model houses or figurines for reconstructing the life of the deceased in the underworld. The only mark of the family's lofty status is the presence of precious imported glass cups, a diamond ring, and a vessel made of shell, pearls, and amber and turquoise beads.

Han dynasty Chinese family graveyards have also been found along the northwest frontier zone, at Jiayuguan, Jiuquan, and Dunhuang.[4] Stone rings or earthen ramparts demarcated groups of graves belonging to the same lineage. Within the ring the tombs were arranged according to the hierarchy of kin ties. Many graves used a painted screen wall at the tomb entrance to symbolize the limits of the individual household. In addition to the joint burial of husband and wife, typical of the Han, some of these tombs included a second generation, perhaps indicating an increased frequency of married children living with their parents in this period.

Family graveyards figure in the poetry of the Northern and Southern Dynasties. Pan Yue (247–300) in his "Rhapsody on Recalling Old Friends and Kin" describes visiting the clustered tombs of his father-in-law and his two sons about fifty miles south of Luoyang:

> The Lord of Dongwu was entrusted here;
> They opened up a plot and built a grave.
> Tall and stately stand twin grave markers;
> Neatly arrayed, a row of catalpas.
> Gazing upon the catalpas
> Moves me to deep thought.
> Having offered respects to Lord Dai,
> I also mourn Yuan and Si.
> Their graves rest one upon another, mound touching mound;
> Cypresses, lush and luxuriant, in thick clusters planted.

A few decades later Tao Yuanming described a picnic celebrated in the shadow of the cypresses lining the tombs of the Zhou family, most likely the same tombs discussed above.[5] Thus the family cemetery had become a standard feature in the life of the elite, who alone were in a position to create and enjoy them.

People in this period also invented the "merit cloister," a plot of land formally donated to the Buddhist monastic order to serve as a family graveyard. As monastic property, it was free from taxes and held in perpetuity, but in practice it served the needs of the donor family. The family appointed monastic administrators for "their" cloister, so repeated gifts allowed them to control the monastery as a front for their own economic and cultic activities. This was distinct from the conventional family graveyard, in that only two or three kin participated in the seasonal graveside offerings performed by monks.[6]

Before the Tang, no evidence indicates collective worship of ancestors outside the residential family. Children made offerings at the graves of parents or grandparents, but descendants of more distant ancestors never gathered for any collective worship that would have established them as a meaningful social grouping. However, at the end of the seventh century, or in the early decades of the eighth, paternal kin began gathering to clean and make offerings at the tombs of ancestors removed by four or five generations.[7] These offerings, made at the Qingming ("pure and bright") Festival 105 days after the winter solstice in the late second or third lunar month, mark the beginning of the transformation of distant kin into a self-conscious, organized paternal lineage through shared worship of remote ancestors.

The prehistory of the festival sheds light on this new development. During the Han dynasty, graveside offerings parallel to those in the ancestral temple became common, but there is no record of a single festival on which all kin made offerings at tombs. The *Monthly Ordinances of the Four Classes of People* (*Simin yueling*), written in the late Eastern Han, encouraged grave offerings in each of the four seasons. The spring offering was to be made in the second lunar month, in association with the sacrifices to the local altar of the soil.[8] Several Eastern Han texts also refer to banning fire for several days, or in one text for two months, and consequently eating cold food. The earliest references place this ban in midwinter and declare it to be a memorial to a meritorious seventh-century B.C. official, Jie Zitui, who resigned from office, was burned alive in an abortive attempt to force him to leave his mountain retreat, and received a memorial cult in his native region near Taiyuan. The Han government tried to ban this cold-food practice as a danger to health, and in 206 Cao Cao issued an edict against it, stating that it was celebrated 105 days after the winter solstice, that is, on the Qingming Festival. This date was also recorded a few decades later by a native of Taiyuan.

Further unsuccessful attempts to ban the cold-food cult were made by Shi Le in 317 and by the Northern Wei in 474 and 496. Two mid-sixth-century texts describe an empire-wide cult celebrated 105 days after the winter solstice that *Essential Methods of the Common People* explains as a memorial to Jie Zitui. *Seasonal Records of the Mid-Yangzi Region* (*Jing Chu sui shi ji*) cites the *Rituals of Zhou* (a late Warring States or early Han composition) to the effect that in the second month of spring an emissary used a "bell with a wooden clapper" to announce a prohibition of fire in the state's capital. The ruler's calendar, preserved in several late Warring States and early Han texts, records the use of such a bell to announce a ban on sexual activity and any use of fire "to burn mountain forests," precisely the act that killed Jie Zitui. Bans on fire and sexual activity also figure in accounts of the summer solstice from the same period.[9] These texts clearly link the supposed commemoration of a historical event with a broader ban on fire that was part of the ritual closing of the old year and the starting of the new. This annual cleansing marked by extinguishing old fires, briefly banning them, and then resuming new ones could have facilitated the emergence of the Sui-Tang festival for cleaning graves.

By the early Tang, the Cold Food Festival had become an occasion for families to gather at the tombs of their ancestors to clean them, make offerings, and enjoy a feast. The earliest anecdote linking the festival with graveside offerings appears in a text dating from the 660s relating a story set in the Sui dynasty. By the eighth century the practice had become widespread, as indicated by a decree of 732 noting that while the classics did not mention the practice of visiting graves at the Cold Food Festival, it had become customary and should be encouraged: "For gentlemen and commoners who do not get together to make offerings at family altars, how else can they exhibit their filial sentiments? They should be allowed to visit the graves and together perform the rituals of bowing and sweeping at the tombs." Writing some decades later while in exile, Liu Zongyuan lamented that even the ancestors of the horse doctors and humble field laborers around him received offerings at their graves, while he alone could not visit the tombs of his ancestors.[10]

These developments had two major consequences for ancestor worship. First, the construction of family cemeteries encouraged making offerings to early ancestors. Since the more distant the common ancestor, the more people who could recognize themselves as kin, this increased the potential size of kin groupings. Second, the Cold Food Festival became an occasion for descendants of a common ancestor to come together and hence become familiar with one another. This increased the possibility of larger, self-conscious groups who could act together or provide mutual assistance in times of trouble. However, the impact of the festival should not be exaggerated, because there is no evidence that substantial numbers of kin actually gathered at individual graves. A few poems and essays suggest that care of graves remained largely the affair of individual households.[11]

In addition to family graveyards and annual festivals for extended family, another feature of the late Tang can be traced back to the Northern and Southern Dynasties: communal families which stayed together for generations—in one case for thirteen—without dividing property. This Tang practice seems to have been a recurrence of the pattern found earlier in northern China in which families dwelt together for generations in close association with neighbors as a form of local self-defense. By not dividing property over many generations, families became quite large; some numbered nearly eight hundred individuals.[12] The vast majority of such cases were commoners, with multi-generation scholar households being much rarer and never becoming this large. Such families steadily declined from the early Song (late tenth century). Although these families were praised by Confucian moralists and rewarded by the emperor, the fact that they consisted of poor commoners rather than literati indicates that they were organized for self-defense rather than out of a desire to construct a ritually proper kin system. That the restoration of social order in the Song was linked to their decline points to the same conclusion. Rather than being a stage in the development of the classic Song lineage, with its ancestral temples and lineage endowments, communal families were an archaic form that appeared in times of disorder, such as in north China in the fourth and fifth centuries.

Writing the Lineage

The expansion of self-conscious kin groups was furthered by new forms of writing, most notably "family instructions" and genealogies. While oral and even short written deathbed instructions are recorded in earlier texts, and a few Han sources refer to "family regulations," the Northern and Southern Dynasties produced the earliest surviving model of an extended composition addressed to descendants and stipulating the forms of conduct that distinguished the family and were essential to its prosperity. The classic case is *The Family Instructions of the Yan Clan,* composed by Yan Zhitui (531–591).[13] This book used written instructions to sons to offset the physical and oral power of women in the household. It thus sought to strengthen the paternal lineage both among members of the nuclear family and among a larger number of males sharing a common surname.

The text features advice for anyone trying to maintain a family for generations. Examples include strictures on the danger of remarriage, warnings that brothers who love one another can be pulled apart by the ambitions of their wives, insistence on the constant disciplining of children, and calls on parents to avoid excessive intimacy with their offspring, which undercuts parental authority. Yan Zhitui also discusses the need to carefully manage the family's material resources and not to be overly trusting of servants. Being a scholar, he emphasizes the importance of treating books well and devotes several chapters to the importance of study and skillful writing.[14]

In addition to giving advice, the book describes and assesses regional variations in households, the conduct of their business, and familial values. An entire chapter specifically devoted to "customs and conduct" deals with issues such as taboos on uttering the names of deceased parents, the celebration of festivals, mourning the dead, and related matters. The book often contrasts conduct in the north and in the south, cites strictures from the canonical sources, and judges which region's behavior is preferable, as in the following example:

> At the winter solstice and New Year's day, southerners would not call on a family in mourning. If they did not write a letter of sympathy, then after the festivals they would extend condolences by wearing a formal mourning band. Northerners on these same days would solemnly perform the ritual of a consolation visit. As the ritual classics say nothing explicit on this matter, I do not choose between them. When guests arrive, southerners do not go out to welcome them. When meeting they raise their clasped hands but do not bow. When guests leave they would do no more than get off their mats. Northerners go all the way to the gate both to greet and to send off. When they meet, they bow. These latter are the ancient ways; I prefer both to welcome and to bow.[15]

Southerners insisted on discussing their family histories only in writing, while northerners would talk about them face to face and even pose what Yan Zhitui regarded as intrusive questions about a guest's family background. Yan's discussion expands into the broader question of who could be recognized as kin in the south and the north, and what terms should be applied to them:

> Customarily, south of the Yangzi one calls all those who held high office "venerable." Those of the same generation, even if linked by a common ancestor of a hundred generations before, are all called brothers. When speaking to non-kin they are all called "clansmen."

Scholars north of the Yangzi, even if related as distantly as twenty or thirty generations, still call one another "collateral" older or younger uncle. Emperor Wu of the Liang once asked a man from the central plain, "You are a northerner, why are you not aware that there are clans?" He replied, "Flesh and blood are so easily parted, I cannot bear to speak of such a thing as a clan." At the time this was regarded as a brilliant reply, but he showed he was ignorant of ritual.[16]

While some of the disputed issues are unclear, Yan Zhitui's text demonstrates several points. Both in the north and the south, members of the elite were tracing kin back across dozens, if not literally a hundred, generations, which was only possible with detailed written genealogies. The exact relations of people to one another and the terms describing those relationships were issues of central concern. As to the dispute between Emperor Wu and the northerner, it appears that the latter regarded the undefined notion translated here as "clan" to be an artificial construct that in some way denied the physical and emotive ties that bound kin together. This would fit well with the southerners' preference for constructing kin ties in written accounts, in contrast with northerners who expected a lived, working knowledge of family relationships.

A final type of material in the *Family Instructions* is addressed to Yan Zhitui's descendants specifically as members of the Yan family. Yan takes pains to point out rules for conduct and belief that characterize his particular family. One example of this is his warning against involvement in military affairs. While he offers general reasons for avoiding warfare, these are preceded by an enumeration of members of the Yan family who had been literary scholars from the time of Confucius down to the present day. Only two members of the family had opted for the military life, and both had met disaster. Thus, avoiding a military life was a family obligation, out of respect for ancestral traditions.

Another example is the opening of his chapter urging a belief in Buddhism: "The matter of transmigration through past, present, and future lives is believable and has proof. Our family for generations has sought refuge for the heart/mind in Buddhism. Do not neglect this."[17] While Yan devotes the chapter to proofs for the veracity of Buddhism, immediately after a chapter attacking Daoism, the primary appeal here is to family tradition. To be in the Yan lineage meant to believe in Buddhism.

Yan insists on the centrality of scholarship and literary activities to a proper life and a proper lineage. He notes that his sons grew up among barbarians in the north, so they could learn proper customs and correct family practices only from texts. Later, he justified a reduction of his own standard of living in order to support his sons' educations in terms of "devoting ourselves to the Way of former kings and carrying on our family's hereditary enterprise/calling." In discussing literary composition, he refers to a family tradition in which for generations the writings of the Yan family have been "extremely classic and correct, not following current fashion." Such references to family traditions of scholarship and writing also figure in his insistence on the importance of calligraphy, which he describes as a "family tradition" crucial to his own survival. Yan Zhitui several times cites writing as a basis of kin ties, and advocates receiving criticism and correction from older relatives in order to learn how to write.[18] In short, through instruction from kin the men in his family formed their own traditions of writing that then became essential to the lineage's survival as a distinctive entity across generations.

The theme of writing as a means of maintaining a family also figures in Yan Zhitui's critique of the intimate physical and oral world dominated by women. The most extensive discussion of this theme is in the chapter "Exerting Oneself in Study." He argues that people's tendency to encourage children to admire and imitate eminent neighbors is folly, because the highest models for conduct are in the texts that preserve the wisdom of antiquity. More generally, throughout the text he asserts the superiority of wisdom or knowledge derived from the eye to that derived from the ear. At one place this refers to the primacy of direct observation over hearsay, but elsewhere it recommends relying on texts over trusting what one is told.[19] While these arguments do not explicitly deal with the theme of men versus women, they justify the text's stated project of supplanting potent words with a written text, and they make textual transmission and study fundamental to the survival of a lineage.

This last point is elaborated throughout the text in an argument that textual study provides the best, if not the only, economic foundation for a lineage's survival. Knowledge gained from study is not lost even when war destroys all one's property or kin, and it will always find a market. It is more valuable than land, which disperses with the passage of generations, or even noble rank, which vanishes with the fall of each short-lived dynasty. He thus posits a socioeconomic rationale for writing as a way to preserve a lineage, although he also piously insists that its ultimate role is moral cultivation.

This economic justification for writing forms the core of the chapter

"Exerting Oneself in Study." After asserting that all people, even sage rulers and high nobles, must study, he locates scholarship within an economic model of society:

> All people in the world ought to have a profession/calling. Farmers plan for ploughing and sowing; merchants discuss and judge goods and prices; craftsmen exert their skill to the limit in making utensils; masters of skills and arts deeply ponder their techniques; warriors train in the use of bow and horse; and literary scholars expound the meanings of classical texts. I have seen many "scholar-officials" who are ashamed to associate with farmers or merchants and embarrassed to deal with craftsmen or artists. In archery they cannot pierce the target, and in writing they can barely manage to sign their names. Idly and without effort they fill themselves with food and drink, and thereby fritter away their time to the end of their days. [20]

After pointing out how such noble idlers perished each time a dynasty fell, he argued that those with a skill can survive anywhere, and writing is the most useful and noble of such skills. This insistence on writing as a saleable skill that could see one through the worst disasters was one of the lessons that he had drawn from his own experience of having lived through youthful poverty, the fall of several dynasties, and captivity in the north. His own experience had "carved on his flesh and bones" the value of this craft.[21]

The notion that study was crucial to the family pervaded the elite of the Northern and Southern Dynasties. Writing in the late fifth century, a member of the powerful Wang family argued that the privileges based on an ancestor's rank would always fade away, so that only hard work could maintain a family's position. He asserted that there was an enormous difference in the worldly position of a father and his sons, or even of siblings, and that the difference depended entirely on how diligently they studied.[22] The argument also runs through *New Account of Tales of the World*, in which even the most eminent lineages, such as the Xie, constantly examine their young children for signs of the literary and scholarly excellence that will guarantee the family's future. Children or young people are subjected to the same competitive evaluations of talent and character that were applied to the selection of adults for office, with some percipient adult foretelling which young son would preserve or restore the family's position through his literary talents or skills in cultivated social discourse. The following is a good example:

> The Director of Works Gu He once engaged in pure conversation with other worthies of the age. Zhang Xuanzhi and Gu Fu, the sons respectively of his daughter and his son, were both in their seventh year and playing by the side of the dais. At the time they listened to the conversation, even though their spirits and senses seemed completely detached from the scene. Then, seated beneath the lamp, the two boys repeated the words of "guest" and "host" without any omissions or mistakes. Getting off his mat and putting his mouth close to their ears, Gu said, "I never imagined that our declining clan would ever again produce such treasures as these."

In a few cases even girls joined in the competition.[23]

In addition to family instructions, the writing of genealogies became important during this period. Although there are references in Han texts to composing genealogies and to their wholesale destruction at the end of the dynasty, during the Northern and Southern Dynasties these family records became a universal feature of elite families and any who imitated them. They allowed lineages to identify their members, and members to secure the prestige of belonging to an eminent line. The state used genealogies to determine who could receive privileges based on family background. Consequently, genealogies became fundamental determinants of the social and political order, as well as of kin structures.

No genealogies survive, but references to them in the histories and essays of the period allow us to reconstruct their basic features. Genealogies described the origins of a family, the different branches and their respective status, the major offices held by members, and marriages. Extracts from genealogies are quoted in a commentary to *New Account of Tales of the World* to provide information about people in the anecdotes. These extracts provide the name a man used in public life (but not his personal name), the place of origin of his branch of the family, the name and highest office of his father and grandfather, his own highest office and other offices, sometimes his age at death, and occasionally his mother's lineage, sisters' names, and other relatives.[24]

The best piece of evidence is the "Later Preface to the Family Genealogy of the Yu Line of Henan," written by Yu Shao in the third quarter of the eighth century. In this preface he explains that his family's genealogy dated back to the family's receipt of a new surname and a fief under the Northern Wei, which had granted these honors to one Yu Jin. The family had kept a record of offices and marriages for over one hundred and seventy years but then lost it during the catastrophic An Lushan rebellion in 756. Yu Shao was now reconstructing it, and, as he explains, the family was divided into nine branches, each descended from one of the nine sons of Yu Jin. Each branch was described in two scrolls, the first of which recorded the line's founder and the subsequent four generations. These five generations matched the number that would receive sacrifices in an ancestral temple. The second scroll recorded the present head of the branch, his father, and their descendants.

This discussion shows the breadth of those who could be included, but Yu Shao then appended a crucial modification:

> The branch founded by the fourth son of Yu Jin, Yu Li, has very few officials compared with the three eldest branches. Therefore I have put it and the branches founded by the fifth, sixth, seventh, eighth, and ninth sons—six branches in all—into one scroll. In that scroll I have simply copied out the old genealogy for the fifth branch on down, since their descendants' offices were insignificant and they married no one of consequence. They have sunk into obscurity, and nothing whatever is heard of them.[25]

In short, the genealogies that emerged in the Northern and Southern Dynasties, as well as those of the Han, were not complete lists of all kin defined by a certain degree of blood ties but only kin whose status, gained through successful careers or marriages, made them worthy of being recognized and remembered.

These twin principles of casting one's net as widely as possible and then tossing out all those fish too small to be of use are indicated in anecdotes scattered through the dynastic histories. As examples of breadth of knowledge, a man named Wei Ting told the founder of the Sui dynasty that his lineage had become divided into southern and northern branches that had no contact, but his records still allowed him to trace their kin ties. A preface of a Tang genealogy preserved in Japan tells how the author kept a detailed genealogy so that branches that had grown distant from one another could more easily trace their common ancestry. Conversely, anecdotes tell of poor orphans disavowed by successful relatives who refused to count them as kin. In one celebrated case Man Zhangzhi's attempt to marry his son to the daughter of an eminent family was blocked because investigators found that Man's genealogy included commoners as well as officials.

The practice of excluding unsuccessful kin is articulated as a general rule in one of the Tang dynasty's official histories: "Every surname group [among the great lines of Shandong] ranked its branches. Though their choronym [place of origin] was the same, within the line there was a substantial difference between high and low."[26] In the crucial matter of constituting their membership, the great lineages of the Northern and Southern Dynasties did not allow sentiment to interfere with a ruthless calculation of worldly advantage. Only those who made their way in the world through office or marriage could be counted as members of the true elite.

This approach to lineages is the social form of the Nine-Rank appointment system that enabled hereditary claims only to entry-level posts; maintaining a high position from generation to generation depended on a family's members securing continued promotions from the state administration. In the same way, remaining members of a lineage that enjoyed a hereditary claim to office depended upon success in each generation in securing higher posts. Easy access to office came through lineage membership, but, conversely, lineage membership came through obtaining high office.

The only thing holding the great families together was their consciousness of being kin, a consciousness embodied in their genealogy.[27] The sole exception was those northern families that remained masters of forts in their localities, men who did not rise above the local elite. Since the genealogies were based on the principle of excluding lines that failed to attain office, elite kin structure, beyond the level of the individual household, was formed through the nexus of the state. The great families' domination of high office in the period thus came at the cost of making their own existence dependant upon the workings of the political bureaucracy. An individual's stylized retirement from the court to become a "hermit" was a luxury that in the long run depended on family status and the income of periodic access to office.

Kinship and Buddhism

While developing larger kin units under the Northern and Southern Dynasties entangled the great lineages in the state structure, families in the period also increasingly entrusted to emergent religious institutions the rituals that defined their existence. Specifically, the Buddhist order with its new model of the afterlife and the rituals necessary to secure a happy existence for the dead increasingly made itself essential to maintaining links between a family and its ancestors, and hence to the structure of the family itself. In certain times and places the Daoist church, particularly devotees of the syncretic Lingbao tradition, played a similar role.

The earliest evidence of using the Buddhist and Daoist religions to serve the family derives almost entirely from images and their accompanying inscriptions. Consequently it is difficult to generalize about the spatial and temporal ranges of these developments; many changes were probably regional. The first clear evidence of using Buddhism to secure a happy afterlife for ancestors, as well as a prosperous present and future for the family as a whole, comes from the walls of caves and the sides or back of freestanding stupas (domed or pyramidal funerary monuments containing Buddhist relics) or steles (carved stone slabs erected for commemorative purposes). Images of the Buddha appear in Han tombs and on funerary jars from the third century, but it is unclear whether these images were invoked as adjuncts of a specifically Buddhist belief or whether the imported Buddha figure was adopted as one deity among many. In some cases the Buddha was specifically associated with the west and hence linked with the Queen Mother of the West, who was carved or painted in tombs to assist its inhabitants to secure a happy afterlife. Thus, the first century and a half of Buddhist figures in China likely formed an iconographic extension of traditional Chinese beliefs.[28]

These early Buddhist mortuary images largely vanished in the fourth century, replaced by what became classic icons of the religion. While literary references to stone sculptures of the Buddha date back to the fourth century, the earliest surviving statues come from the early decades of the fifth century.[29] Of thirteen votive stone stupas—varying in height from seventeen centimeters to one meter—from Liangzhou in the northwest of China, seven are dated by inscriptions to 426–436, when the area was ruled by a family of Xiongnu descent who were devotees of Buddhism. A monastic community had been established there since the third century, and the earliest of the celebrated Buddhist caves at nearby Dunhuang were constructed in the same period.

Yet tombs from this period in this region do not show any Buddhist influence. The painted bricks from the tombs at Jiayuguan contain numerous scenes of families and daily life, while religious images include such traditional figures as the Queen Mother of the West, the King Father of the East, Fuxi and Nugua, tomb-protecting monsters, and the tree associated with the altar of the soil. Several tombs, including several without decorations, include "tomb-protecting texts" similar to those found in the Han. One type of text refers to jars of grain and small lead figurines that will assume any guilt incurred by the living. Yet two deities—Master Green Bird and the North Star—guarantee that the dead will bear responsibility for their own guilt and henceforth be completely separated from the living. A second type of text invokes two clusters of stars that will take responsibility for the dead, purge away death pollution, and maintain their separation from the living. These all have Han precedents, and apart from a single character "Buddha" on a pottery shard, there is no evidence of any Buddhist impact on funerary ritual.[30]

Given that traditional funerary practice survived in this region, the thirteen votive stupas provide striking evidence of the fusion of Buddhism with earlier conventions (Fig. 19). The stupas seem to have been stock items manufactured in workshops and subsequently purchased for use. They have an octagonal base, a round drum, a dome with image niches, and a projecting crown with a series of tapering stories that are an abstract version of the parasols that conventionally topped a stupa. Some have an image of the Big Dipper carved on top of this register. The dome has eight niches that correspond to the sides of the octagonal base. Seven of the niches are occupied by identical Buddha figures, and the eighth by a crowned and bejewelled bodhisattva. These represent the six Buddhas of the past, the historical Buddha Sakyamuni, and the future Buddha Maitreya. The round drum contains an extract from a canonical sutra—a feature unique to these pieces—followed by the dedication, which typically includes the name of the donors, the date, the circumstances of the purchase, and the wishes of the donors. Each side of the octagon contains the image of a haloed figure, four male and four female, clad in attire that indicates an Indian or Central Asian origin. In the upper right corner of each of these images is one of the eight trigrams from the *Canon of Change*.[31]

These objects represent an early example of a clearly Buddhist object combined with elements of traditional Chinese cosmology. The Dipper and the hexagrams were linked in divinatory procedures under the Han and still used in this way under the Northern and Southern Dynasties.

Fig. 19   Drawing of a Northern Liang votive stone stupa. Near Dunhuang.

The trigrams were conventionally correlated with family members: father, mother, three sons, and three daughters. The embodied trigrams on
the stupas are likewise divided into four females and four males.

The inscriptions on these objects fusing Buddhism and received Chinese culture demonstrate at least two points. First, with one exception,
lay people paid for their carving. Several of them cite an entire family as
patrons. Since no individuals announce titles, probably none of them
were officials, although reference to a hired calligrapher and a servant indicate some degree of wealth. Second, the dedications devote the merit of
the deed first to the emperor and then to various groups of kin including
"fathers and mothers for seven generations," brothers, unspecified ancestors, and other kin. They express the wish that family members should all
have a future encounter with Maitreya, that is, be reborn in the Tushita

Heaven where the future Buddha dwells. Thus the primary function of these clearly Buddhist pieces was to secure a better rebirth for deceased kin and prosperity for the family.[32] While the form of the pieces is unique to the region, the creation of Buddhist images to secure blessings for ancestors and the family exemplifies the major role that the new religion would play in the lives of much of the population.

Almost contemporary with these stupas was a memorial stele carved at the behest of a man named Wei Wenlang in 424. This object employs many elements from Han funerary art depicting the passage of the soul to the afterlife. What is strikingly different is that these images are surmounted by a pair of figures making the Buddhist hand gestures that mean "fear not" and "the granting of wishes." Moreover, one figure's attire indicates a Daoist deity, although the patron describes himself as a "Buddhist disciple."[33] Other steles also combine Buddhist and Daoist divinities in a single piece, or depict Daoist divinities in the positions and postures of Buddhas. Several are inscribed with the wish that the merit of making the object should benefit their ancestors and relatives, a distinctively Buddhist form of piety.[34]

Early cave carvings at Dunhuang, dating from the same period, suggest a use of Buddhist images for political purposes that is linked to care for deceased relatives. The conquest of Dunhuang had culminated in a large-scale massacre. Shortly afterward, the conquerors commissioned a set of three caves decorated with scenes for use in visualization practices by meditation masters. The central statue depicted the future Buddha Maitreya, who both assisted meditation and formed a goal for the practice, while the walls were painted with scenes from the life of the historical Buddha and his earlier incarnations. These images are notable in that they all depict cases in which those who later became the Buddha underwent physical suffering and mutilation: being punctured by a thousand nails, having one thousand pieces of flesh cut from his body, giving his own flesh to a hungry hawk to save a pigeon, or giving up his head to fulfill a vow. This probably aimed both to mitigate the crimes of the victors and to suggest to the vanquished new modes of visualizing the fate of their kin, whose violent deaths could lead, with the help of the new religion, to a blessed fate.[35] While the use of such stories to decorate caves was already a commonplace practice at Kucha (the immediate model for the Dunhuang caves), the selection of these specific stories could be related to the recent political events.

Using Buddhism to guarantee happy rebirths for dead kin continues in inscriptions on stone and bronze statues produced under the Northern Wei, Zhou, and Qi dynasties. Thus in 495 a woman named Zhou dedicated images of Sakyamuni and Maitreya for her "deceased husband, Tian Wenhu, the governor of Changshan; her deceased son Sixu; and her deceased daughter Ajue." She prayed that they all in subsequent lives would "encounter the Three Treasures [the Buddha, the monastic order, and the scriptures] and the descent into the world of Maitreya [as the next Buddha]. If they should fall into the Three Evil Paths [animal, hungry ghost, hell], may they be quickly saved and delivered." Again, Buddhism was invoked to secure a happy afterlife for family members.[36]

Images sponsored by village associations of pious lay Buddhists likewise indicate that their primary concern was to gain religious merit for themselves, their living kin, and their ancestors. The well-being of the emperor and state were secondary.[37] Some steles refer to methods by which children, too, could attain enlightenment. One from 540 features a cartouche describing a scene thus: "This is Dingguang Buddha teaching three children to make charitable contributions. All three achieved the stage of 'stream-winner,'" that is, they were guaranteed eventual enlightenment with no retrograde births.[38]

During the subsequent Sui dynasty, images of paradises painted on cave walls depicted the blessed realms in which family members should be reborn. This practice grew even more common in the Tang period, when the tradition of the "family cave" reached its apogee.[39] A final piece of art-historical evidence for the intimate link of the Buddhist religion with concern for the dead is the manner in which the structure of tombs from the third century on was reshaped to resemble Buddhist monastery complexes or cave temples, which had initially been patterned on the model of Han tombs.[40]

Evidence from art and inscriptions of the central role of Buddhism in defining relations between the living and the dead can be supplemented by textual evidence demonstrating how the Ghost Festival became a major event on the Chinese ritual calendar around this time.[41] While father-son ties constituted the lineage in China, the story underlying this new festival focused on the devotion of a son to his mother. The Ghost Festival ultimately derives from fifth-century accounts of how the Buddha's disciple Mulian rescued his mother from hell and rebirth as a hungry ghost by invoking the collective power of the monastic order. This was achieved through offerings to the assembled monks on the fifteenth day of the seventh month at the end of their summer retreat, when a season of austerities had brought their spiritual powers to a peak. Their collective merit was sufficient not only to rescue his mother but also "seven generations of relatives and six kinds of relatives," the same formula that appears on many of the votive inscriptions.

This story became the prototype for an annual festival in which lay people donated part of the fruits of their harvest to the monastic community in exchange for the post-mortem well-being of their kin and aggrieved spirits. The *Record of Seasonal Observances in Jing and Chu*, completed around 561, indicates that by the middle of the sixth century the Ghost Festival was celebrated throughout south China and entailed the elaborate decoration of temples and collective festivities with music and song.[42] The festival and its founding myth dramatized what was implicit in inscriptions and images: for its believers, Buddhism had become essential for assuring the well-being of ancestors and hence for constituting a family. Traditional ancestor worship had been exclusively a matter for kin, and the only offerings to nonrelatives were those made to the state. In the new order, offerings to ancestors had to pass through the monks to be effective, making the Buddhist establishment indispensable to kin structure.

New Roles for Women

The story behind the Ghost Festival was retold and elaborated over the centuries, becoming the best known account of mother-son ties in all of Chinese civilization. The figure of Mulian spread from Buddhism into popular religious belief and conventional ancestral worship. The story also became one of the most popular themes for ritual plays performed in association with funerals. In all these ways it gave formal and literary sanction to a fundamental tie in the Chinese household that had hitherto been ignored in texts.[43] In giving pride of place to mother-son ties, the Mulian story and the Ghost Festival were part of a centuries-long process that increasingly emphasized the emotional bonds that defined the family.

In third-century tombs at Jiayuguan and Dunhuang, archaeologists have discovered numerous paintings that depict doting parents carrying or playing with small children, who form the center of attention. Parents hold children on their laps, fix their hair, and entertain toddlers by swinging a ball on a string, in at least one case with grandparents looking on.[44] These scenes depict the household as a nuclear unit of parents and children held together in physical intimacy by bonds of affection and care.

Increasing emphasis on the mother also altered depictions of the story of Guo Ju. He was a poor man who decided that, in order to have enough food for his mother, he had to kill his infant son. When digging the grave, he found a pot of gold as a reward for his devotion to his mother. The earliest versions of the story treat Guo Ju as exemplary for his filial piety, and the mother of the infant plays no role. However, a depiction of this story from a Northern Wei coffin lid now at the Nelson Gallery tells the story entirely in terms of the mother-son relation. The first scene depicts the child's mother seated on a dais holding her child while two maids tell her of the impending sacrifice; the second shows her kneeling with the child in her arms while her husband digs; and the third shows her returning triumphantly with the child in one arm and the pot of gold carried on a pole carried by her and an unidentified older man. The entire story thus becomes one of motherly loss and redemption, in which the child never leaves its mother's arms. A less elaborate tile from Dengxian shows the pot of gold flanked by Guo Ju with his spade on one side and the mother holding the child on the other (Fig. 20). Again, it is the mother's relationship with the child that is highlighted.[45]

A final artistic theme emphasizing the emotional ties of mother and son, although not to the exclusion of those with the father, is the story of Syama ("Shanzi" in Chinese). In this story the future Buddha became the son of an old, blind couple. One day when he had gone to the woods to fetch water for them, he was accidentally shot by a king. He cried out that in killing him the king had killed three people. Hearing this the king was duly repentant and went to tell the old couple that he would serve them as their son Shanzi once did. The grief-stricken parents swore a vow of truth that as evidence of the moral perfection of their son, the poison from the king's arrow should leave his body. In response the god Indra poured an elixir into Shanzi's mouth that expelled the poison. This story, popular in India, was soon transported to China, where it was carved or painted on numerous steles or cave walls. The climactic scene and center of attention always depicted the two parents mourning the body of their dying son, again making the sentimental ties of parent and child central to the definition of an ideal family.[46]

Especially among non-Chinese peoples, who had always granted a larger role to women, female political power gained greater recognition

Fig. 20   Top: Rubbing of the side of a coffin depicting the story of Guo Ju.
Northern Wei, sixth century. Nelson Gallery, Kansas City. Bottom: Drawing of a
tile depicting the story of Guo Ju. Dengxian, southern Henan, late fifth to early
sixth centuries.

during the Northern and Southern Dynasties. This phenomenon was tied to Buddhism, for the dominant dowager empresses—such as the Dowager Empress Wenming who controlled the Jin court of Emperor Xiaowen in his youth and the Dowager Empress Hu who controlled the Northern Wei court from 515 to 520—were major patrons of Buddhism. After Dowager Empress Wenming's death her son continued to sponsor major Buddhist construction projects for her salvation, a practice that had become standard in the period and again emphasized the mother-son tie.

The negative correlate of this increased female power was the Northern Wei practice of putting to death the mother of an heir to eliminate the threat she posed, though Dowager Empress Hu escaped this fate. She figures prominently in the *Record of the Buddhist Temples of Luoyang*, where she was both the major patron of the greatest temple in the capital and a leading actor in the civil war that destroyed the dynasty.[47] The Tang, while not strictly a conquest dynasty, nevertheless witnessed the apogee of female power when Empress Wu became the only woman to rule China in her own name, from 690 to 705. Even after her deposition powerful women dominated China for a decade, until the forced suicide of the Taiping Princess in 713. All of these women were major patrons of the Buddhist order.

In addition to this formal recognition of older roles, new public roles as nuns and priestesses emerged within the institutional religions. A religious niche for women had existed, and would continue to exist in the role of shamans, but the new offices in the institutional faiths enjoyed a far greater prestige and legitimacy, as evidenced by the ordination of imperial princesses and even retired empresses. Such female religious specialists could even, especially in Daoism, be treated as saints whose spiritual attainments helped to save the world, and some of them became the founders of later religious lineages.[48] In addition to their religious activities, both Daoist and Buddhist nuns were among the first women to become celebrated authors and leave appreciable bodies of verse behind at their deaths.[49]

Buddhist nuns also became patrons of religious art, as did other women acting either as individuals or as members of religious associations. This is particularly notable in the countryside, where women's names often figure in lists of members of the sponsoring lay society engraved on the backs of Buddhist steles. Indeed at least two steles were sponsored by organizations consisting entirely of village women. One was donated by an association of thirty women, and the second by a group of seventy-five.[50]

This prominence of women in religious societies in the north may also reflect the fact that women there often controlled their family's finances.

Buddhist nuns were also notable for establishing the precedent that women could reject marriage. Biographies of nuns relate how their commitment to the Buddha led them to resist all family pressure. The power of their devotion and prayers induced divinities to support their resistance, and this support sometimes took surprising forms, as in the following story:

> Sengduan had vowed that she would leave the household life rather than be married off. Nevertheless, her beauty of face and figure were well known in the region, and a wealthy family had already received her mother and elder brother's agreement to a betrothal. Three days before the marriage ceremony Sengduan fled in the middle of the night to a Buddhist convent whose abbess hid her in a separate building and supplied her with everything she needed. Sengduan also had a copy of the *Bodhisattva Guanshiyin Scripture* that she was able to chant from memory after only two days of study. She rained tears and made prostrations day and night without ceasing. Three days later, during her worship, she saw an image of the Buddha, who announced to her, "Your bridegroom's lifespan is coming to an end. You need only continue your ardent practice without harboring sorrowful thoughts." The next day her bridegroom was gored to death by an ox.[51]

While the text does not credit the Buddha for the groom's violent death but only for foretelling it, violence to suitors and even parents became a recurring theme in tales of marriage resistance.

The presence in texts of Guanyin, who later became the patron of resistance to marriage in tales of such celebrated would-be celibate women as Princess Miaoshan and Chen Jinggu, suggests another possible female role, that of goddess.[52] While no important new female divinities developed under the Northern and Southern Dynasties, older figures were significantly elaborated.

The Mysterious Woman was a goddess in the Han dynasty who oversaw warfare, sexuality, and long life, and who revealed texts and talismans pertaining to these arts to the Yellow Emperor. In the fourth century she appeared in several Daoist texts as a body god (a divinity who inhabits the human body) conceived as a microcosm of the universe and whom the adept could visualize, meditate on, and petition for aid. She prepared alchemical elixirs, including sexual potions, with which she had been identified since the Han. While her role as a revealer of texts is less prominent, several of the major Daoist textual traditions claimed to receive their initial textual revelations from divine women. Notably, these women were not strictly goddesses but mortal women who had attained immortality and a rank among the Perfected.[53]

Han dynasty tomb art had included two powerful cosmic goddesses, the Queen Mother of the West and Nugua. Nugua was paired with her consort Fuxi as an intertwined couple who generated the cosmos and embodied the correlate powers of yin and yang. The Queen Mother of the West was a goddess who likewise generated the cosmos, ruled over a court of immortal beings in the distant west, and may have symbolically represented the matriarch of the household.[54] During the Northern and Southern Dynasties, the Queen Mother of the West was elevated to the position of highest goddess in the Shangqing tradition of Daoism. In this context she revealed essential scriptures, became the object of visualization and meditation exercises, and served as a body god. Her western paradise—already central in her Han role—became much more elaborate and detailed. Her periodic meetings with her consort to maintain the cosmos were also described in detail.

As a consort or sexual partner, the Queen Mother of the West became linked with a series of Chinese sage rulers just as she had been linked to King Mu in the earlier *Biography of Mu, Son of Heaven* (*Mu tianzi zhuan*). These rulers included the Yellow Emperor, Shun, and Yu. But her most important role was as the central figure in a set of stories dealing with her visit to Emperor Wu of the Han, to whom she offered the techniques of immortality. In these stories the Queen Mother assumed the role as the combined sexual partner and giver of immortality that dominated her image in Tang poetry.[55]

This idea of the goddess as an erotic figure had appeared as early as the Warring States *Songs of the South,* where she was the archetypal figure of the desirable female. Poems about actually encountering a goddess became the earliest form for writing explicitly about eroticism and desire. Examples include the "Rhapsody on the Gaotang Shrine" and "Rhapsody on the Goddess" attributed to Song Yu, a semi-mythic poet supposedly of the late Warring States period, though in reality these poems probably date to the Eastern Han or later.[56] In both of them the poet leads the king to desire union with the goddess by narrating tales of earlier such encounters in history or in a dream.

The earliest datable poem on this theme is the celebrated "Rhapsody on the Goddess of the Luo River" by the Wei prince Cao Zhi in the early third century. In this poem the prince on the riverbank encounters the beautiful goddess, who signals him to join her in the depths. His caution overcomes his passion, and he is left mournful and abandoned. This conflation of the goddess and eroticism became a standard theme of Chinese literature and also figured in the transformation of the Queen Mother of the West from a religious figure to an erotic figure in Tang poetry, where she served as the patron divinity of prostitutes, musicians, and related performers.

8

DAOISM AND BUDDHISM

THE Eastern Han dynasty and the Northern and Southern Dynasties witnessed a revolution in Chinese religion, with the appearance of large-scale, organized religious movements. These faiths provided both new visions of the place of humankind in the cosmos and new institutions that transcended ties of kinship, locality, and political hierarchy. They met social, emotional, and intellectual needs not satisfied by the old cults of the ancestors, gods of soil and grain, and sacrifices to Heaven. Moreover, these earlier religious practices tied to family and state were transformed by the elaborate theologies of the two great institutional religions that developed during the Northern and Southern Dynasties: Daoism and Buddhism. The rise of temples as semi-public urban spaces, the development of gardens as images of paradise, the emergence of a pan-Asian world linked by a shared Buddhist faith, and the impact of Daoism and Buddhism on the family were just a few of the ways these new forms of thought and conduct changed forever the intellectual, social, and political structures that had characterized China prior to their appearance.

Buddhism was an alien faith brought into China during the Eastern Han by merchants from Central and Southeast Asia. This new religion found favor among elements of the elite and gradually spread throughout society until it permeated every aspect of Chinese life. The history of Daoism in China went back much further, to cults and beliefs that had existed since at least the Warring States period. It formed organized movements at approximately the same time that Buddhism entered China, but it did not develop temples, a hierarchy of clerics, and a canon until later, after Buddhism provided the model.[1]

Institutional Daoism

The idea that humans could become immortal emerged in the late War-ring States period and figured prominently in motivating the *feng* and *shan* sacrifices of the First Emperor of Qin and Emperor Wu of the Han. Immortality was also a major theme of Han tomb art, including depic-tions of the court of the Queen Mother of the West and of winged im-mortals soaring through the skies, riding on beasts, or playing the *liu bo* board game on the peaks of mountains. The idea that people could trans-form their bodies to attain longevity also appeared in some philosophical and macrobiotic hygiene texts, and was criticized in the first-century A.D. works of Wang Chong.[2]

A second early idea that became fundamental to Daoism was that of the revealed text. In some accounts, a god such as the Mysterious Woman or the divinized philosopher Laozi presented a text to a sage-king or some other mortal who used it to bring order to the world. In an-other version, certain texts came not from anthropomorphic deities but emerged directly from the incipient patterns of the natural world. This idea appears most clearly in accounts of the origins of the *Canon of Change*, and also those of the "apocryphal" texts that emerged in the late Western Han and flourished in subsequent centuries. One such revealed text that emerged in the Eastern Han, the *Canon of Great Peace (Taiping jing)*, became the foundational sacred text of the first organized Daoist movement.[3]

A third root of religious Daoism was belief in an afterlife dominated by a celestial bureaucracy resembling that of the earthly empire. Evi-dence of this belief appears in a few Warring States texts and in Eastern Han "tomb ordinance" texts, which refer to a celestial monarch who commands such officials as the assistant of the sepulcher, assistant of the mound, sire of the tomb, the squad chiefs of Haoli (realm of the dead), and so on. This bureaucracy protected the denizen of the tomb from evil forces of the underworld, but also guaranteed that the deceased could not return to trouble the living. This approach to funerary rit-ual was thus essentially exorcistic, involving first the expulsion of evil influences from the tomb, followed by the expulsion of the recently de-ceased from the realm of the living. The emergent Daoist religion adopted this bureaucratic model but added an element of salvation, allowing a purified spirit to be transferred to paradise, in some cases to take up a bureaucratic post.[4]

The first organized, mass, popular religious movement in China of which we have any record occurred in 3 B.C. During a great drought in the north China plain, many people assembled on the roadsides and proceeded through the countryside carrying branches or stalks of hemp and straw. They proclaimed that these objects were the talismans of the Queen Mother of the West and that those who wore them would not die. Throughout that summer they gathered in the towns and cities, where they held mass worship services. In the capital, these included singing, dancing, and the staging of torch-lit processions through the streets and across the rooftops, all in the expectation of the imminent arrival of the Queen Mother. In the fall the drought broke, and the movement disappeared from official histories.

The few brief accounts in the histories are our only literary evidence for the popular cult of the Queen Mother, but from other sources we know that in the time of Emperor Wu she was believed to reside at the western edge of the world and to be able to grant immortality. During the Western Han she became associated with the myth of Kunlun, the great mountain that linked Heaven and Earth, which was likewise in the distant west; at its summit dwelt immortal beings. Because of their shared geographic location and the common association with immortality, these two myths merged, and in the tomb iconography of the Eastern Han, where she frequently appears, the Queen Mother is the presiding deity of a paradise in the far west where peaches of immortality grow and no one dies. Fragments of an early Eastern Han divinatory text show that the Queen Mother had also become a powerful protective deity who was able to bless people with wealth and children, and that through certain esoteric techniques people could transcend space and time to travel to the Queen Mother's paradise. From the accounts of the popular movement in 3 B.C., we also know that she was invoked with songs, dances, and the manipulation of magical plant talismans.[5]

The cult of the Queen Mother antedates Daoism, but it reveals a major reason for the rise of institutional creeds. In Han cosmology, Heaven was a moralized divinity tied to the emperor. As the Son of Heaven, he alone could worship it, and when he acted improperly, Heaven sent down droughts and plagues. The people suffered and died, but they could not avert disaster through good conduct nor appease Heaven through sacrifice. The Queen Mother was an alternative high divinity who was open to appeal from the populace and who would save those who called on her. She thus anticipated the religious function of popular Daoist divinities, as well as the Buddha and bodhisattvas. Moreover, several features of her cult—the hope of immortality, the transcendence of time and space in magic journeys, the use of magical talismans, the incorporation of song, dance, and spirit travel in trance that had characterized the religious practice of the shamans of ancient China—became important in later Daoism. Consequently, the cult of the Queen Mother can be regarded as a proto-Daoist movement and an immediate ancestor of institutional religion in China. She was incorporated into the Daoist hierarchies of divinities, where she played a major role both for clerics and the interested laity.

The millenarian rebellions of the Yellow Turbans in Shandong and the Five Pecks of Grain in Sichuan incorporated two new features of later Daoism: divinely revealed texts and a vision of the end of time that prophesied the sweeping away of the old order and its replacement by a realm of Great Peace inhabited by the faithful. The earliest record of a revealed text proclaiming the Great Peace was 7 B.C., when a book of that name was presented to the Han court. Another book with the same title was revealed in the middle of the second century A.D., and this became the central scripture of the Yellow Turbans. This movement and the closely related Five Pecks of Grain, founded on the basis of a nontextual revelation supposedly made in 142, organized their followers into military units for collective worship and action. Their primary religious practices included healing diseases and prolonging life through confessing sins and performing penance (in the belief that illness was caused by misconduct and the violation of taboos).

These two movements taught that, in addition to individual sins, people also suffered from an inherited collective evil accumulated over the centuries that could be expurgated only through communal mobilization, missionary work, and even secession or the creation of a new state. They also used meditation, breathing exercises, and other hygienic and dietary practices to extend life. Both movements apparently worshipped Laozi, the putative author of the *Canon of the Way and Its Power,* who by this time was understood as a cosmic being periodically reincarnated to rescue suffering humanity. The Five Pecks of Grain recited his text as a revealed scripture whose words had magical powers.[6]

Although the Yellow Turban rebellion was suppressed in 184, the Five Pecks of Grain movement established a Daoist kingdom in Sichuan ruled by the so-called Heavenly Masters of the Zhang family. This state was organized into parishes that kept population registers and were administered by men with titles such as "libationer" that were adopted from Han local society. The registers listed and ranked people according to the number of spirit troops and generals who were placed at their disposal in the rites of initiation into the church and subsequent periodic ceremonies. The state also had a ritual calendar structured around general assemblies on the fifteenth day of the first, seventh, and tenth months. At these gatherings, officials taught the precepts and prohibitions of the movement. There was also a general fast of penance in which believers pursued universal salvation through daubing their bodies with mud and charcoal, tying their hands, and reciting long lists of sins. Personal penance included work on repairing roads, an activity made sacred by its identification with the Way, and the erection of hostels that were both local administrative centers and lodging places for traveling officials. The state erected special "quiet rooms" in which people could meditate upon their transgressions.[7]

The Five Pecks of Grain movement under Zhang Lu submitted to Cao Cao in 215, and large numbers of its followers were resettled around Luoyang, Ye, and other parts of the northeast. This resettlement spread Daoism into the central plain. Daoist leaders seem to have exerted some influence on the Cao family and to have played a role in the establishment of the Wei dynasty.[8] At the end of the third century, when the Jin dynasty began to collapse, resettled followers of the movement led by a Li family returned to Sichuan and founded a Daoist theocratic state named Great Perfection (Da Cheng). The repeated establishment of Daoist kingdoms in Sichuan made this region, ringed by mountains, a world apart from the greater Chinese realm. The kingdom of Great Perfection lasted until the middle of the fourth century when it was destroyed by Huan Wen.[9] The church was again scattered, but later Daoism descended from this theocracy in Sichuan, and all later Daoist schools traced their roots back to the Way of the Heavenly Masters founded by the Zhangs.

While popular movements preached millenarian visions of collective redemption, the pursuit of individual immortality that had obsessed Qin's First Emperor and Emperor Wu of the Han continued among the Eastern Han elite, notably in southern China. This tradition culminated in the mid-fourth century in the *Master Who Embraces Simplicity* (*Bao Puzi*) by Ge Hong (284–363).[10] He compiled a library of works received from his teacher, which indicates the existence of a substantial tradition among the literate population, but unfortunately virtually all were lost. Thus, his lengthy but unsystematic work on techniques of immortality remains the sole surviving evidence on the practice as it existed before the rise of religious Daoism.

The ultimate ideal was to become an immortal, a transformation comparable to such natural changes as the shedding of a snake's skin or the emergence of a butterfly. Part of Ge Hong's work is a polemical attempt to persuade readers that immortal beings exist, an argument with many echoes in the writings of his acquaintance Gan Bao. He argued that due to the declining moral character of the age, immortals no longer dwelt among men. The highest immortals were celestial transcendents who rose into the Heavens, where they assumed posts in the celestial hierarchy. Next were earthly transcendents who wandered through the mountains. The lowest were those who simulated death by providing a substitute body that acted as a corpse to deceive the spirit bureaucracy. Sometimes the latter two categories were transitional stages to provide enough time for the faithful to finally be able to ascend to the Heavens. Ge Hong insisted that adepts must withdraw from society to the mountains in order to cultivate the arts, thus imitating the conduct of hermits in this period.[11]

Among the techniques for achieving immortality, the lesser arts focused on the retention and circulation of the body's spirit energy (*qi*) through breathing, gymnastic, and sexual exercises that had emerged in the earlier tradition of "nourishing the life."[12] These aimed at the retention of the body's own positive energies, the expulsion of negative ones, the absorption of energy from the outside, and the removal of all internal blockages to their flow. The flesh was purified through dietary restrictions: not consuming meat, wine, strong-smelling vegetables, or cereals. Such foods nourished the Three Worms, cadaveric demons who were trapped in the human body and released through its death. Instead, the devotee should live on a natural diet of tree bark, fungi, dew, herbs, and assorted chemical concoctions that would either kill the Three Worms or replace the fleshly body with a more permanent one. Once they became immortals, they would dine on the wind and cosmic ether.

The most exalted method of attaining immortality, and Ge Hong's principle interest, was alchemy. Many substances could purge the body of noxious influences and cause it to revert to the purity of the primal state of nondivision. These substances were subjected to assorted procedures and rituals that transmuted conventional elements into their precious essences, which were then ingested. The most important substances were gold, which never rusted and hence was itself immortal, and cinnabar, a natural mineral believed to be potent because of its fiery red color. Natural cinnabar was usually replaced by a synthetic variety concocted from sulfur, saltpeter, and mercury (which are also ingredients of gunpowder, the invention of which resulted from Daoist experiments). The use of mercury in Daoist alchemy led to many deaths through poisoning, whether deliberate (as a step to immortality or in a court intrigue) or accidental. The chemicals were accompanied by many medicinal herbs and fungi.[13]

Because such "external alchemy" was too expensive for many practitioners, including Ge Hong himself, it was gradually replaced by "internal alchemy." This was a meditative practice, closely related to breathing exercises, in which the devotee created an inner furnace and crucible through intense visualization of certain trigrams from the *Canon of Change*. This internal furnace and crucible produced their own purifying compounds, which circulated through the body.

Ge Hong's book was completed just as northern émigrés fled south at the fall of the Jin, taking Daoism along to their new home. With the establishment of the Eastern Jin court, several old southern families found themselves reduced to a secondary position in politics. Seeking an outlet for their ambitions, they formed what would become the most important branch of southern Daoism, the Maoshan school, also known as Highest Clarity (*Shangqing*) Daoism.[14] This cult developed around documents revealed to Yang Xi in the years 364–370, which attracted the attention of elites through the exalted literary style of their ecstatic verse and by their brilliant calligraphy. These texts offered an aesthetically pleasing mechanism by which old southern families could accept Daoism without assuming an inferior place to the Heavenly Masters in the spiritual hierarchy.

These texts revealed what became the standard cosmology of later Daoism: a hierarchy of Heavens, with more exalted and powerful immortal intercessors than had hitherto been imagined. The Perfected Men and Women who had spoken to Yang Xi were far superior in rank and more refined in substance than the mere immortals who had been the ideal of men like Ge Hong, and the Heaven of Supreme Purity from which the revelations came was far higher than the Heaven of Great Purity promised by the Sichuan Heavenly Masters or Ge Hong. The writings revealed to Yang Xi included verses such as:

The luminous glows within,
Then spurts forth as a bridge across dark waters.

Present me with writings and jade slips,
Inscribe my name in the cloudy chambers.
I now feed on the lunar efflorescences,
Joining thereby with the perfected.
I will fly as a transcendent to Purple Tenuity,
There to pay court to the Grand Luminaries.[15]

Key practices of the Heavenly Masters, especially sexual ones, were de-nounced or relegated to an inferior status as preliminary exercises. The healing function of earlier confessional rites still figured in Yang Xi's works, but these claimed to heal by identifying the underworld entangle-ments of deceased kin, sometimes due to their crimes in life. This had re-sulted in spirit complaints against them, which were resolved by invoking assorted deities to pacify the dead or secure for the living an ascent to a kin-free paradise.[16] Thus the texts revealed to Yang Xi, which the old southern elite preserved, reworked, and expanded (as later figures re-ceived new revelations), claimed to be more refined and complete than earlier Daoist writings.

The Maoshan revelations also inverted the apocalyptic expectations of the popular movements. According to Yang Xi's texts, the present world was under the authority of the Six Heavens, that is, the nonimmortal dead ruled by spirits of fallen generals who required blood sacrifices from the people of the Yangzi region.[17] Followers of the Maoshan tradition re-jected these cults, forming a spiritual elite by swearing oaths of loyalty to masters who had received sacred texts and purifying themselves through meditation. As "seed people," they would survive the cataclysmic fall of the Six Heavens, when the vulgar practitioners of blood sacrifices per-ished, and then would repopulate the redeemed world. This earthly para-dise was reserved for the noble and refined few, those of sensitivity and literary cultivation who could grasp spiritual subtleties and who appreci-ated good calligraphy and poetry. The Maoshan school found great favor with the imperial house of the Southern Qi dynasty in the late fifth cen-tury, and the movement's ninth patriarch, Tao Hongjing, developed close ties to the founder of the subsequent Liang dynasty.

While this elite Daoism won favor with southern literati and dynasts, another purified version found fertile ground in the north. Kou Qianzhi, whose family had followed the Way of the Sichuan Heavenly Masters, re-ceived a series of revelations in the first decades of the fifth century in which the deified Laozi told him that the true Way had become corrupt.

All blood sacrifices and sexual exercises were to be halted, so Daoists should use only meditative, dietary, respiratory, and gymnastic techniques to secure immortality. Another revelation told him that the emperor of the Northern Wei was the Perfect Lord of the Great Peace.

Armed with this news, Kou Qianzhi went to the Northern Wei court and, in alliance with a Chinese clique hoping to reassert the superiority of native culture over the alien faith of Buddhism, persuaded the emperor in 442 to convert to Daoism, adopt the title of Perfect Lord of the Great Peace, and rule as a Daoist sage.[18] The emperor received magical talismans from Kou Qianzhi, who became a leading minister at court. The ruler also promulgated a new code composed by Kou Qianzhi to purify Daoism. Between 444 and 446, the emperor denounced Buddhism, although this seems to have been at the behest of Cui Hao's Chinese faction rather than Kou Qianzhi. The death of Kou Qianzhi in 448 and the assassination of the emperor in 452 ended both the Daoist theocracy and the suppression of Buddhism.

Thus what had begun in the second century as the millenarian expectations of rebels had, by the early sixth century, become a philosophical religion catering to the world vision of the elite and the needs of the state. In the north it consisted of a state-sponsored cult with temples and ordained priests, while in the south it circulated among the elite in the form of sacred texts transmitted from teachers to sworn disciples, among them members of the imperial clan and even some emperors. When the Tang dynasty was established in the early seventh century, the imperial clan, claiming to be descendants of Laozi, established Daoism as the highest state religion, with official temples and ordained priests in every major city.

Institutional Buddhism

While organized Daoism began as a popular movement and ended as a state-sponsored religious organization, Buddhism followed the opposite trajectory. It entered China among the elite but became a mass religion. Central Asian merchants, along with sea-traveling traders arriving in Jiangsu, first brought the new religion to China. We do not know the exact date of its introduction, but the first written reference to Buddhism, in A.D. 65, shows an established community of monks and laity under the patronage of a brother of the emperor. This text links the brother's worship of the Buddha with his worship of Huanglao, a Daoist divinity closely related to Laozi, and examples of the Buddha in Han tomb art generally appear together with, or in the place normally assigned to, the Queen Mother of the West. In 166 the emperor himself sacrificed to the Buddha, this time in association with Laozi. This pattern suggests that the Buddha was at first regarded as another Daoist divinity who, like the Queen Mother, dwelt in the west and protected those who worshipped him.[19] For most of the Chinese people, the Buddha would remain a figure of devotion, whose image was worshipped to secure protection or good fortune, and not a teacher of philosophical truths.

Several foreign monks settled in the Eastern Han capital and began the difficult task of translating Buddhist scriptures into Chinese, but only in the Northern and Southern Dynasties were the metaphysical and doctrinal beliefs of Buddhism recognized and appreciated by Chinese elites. A vogue for metaphysical speculation in the early third century was associated with renewed interest in the Warring States classics of philosophical Daoism: the *Canon of the Way and Its Power* and the *Master Zhuang (Zhuangzi)*. Many devotees of "pure conversation" also engaged in "Dark Studies," a discourse devoted to such topics as the relation of words to reality, the one to the many, and existence to nothingness. The elaborate psychological and metaphysical vocabulary of Buddhism fed directly into discussing such questions, so Buddhist monks began to participate in the debates and conversations of the Chinese elite. Sons of eminent families sought instruction in Buddhism or became monks in order to refine their debating skills, particularly after the flight south in 317. Eminent monks like Zhi Dun became leading lights in pure conversation circles at the Eastern Jin court, composed lyric poetry, practiced calligraphy, combined Buddhist studies with commentaries on the *Master Zhuang*, and sought to reconcile Buddhist doctrines with Chinese intellectual traditions.[20]

Meanwhile, several barbarian states in the north adopted Buddhism, sometimes because it was a non-Chinese intellectual faith, sometimes because Buddhist monks could work small miracles, like Fotudeng, who served under Shi Le of the Later Zhao dynasty. Remaining in contact with Buddhist Central Asia, these states brought in new ideas and sponsored translations of most of the Buddhist canon into ever more fluent Chinese. The most celebrated translator was Kumarajiva, who was brought from the Dunhuang region to Chang'an by the successors of Fu Jian in 401. Other monks, notably Huiyuan, introduced new practices such as the worship of Amitabha, who promised rebirth in his Western

"Pure Land" paradise to anyone who visualized his image or called on his name. Such a devotional practice was much easier for lay people than the arduous exercises of mental purgation and controlled breathing prescribed for monks. The chanting of Amitabha's name thus became one of the most popular devotional practices in China.[21]

In the fifth century the restoration of imperial power by military dynasts in both the north and south led Chinese Buddhism into an era of major state patronage. In the south the Eastern Jin court, after several debates, ruled that Buddhist monks need not bow to the emperor. This reflected to an extent the weakness of the emperor and the avid patronage of Buddhism by several leading families, but the precedent was respected even by the southern military dynasts, who generally refrained from regulating the Buddhist order.[22] This hands-off policy, however, did not stop southern emperors from using the spiritual power of the Buddhist order to strengthen their own position. Emperors took bodhisattva vows, built temples and procured images, ordained monks, organized vegetarian feasts for monks and officials, and sponsored public readings and expositions of sutras.

The aim of Mahayana Buddhism (the sole variety of Buddhism to reach China) is the redemption of all living beings from the cycle of rebirth. A bodhisattva is a being who, after attaining enlightenment, does not enter Nirvana but instead vows to remain in the world until he or she has redeemed all living things. In formally taking the vows of the bodhisattva, the rulers of the southern dynasties not only expressed their devotion to Buddhism but also asserted their own status as redeemers and saviors. This gave the already sacred position of emperor an additional splendor as a *cakravartin*, "wheel-turning" king or cosmic overlord. Thus emperors invoked the rhetoric of Buddhism to articulate the newly revived imperial power, even as they accrued spiritual merit for their dynasty and people.

The most celebrated (or notorious, depending upon one's taste) imperial patron of Buddhism in Chinese history was Emperor Wu of the Liang dynasty.[23] By declaring his status as bodhisattva as well as emperor, he claimed power over both monks and laymen, and sought to extend the sacred and secular authority of the dynasty. He assembled thousands of people to witness his vows, and he periodically restaged great assemblies to perform sutra lectures, public confessions, renewals of vows, and related rituals. At these events, the emperor promised to devote all the merit that he earned not only to the well-being of his people but also to the redemption of beings suffering in hell and those who had fallen into other bad rebirths. Several later southern emperors performed similar vows, as did Empress Wu during the Tang dynasty, for whom the roles of *cakravartin* ruler and bodhisattva were essential in becoming the only female ruler in Chinese history.[24]

In the north, state sponsorship of Buddhism was associated with more vigorous regulation of monks. The first step to state absorption of the Buddhist monastic order took place in the late fourth century, when the Northern Wei ruler appointed a chief monk. Whereas southern monks had gained the privilege of not bowing to the emperor, this chief monk took the opposite position, by propounding the doctrine that the Wei ruler was in fact an incarnation of the Buddha, so that all monks should bow to him. This identification of the Wei rulers as Buddhas may have been facilitated by the belief of many steppe-dwelling nomads that the ruler was a manifestation of the deity. At any rate, it become part of the self-image of the Northern Wei dynasty, which like the southern dynasts added the spiritual power of the Buddhist order, along with claims of Buddhahood, to the already formidable powers of a Chinese Son of Heaven.

After a brief interval when the third Wei emperor adopted Daoism and sought to suppress the Buddhist order, the Northern Wei court resumed its close identification of the ruling house with the Buddha. One Wei emperor had five images of Sakyamuni Buddha cast in bronze, one for each of his predecessors. The first five caves built at Yungang, just outside the Wei capital, may also have commemorated the Wei rulers as Buddhas (see Fig. 11). The Wei emperors established a government department to supervise Buddhism, with a chief monk who appointed officers for the major monasteries of the realm. Between 470 and 476 the Wei established samgha households, in which captives taken in the northeast were attached to Buddhist monasteries and required to pay them a set amount of grain, and Buddha households, wherein convicts and slaves were given to the monasteries to work their fields. The wealth accumulated by the monasteries was to be used to relieve suffering in times of famines or floods, but the monasteries were enriched from these programs as well. With enthusiasm for the faith spreading among the common people, donations of land and money made many Buddhist monasteries extremely wealthy.[25]

The Wei tried to limit the number of monks ordained, but the limits were constantly raised, and even these were vastly exceeded. Restrictions on building monasteries were also issued, but then ignored by the imperial clan itself, along with their subjects. Patronage under the Wei reached its apogee in the first decades of the sixth century, when dowager empresses passionately committed to Buddhism erected spectacular temples in the capital and regularly gave lavish donations. Eunuchs and courtiers followed suit, and by the time civil war broke out there were more than 1,300 monasteries in Luoyang, more than one monastery for every hundred households (while the law stipulated that the city should have only one monastery). Nor was this efflorescence limited to the capital. According to government records, at the end of the dynasty there were thirty thousand monasteries in the empire, and more than two million monks. Even allowing for vagueness and exaggeration, the numbers are significant.

Many of these two million monks were just avoiding taxes, and many "monasteries" were small buildings with a couple of monks. Nevertheless, piety in the sixth century in north China was both widespread and deep. Evidence for this comes from Yang Xuanzhi's *Record of the Buddhist Temples of Luoyang*, which describes a capital city filled with more than a thousand temples founded by lay patrons for the public worship of images. Miracles associated with these wonder-working images, including miracles tied to political events of the day, attracted huge crowds.

Buddhist deities and other spirits also populated local lore and urban legends, as this example makes clear:

> Hou Qing, a native of Nanyang, had a bronze image of Buddha that was more than one Chinese foot high. He owned an ox that he wanted to sell to get money to cover the statue in gold leaf. However, because of an emergency he used the money for other purposes. Two years later his wife, a woman of the Ma family, suddenly had a dream in which the statue said, "You and your husband have owed me a gilding for a long time, but I have not demanded the recompense. Now I am taking your son Chouduo as compensation for the unperformed gilding." The woman awoke feeling uneasy and at dawn Chouduo fell ill and died. Qing was then fifty years old, and this was his only son. The sound of their mourning moved even passersby. On the day of Chouduo's death the image turned into gold and its light shown on the neighboring houses in all four directions. Those who lived in the same ward all smelled something fragrant.[26]

Further evidence of a belief in the power of images comes from inscriptions for statues and paintings in the two great Wei Buddhist cave complexes at Yungang and Longmen (Fig. 21). In addition to inscriptions by the imperial clan, officials, and monks, there are numerous examples from religious societies, groups of laymen who pooled money to commission images as a means of attaining merit. These inscriptions reveal what Buddhism meant to the urban people of the capital, for whom the philosophical speculations on the nature of perception or reality were of little interest: a pious belief in a merciful god who would redeem living creatures, rescue them from suffering, and transport them to a blessed realm of salvation. Most inscriptions offered formulaic prayers for the dynasty,

Fig. 21   The great *kang* at the Longmen caves. Near Luoyang, early sixth century.

but their primary concern was for the redemption of parents and their rebirth in paradise. Other inscriptions express the desire to acquire merit for rebirth in Amitabha Buddha's paradise, to thank the Buddha for fulfillment of a wish (such as the birth of a son or recovery from illness), or to pray for some material benefit. In short, to the common people, the Buddha continued to play the same role he had played in Han tomb art, a loving god who rescued the suffering, like the Queen Mother of the West.[27]

The Yungang and Longmen cave inscriptions reflect primarily the interests of the court and secondarily those of an urban elite. The interests of pious commoners are expressed in numerous inscriptions on movable steles or statues purchased with money collected by pious lay associations in the countryside. These inscriptions indicate a primary interest in invoking the powers of the Buddha and bodhisattvas to secure personal well-being, the health of relatives, and the superior rebirth of deceased kin.[28] They also list the names of donors, including women, and the key leadership role of monks and nuns who moved through the countryside to spread the faith. Many inscriptions indicate that the stele was either built by traveling artisans hired by the monks or, more frequently, purchased ready-made from urban workshops. In the latter case, the artisans left blank spaces where the names of donors and their wishes could be inscribed. Some steles also featured cartouches identifying the scenes being portrayed, thus serving as a mode of education. Finally, some texts, and occasionally inscriptions on the steles themselves, identify the sorts of rituals that could be performed with such objects.

Textual evidence also shows that combinations of Buddhism with conventional family piety were quite popular. The earliest and best-documented example is the Heaven-Man Teaching in sixth-century China.[29] This Buddhist folk religion taught that those who followed the five moral precepts—not to kill, steal, commit adultery, drink, or lie—and chanted a simple formula of praise to the Buddha while circling a Buddhist statue would secure a better rebirth on earth and enjoy health and prosperity. This utilitarian creed employed a radically simplified form of Buddhism to secure worldly happiness. It eschewed any mention of Nirvana, bodhisattvas, the transfer of merit, the redemption of all living creatures, and any of the other principles of Mahayana Buddhism. It passed over in silence the practices of meditation or the enunciation of philosophical principles that would have been central to monastic practice. The Heaven-Man Teaching instead offered basic moral prohibitions supplemented only by devotion to the name and image of the Buddha. This stripped-down form of lay Buddhism appealed to the widest possible audience, and its practitioners formed pious groups apparently associated with the samgha households established by the Northern Wei dynasty to aid in propagating the faith and practicing public charity.

Evidence indicating the spread of Buddhism through the countryside of north China from the fifth century on largely takes the form of stories of wandering monks, often persecuted by authorities, who mingled with the peasants to propagate the faith.[30] Many monks apparently acted as village exorcists, magicians, or mediums, just as some of their more exalted predecessors had performed magic for rulers such as Shi Le. They also took the lead in buying steles and in charitable works described in their inscriptions, such as building bridges. Other itinerant monks went into trances in which they burned parts of their body or drove nails through their flesh without feeling pain, often in association with public festivals, as still happens in China today.

One story tells of a monk who tried to redeem some pigs from slaughter by buying them and, when the peasants refused to sell, began to slice off pieces of his own flesh to exchange for the pigs. While such figures were the targets of frequent hostile decrees banning these practices, they also seem to have shared in the positive image of the untrammeled, wandering life of the Daoist sage that justified the eremitic ideals of the period. The free mingling of monks and laymen became a prominent feature of certain strains of Mahayana thought, particularly in association with apocalyptic scenarios.

Hostile government memorials testify to the spread of small shrines, votive towers, and hermitages throughout the countryside. Officials complained that small, illicit establishments were found in mountain forests, in the countryside, and in every village. The seventh-century official Di Renjie (Judge Dee), who became a celebrated detective in Chinese and Western fiction, noted the presence at the gates of villages of shops for copying sutras and making images. Many villages staged vegetarian feasts. One Northern Wei official argued that all the villagers in the Guanzhong region engaged in such activities, and that these banquets provided occasions for open criticism of the government. Banquets were also organized by local associations such as those that propagated the Heaven-Man Teachings, as described in donor lists on inscriptions. Accounts of the activities of such associations of pious lay people and of the rules for membership appear among the documents at Dunhuang. The associations at

Dunhuang brought lay people and Buddhist monks into regular contact for a whole range of religious activities.[31]

Overlap and Borrowing between Daoism and Buddhism

Despite their different origins, in practice there was considerable blurring between Daoism and Buddhism in China. Both religions ordained religious specialists, established residential institutions, compiled canonical scriptures, and elaborated theological systems. These all entailed borrowing, though in most cases Buddhism provided the model for the full-blown Daoist institutions and practices. The two faiths developed a considerable common vocabulary, including terms for lay associations, and images of Buddhist and Daoist deities combined in sculpture and painting. Certain inscriptions refer to Buddhism as "the teaching of the Way," which could also refer to Daoism.[32]

More significant is the fact that both faiths participated in several major intellectual developments of the period, notably millenarianism and belief in reincarnation. One of the key ideas to emerge in the period was the millenarian doctrine of the imminent destruction of the world, or its old order, followed by the emergence of a new and purified world controlled by the faithful. This idea appeared in the apocalyptic teachings of the late Han Daoist rebels and in the transmuted apocalypse envisioned by Daoists among the great families of the south. In the same period the idea of an imminent, world-destroying cataclysm also became prominent in Buddhism. The notion that all worlds eventually perished was a standard Buddhist theme, but in third-century China it became associated with the vision of great disasters such as fires and floods marking the end of the world.[33] In the fourth and fifth centuries this link became widespread in Buddhist traditions.

The *Lotus Sutra,* one of the most influential Buddhist scriptures, translated five times between 255 and 406, describes an apocalyptic scenario of imminent world destruction in which only those who escape to the Buddha's paradise survive:

> Ever am I on the Vulture Peak
> And in my other dwellings.
> When the beings see the kalpa ending
> And being consumed in a great fire,
> This land of mine is perfectly safe,

Ever full of gods and men.
In it are gardens and groves, halls and towers,
Variously adorned with gems,
As well as jeweled trees with many blossoms and fruits.[34]

This scene, combining belief in a looming apocalypse with detailed visions of a garden paradise, appears in several wall paintings drawn from the *Lotus Sutra* in the fifth and sixth centuries.[35]

Even more widespread were millenarian visions linked to the future Buddha Maitreya and above all to the bodhisattva Prince Moonlight. While Maitreya generally figured as the presiding Buddha of a paradise in which the pious hoped for rebirth, or as the one who in a distant future would create a blissful paradise for the faithful on earth, in a few texts from the sixth and seventh centuries he became a messianic savior who would lead his followers into a renewed world following an apocalyptic battle. The absence of any such scenario in canonical texts has led to speculation that it was adapted from Daoist models.[36] As for Prince Moonlight, he appeared in several texts composed in China that prophesied a world-destroying deluge ending in his creation of a purified realm of the faithful. Significantly, this figure in India was simply a pious son who converted his father to Buddhism. The apocalyptic scenario is entirely a Chinese invention and includes events in specified years that are identical with those found in Daoist prophecies of an impending end of the world. Consequently, it is almost certain that major elements of this Buddhist apocalyptic lore derived from Daoist antecedents.[37] Both Maitreyan apocalyptic prophecies and those associated with Prince Moonlight were regularly invoked in political uprisings involving Buddhist monks and laymen, in the same way that apocalyptic scenarios in early Daoism had been used to support political programs.

Another line of Buddhist millenarian prophecy focused on the disappearance of the Buddha's teachings from the world. This doctrine had developed in India, but in China, under the impact of Daoist millenarianism, it became both more elaborate, as a three-stage decline, and more immediate, as people proclaimed that the Buddha's teachings had vanished or were about to do so and to draw practical consequences. In the earliest examples, such as a Liang votive stupa from 434, it seemed to amount to little more than a lament for being in a world without a living Buddha and the consequent necessity of recourse to the adoration of images.[38] In the sixth century, however, it led to more extreme actions.

Several monks began carving the complete Buddhist canon in stone to preserve it for later ages when a new Buddha would appear.[39] The sixth-century *Scripture for Humane Kings* (*Ren wang jing*) argued that the decline of the Buddha's law meant that kings would replace monks as the primary defenders of Buddhism and that the recitation of the scripture to protect the state would become the central ritual of Buddhism. Reworked in the eighth century by Bukong to prepare for a Tibetan invasion, the *Scripture for Humane Kings* became a central text of esoteric Buddhism, and the monks who performed it became an arm of the government.[40]

The most radical approach to the end of the law came from the Sect of the Three Stages that emerged in the late sixth century. This movement preached that the disappearance of the Buddha's law abolished all religious distinctions, including those between monk and layman. It advocated a great fusion of monks and laymen like that anticipated in the universal assemblies orchestrated by Emperor Wu of the Liang. In place of conventional, institutional Buddhism, its preachers offered a program of universal reverence for the Buddha nature of all living creatures. They also made the classic lay obligation of charity central to their practice, and consequently founded the institution of the Inexhaustible Treasury to which all people would make donations to rescue the poor and suffering. This charitable institution operated throughout the Sui and Tang empires until it was finally abolished in the middle of the eighth century.[41]

Alongside millenarianism, the second major idea shared by Buddhism and Daoism during this period, one even more crucial to the development of Chinese civilization, was reincarnation. Though imported into China with Buddhism, it was gradually adopted by various strands of Daoist thought, which facilitated its general acceptance throughout Chinese society.[42] The full-fledged Chinese acceptance of reincarnation came with the emergence of the Lingbao tradition of Daoism at the end of the fourth century, a watershed event in the history of Daoism. In the Lingbao school, Buddhist concepts and terminology became such major and permanent elements in Daoist texts that some scholars treat this tradition as simply a straightforward adoption of Buddhism.[43] However, the notion of reincarnation in the Lingbao scriptures was specifically formulated to account for a perceived contradiction in Buddhist teachings, a contradiction that highlighted tensions in the relations of the living and the dead.

On the one hand, Buddhist apologists such as Chi Chao (339–377) had argued that the doctrine of karmic reincarnation meant that each individual was responsible only for the consequences of his own acts. But other

Buddhists claimed that merit could be transferred to one's ancestors to secure them a better rebirth, a belief underlying the making of Buddhist images and the Ghost Festival. Through an elaborate, Daoist-based analysis of the constituent elements of the body, and a model of declining stages of history where the practice of invoking ancestors in oaths implicated kin in one another's deeds, the Lingbao tradition formulated a theory of reincarnation that insisted on kin's mutual responsibility and the enduring nature of their ties. It also developed elaborate rituals that invoked this theory in the service of redeeming one's unhappy ancestors.[44] The idea of reincarnation thus became part of the common religious inheritance of later China.

The rise of Buddhism and its interplay with Daoism permanently altered several features of the Chinese religious universe. First, the rather nebulous afterlife of Han China was replaced by graphic, detailed visions of layer upon layer of paradises and hells. Also introducing belief in hungry ghosts (beings punished for their sins by being unable to eat sacrificial offerings) and new types of demons, Buddhism greatly enriched the Chinese vision of the afterlife. Second, it also radically moralized the spirit world. There is little evidence that the Han believed in reward and punishment in the underworld. The most common operative principle seems to have been that with proper burial people received treatment in the underworld that corresponded to their positions in life; ritual rather than conduct determined one's fate. A simplified vision of the Buddhist doctrine of karma, however, in which people's conduct resulted in rebirths in better or worse lives, in a heaven or a hell, pervaded Chinese visions of the afterlife in the Northern and Southern Dynasties and beyond. Linked to this was a third major change: the indispensable role that the Buddhist order came to play in Chinese funerary ritual and in festivals for the redemption of the dead. Buddhist rituals brought to bear the spiritual power of monks and Buddhas to redeem ancestors from hell and secure for them a rapid rebirth in a pure-land paradise.

Despite an attempted suppression by a Northern Zhou ruler in 574–578, the Buddhist order emerged as the primary state religious institution under the Sui. The dynasty's founder, a pious believer who attributed his rise to the Buddha, instituted the full panoply of state Buddhism that had developed in the Northern and Southern Dynasties: the emperor's bodhisattva vows, the establishment of state temples with endowed estates, the ordination of monks, the sponsored readings of scripture, and regular charity to the Buddhist order. He also built more than one hundred stupas containing relics of the Buddha, hoping thereby to win merit for his dynasty and preserve it.[45]

His prayers were not answered, however, and the Sui did not survive the reign of his son. The succeeding Tang dynasty granted ritual priority to Daoism, and although it continued to support Buddhist monasteries, the heyday of state-sponsored Buddhism was probably already past. Nevertheless, the Tang empire marked the high point of Buddhism as a philosophical force in Chinese society, and the mental universe that Buddhism had disseminated to the common people, with its inevitable retribution, its heavens and hells, its festivals of redemption, and its vision of merciful, saving gods, has remained part of Chinese civilization down to the present day.

Taming the Wilds

The Northern and Southern Dynasties' religious incorporation of the wilder regions of the earth, both the uninhabited mountains and the deeper south, required more than the construction of religious buildings on hillsides and in forests. Bringing these sites into the civilized world also entailed taming local religious powers. Accounts of this process by Daoists and Buddhists took two forms: tales of the conquest or conversion of animal demons that inhabited an area, and tales of the conquest or conversion of a local divinity, who was often the recipient of blood sacrifices.

Already in the fourth century B.C., the *Transmission of Master Zuo* (*Zuo zhuan*) posited a physical and moral concordance between the character of a region's soil, water, and winds and the creatures that fed on them. This congruity between a territory and its animals was written into patterns of diet, sacrifice, and agriculture.[46] In the Han period this same idea emerged in depictions of topography on "hill censers" and related art, where the flowing, dynamic lines of hills intertwine with the strange creatures that fill the landscape. Texts from the same period describe how different types of terrain produce distinctive types of flora, fauna, and humanity. The transmutation of landscape into animals and then back again was also enacted in magical pageants performed in the capital, as described in the poetry of the period. This idea carried forward into Buddhist art and texts, which depicted the Vulture Peak where the Buddha preached as a mountain in the shape of a great bird and insisted on the presence there of birds, beasts, and local divinities embodying the landscape.[47] This identification of landscape with its inhabitants meant that incorporating a territory into civilization took the form of domesticating its wild creatures.

The clearest evidence of a tension between Daoism and local animal deities comes from the history of Sichuan, where the institutional Daoist faith emerged. When Zhang Daoling established the Way of the Heavenly Masters at the end of the Han, Sichuan was still inhabited by peoples with distinct cultures, the most numerous of which were the Ba. These people were celebrated warriors who hunted white tigers but also worshipped these fierce, powerful animals who shared their region and their love of hunting. An origin myth of the Ba people concludes with the founder transforming into a white tiger, and some Ba groups sacrificed humans to this tiger god. It is also likely that the religion involved spirit possession in which a shaman took on the role and aspect of the tiger.

Since pre-imperial Qin the Ba had been locked in perpetual conflict with expanding Chinese states, and one story of political accommodation with the Qin features the killing of a marauding white tiger and the pack that followed it. Consequently, the Ba flocked in the thousands to join the Daoist rebel movement, which shared their resistance to Chinese exploitation. While we have no explicit records of how these Ba people in Sichuan converted to Daoism, the early Daoist critique of blood sacrifices to local, demonic gods certainly entailed an abandonment of any worship of wild animals.[48]

Another cult that converted from worshipping animal gods to Daoism was that to Wenchang. In its earliest form this local cult in the town of Zitong in northern Sichuan was devoted to a great snake that dwelt in a cave on nearby Sevenfold Mountain, from which it controlled rain and thunder. This mountain lay beside the main road connecting Chengdu to the Qin, and later Han, capital in Guanzhong, and by the fourth century it also figured in a story relating how the snake god brought down its mountain on top of the Five Stalwarts escorting five maidens sent to distract the king of Shu (Sichuan) while Qin plotted its invasion. However, in the sixth-century *Chronicle of the Sixteen Kingdoms* (*Shiliu guo chunqiu*) the mountain god was not a snake but a man named Zhang, who in later Tang poetry was celebrated as a fallen war hero. This is another case of taming a wild animal spirit, possibly at first under the aegis of Sichuan Daoism and finally under the state cult. However, here the act of domestication entails the transformation of the god into a human.[49]

Daoist hostility to local cults also took the form of attacks on their performance of blood sacrifices to deviant local gods often identified as the ghosts of defeated generals or others who had died violent deaths. Throughout the Northern and Southern Dynasties and beyond there are records of former devotees of such heterodox local cults who converted to Daoism, because it provided a sublimated and better-organized version of the practices with which they were familiar. Such luminaries of Daoism as Zhang Lu, Kou Qianzhi, and the Lingbao founder Lu Xiujing all claimed to offer a purged form of the practices that surrounded them. Ge Hong likewise recorded cases of converting the followers of deviant local cults to the elite, text-based forms of which he approved. Although the records are too scattered to produce a detailed history, they indicate that throughout the south of China, and sporadically in the north, text-based institutional Daoism evolved in constant tension with local cults from which it borrowed ideas and practices but whose major gods and rituals it sought to suppress.[50] In this way much of the history of Daoism in the period is a religious incorporation of the southern frontier into the Chinese textual universe.

Buddhist stories of the domestication of wild spaces through the conquest, expulsion, or conversion of local animal spirits are also abundant. Dozens of stories in the sixth-century *Biographies of Eminent Monks* (*Gao seng zhuan*) tell of monks entering an area where the inhabitants worshipped a local god, sometimes an animal spirit, who then converted to Buddhism. If the animal god was in a mountain, it would relinquish its cave to the monk. Other stories tell of dragons that inhabited mountain springs and were converted to Buddhism as a first step in the establishment of a monastery there. In some stories the conversion of the dragon brought needed rain. Sometimes the monks used their magical powers to expel, rather than convert, the local animal gods. In yet other cases the monks expelled snakes and other animals prior to the building of a temple, but the expulsion was carried out so that the animals were not harmed in the digging of the foundation.[51]

The expulsion of animals also took the form of self-sacrifice, in which the monk fed himself to the animal prior to becoming the guardian spirit of a village:

> At the beginning of the Song dynasty [420–479] a tiger ran wild at the foot of Mount Jia in the district of Pengcheng [modern Tongshan in Jiangsu]. Every day several villagers were attacked. "If the tiger ate me," said the monk Tangcheng to the villagers, "this scourge would certainly disappear" . . . At the third watch they heard the ti-

ger seize the monk. The villagers followed the beast as far as the mountain. There they saw that it had devoured the monk's entire body, except his head, which they buried. On that place they erected a stupa, and from then on the ravages of the tiger ceased completely.[52]

In addition to civilizing spaces through converting or expelling savage local deities, Buddhist monks also brought certain mountainous regions into the human world through identifying these locations as the dwellings of powerful bodhisattvas who would bless pilgrims. The earliest of these places was Mount Wutai, supposedly inhabited by the bodhisattva Manjusri. This belief made the region around the mountain a major pilgrimage site by the early seventh century, and it led to substantial imperial patronage.[53]

A final element in Chinese religious conquests of the wilds was the appearance of the city god cult. With one exception, the earliest such cults were in the Yangzi valley or points south, and even later, when the city god became widespread, more than two thirds of the examples come from the south.[54] In the earliest recorded cases, from the middle of the fifth century through the eighth, the god was a named human being usually associated with military achievements and credited with building the city walls. This recurring attribute reinforces the identification of the god as the spirit "of the city walls and moats," who was thus identified with defending the people and imposing order on a recalcitrant nature. In several cases in the southern dynasties the god was also given credit for opening up wastelands by building reservoirs and irrigation systems. City gods were invariably humans who were credited with a pacifying or civilizing mission. Some of the gods were historical figures from the Warring States period or the Han founding, while others are otherwise unknown local people whose achievements were located in the Sui or Tang.[55]

The origins of city gods often involved the conversion or defeat of local animal deities. This is particularly striking in the case of the city god of Taizhou (in eastern Zhejiang), originally a dragon spirit who received sacrifices from the population. This creature was humanized in later legends telling how a member of an important local family retired to the hills and turned into a dragon that protected the city. An origin myth of a city god from Jiangxi tells how a hero first defeated a local warlord during the civil war after the collapse of the Sui, and subsequently as prefect eliminated an enormous water buffalo with a golden hide and vermillion tail that emerged at night from a deep pool to harm people and their crops.[56] These and similar examples of city gods that quell, expel, or convert animal gods show that this urban cult played a role in state or popular religion parallel to that of Buddhism and Daoism in the religious incorporation of hinterlands and frontiers.

As in the case of Buddhism and Daoism, the city god cult also aimed to regularize and humanize religion through the elimination of local sacrifices to blood-drinking ghosts and earth gods. One such conflict between the state and local cults, beginning in the early decades of the fifth century and lasting for more than a century, pitted the ghost of Xiang Yu, the defeated archrival of the Han dynasty's founder, against all officials who took up office in Wuxing (just south of Lake Tai). The ghost of Xiang Yu had become conflated in a popular cult with the god of Bian Mountain, and he received blood offerings at the base of this mountain on the edge of the prefecture. The deaths of prefects while in office led to the belief that Xiang Yu had occupied the *yamen* (building housing the local government), so officials began to refuse to enter. At some point the local people even erected Xiang Yu's statue there. Several officials, including one who was a pious Buddhist, attempted to ignore or expel the ghost, but they soon fell ill and died. Although Xiang Yu's statue was finally removed by an official, his cult continued, so when a city god cult was established in the town, Xiang Yu was pointedly excluded from consideration for the role.

The case of Xiang Yu is historical, if perhaps embellished, and there are other accounts in the histories of officials who fell ill and died because they whipped statues of local gods for failing to bring rain. Popular fiction also includes stories like that of Zhen Zhong, who when going to take up a new post was intercepted by the local earth god, who had chosen him as a son-in-law. The already married Zhen declined, but under attack from the demon followers of the earth god he fled back to his home and soon perished, carried off by the god to marry his daughter.[57]

These malevolent ghosts, earth gods, and animal spirits were ultimately tamed by the benignly human city god. As an ally of imperial officials and subject to punishment at their hands if he failed, the city god represented a domestication and moralization of the local religion. In part this triumph of orthodoxy extended the norms of elite, imperial culture into the frontiers and the hillsides from which it had been excluded. But even more, it represented the ability of the imperial elite to command ideological support from the new urban classes, and the success of the court in communicating the image of the empire as a divine force.

9

WRITING

AS WITH so much of Chinese culture during the Northern and Southern Dynasties, writing and literature were characterized by the opening of new, autonomous spaces. Paralleling the emergence of sites for collective composition of verse and conversation, institutional religions, temples and gardens in cities, villas and hermits' caves in the hills, the literati created a more autonomous "aesthetic" realm no longer subordinated to the moral project of the classics, philosophy, and historiography.[1] This new realm of writing and images gained an intellectual grounding with the emergence of "Dark Studies."

Explorations of the Mysterious

"Dark Studies" (*xuan xue*) loosely refers to the activities of a group of writers working in the middle of the third century and their intellectual descendants. With the official textual orthodoxy of the classics compromised by the fall of the Han state, these writers explored the *Canon of Change*, the *Canon of the Way and Its Power*, and the *Master Zhuang* to provide fresh insights into language, society, and the cosmos. They framed arguments around a series of binary oppositions: being and non-being, name and reality, language and meaning, one and many, character and talent. These played into an overarching debate between the "teaching of names" (*mingjiao*, received teachings on social roles) and the "self so" or "spontaneously natural" (*ziran*, the natural course of things without conscious interference). The key thinkers include He Yan, Wang Bi, Xiang Xiu, Guo Xiang, Zhong Hui, and the poet-essayists Ruan Ji and

Xi Kang, who are linked as the two greatest of the Seven Worthies of the Bamboo Grove.[2]

As a cosmological or metaphysical alternative to the moralized Heaven of official Han Confucianism, the roots of Dark Studies go back to the end of the Western Han. The ultimate intellectual ancestor was Yang Xiong (53 B.C.–A.D. 18), who wrote a revised version of the *Canon of Change* entitled *The Great Dark*. He described the "dark" in his title as an undifferentiated, ineffable principle preceding the primal division into yin and yang that thus pervaded all things. It resembled the Way described in the *Canon of the Way and Its Power,* or the "nothingness" (*wu*) that Wang Bi posited as the ground of all being. Indeed, Yang posed the question of whether the "dark" somehow produced all things out of "emptiness and nothingness."[3]

Yang cited his intellectual debt to the Daoist *Canon of the Way and Its Power,* while still defending the ultimate authority of the morality espoused by Confucius. Subsequently, several scholars—including Yan Zun, Huan Tan, and Wang Chong—articulated a cosmos with no "Heaven" intervening in human affairs as a moral, personified agent.[4] These thinkers, particularly Wang Chong, whose writings were embraced by the leading late Han scholar Ma Rong, provided the intellectual background from which Dark Studies emerged.

These earlier ideas developed into a major intellectual discourse in response to the political and social changes at the fall of the Han dynasty. The empire's collapse undercut an official orthodoxy that had already lost most of its intellectual authority, apart from that imparted by the state. Increasing interest in the eremitic life called for ideas that rationalized activity outside the state sphere and justified aesthetic self-cultivation. The interlinked rise of "pure conversation" and interest in judging character provoked questions about the relation of names to reality, or character to talent. Dark Studies flourished, at least in part, because it met these needs and addressed these questions.

Dark Studies also emerged together with a north-south division in Chinese thought during the Three Kingdoms period. Innovative readings of the *Canon of Change* and *The Great Dark* that emphasized natural spontaneity (*ziran*) developed in Jingzhou in the central Yangzi valley. Scholars who remained with the court in the north, such as Liu Shao, who authored the *Study of Human Abilities*, elaborated earlier concerns about the relation of names and forms (or offices) that had developed within the Legalist and Confucian traditions. After Cao Cao occupied

Jingzhou and brought the leading scholars of the central Yangzi north, contact between these diverse regional traditions culminated in the classic works of Dark Studies in 240–249.[5]

The leading thinkers of this decade were He Yan, who was also chief minister in charge of appointments, and Wang Bi, who made the greatest impact and whose works are best preserved. These consist of commentaries on the *Canon of the Way and Its Power* and the *Canon of Change,* as well as more synoptic writings on the latter work and the *Analects* of Confucius. Wang Bi is best known for his argument that *wu*—variously interpreted as nothingness, nonbeing, or negativity—was the ultimate basis of reality. He maintained that all existing entities had to have a cause which itself could not be another entity. Explaining the existence and actions of things in terms of some other thing led to an infinite regress. There had to be an ultimate origin or cause, which he identified with the universal Way or the nonexistent potentiality prior to all specific existences. As a nonobject lacking all specificity and characteristics, it was prior to and hence above the active, moral Heaven of Han cosmology. It also lay beyond the reach of images or language in the realm of the "mysterious" or "dark," a word that thus defined this line of argument. This discussion of the relation between negativity and entities thus became an argument about the ability of language to articulate ultimate meanings, and hence of names to apply to realities.[6]

These ideas about being and a language that could describe it, or rather describe its own limits, also developed into a political theory. Just as the multitude of entities derived order and sense from the single dark negativity that preceded and produced them, so the multitude of humans achieved stability only through the existence of a single ruler who remained beyond the conventional social order and thus could act as ultimate cause.[7] However, for the ruler to function he had to relate to the people not as their opposite, as one man opposing a myriad, but as a radical "other" totally outside the ordinary realm of desire and contrivance. In this way, Wang Bi philosophically justified the old ideal of rule without purposive action (*wu wei*) and also articulated a veiled critique of the Cao-Wei state's surveillance and repression of the great clans, as well as its constant warfare against the southern kingdoms of Shu and Wu.[8]

Besides emphasizing the ultimate priority of the negative or nonexistent, Wang Bi also asserted that Confucius was a greater sage than Master Lao (Laozi). This position, together with his insistence on the necessity for a single ruler, has led modern scholars to argue that Wang Bi was a conservative and a "Confucian" (to the extent that such a term meant anything in an age that aimed to synthesize its entire intellectual inheritance). However, for Wang, Confucius's superiority lay in his ability to "embody" nothingness, while Master Lao merely "spoke" of it. What is thus at stake was Wang's insistence on the absolute priority of nothingness, and his denial of the possibility of a language that could express ultimate things. Wang Bi criticized the "teaching of names," i.e., classic Han Confucian values, because "names" could not capture the fundamental nature of existence, and names encoding social positions imposed uniformity. The only useful names flowed spontaneously from nature and achieved fruition in a sage ruler.[9]

Wang Bi, and apparently He Yan, thus used the Daoist classics and the *Canon of Change* to justify the overall political order while criticizing specific policies. The poet-essayists Xi Kang and Ruan Ji, by contrast, employed the same texts to formulate more radical critiques. In a series of essays on the pursuit of immortality, the absence of emotions in music, and the dispelling of self-interest, Xi Kang articulated a radically physical vision of human life that rejected the ideal of a sage devoted to public service and instead celebrated the Daoist "Perfected Man" who rose above concern for the mundane world to work toward self-perfection.[10] He became noted for avoiding political service, neglecting personal cleanliness, and devoting himself to a life of wine and music among the hills and streams.

Ruan Ji was less intellectually consistent, denouncing ritual and proclaiming the philosophy of the *Master Zhuang* as his model, while still endorsing received ideas about music and the *Canon of Change*. However, in his personal conduct he was celebrated for the wild and unconventional behavior associated with natural spontaneity. His ultimate ideal was the Great Man who mocked Confucian morality and devotion to public service, instead escaping from the world to embark on a transcendent spirit journey.[11] The men who became legendary as the Seven Worthies of the Bamboo Grove embodied this vision of life, and it was as exemplary figures rather than as thinkers that they were invoked by members of the southern elite as models for a life of spontaneity amidst the beauties of nature.[12]

Guo Xiang (ca. 252–312) was best known for his commentary on the *Master Zhuang*, which may or may not have been largely based on an earlier commentary by Xiang Xiu. Guo developed the idea, articulated earlier by Pei Wei, that the notion of "nothingness" or "negativity" is meaningless because all existence consists of entities. Whereas Pei Wei had denied "nothingness" in order to assert the validity of received morality, Guo Xiang insisted that all entities were spontaneously self-generated, so that the whole universe was naturally self-so (*ziran*). In the Han universe, society and nature had been united in a purposive, conscious, teleological, and moral whole. Eastern Han critics like Wang Chong had divided the two, with nature lacking the goals or morality that characterized human society. Guo Xiang's "dark" commentary reunited nature and humankind by making both purposeless, unconscious, nonteleological, and amoral.[13]

He further argued that conventional morality and the state remained grounded in nature, but they, like everything else, emerged through spontaneous self-generation. Every being in Guo Xiang's universe acted of its own accord, but in doing so formed a coherent order in which everything had its place. Ruler and serf both spontaneously performed the role dictated by their positions, thereby preserving the Daoist ideal of noncontrivance within a functioning social order.[14] However, in contrast to Wang Bi, Guo Xiang no longer treated the ruler as a unique philosophical necessity within the ontological order, a transcendental One set against the mundane Many, but simply one self-generated position in a universe of such beings.

Whereas Guo Xiang, like Wang Bi, cited the dark origin of things to justify the political order, other writers and political actors applied the same ideal of spontaneity to different purposes. The Seven Worthies and those who emulated them valorized spontaneity to justify the rejection of some, or all, conventional moral values in the name of radical individualism. Throughout the Northern and Southern Dynasties, the ideal of natural spontaneity elaborated in Dark Studies was used by aesthetes and dilettantes to rationalize either a life of retired self-cultivation or claims to a monopoly of court office based on their supposed superiority of spirit and style.[15] The increasing autonomy of artistic pursuits was justified in part through appeals to the ultimate value of the spontaneously "self-so." In a world where everything was self-generated, each activity or object justified itself without appeal to a single source of value grounded in Heaven or the state.[16]

Lyric Poetry

Lyric verse emerged in the Han as anonymous Music Bureau (*yuefu*) ballads and "ancient poems" (*gu shi*). The former dealt with many aspects of human life, among both the common people and the elite, while the latter dwelt on the melancholy elicited by the brevity of existence and the fleeting solace of sensual pleasures. While these forms provided the foundation for the emergence of lyric poems written by named authors, they continued to evolve as anonymous songs. One striking feature of this evolution was the marked differences between northern and southern Music Bureau ballads after the division of China.[17]

The songs of the north, produced under non-Chinese warrior dynasties, emphasized masculine heroism and military affairs.

> I just bought a five-foot sword,
> From the central pillar I hang it.
> I stroke it three times a day—
> Better by far than a maid of fifteen.

This period also produced the earliest surviving version of the story of Mulan, a woman who dressed up as a man to provide military service in place of her father. While some of these songs about valor were actually written in the north, the notion of a heroic "northern" style soon became conventional, and many southerners wrote verses on these themes in the imagined voice of a typical northerner.[18]

The most distinctive anonymous popular verses written in the south were love songs in quatrains, apparently sung to tunes indicated by the title. Some were clearly written for a female voice, whereas others seem to have been performed by either a male or a female. They were often erotically explicit but also employed double-entendres based on puns such as "lotus" for "passion," or "silk" for "longing." In the sixth century these erotic songs became very popular in the courts, where choruses of women were trained to sing them. The best known were called the Ziye songs, a word that meant "midnight" but was also said to be the name of a famous courtesan. A typical example is:

> I held my dress, not tying the sash;
> I painted my brows and went to the window.
> My gauze skirt is easily whirled by the breeze—
> If it opens a bit, just blame the spring wind.

These songs were influential both in the evolution of palace-style poetry in the southern courts and in the emergence of the quatrain as a major poetic form.[19]

Music Bureau and related songs began to be written by known authors at the end of the Han dynasty, when actual power was in the hands of Cao Cao and other warlords. Cao Cao himself became a celebrated writer of songs noted for martial spirit and bold simplicity of language. He also gathered some of the finest writers of his time, the Seven Masters of the Jian'an (reign period, 196–219).[20] Two of his sons, the heir Cao Pi and a younger son Cao Zhi, also became celebrated poets. Cao Pi was the first major literary theorist in China, while his younger brother most clearly exemplified the use of lyric verse to express one's innermost thoughts and feelings, and the lyric poet as the exemplary cultivated man.[21]

Interpretation of Cao Zhi's poetry has been dominated by his rivalry with his brother and the unsuccessful political career that led to his early death. Consequently, assessments of his verse have been intertwined with judgments about his character.[22] To a certain extent this is an obstacle to the evaluation of his significance in the history of Chinese poetry, but it also suggests something of the nature of his achievement. Cao Zhi was among the first Chinese lyric poets to emerge from anonymity by making his own experiences the centerpiece of his poetry. In the process of creating a tragic self whose multiple aspects were transmuted into a body of verse, he set a precedent for the basic presuppositions of Chinese lyric, which subsequently was read as the true articulation of the responses of a cultivated sensibility to actual experiences.[23] The insistence of Chinese readers on viewing the poetry of Cao Zhi through the prism of his biography was a consequence of the emergence of a new mode of verse, of which he was the first exemplar.

Cao Zhi's intertwining of self and poetry takes several forms that came to characterize the Chinese lyric. He and the comrades in his poetic circle modified the Han "old poems" to create the new subgenre of "poetry of presentation and reply." This demonstrated most clearly poetry's role as a mode of social exchange. Whereas in the "old poems" the author had described some standard scene—a bustling street, a lonely tower—and then stated the feelings evoked, in the "poetry of presentation" Cao Zhi described a scene that he witnessed, associated the scene with the plight of a friend, and then offered consolation or encouragement.

The detail of description, which usually constitutes most of the poem, conveys the sense that the author had witnessed the opening scene, while his reflection on it, and his address to a friend, also ties the poem to the author. In Cao Zhi's hands, verse became a mode of conversation as well as a testament to the writer's experiences and feelings. Following the deaths of most of his friends and his own political exile, Cao Zhi largely abandoned this subgenre of "presentation and reply." His longest and probably last poem in the form is an extensive lamentation on the sorrows of parting, the horrors of travel, and how a person's state of mind permeates every aspect of the surrounding landscape.[24]

Cao Zhi also followed his father in developing the Music Bureau ballad.[25] While Cao Cao had modified the form to recount personal aspects of his political struggles, Cao Zhi first reworked the ballad to project visions of an idealized self. His version of the classic "Mulberry on the Bank" differs from the original by presenting the observations of a single observer, instead of describing the beautiful Luofu from several viewpoints. Whereas the original Luofu emerged through the enumeration of garments and attributes, Cao Zhi makes her a unitary character by tracing the recurring theme of her physical grace and mobility in every aspect of her bearing and attire. At the end of his poem, Luofu (who in the original was married) emerges as a single woman who refuses all suitors while waiting for a man of true virtue. Luofu, of course, stands in for the poet himself, and Cao Zhi thus turns the entire ballad into a meditation on his own condition.[26]

Ballads on heroic youths similarly allow for meditation on the ideals of the poet and his sufferings. References to past sages and virtuous ministers become vehicles for reflection on the ironies of history or twists of fate, but ultimately to reveal the injustices and sorrows of the poet's own situation. Even his verse about a topic as mundane as cooking beans was a veiled reference to his fraught relationship with his ruler-brother, Cao Pi. In reworking the long-established genre of the banquet song, he turned the old ballad form with its rapid shifts in mood and topic into a sustained meditation on the scene of the banquet and its impact on the participants. But his most frequently employed Music Bureau theme was "wandering with immortals," which he adapted from the *Songs of the South*. In these poems, his soaring journeys to the realms of the immortals served to criticize the failings of his own world and seek emotional release from its miseries. Whether he actually believed in the possibility of such transcendence is unclear.[27]

The next generation of poets was dominated by the figures grouped, retrospectively, as the Seven Worthies of the Bamboo Grove. Some of these men actually had relations, but as far as we know they were never all physically in the same place, and some of them probably never met.

The greatest poets were Xi Kang and especially Ruan Ji, whose celebrated series *Songs of My Cares* marked the next major innovation in the
Chinese lyric. Ruan Ji was an epoch-making figure because he deepened
lyric verse to make it "universal." He showed how a skilled poet could
not only sing his feelings in response to the events of his own life, but
could also provide insights into the human condition by portraying the
world or history through the prism of a distinctive personality.[28] Instead
of simply responding to his own specific circumstances, or offering gener-
alities on human life, Ruan Ji used his anguished search for personal
meaning to reflect on the varieties of human sorrow or frailty.

Ruan Ji achieved this new effect primarily by replacing narrative se-
quences or linear expositions with a mental landscape in which natural
images and literary references were freely combined to evoke the poet's
moods or feelings. Rather than being bound by a single figure or scene to
which the poet responds, most of Ruan Ji's verses define a mood or sentiment by accumulating disparate images, as in the following poem, number seventy-one in the series:

> Hibiscus overgrows the grave mounds,
> Sparkling in lustrous shades.
> But when the bright sun sinks in the forest,
> Its petals fall to the roadside.
> Crickets chirp by doors and windows,
> Cicadas hum amidst the brambles.
> Mayflies play for only three mornings,
> Yet they preen themselves, working their wings.
> For whom do they display their finery,
> Flying up and down, sprucing themselves up?
> How short life is,
> But everything, full of ardor, labors on.

Here a whole range of plants, animals, temporal aspects of nature, and
signs of human mortality that could never form a single scene—being
drawn from different seasons and settings—nor be linked in a narrative
sequence are combined to form a meditation on the vanity of existence.
In other poems, images of the frail human body are linked to social or political collapse, so characteristic of the age in which he lived.[29]

After the rise in the fourth and early fifth centuries of the poetry of
landscape and reclusion touched on earlier, poetic circles in the Qi and

Liang dynasties moved into the palaces of the imperial princes, which became the literary as well as political centers of southern China. The next great innovative poetic circle formed at the end of the fifth century around the Qi dynasty imperial prince Xiao Ziliang at his celebrated Western Villa during the Yongming reign period (483–493). This circle was collectively known as the Eight Friends of Prince Jingling, and its most eminent members were Shen Yue, Xie Tiao, and Wang Rong.[30] These poets were best known for introducing the systematic use of tonal prosody, a complicated practice that culminated in the Tang dynasty codification of "regulated verse" as the ideal model of Chinese poetry right down to the present.

The prosodic rules were summed up under the title "four tones, eight prohibitions." The "four tones" refer to the level, rising, parting, and entering tones that characterized the phonetic system of the period. In Tang dynasty "regulated verse," the tones were divided into only two, level and oblique, but statements from the earlier period, confirmed by current research, show that the Yongming poets actively distinguished all four tones in their prosody.[31] The "eight prohibitions" refer to specific combinations of rhyme or tone that were regarded as defective or inferior. Whereas Tang verse was tightly bound by positive regulations, these earlier rules consisted largely of bans on certain features. The entire system aimed to avoid repetition and encourage variation, in the name of phonetic liveliness and flexibility. It derived from a new concern with the importance of sounds, as indicated in discussions by the contemporary literary theoretician Liu Xie:

> In our time when someone plays a zither and the sound is out of tune, he definitely knows how to change and tighten [the strings]. However, when he produces a literary composition and it sounds odd, he does not recognize the way to smooth it out. Although coming from the strings, the zither is able to attain euphony, but the sounds that sprout from the heart/mind may still lose harmonious rhythm. Why is this? It is probably because listening inwardly it is difficult to hear well.[32]

This assumes that the sounds of the poem, like its words, are rooted in human speech and are the product of the poet's heart/mind. The sounds themselves are thus inextricably tied to the poem's meanings.

This new concern with sound emerged for several reasons. By this time poetry had largely become separated from music, leading the critic Zhong Rong to attack the new prosodic system with this rhetorical question: "Now that we no longer set our poems to music, how do we benefit from tonal prosody?" But this was precisely the reason for the new tonal system, to create an aural harmony independent of music. In arguing for regulated prosody, Shen Yue pointed out that Chinese speech had four tones, while the musical gamut had five notes. The new prosody allowed poetry to remain harmonious or musical when freed from the alien confines imposed by musical structures.[33]

The new interest in tonal patterns also reflected the influence of Indian literature that had entered China together with Buddhism. Prolonged contact with Indian and Central Asian languages, along with extensive work in translation from them, made Chinese scholars and poets more conscious of their own language and encouraged them to articulate its characteristics in their theories of verse. Buddhist monks in south China chanted scriptures on a system modeled after their understanding of the "three tones" (more accurately "pitch-accents") used in chanting Sanskrit. Prince Xiao Ziliang, the imperial patron of the poets who introduced formalized tonal prosody, also sponsored the public chanting of scriptures at his Western Villa. The emphasis on chanting and pitch-accents as fundamental to verse provided a model for theorizing Chinese tones. Sanskrit literature provided not only new meters that the Buddhism-influenced poets of the period adapted, but also its own theories of prosody, including enumerated lists of "faults" or "prohibitions" that provided the model for the new Chinese theory.[34] Thus the massive influx of Indian texts and theories stimulated more systematic thinking about the musical character of the Chinese language.

The circle that formed around Xiao Gang (503–551), who became Emperor Jianwen of the Liang, developed the "palace-style poetry" that became an object of criticism and censure through much of Chinese literary history. Nevertheless, it was the major verse form of its day, and it made a major contribution to the poetic techniques of the celebrated high Tang verse.[35] "Palace-style" verse was in many ways the extreme expression of the southern dynasties' trend toward establishing poetry as an autonomous field. In his writings on verse and in his own verse, Xiao Gang explicitly rejected the moral/political program that had dominated Han poetic theory and continued in weakened form in the work of post-Han poets. He even denounced the critical remarks of Cao Zhi, whom the contemporary critic Zhong Rong rated as one of the greatest poets of all time. Arguing that poetry was entirely a means of expressing feelings and that its distinguishing virtue was a refined and ornate language, Xiao Gang concluded that it should never touch on weighty, public affairs. These subjects were too solemn for the playful language of verse, and they already had their own genres, such as memorials and essays. Poetry should serve as an elegant and mildly erotic linguistic game that articulated and enhanced the pleasures and passions of life at court.[36]

Literary Theory

Even as composing lyric poetry became a measure of literati status, authors articulated new justifications for literary writing as a noble pursuit in its own right. The first of these appears in a surviving fragment of the section on literature from Cao Pi's *Authoritative Judgments (Dian lun)*.[37] This asserts that literature, rather than serving morality, is the highest form of human activity and the chief means of justifying a person's life:

> Literary works are the supreme task in the regulation of a state, a splendid work that never decays. A time will come when life is finished; glory and pleasure end with the body. To make certain that both reach their fullest possible extent, nothing is better than undying literature. So ancient writers entrusted their persons to ink and brush, and displayed their thoughts in compositions. Without relying on the words of a fine historian or support of a powerful patron, their fame transmitted itself to later times.[38]

This marks a new era in literary thought. The standard early discussion of achieving immortal fame had posited a hierarchy of "establishing virtue," "establishing deeds," and "establishing words," but even there "words" had referred to political speeches or the moral teachings of a sage. While earlier writers such as Sima Qian had insisted on the importance of literature in transmitting one's name to posterity, this had been treated as a poor substitute for the ideal of a successful political career. The idea of immortality through literature takes on special poignancy in the case of Cao Pi, for as we know from his letter on the social function of poetry, all of his poet friends had died in plague or war. His essay concludes with a reflection on the brevity of life and parting from his friends.

In addition to this novel assertion of the centrality of literature, Cao Pi's essay provided the first clear discussion of how literature expressed its author's character: "In literature bodily energies [*qi*] are the decisive factor. The purity or turbidity of these energies has a fixed form, so they cannot be attained by force or effort. Compare it to music: even if the melody is the same and the tempo identical, when it comes to differences in drawing on one's energies, skill or ineptitude are innate. Although they may be found in the father or elder brother, they cannot be transmitted to a son or younger brother."

This assertion that "bodily energies are decisive" followed an enumeration of the strengths and weaknesses of the leading writers of his day in which their tendencies were frequently explained in terms of their *qi* energies.[39] Each writer had a distinctive, inborn endowment of *qi* that led him to develop certain aspects of verse and slight others. Thus, the argument here traces the style of a person's compositions to his inborn character, so that writing became not only the high road to immortality but the ultimate expression of a man's nature.

The next great work of literary theory was Lu Ji's "Rhapsody on Literature" (*Wen fu*), which established the fundamental issues for most Southern Dynasties discussions of literature.[40] The key innovation of this rhapsody was to focus on the act of composition. Since epideictic rhapsodies aimed for an exhaustive account of a topic, Lu Ji attempted to describe the entire process of writing a literary work. He began with an account of its mental preconditions, followed by the meditation undertaken before beginning a work, and then described the act of composition itself. In the Jin dynasty it had become conventional in the name of completeness to situate a rhapsody within a cosmological frame, so Lu Ji also pioneered the idea that the highest literature expressed the ordering principles of the universe. Consequently, Lu expounded a model of literary composition based on the theories of mind and cosmos elaborated by Wang Bi, Guo Xiang, and other writers in the Dark Studies tradition.

Lu Ji was one of the first writers to make emotions central to lyric. In a catalogue of genres, he wrote, "Lyric [*shi*] follows from the emotions and is sensuously intricate." Here he replaced the canonical and highly moralized "fixed intent" (*zhi*) that had justified verse in the Confucian commentarial tradition with the broader and more suspect "emotions," which led directly to an insistence on the poem as an object of sensual and seductive beauty.[41] Many subsequent writers identified the expression of emotions as the defining role of verse, such as the early sixth-century critics Zhong Rong and Liu Xie. This unprecedented interest in the emotions marked a shift in emphasis from poetry as a form of efficacious public speech to poetry as an expression of the inner state of the author.[42]

Another point in Lu Ji's argument, also elaborated in the following centuries, was that the emotions invoked by the poet were responses to encounters with the world and its objects. Thus the poet should begin by situating himself at the center of the cosmos, after which he:

> Grieves for the falling leaves in the severe autumn,
> Delights in the young branches of fragrant spring.
> His heart shudders in thinking of the frost;
> His intent soaring, he gazes down on the clouds.[43]

Here the poet's mind is mapped onto the annual cycle, as his feelings rise and fall in accord with the objects that appear in each season.

This intimate linkage of feelings with objects is mentioned in many third-century poems, and theorized by later critics. For example, Liu Xie devoted a chapter of his treatise on literature to the impact of the physical world on verse, and he elaborated some of the same themes as Lu Ji: "The year has its objects and every object has its appearance; human feelings change following the objects, and literary expression is triggered by the feelings thus evoked. A single leaf might be in perfect rapport with the mind. Similarly the sound of insects might touch the heart." This insistence on the pivotal role of objects and their interplay with the mind is also linked to the rise of poetry devoted to their description and to the new centrality of landscape as a theme of poetry.[44]

Lu Ji's rhapsody also describes how the poet readies his mind for the task of composition, suggesting the almost supernatural powers of perception and creation developed though proper preparation. The poet first engages in the meditative exercise of cleansing his mind of extraneous thoughts, sealing out visual or auditory distractions. This leads to a state of illumination, in which the imaginative power of the perfected mind transmutes the surrounding world of objects:

> Thus it begins:
> Complete retraction of vision and reversion of listening,
> Immersed in thought, seeking on all sides,
> The essence gallops to the world's eight limits,
> The mind roams myriad leagues up and down.

When it is attained:
Emotions, like the sun about to rise, grow brighter;
Things, fully illumined, vie to enter the mind.[45]

This insistence on stilling or cleansing the mind derives from the early Daoist classics, most importantly the *Master Zhuang,* in which the sage's tranquility enables him to embrace all of Heaven and Earth and its myriad creatures. Lu Ji's recourse to these texts indicates the impact of their revival by the Dark Studies masters who wrote a few decades earlier. The final lines, which invert the classic pattern of emotions being elicited by the perception of things, suggest the power of the poet's inspired mind to fuse with the objects that motivate his song.[46]

The next major writer on literary theory, Zhong Rong (459–518), made few original contributions, but his *Rankings of Poetry* (*Shi pin*) placed all the poets up to his own day into hierarchically graded categories of merit. This derived from the numerical rankings of men by their moral character pioneered by Ban Gu in the Han, which fed into the numerical ranking of men's talents and characters in the Nine-Rank system that underlay official recruitment and elite status in the period.[47] This move from rating on the basis of moral character or political talent to rating on the basis of poetic skill demonstrates the increasing tendency to treat literary art as an accomplishment in its own right, rather than an adjunct of ethics or politics.

Zhong Rong was also the first critic to emphasize the importance of immediacy in verse. He argued that the writer should avoid using too many allusions to earlier works but instead depict his immediate reality. Closely related to this was his emphasis on the detailed and skillful depiction of physical objects as a virtue of poetry. This was particularly true of poets from the late third century and subsequent periods. Thus he classified Zhang Xie (d. 307) as a poet of the highest rank in part because of his artful depiction of external reality. This emphasis on descriptive language became a major feature of poetry in the Northern and Southern Dynasties.[48]

However, Zhong Rong was also one of the first critics to emphasize that description was not valuable in its own right but only to suggest something beyond the object. Thus he states that the ultimate merit of Zhang Xie's poetry lies in the "flavor" attained by its colorful language and musical rhythms. Similarly, the value of Yan Yanzhi's poetry is said to lie in the powerful feelings evoked by his artful descriptions. The idea of a "meaning beyond the words," a suggestive or profound quality often described as "flavor," which could only be appreciated through protracted reflection, became fundamental to the appreciation of poetry. It is reflected in Zhong's reworking of the notion of *xing,* "evocation." In Han readings of the *Canon of Odes* (*Shi jing*) this term indicated a natural image usually found at the beginning of a poem; in the writings of Zhong Rong and subsequent critics it became closely linked to the notion of "flavor" and meant something like "mood," as in the following passage:

> Poetry has three principles: *xing* [evocation], *bi* [comparison], and *fu* [presentation]. When the words are over but the meaning still lingers, this is *xing.* Using an object as a comparison to express the poet's intent is *bi.* Directly presenting a fact, describing an object that bears a meaning is *fu.* Apply these three with appropriate proportion, infuse the poem with emotional energy, and decorate it with colorful language in order to make those who read it savor its infinitely lingering flavor, and those who hear it are touched to the heart. This is the ultimate of poetry.[49]

Here "evocation" is no longer a simple poetic technique but rather the first and encompassing principle of versification, a principle defining the ultimate virtue of a language that lingers and resonates in the mind of the reader.

Liu Xie's work of criticism, *Literary Mind and the Carving of Dragons* (or *Literary Mind and Ornate Rhetoric, Wenxin diao long*), was of secondary importance in its own time, but in the twentieth century it came to be regarded as the greatest work of Chinese literary theory. This shifting evaluation reflects the anomalous character of the work, which was a systematic treatise in a tradition consisting of essays, letters, prefaces, and scattered remarks. This unprecedented composition of a structured treatise—analytically narrating the history of literature, expounding the process of literary creation, and enumerating the forms it produced—was almost certainly inspired by the model of Buddhist and other Indian theoretical texts. Examples that had entered China in preceding centuries demonstrated the use of a detailed, numbered format for an exhaustive analytic exposition of a topic. The division of the text into two parts, one dealing with specific genres and the other with matters of style and lan-

guage, was also typical of Sanskrit treatises on poetics. Liu Xie was an or-
phan raised in a Buddhist temple who became a lay-scholar and disciple
of the monk Sengyou, and wrote substantial treatises on aspects of Buddhism. Thus, although there is only one term of clearly Buddhist origin in
the *Literary Mind*, and a handful of other neologisms perhaps created to
translate Sanskrit originals, the systematic organization of the text and
the mode of thought that underlies it, both without precedent or heirs in
the Chinese literary tradition, are clearly a result of Liu's immersion in
Buddhist texts.[50]

Although the organization of Liu Xie's work was unique, much of it
consisted of the fullest and most systematic exposition to date of ideas
about literature that had developed in the preceding centuries. In addition to discussing all known genres, the work includes chapters on such
themes as the cosmic origins of writing, the importance of the physical
appearance of objects, the role of emotions, the relation between the
character of an author and his compositions, and the almost superhuman
ability of a cultivated mind to transcend time and space through the powers of imagination. The chapter on this last theme is one of the most influential. After a brief introduction on the ability of "spirit thought" to
move freely through space and time, the text continues:

> When the basic principle of thought is at its most subtle, the spirit
> wanders freely together with objects. The spirit dwells in the breast;
> fixed intent and bodily energies control the bolt to its gate. Objects
> enter through the eye and ear; in this process language controls the
> hinge and trigger. When hinge and trigger open, then no aspect of
> objects remain hidden. When the bolt is closed, then the spirit retires
> into the heart/mind. Thus in shaping and turning [as on a potter's
> wheel] literary thought, the most important thing is emptiness and
> stillness.[51]

Here Liu Xie develops the observations of Lu Ji and others into an elaborate and systematic discourse on how the mind and material world inter-
act to produce literary works. The entire process is based on theories of
mind and the cosmos derived from Dark Studies.

One aspect of Liu Xie's thought that reflects new ideas about the autonomy of literature is his discussion of the classics.[52] His chapter "Re-
vering the Classics" argues that the Five Classics were the perfection of
the Way and the source of all literature. This aspect of the argument was

conventional, for the Han catalogue of the imperial library had already traced every genre of literature back to the classics. However, the Han argument had been based on the assumption that the classics, and the genres derived from them, were all produced by rulers and their officials, so that the textual realm was mapped onto the political one.[53] Liu Xie, in line with the tendency of his age to treat writing as independent, insisted that the classics were not merely exemplary texts but exemplary *literature*. Thus, he argues that the classics were "replete with style/pattern," citing the Han scholar Yang Xiong's remark that the literary style of the classics was like "carved jade." He also asserts that it was the power of Confucius's literary expressions, which he describes as "richer than the mountains and seas," that made him immortal.[54] In this way the power of literature becomes the basis of social order, rather than the reverse, as had been argued in earlier periods, and literary attainments become central to social authority.

A final aspect of the emergence of a largely autonomous literary sphere was the compilation of anthologies consisting entirely of verse and literary essays. Principles for selecting and arranging literary pieces in collections always reflect ideas about the nature of literature, ideas that the anthologies in turn help shape. Thus the *selection* of songs in the Mao version of the *Canon of Odes* anthology, the sole surviving Han commentary on that classic, reflected the idea that poetry expressed a normative authorial intent, while the *arrangement* constituted a theory of both the geographic structure of the Zhou state and its temporal career. Similarly, the *Songs of the South* brought together songs from different genres and several eras that were reread as the works of a single author. These readings of the anthology formed a new model of literature as the impassioned testimony of an unhappy consciousness.[55] Similarly, the compilation of anthologies consisting entirely of *belles lettres* marks the emergence of an idea of literature as autonomous, and the content of those anthologies reveals how that autonomous realm was defined.[56]

The earliest known anthology devoted to literature as an art was compiled by Cao Pi, also the first exponent of the idea of an autonomous literary realm. In 217 or shortly afterward he compiled a collection of the poems of four of his friends who had died that year in a plague. By the early fifth century Xie Lingyun had compiled an anthology that consisted primarily of lyric poems written in five-character lines, and this anthology was adopted and modified by several subsequent writers.[57] The monograph on texts in the seventh-century *Book of the Sui* lists 107 anthologies in 2,213 scrolls, although some of these appear to be literary criticism. Most were compiled during the Liang dynasty, and the two surviving examples from that period provide our only real information on the composition of these collections.

The most influential of the surviving anthologies was the *Selection of Refined Literature* (*Wen xuan*) compiled under the auspices of the imperial heir Xiao Tong (501–531), a leading patron of literature. This anthology contained 761 works of prose and poetry by over 130 writers dating from the third century B.C. to the sixth century A.D. It represented a moderate position on the nature of literature, in that its preface reiterated the classic strictures on the social and political role of writing, but at the same time the contents excluded the classics, philosophy, and history. It thereby presented an image of "writing" that consisted entirely of literary works of poetry and prose, thus corresponding to the bibliographic category of "literary collections" that had emerged by the Qi and Liang dynasties.[58] The development of this category, and the creation of an anthology based on it, clearly marked the emergent belief in a largely autonomous literature.

The anthology's arrangement reflected the same mix of a conservative, pragmatic view of literature with the more modern, aesthetic vision. The section on poetry was divided into rhapsodies and lyrics, with the former, the most honored genre in the Han, coming before the latter, the most prestigious in preceding centuries. The subsection on rhapsodies began with the poems on imperial themes such as the capital and hunting park, and proceeded to more private matters such as journeys, music, the arts, and finally the emotions. The subsection on lyric began with poems of moral exhortation, followed by social poems on banquets, poems on history, and finally poems devoted to the expression of personal sentiments and the description of landscapes. Liang court poetry, such as that composed by Xiao Tong, lyrics on objects, and the erotic verse so popular in the period were excluded. The section on prose was organized in the same manner, moving from the more "public" and "serious" (decrees or memorials) to the more "private" and "emotional" (most notably personal letters). Thus the anthology as a whole enshrined the centrality of *belles lettres,* but the internal organization delivered a more conservative message of the priority of the public and political.

When Xiao Tong died in 531, he was replaced as heir apparent by his brother Xiao Gang, who espoused a different vision of literature that was also expressed in an anthology, *New Songs from a Jade Terrace.* Xiao

Gang was the leading patron of what came to be called palace-style poetry. This consisted of verses on life in a princely palace, including poems
on buildings, precious objects, gardens, and above all palace women. The
focus on women is indicated in the preface, which describes the physical
features of palace beauties, tells how they composed fine poetry (including some historical cases of women poets), and then discusses their motives for writing:

> Languidly idle with few distractions,
> In tranquility with hours of leisure,
> They loath Eternal Joy Palace's tardy bell,
> Are weary of Central Hall's slow arrow of time.
> . . .
> Unable to delight her spirit in idle hours,
> She devotes her mind to the latest verse.
> This serves as a substitute for the flower of oblivion,
> And relieves somewhat the malady of melancholy.[59]

The preface indicates that the editor has compiled the anthology for the
diversion of these palace women, and to provide models for their compositions. This announces the theme of poetry as a social diversion or entertainment, and provides a twist to the classic trope of the courtier who
writes in the voice of a woman.[60]

The contents of the anthology match the program of the preface. In
contrast with the *Selection of Refined Literature,* which included primarily pieces from the Han, Wei, and Western Jin, three quarters of the *New
Songs* date from no more than a century prior to its compilation. Two
chapters consist of the works of living poets, and the best-represented author was its patron Xiao Gang. The poetry also reflects contemporary
taste, with an emphasis on erotic verse, skillful wordplay, and elaborate
descriptions of objects. Han Music Bureau ballads are largely excluded,
while there are many examples of southern popular song traditions such
as "music of Wu" from the capital region and "western songs" from cities of the central Yangzi region such as Jiangling and Xiangyang. These
were primarily quatrains, dealt largely with love and courtship, and were
full of local dialect. What defines the anthology, above all, is its rejection
of any serious moral or political purpose and its devotion to literary art
as a mode of refined, elite entertainment.

Calligraphy

Claims for an autonomous aesthetic realm also figured in the rise of calligraphy as the leading visual art. While calligraphy had been a necessary skill for holding office as early as the Warring States period, and distinct calligraphic styles for different functions emerged in the Han, there was no sense for the first three centuries of the Han dynasty that calligraphy was essential for a scholar. To the contrary, it was often associated with the detested lesser officials or "clerks," who manipulated the letter of the law to benefit themselves or their superiors and wielded their brushes and knife erasers to destroy noble and generous souls. Even after calligraphy became a literati art form, it remained associated with a menial or degrading position. This figures in an anecdote from *New Account of Tales of the World* and remarks in *Family Instructions for the Yan Clan,* both of which argue that a skillful calligrapher will be subjected to constant demands from superiors and friends, which the authors equate with servitude or corvée labor.[61]

Calligraphy was first linked to individual character as a form of elite self-expression in the career of Cai Yong (132–192). A celebrated poet, musician, and composer of essays, he was the first person to be celebrated for the quality of his calligraphic brushwork.[62] Because he combined literary skills with fine calligraphy, he received many requests to compose funerary inscriptions and brush them onto stone, where the carvers could then inscribe them. In 171, as a collator of texts in the imperial library, he put these same skills to work in fixing on stone authoritative versions of the Five Classics.

At this time Cai was involved in the struggles of the "pure criticism" movement. In 169 he composed his most celebrated stele inscription for Guo Tai, the leader of those protesting against court corruption and one of the first men celebrated for his ability to evaluate character. In 178 Emperor Ling established the Hongdu Academy as an alternative to the existing Imperial Academy, so that he could recruit skilled writers not tied to the established scholarly groups. The new academy included training in the composition of rhapsodies and the writing of graphs in the "bird seal" script, which was marked by curving lines and tendril-like appendages, in contrast to the square, geometrical official script. Cai denounced these men and the idea of employing people on the basis of a technical virtuosity detached from moral character. He also composed essays and a

rhapsody praising the sacred origins and efficacy of the conventional clerical and seal scripts, linking these to the establishment of a unitary state.
Thus, although Cai combined the talents of a literati with great calligraphic skill, he still defended the idea that calligraphy was a minor art
devoted to state service.[63]

Calligraphy emerged as a literati art in part because of the Han dynasty
development of running and cursive scripts. These allowed for greater
freedom of brushwork and made it easier to perceive the calligraphic line
as a direct extension of the bodily action of the writer. One could thereby
read script as an extension of the person. Particularly notable was the use
of cursive script, which began as flowing, simplified writing that could be
set down at high speed, but evolved into a fluid and dynamic artistic form
that allowed each writer to develop his or her own variants.

The first theoretical treatise on calligraphy was Zhao Yi's diatribe
Against Cursive Script (late second century A.D.):

> Among those of my commandery were two men: Liang Gongda and
> Jiang Mengying . . . In emulating the cursive script of Zhang Ji they
> surpassed Yan Hui's imitation of Confucius. Gongda would copy
> out manuscripts and show them to Mengying and together they
> would recite the texts and copy them without ever growing weary.
> Later scholars began to vie with one another in emulating these two
> brilliant men . . . Now each man has his own particular energies and
> blood, and different sinews and bones. The mind is coarse or fine,
> and the hand is skilled or clumsy. Since the beauty or ugliness of a
> piece of writing depends on the mind and hand, how can one make
> beautiful writing by force of effort?[64]

From the fact that calligraphy is an extension of the body, Zhao Yi concludes that it expresses a unique character and thus cannot be mastered
through imitation.

His essay shows that by the end of the Han many scholars imitated
beautiful calligraphy in order to master the skill. This practice leads
to one of the key issues for calligraphy in the Northern and Southern Dynasties: copies and forgeries. This was the one question unique to
calligraphic theory in the period, which otherwise borrowed from poetry, painting, and medicine (since calligraphy was an expression of the
body).[65] As indicated in Zhao Yi's essay, imitation was essential to learning calligraphy, so making copies was part of normal literati life. How-

ever, anecdotes from the Northern and Southern Dynasties show that trying to pass off a copy as an original was regarded as a fraud or deception
(*wei*) that sought to "confound the real" (*zhen*). Like other aspects of
critical theory from the period, these terms seem to have been borrowed
from the *Master Zhuang,* where *zhen* denoted what was genuine or inborn and marked human perfection, while *wei* meant the false or hypocritical. The terms entered Chinese poetics in the writings of Tao Qian,
who held up *zhen* as the ideal to which he devoted himself.

This dichotomy was first applied to calligraphy in anecdotes in Yu
He's (d. 366) *Memorial on Calligraphy* about the celebrated Wang Xizhi
(303–361), whose style had already become the standard for all calligraphy and consequently the constant target of copyists. One anecdote tells
how one member of the imperial house, Liu Yizong, spent large sums of
money to buy outstanding examples of calligraphy: "Base fellows cun-
ningly made copies. They used the drippings from thatched roofs to
change the color of the paper and age it, making it like old calligraphy.
Real and fake [*zhen wei*] were mixed together, and no one could tell
the difference. Therefore, among the many works accumulated by Liu
Yizong, there were many that were not authentic [*fei zhen*]."[66] Calligraphy had become a prestigious art in the highest circles, and therefore a
market for it had developed, but in response to this market forgery had
become a major industry as well, with many skillful techniques.

The very notion of "forgery" entails beliefs about what is of value in
calligraphy. An anecdote in which Wang Xizhi does not at first recognize
a copy of his own writing as a forgery shows that even pieces that could
not be visibly distinguished from an "original" were regarded as fakes.
This means that the crucial factor in valuing calligraphy was the belief
that it was an extension of its author; what made the writing precious
was the link to the man himself. This is our clearest evidence of how
much calligraphy had evolved from being a mere clerical skill into a high
art, in which the lines of the graphs testified to the lofty spirit of the person who brushed them. This idea that calligraphy transmitted spirit explains why *New Account of Tales of the World* gave poetic accounts of
the calligraphy of Wang Xizhi and his son Xianzhi, as well as their character, and why the supposed personal character of Wang Xizhi became
essential to the later hypervaluation of his work.[67]

A final aspect of calligraphy linked to the pursuit of the "genuine" was
its role in the formation of Daoism. The texts revealed to Yang Xi, which
underlay the formation of the Highest Purity tradition in the south, had

been distinguished by their brilliant poetry and calligraphy. Tao Hongjing, who had become a judge of calligraphy for Emperor Wu of the Liang and wrote on how to recognize the genuine, used his ability to discern the calligraphy of Yang Xi to distinguish the true revealed texts from later accretions. Thus the difference between true calligraphy and false here distinguished sacred canon from profane, a point made by Tao in his postscript to the *Declarations of the Perfected* (*Zhen gao*) that he assembled from Yang's texts. However, while Yang Xi's texts were written out hastily in cursive form, which itself seems to have influenced calligraphers of the period, they were transcribed into a careful clerical script. This shows the continued influence of the idea that solemn, public texts should be written in a formal, clerical style.[68]

The *Declarations* divided graphs into three levels. The highest exist at the primordial origins of the world and can be written and read only by celestial beings. The second, described as "cloud-seal script," is used to write talismans that command spirits. These cannot be read by ordinary mortals and are the privilege of ordained Daoists. The third level is the regular script used by ordinary people. Unlike the earlier forms, these have been forced into fixed, definite shapes that make them recognizable but deprive them of numinous power. Later Daoist texts elaborated this idea of potent, living graphs that existed since the beginning of time; in some accounts the tangible world derived from them. This theory of the divine nature of graphs and the role of connoisseurship in constituting the Daoist canon both show the importance of calligraphy in the religious history of the period.

Prose Narrative

One final aspect of the development of writing in the Northern and Southern Dynasties was the transformation of the forms and uses of prose narration, beginning with histories. The most important development in the writing of history was its establishment as a distinct bibliographic category. In the Han, all histories written in the period were treated as offshoots of the *Spring and Autumn Annals* within the category of classics. History was first set apart as a category, not yet named "history," in a four-part bibliographic scheme used in the *New Catalogue of Palace Texts* compiled by the Cao-Wei dynasty scholar Xun Xu.

"History" was formally established as a separate category during the reorganization of the Imperial Academy in 438, when the Southern Song dynasty established four academies: Confucian studies, Dark Studies, historical studies, and literary studies. Thus, history emerged as an independent discipline roughly in tandem with the idea of an autonomous literature. The establishment of history as a distinct genre also coincided with discussions of the nature of historical practice. The first clear case of this was Qiao Zhou's (d. 270) *Examination of Ancient Histories,* and the practice culminated in the inclusion of a chapter on history in *The Literary Mind and the Carving of Dragons* (ca. 500).[69]

Whereas the Han catalogue of the imperial library listed twelve titles under the *Spring and Autumn Annals,* the category "history" in the *Book of the Sui* (completed in 656) listed 874 titles, of which 817 were still extant. More histories were composed in the Northern and Southern Dynasties than in any period until the last dynasty, the Qing (1644–1912). Many historians, notably Sima Biao, Yuan Hong, and Fan Ye, wrote histories of the Han dynasty to explain its downfall. Others wrote accounts, both private and state-sponsored, of post-Han dynasties. Many tried to distinguish the legitimate successors of the Han from mere rebels or usurpers. Notable examples are Chen Shou's *Records of the Three Kingdoms,* Shen Yue's *Book of the Song Dynasty,* Xiao Zixian's *Book of the Southern Qi,* and Wei Shou's *Book of the [Northern] Wei.* The histories by Shen Yue and Xiao Zixian were officially sponsored histories of the dynasties immediately preceding those that the authors served, which set the pattern for later Chinese official historiography.[70]

The period also saw the rise of histories that did not take the dynasty or state as their unit of study. There were histories of regions, such as the *Record of the States South of Mount Hua* (*Huayang guo zhi*), and histories on religious topics. These included *Biographies of Eminent Monks* written by Huijiao, accounts of temples and wonder-working statues, colophons describing events leading to the writing or revelation of a text, and such anomalous works as *Record of the Buddhist Temples of Luoyang.* Writers also developed an interest in miscellaneous biographies and collections of anecdotes, a genre pioneered by Pei Qi, whose *Forest of Conversations* (*Yu lin,* dated 362) provided the model for *New Account of Tales of the World.* This work, in turn, inspired anecdote collections over the centuries in China and even Japan. Like other narratives about the past that did not conform to the model of political historiography, *New Account of Tales of the World* was denounced by many Chinese writers and often classified as "petty talk" (*xiao shuo*), which would later be used to translate the English word "fiction."[71]

The most important development at the boundaries of history and fiction was the rise of a new kind of text, the "anomaly account" or "record of the strange" (*zhi guai*).[72] This genre, largely tales or descriptions of ghosts, strange creatures, or bizarre events, is conventionally treated as the origin of fiction in China, but those who wrote the texts justified them as extensions of three classically-sanctioned modes of factual writing: cosmography, omen records, and history. Early Chinese cosmographies (written accounts of the world's structure) included such texts as the "Tribute of Yu," the *Biography of Mu, Son of Heaven* (*Mu tianzi zhuan*), and the *Canon of Mountains and Seas* (*Shan hai jing*).[73] Dealing with distant regions and high mountains, these texts contain stories of strange beings that serve to confirm the normative status of the central regions. Omen records were collected in official histories, including numerous accounts of bizarre phenomena that presaged disorders in the world. Finally, key figures such as Gan Bao justified their tales of prodigies and ghosts as a means of filling in what was omitted in more conventional histories.[74]

As supplements to history, anomaly accounts emphasized what was "peripheral" because it came from distant regions, high mountains, or the hidden realm of spirits. Most writers of these accounts, which largely circulated in the area controlled by the southern dynasties, were southerners, and a large proportion of the anomalous events occured in the south and southwest.[75] They thus provided written accounts of the regions that were being physically incorporated into the Chinese world through expansion southward or up into the mountains. They also sometimes modified relations between the center and the periphery, thereby challenging social hierarchies. In certain texts the esoteric skills or personal knowledge of distant regions claimed by the author meant that it was he, rather than the ruler, who mastered the periphery and incorporated it into the human world.

This theme of the superiority of the adept who had retired from the human world became even stronger in more explicitly Daoist collections of anomalies, which emphasized the autonomy of those dwelling at the edges of the world and their superiority even to the rulers of men. The adept's ascent to higher regions, beyond the dreams of noblemen and kings, translates into claims for the supreme status of whoever is most remote. In texts narrating the meetings of the Han Emperor Wu with immortals, the adept Dong Fangshuo mediates between the ruler and these beings from the edges of the world, and the mediator, not the ruler, is master of the game. The exception to this pattern was Buddhism-inspired works, which, out of sensitivity to the charge of their alien origins, insisted on the potential wonder-working abilities of any person of true faith.[76] Nevertheless, popular accounts of Buddhist magic emphasized the remote origins of its practitioners.

The major works of the genre represent a cosmic expansion of Han dynasty perspectives on Heaven and humankind.[77] Under the Han, the human and divine had combined in a moralized world where Heaven acted as a supreme judge, imposing conventional values. "Records of the strange," however, extended the spatial and moral range to include everything within the cosmos. The divine revealed its connections not only to the ruler who had previously been the unique link between Heaven and man, but to all people and even to animals. Although the world of the "strange" might appear to be chaotic, underlying stable relations and patterns emerged in seemingly anomalous events that revealed clear connections between all species between Heaven and Earth, both visible and invisible. The ultimate message of these texts was thus a universal "reciprocity across boundaries," where the old Han ritual-based order gave way to a realm that included the most distant and alien creatures, the mountain peaks and hidden caverns of the immortals, and the worlds of all the living and the dead.

CONCLUSION

THE reunification of China in 589 under the short-lived Sui dynasty after four centuries of division, and the subsequent centuries under the Tang dynasty (618–906), reimposed unitary imperial rule on a Chinese society that had been transformed since the fall of the Han dynasty. While claiming to be the successor or rebirth of the Han, the Sui and Tang dynasties incorporated numerous institutions and practices developed by their "barbarian" predecessors who had ruled north China in the fifth and sixth centuries—the Wei, Zhou, and Qi.

The inheritance from the Northern and Southern Dynasties included the equal-field system, the last system of state-owned land; the divisional army, the last form of a hereditary soldiery; the collection of taxes in grain and cloth; state sponsorship of institutional Daoism and Buddhism; regular foreign relations with the more distant realms to the east and the south that had emerged since the Han; and the incorporation of foreign peoples within the ruling house, for both the Sui and Tang imperial families had intermarried heavily with non-Han peoples.

Major innovations included the abolition of the Nine-Rank system of recommendations that had facilitated the emergence of a semi-hereditary aristocracy; the building of capitals with novel features at Chang'an and Luoyang; the incorporation of south China, where nearly 40 percent of the population now lived, into the empire; and new patterns of international relations that both consolidated the developments of the preceding centuries and anticipated the dominant patterns of the late imperial period.

The Sui's conquest of the south was rapid. Having replaced the Northern Zhou by a *coup d'état* in 581, the founder, Emperor Wen (r. 581–604), inherited a position of unprecedented strategic strength. Sichuan had been occupied in 552 by the Zhou's predecessor, the Western Wei, which two years later conquered much of the central Yangzi region around Jiangling. The southern Chen court, heir to the devastation of the Hou Jing rebellion, had joined the Zhou state for a joint attack on Qi in 575, but once Qi was destroyed in 577 the Zhou armies attacked their former allies, destroyed much of their forces, and pushed them back to the line of the Yangzi River. At this point Chen seemed ready to fall, and only the struggles at the Zhou court leading up to and following the Sui seizure of power delayed the conquest.

By 587, however, Emperor Wen's position was secure, and he began preparations for conquering the south. The primary obstacle that had blocked previous northern armies was their lack of a strong fleet. The Sui generals set to work assembling and training a major fleet in Sichuan, as well as smaller ones in the central Yangzi region and at the seacoast. Large land forces were also assembled. In late 588 the invasion began under the titular command of Prince Yang Guang, who would become the second Sui emperor, and in a series of battles it swept the Chen forces from the river, crossed the Yangzi, and occupied the capital at Jiankang. The Chen ruler was taken prisoner and commanded his forces to surrender. An uprising of leading southern families, who feared that the new regime would eliminate their privileges, broke out in 589, but it was savagely suppressed, bringing to an end the political division between the north and south. While tensions between the two regions continued, the benevolent rule of Yang Guang in the south gradually diminished resistance. He partially rebuilt the destroyed southern capital under the new name of Danyang and became an industrious patron of southern Buddhist monasteries and literary gatherings.[1]

Like other new dynasties, the Sui established a set of institutions that were considered essential to imperial rule. In addition to reasserting state patronage of canonical textual studies, Emperor Wen also supported institutional Buddhism and Daoism, which had been the targets of an attempted suppression in the north between 574 and 578. This included recognizing major temples as state-supported institutions, permitting specified numbers of ordinations, presenting gifts to temples, and sponsoring banquets on certain occasions. Emperor Wen distributed relics to the major cities of the empire and instituted a legal code, a tax structure, a system of state-controlled redistribution of lands, and a military organi-

zation based on the Zhou Divisional Army. Finally, he and his son contin-
ued to develop relations, which had begun in the Han, with the states of
Korea and Central Asia, and also with several states in what is now
Southeast Asia and with the distant islands of Japan.[2]

The first great reform of the Sui was the abolition of the Nine-Rank
system of recommendations that had favored established families in the
pursuit of official appointments. The Sui launched a series of bureaucratic reforms at the central and local levels, including a restoration of
Han titles and a return to the principle of having only two levels of local
administration. Both of these were part of the Sui project to restore the
classic Han model of a unitary state. However, far and away the most important single administrative reform was the elimination of the office of
impartial judge and the associated practice of relying on recommendations based on family background to fill entry-level positions at court.
This system had become the key mechanism by which certain families
had guaranteed their access to office and maintained their predominance
in Chinese society for centuries. While they had not formed a closed aristocracy and had been unable to secure political control in a world
dominated by military power, the great families had enjoyed unchal-
lenged social prestige and had prevented rulers of short-lived dynasties
from asserting control over appointments. The abolition of this practice
in 583, and its replacement with appointments made by a Board of Civil
Office in the central bureaucracy and controlled through annual reviews,
marked the first step in the formal reassertion of imperial power over the
great families.[3]

The Sui also moved toward the introduction of an examination system,
which would become the primary route to office from the Song dynasty
onward. In 587 Emperor Wen decreed that each prefecture should annu-
ally send up three candidates for office who had been chosen for their talent and knowledge of the classics. These seem to have been selected by
some form of local exam. While Emperor Wen carried out a large-scale
elimination of local schools in 601, in association with his distribution of
Buddhist relics among the prefectures, his successor Emperor Yang
(r. 605–618) revived the schools and also introduced the *jinshi* examination degree, which became the most prestigious degree in the subsequent
Tang dynasty and much of late imperial China. In addition to local and
prefectural schools, three academies had been established in the capital
under the Jin and the Northern Wei. Scattered records indicate that candidates from the schools had to pass an oral examination at the local

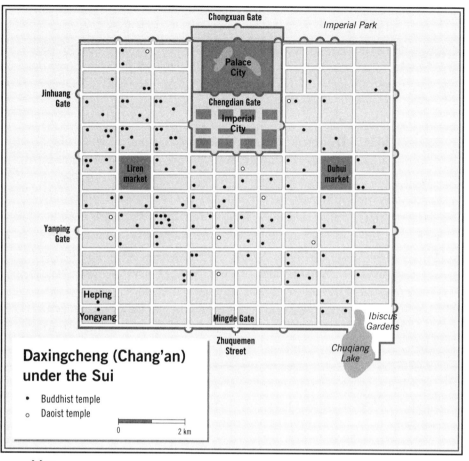

Chongxuan Gate

Imperial Park

Palace City

Jinhuang Gate

Chengdian Gate

Imperial City

Liren market

Duhui market

Yanping Gate

Heping

Yongyang

Mingde Gate

Ibiscus Gardens

Zhuquemen Street

Chuqiang Lake

Daxingcheng (Chang'an) under the Sui

• Buddhist temple
○ Daoist temple

0   2 km

MAP 15

level and then a written one at the government agency to which they were assigned.[4]

Another great Sui innovation was the building of a new capital, named Daxingcheng, just to the southeast of the old capital Chang'an in the Wei River valley (Map 15). Although the ancient city had fallen into decay over the centuries, its geographic setting had made it a secure base for many earlier rulers. It had served as the capital of several short-lived regimes in the northwest, including the Northern Zhou, and the Sui founder himself had first seized power at this site. By choosing this location for its new capital, the Sui clearly linked their feat of reunifying China to the Han, which had been the last dynasty to rule a united Chinese state for a sustained period.

Han Chang'an had been an irregular city defined in the north by the course of the river. The new city was to be a giant, canonically-prescribed rectangle measuring between five and six miles on a side. To the north of the city was a large imperial park. Within the city walls, backing directly onto the north wall, was a compound with the imperial palaces. South of this was another walled enclosure containing an administrative city with all the government offices. This was a new feature of Chinese imperial capital design. The rest of the area within the outer wall was to be divided into 108 walled compounds, of which two would serve as markets and 106 as residential wards. In actual practice the outer wall was built first, followed by the palace compound, so that the emperor moved into a largely empty capital in 583. Members of the imperial family then built their palaces in the city, and imperial name-plaques were granted to anyone who endowed a Buddhist temple. This resulted in the rapid founding of more than a hundred temples. The conquest of Chen was followed by the forcible resettlement of a large population in the capital. Nevertheless, much of the city was still empty when the Sui fell to the Tang. The new dynasty transformed it from a primarily religious and administrative center into a vibrant residential city.[5]

The Sui founder's successor, Emperor Yang, reconstructed the second Han political center, Luoyang, which had been capital of the Eastern Han and, for some decades, of the Northern Wei (Map 16). The project was carried out in the first year of his reign, and although the city was only a bit over half the size of Daxingcheng, it contained much elaborate and expensive architecture, setting a pattern for the conspicuous expenditure that was ultimately to doom the ruler and his dynasty. Because the city was bounded on the north by hills and old imperial graves, the imperial park was established to the west of the city, and the palace compound was moved to the northwest corner for ease of access. As in Daxingcheng, a new-style administrative center was built just south of the palace compound, and an axial road ran straight from the south gate of the administrative center to the southern city wall. Because of the placement of the palace and administrative compounds to the west, however, this axial road did not bisect the city as did its equivalent road in Daxingcheng.

What bisected Luoyang into northern and southern parts was the Luo River, and this resulted in some irregularity in the distribution of residential wards and markets. The area north of the river that was not occupied by palaces and government buildings was divided into thirty walled

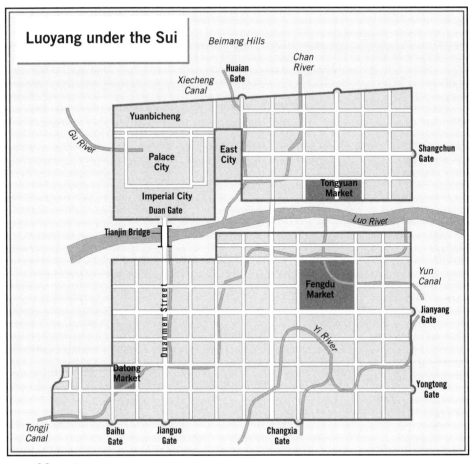

Luoyang under the Sui

Beimang Hills

Chan River

Huaian Gate

Xiecheng Canal

Yuanbicheng

Gu River

Palace City

East City

Shangchun Gate

Tongyuan Market

Imperial City

Duan Gate

Luo River

Tianjin Bridge

Duanmen Street

Fengdu Market

Yun Canal

Jianyang Gate

Yi River

Datong Market

Yongtong Gate

Tongji Canal

Baihu Gate

Jianguo Gate

Changxia Gate

MAP 16

wards, of which two were combined to form a market abutting the river. The area immediately south of the river was lined by a series of half-sized wards, and the area to the south of these was divided into a grid of sixty-six regular wards. However, four of these were combined to form another market just to the south of the river wards and connected to the river by canals. After 610 a ward in the southwest corner of the city on the Tongji Canal was dedicated to a third market.

The Sui's eastern capital of Luoyang differed from Daxingcheng in several ways. It was marked by the irregular placement of the government compounds, with the resulting skewed axiality. It had far fewer religious establishments, and indeed Emperor Yang engaged in a limited purge of Buddhist establishments in the western capital. Most important, unlike

Daxingcheng, which had two markets lying in symmetrical balance on either side of the palace district, Luoyang had three markets whose placement was determined by access to water. These pragmatic locations made
them far more suitable for actual trade than the markets in Daxingcheng,
which were situated in sites determined by cosmological and political
models.[6] The centrality of trade, and above all of water-based trade, in
the structuring of the city was an important new feature, and a key development in the physical evolution of the Chinese state.

The new importance of water transport was embodied in the most significant innovation of the Sui, the building of the first Grand Canal to
provide efficient shipping of bulk commodities from the south to the
north and from the east to the west. By facilitating the large-scale movement of men and goods, this massive engineering project aimed to bind
together the regions of the two great river systems of China, which had
been separated politically for four centuries. Above all it sought to allow
the movement of grain from the south, which was now the most productive region of the empire, to the north, which had been established as the
political capital by conquest and military domination.

The Grand Canal is usually attributed to Emperor Yang, but in fact the
project, which connected several older canals and waterways, was begun
by his father in 584. Emperor Wen decided to restore an old Han canal
(called the Guantong Canal) that had run parallel to the Wei River, which
was prone to silting and seasonally shallow, so that bulk commodities including grain could be shipped from the more fertile flood plain of the
Yellow River in the east to the over-populated capital region of Guanzhong within the passes (Map 17). The second leg of the canal, in which
the Tongji Canal linked Luoyang to the Huai River and then via an
old canal (called the Han Conduit) to the Yangzi near Jiangdu (modern
Yangzhou), was begun in 605 by Emperor Yang. A third leg, again largely
following older canal routes, went from the Yangzi near Jingkou (modern
Zhenjiang) along the Jiangnan Canal to the head of Hangzhou Bay at the
town of Yuhang. Several major granaries in the capitals and at key points
along the canal allowed for the storage and trans-shipment of grain.

A final leg of the Grand Canal, begun in 608, led northeast from the
confluence of the Luo and Yellow rivers near Luoyang to the vicinity
of modern Beijing. This was the only section that entailed substantial
new digging.[7] It connected the northeast to the central plain and thus to
the south, thereby linking all the regions of China by water. It also allowed for the provisioning of the disastrous military expeditions against
Koguryo (North Korea) that ultimately led to the fall of the Sui dynasty.

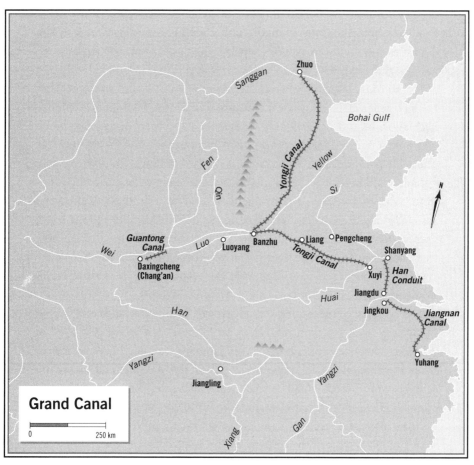

MAP 17

After the Sui collapsed under the strain of Emperor Yang's expenditures, Chinese historians savagely criticized the building of the Grand Canal. But its importance to the long-term political unification of China can scarcely be exaggerated. Together with the already-existing canal network in the south, it allowed shipment by water to the capitals from every productive region in China except Sichuan, which was linked to Chang'an by a well-established road and by river to the now populous lower Yangzi region. As both a symbol and an actual mode of transport, the Grand Canal joined into a unified polity two regions that for four centuries had developed independently. This linkage became ever more important as economic and demographic growth made the south the most populous and the most productive region of China, and as provisioning the militarily, and hence politically, dominant north came to depend primarily on the canal. The emergence of Beijing as the capital of a united China under the Mongol Yuan, the Ming, and the Manchu Qing dynasties was an outgrowth of Emperor Yang's decision to extend the canal into the northeast.

For all of its importance to posterity, the Grand Canal was a disaster for its builder. Its construction consumed substantial amounts of money and labor. In and of itself this would not have been disastrous, but it was linked to a broader pattern of conspicuous expenditure by Emperor Yang. He paid for huge, elaborately decorated buildings in both the capital and elsewhere. These included richly ornamented palace compounds in the park to the west of Luoyang, at several key points along the canal system, along the northern frontier, and in or near key cities in the south such as Jiangdu and Danyang. These imperial palaces provided suitably rich accommodation wherever he moved throughout his realm, but despite their political and strategic uses they represented an extraordinary drain on the treasury.

The building of these compounds inspired the myth of Emperor Yang's "labyrinth of desire," an imaginary structure in his "River Capital" at Jiangdu, where he could indulge every fantasy of sensual pleasure deep in his hidden chambers. In late imperial fiction this building and its inhabitant became a stock image of wayward sensuality.[8] Even as he bankrupted his court with massive construction projects, Emperor Yang undertook a series of military campaigns against Koguryo in the northeast, which finally triggered the collapse of the Sui.

Unlike the rest of the canal system, the northeastern leg had been designed to carry supplies away from the central regions to the armies at the frontier, and thereby bind this region to the empire. While northeastern armies had initially provided defense, foreign developments led them into a series of disastrous offensives. As the Sui began to feel more secure after almost three decades of rule, they attempted to restore China to its supposed rightful place at the center of the East Asian world. They launched several unsuccessful, but not calamitous, campaigns in the south, and more successful ones into Central Asia, where they secured tribute and recognition of suzerainty from Gaochang and several other leading states. They also pursued an initially successful political campaign to divide the Turks, who now controlled vast regions to the north of China, into two empires and to manipulate a succession struggle in the eastern empire in modern Mongolia.[9]

However, at a triumphant meeting of Emperor Yang and a formally submissive eastern Turkish ruler in 607, the Chinese encountered a delegation from the state of Koguryo. Fearing an alliance between these two potential northern enemies, the Sui sent a message demanding formal submission from Koguryo. When this demand was rejected, Emperor Yang waited for the completion of the northeastern leg of the canal in 609 and then assembled a force to invade Korea in the early summer. The Chinese forces were blocked by a series of walled towns along the Liao River, however, and the arrival of rains in late summer made further advance impossible.

A second mass mobilization in 613 provoked numerous rebellions in areas of the Sui empire that had been struck by flooding, and the campaign was interrupted by a major uprising not far from Luoyang itself. Persisting in what now seems to have become a personal obsession, Emperor Yang called for a third campaign in 614, even as his realm was disintegrating into open rebellion. He and his forces reached the Koguryo capital and elicited a promise from the king to submit. When this promise was not honored, the emperor commanded yet another campaign, but by this time virtually all of China was in open rebellion, and no forces responded to the emperor's call. As the country disintegrated into civil war, the emperor fled to his beloved south; in 618 he was murdered at Jiangdu by the son of his favorite general. In spite of his real achievements, Emperor Yang went down in Chinese history as a cruel megalomaniac who destroyed his dynasty.[10]

While the political debacle of Emperor Yang and the consequent collapse of the Sui can in part be attributed to failings of character, they also foreshadowed in miniature some basic structural tensions of late imperial Chinese geography. Emperor Yang's willingness to employ a classic strategy of division and domination against the Turks, while insisting, beyond reason, on the actual conquest of northern Korea, probably stemmed from his belief that nomads remained alien, while sedentary peoples belonged within the Chinese realm.[11] However, this same sedentary or mixed character of the northeastern peoples had allowed them to establish the Yan, Wei, Zhou, and Qi states in northern China and would later facilitate their resistance to China's repeated attempts to incorporate them into its realm. Consequently, most of the dynasties that conquered all or substantial parts of China during the late imperial period— the Liao, Jin, and Qing—came from the northeast. The military tensions between these people and China led to the establishment of Beijing, near the northeastern frontier, as the primary imperial capital.

While Emperor Yang unknowingly laid the initial infrastructure for a later political center in the northeast and made direct rule of that region central to his vision of China, he placed his own capital at the busy confluence of canals and rivers in Luoyang, and clearly favored life in the richer, more cultivated lower Yangzi, where he spent more and more of his time. He rejected the more strategically secure capital of Daxingcheng, the center of the Guanzhong region, which had been the local base for the ruling elite of the Northern Zhou and Sui states. Emperor Yang not only refused to dwell in the old capital region but he employed men from the Yangzi region as de facto chief ministers—the highest officials in his government. At the end of the dynasty, when his state was collapsing and officials urged him to retreat to the safer region of Guanzhong, the homeland of his best generals and troops, he still refused and opted instead for certain defeat and death in Jiangdu.[12]

Although Emperor Yang's commitment to the south seems to have been based on sensibility and emotion, the Yangzi region in subsequent centuries did become the demographic, economic, and cultural center of China. Thus the personal and political tragedy of Emperor Yang, torn between a military obsession with the northeast and a personal life centered on the south, prefigured in miniature the central geographic tension of late imperial China, divided between a militarily dominant north and an economically and culturally dominant south. However, between the tragedy of the Sui and the emergence of the basic elements of late imperial China lay the eventful history of the Tang dynasty.

DATES AND DYNASTIES

PRONUNCIATION GUIDE

NOTES

BIBLIOGRAPHY

ACKNOWLEDGMENTS

INDEX

DATES AND DYNASTIES

THE NORTHERN AND SOUTHERN DYNASTIES

196 First military colony established by Cao Cao
208 Cao Cao defeated at Red Cliff, ending possibility of reunification
220 Formal abdication of last Han ruler and beginning of the Wei;
        Nine-Rank system established
222 Wu state founded; beginning of the Three Kingdoms period
249 Sima *coup d'état*
265 Jin dynasty replaces the Wei
280 Jin conquers Wu and reunites China
300 Rebellions of the Eight Princes begin
304 Liu Yuan declares himself "King of Han"; first of the non-Chinese
        Sixteen Kingdoms
311 Sack of Luoyang; Jin court flees to Chang'an and to south
316 Sack of Chang'an
317 Jin court established in the south; beginning of Northern and
        Southern Dynasties
322 Wang Dun leads rebellion against the Jin court; first split of lower
        and central Yangzi
337 Establishment of Yan state, first of the northeastern "dual" states
347 Huan Wen conquers Sichuan
350 Ran Min massacres non-Chinese in Luoyang
354 Huan Wen invades the Guanzhong region; repulsed by Fu Jian
356 Huan Wen occupies Luoyang, which Jin holds until 365
369 Huan Wen fails in his final northern expedition but prepares to
        become emperor

376 Xie family establishes the Northern Headquarters Troops
381 Fu Jian completes the reunification of north China
383 Fu Jian's southern expedition fails, and his state soon collapses
386 Tuoba Gui founds the Dai state in the northeast
398 Tuoba Gui conquers the Murong; establishes Wei imperial capital
       at Pingcheng
399 Sun En's Daoist rebellion ravages the lower Yangzi region
402 Huan Xuan occupies Jiankang, purges the Northern Headquarters
       Troops commanders
404 Liu Yu defeats Huan Xuan; military men take control in the south
420 Liu Yu founds the Song dynasty; beginning of the southern
       dynasties
426 Northern Wei takes Chang'an, effectively reuniting the north
439 Northern Wei occupies the Gansu corridor, completing conquest
       of the north
442 Northern Wei establishes "Daoist Theocracy"
446 Northern Wei suppresses Buddhism
450 Purge of Han Chinese from the Wei court, following scandal of
       Cui Hao's history
459 Northern Wei begins construction of the Buddhist caves at
       Yungang
479 Qi dynasty supplants the Song in the south
485 Northern Wei initiates the equal-field system
493 Northern Wei Emperor Xiaowen moves capital to Luoyang,
       launches sinicization policies
494 Northern Wei begins construction of the Buddhist caves at
       Longmen
502 Liang dynasty supplants the Qi in the south; reign of Emperor Wu
       begins
523 Rebellion of the Northern Wei garrisons begins
528 Erzhu Rong occupies Luoyang, massacres court
535 Wei formally divided into two halves, with capitals in Ye and
       Chang'an
548 Hou Jing rebellion begins in the south
549 Jiankang falls; Emperor Wu dies; Western Wei restores Tuoba
       surnames
550 Northern Qi established; Western Wei creates the divisional army
557 Northern Zhou established; Chen dynasty begins in the south
574 Northern Zhou suppresses Buddhism

577 Northern Zhou reunites north China
581 Sui established following a *coup d'état*
589 Sui conquers Chen, reunites China
595 Nine-Rank system abolished
610 Grand Canal completed
612 First invasion of Koguryo
613 Second invasion of Koguryo; beginning of large-scale open
    rebellion
617 Li Yuan, the Tang founder, rebels in Taiyuan
618 Tang dynasty replaces the Sui

CHINESE DYNASTIES

Shang	ca. 1600–1027 B.C.
Zhou	1027–256 B.C.
Western Zhou	1027–771 B.C.
Eastern Zhou	771–256 B.C.
Spring and Autumn Period	722–481 B.C.
Warring States Period	481–221 B.C.
Qin	221–206 B.C.
Western (Former) Han	206 B.C.–A.D. 8
Xin	8–23
Eastern (Later) Han	23–220
Three Kingdoms (Wei, Sui, Wu)	220–280
Western Jin	265–317
Northern and Southern Dynasties	317–589
Sui	589–618
Tang	618–907
Five Dynasties	907–960
Song	960–1279
Northern Song	960–1126
Southern Song	1126–1279
Yuan	1279–1368
Ming	1368–1644
Qing	1644–1912

PRONUNCIATION GUIDE

Pronunciation is as in English unless noted below.

c	as *ts* in *nets*
ch	as in *chat*
g	as in *girl*
j	as in *jingle*
q	as *ch* in *cheese*
x	as *sh* in *sheer*
y	as in *year*
z	as *dz* in *adze*
zh	as *j* in *John*
a	as *e* in *pen* for yan, jian, qian, xian; otherwise as *a* in *father*
ai	as in *aye*
ang	as *ong* in *wrong*
ao	as *ow* in *now*
e	as *e* in *yet* in the combinations ye, -ie, -ue; otherwise as *e* in *the*
ei	as in *neigh*
en	as *un* in *fun*
eng	as *ung* in *rung*
er	pronounced as *are*
i	as in the *i* of *sir* after c, s, z; as in the *ir* of *sir* after ch, sh, zh, r
ie	as *ye* in *yet*
iu	as *yo* in *yoyo*
ong	as *ung* in German Achtung
ou	as in *oh*
u	after j, q, x, and y as *ui* in *suit;* otherwise as *u* in *rule*
ua	after j, q, x, and y as *ue* in *duet;* otherwise as *wa* in *water*
uai	as in *why*
ue	as *ue* in *duet*
ui	as in *way*
uo	similar to *o* in *once*

NOTES

Introduction

1. On Chu, see Lawton, ed., *New Perspectives on Chu Culture*; Li, *Eastern Zhou and Qin Civilizations*, ch. 10–11; Cook and Major, eds., *Defining Chu*. For Han population figures, see Bielenstein, "Wang Mang," pp. 240–242.

1. The Geography of North and South China

1. Skinner, "Marketing and Social Structures"; Skinner, "Regional Urbanization"; Skinner, "Cities and the Hierarchy of Local Systems." On regions in early imperial China, see Lewis, *Construction of Space*, ch. 4. On regions in the late Northern and Southern Dynasties, see Somers, "Time, Space, and Structure," pp. 379–380.

2. Tuan, *China*, pp. 85–86, 88–89; Yang, "Notes on the Economic History," p. 113. On the Yangzi in the Eastern Han, see de Crespigny, *Generals of the South*, ch. 1.

3. Wiens, *China's March*, pp. 100–104; Buchanan, *Transformation*, pp. 17–19. The latter has a table on p. 27 showing the shifting balance of registered population between north and south China.

4. Tuan, *China*, ch. 1; Buchanan, *Transformation*, ch. 2, 4; Tregear, *Geography*, ch. 1, 2, 4; van Slyke, *Yangtze*, 1–3.

5. Fragments of the Han agricultural manual list thirteen crops: spiked millet, glutinous millet, winter wheat, spring wheat, rice, soybeans, lesser beans, hemp, gourds, melons, taro, water-darnels, and mulberry trees. See Tuan, *China*, p. 81. Other texts refer to sorghum, oats, and barley. See Hsu, *Han Agriculture*, pp. 81–91.

6. Hsu, *Han Agriculture*, pp. 111–112.

7. Van Slyke, *Yangtze*, pp. 19–24.

8. Sage, *Ancient Sichuan.*

9. Schafer, *Vermilion Bird.*

10. Holcombe, *Genesis of East Asia,* pp. 13, 18–21.

11. Twitchett, "Monasteries and China's Economy," pp. 532–533. On regional variations of irrigation, see Needham and Bray, *Science and Civilisation:* Vol. 6, *Part II: Agriculture,* pp. 109–113.

12. de Crespigny, *Generals,* pp. 46–58, 311–312, 316–317, 319–323, 377–378, 383. On expansion south along the river lines sketched, see pp. 373–375.

13. Ibid., pp. 18–29, 213, 227, 237, 241–244, 251–258, 267–269, 289–293, 353–407.

14. Van Slyke, *Yangtze,* pp. 54–56; Tregear, *Geography,* pp. 58–61; *Li Bo ji,* p. 199. An earlier poem on the difficulties of the road to Shu was written by Cao Cao in the early third century. See Balazs, "Two Songs," pp. 183–184. On the difficulty of invading Shu, see de Crespigny, *Generals,* pp. 361–363, 369, 372, 376–377, 390–391, 482–483, 487.

15. Gernet, *Buddhism in Chinese Society,* pp. 116–141; Twitchett, "Monasteries and China's Economy," pp. 535–541; Zürcher, *Buddhist Conquest,* pp. 207–208; Ch'en, *Chinese Transformation,* pp. 125–132, provide examples of this phenomenon.

16. Gernet, *Buddhism,* pp. 142–152; Twitchett, "Monasteries and China's Economy," pp. 533–535; Ch'en, *Chinese Transformation,* pp. 131, 138, 151–158.

17. Lewis, *Construction of Space,* ch. 3–5; Lewis, *Writing and Authority,* ch. 8.

18. Ebrey, "Economic and Social History," pp. 626–648, esp. pp. 643 ff.; Lewis, *Construction of Space,* pp. 212–234.

19. Pearce, "Form and Matter," esp. pp. 173–177; Makeham, *Transmitters and Creators,* ch. 1–5, esp. pp. 156–167. The only monograph on commentaries on classics in the period is Kaga, *Chūgoku koten kaishaku shi.*

20. Lin, "Decline and Revival," pp. 135–145; Miao, *Early Medieval Chinese Poetry;* Connery, "Jian'an." On Eastern Han lyrics by named authors, see Holzman, "Premiers vers pentasyllabiques datés."

21. Xiao, *Wen xuan,* vol. 1, p. 339. See also Zhi Yu, "Discourse on the Development of Literary Genres," in Wang, *Early Chinese Literary Criticism,* pp. 63–64.

22. Xiao, *Wen xuan,* ch. 42, p. 925, cited in Spiro, *Contemplating,* pp. 74–75. For an earlier letter to this friend, see p. 924. On Cao Pi's theoretical writings, see Owen, *Readings,* pp. 57–72; Cutter, "To the Manner Born?" pp. 53–71.

23. Spiro, *Contemplating,* ch. 6.

24. Mather, tr., *New Account,* p. 126. Paul Rouzer uses this story to introduce his chapter "Competitive Community." See *Articulated Ladies,* pp. 73–74.

25. Cai, *Matrix,* pp. 95–103; Cutter, "Cao Zhi (192–232)," pp. 1–4.

26. Mather, tr., *New Account*. As examples, see pp. 34, 43, 50, 59, 64, 70, 72, 73, 82, 117, 141–142, 143, 144, 160, 173, 194–195, 202, 217, 218, 232, 239, 242–243, 264, 270–271, 302, 306–307, 332, 333, 360, 368, 373, 382, 387, 388, 389, 395, 397, 398, 402–403, 403–406, 414, 415 (2), 418, 424–425, 434–435, 437 (2), 439, 452.

27. For a complete, if idiosyncratic, study of the Orchid Pavilion gathering, see Bischoff, *Songs of the Orchis Tower*.

28. Needham, Lu, and Huang, *Science and Civilisation*, Vol. 6, *Part I: Botany*, pp. 111, 114, 359, 381, 385, 445–459, 488, 520, 531, 541–542; Campany, *Strange Writing*, pp. 49–52; Greatrex, *Bowu zhi*.

29. Zhou, *Wei Jin Nanbeichao shi lunji*, pp. 390–391, and Lü, "Liang Jin Liu Chao de shixue," pp. 351–352.

30. Kleeman, *Great Perfection*, pp. 108–112; Sage, *Ancient Sichuan*, pp. 10–14, 30, 39–43, 51–55, 76, 127, 138, 143, 171, 200. On the *Shui jing zhu*, see Strassberg, *Inscribed Landscapes*, pp. 77–90; Harley and Woodward, eds., *History of Cartography*, Vol. 2, *Book 2*, pp. 92–95; Needham and Wang, *Science and Civilisation*, Vol. 3, pp. 514, 609, 615, 620; Campany, *Strange Writing*, pp. 31, 44, 187–198.

31. Chen, *Biography of Ku K'ai-chih*. On Gu Kaizhi and landscape painting, see Sullivan, *Arts of China*, pp. 90–95. On Gu as conversationalist, wit, and poet, see Mather, tr., *New Account*, p. 542. On putting lines from Xi Kang's poetry into painting, see p. 368. On the impact and later mythology of Gu Kaizhi, see McCausland, *First Masterpiece*; Sullivan, *Birth of Landscape Painting*.

32. For Gu Kaizhi's remarks on painting, see Bush and Shih, eds., *Early Chinese Texts*, pp. 28–29, 32–36, 39. The passages are on p. 35. On his religious beliefs' relation to painting, see Spiro, "New Light"; Delahaye, *Les Premières peintures*, pp. 6–73.

33. Mather, tr., *New Account*, p. 368.

34. Vervoorn, *Men of the Cliffs and Caves*; Berkowitz, *Patterns of Disengagement*.

35. There are no studies in English of gardens in the Northern and Southern Dynasties. In Asian languages, see Ōmuro, *Enrin toshi*; Wei Jiazan, ed., *Suzhou lidai yuanlin*, pp. 18–49; Wu, *Liu chao yuan lin*; Hou, *Shi qin yu you jing*, pp. 15–36. For subsequent periods, see Yang, *Metamorphosis of the Private Sphere*; Hou, *Tang Song shiqi de gongyuan wenhua*; Hou, *Shi qin*. On gardens in later literati culture, see Clunas, *Fruitful Sites*; Xiao, *Chinese Garden as Lyric Enclave*.

36. Robinet, *Taoism*, pp. 115–119, 150–151, 189, 196; Strickmann, "Alchemy of T'ao Hung-ching"; Strickmann, "Mao Shan Revelations," pp. 3–6, 15–40; Strickmann, *Taoïsme du Mao chan*, pp. 21–57, 115–117.

37. On Hui Yuan and Mount Lu, see Ch'en, *Buddhism*, pp. 103–112; Zürcher, *Buddhist Conquest*, pp. 204–253, 258–263; Tsukamoto, *History of Early Chinese Buddhism*, pp. 759–898; Strassberg, *Inscribed Landscapes*, pp. 67–71.

38. On the religious transformation of mountains by Daoism and Buddhism, see Kleeman, "Mountain Deities in China." On Buddhists who retired to the mountains, see Miyakawa, *Rikuchō shi kenkyū: seiji shakai hen*, pp. 279–288; Berkowitz, *Patterns*, pp. 141–144, 207–217, 238–241; von Glahn, *The Sinister Way*, pp. 87–97. On poetry about mountains as sacred space, see Kroll, "Verses from on High."

39. Strickmann, "Mao Shan Revelations"; Strickmann, *Taoïsme du Mao chan*.

40. On Faxian, see Ch'en, *Buddhism*, pp. 89–91. Boulton, "Early Chinese Buddhist Travel Records," pp. 44–79; Legge, tr., *Record of Buddhistic Kingdoms*. Northern India as the "middle kingdom" is on p. 28. On making China a Buddha realm, see Sen, *Buddhism, Diplomacy, and Trade*, pp. 1–101.

41. Owen, *Remembrances*, ch. 2.

42. Owen, *Great Age*, pp. 147–182; Owen, ed. and trans., *Anthology*, pp. 459–460. On the female frontier captive, see Rouzer, *Articulated Ladies*, pp. 175–200; Frankel "Cai Yan"; Marney, *Chiang Yen*, pp. 132–134.

43. Lewis, *Construction of Space*, p. 387 n. 197; "Record of Wu," quoted in *Taiping yu lan*, ch. 156, pp. 3a–b; Graham, '*Lament for the South*,' pp. 83, 139.

2. The Rise of the Great Families

1. Ebrey, "Economic and Social History," pp. 630–637; Dien, "Introduction."

2. Chen, *Hsün Yüeh*, pp. 19–23. For a Chinese narrative, see de Crespigny, tr., *Emperor Huan and Emperor Ling*. On *qing yi* see Holcombe, *In the Shadow*, pp. 74, 77–78; Tang, "Voices of Wei-Jin Scholars," pp. 118–131.

3. For political background, see Chen, *Hsün Yüeh*, ch. 2–3. On claims to superiority over the emperor, see Chen, "Confucian Magnate's Idea of Political Violence"; Yü, "Individualism," pp. 122–124. On the shift between the Eastern Han elite and the later "great families," see Yang, "Great Families," esp. pp. 125–133.

4. Ebrey, "Economic and Social History," pp. 637–648; Ebrey, "Toward a Better Understanding." See also Mao, "Evolution."

5. Wu, *Wu Liang Shrine*; Liu, Nylan, and Barbieri-Low, *Recarving China's Past*.

6. Ebrey, "Economic and Social History," pp. 645–646.

7. Hendrischke, "Early Daoist Movements," pp. 135–139, 147–157; Michaud, "Yellow Turbans"; Stein, "Remarques."

8. For a Chinese narrative, see de Crespigny, tr., *To Establish Peace*.

9. Chen, *Hsün Yüeh*, pp. 40–47.

10. Ibid., pp. 47–58, esp. pp. 49, 57.

11. There is no substantial published treatment of Cao Cao in a European language. On his rise, see Leban, "Ts'ao Ts'ao." The best treatment remains Kroll, "Portraits." On his poetry, see also Chang, "Generic Transformation," ch. 1; von

den Steinen, "Poems of Ts'ao Ts'ao." In Chinese, see Wang, *Cao Cao*; Guo, ed., *Cao Cao lun ji*. In Japanese, see Takeda, *Sō Sō*.

12. Chen, *Hsün Yüeh*, p. 58–65; Goodman, *Ts'ao P'i*, pp. 4–13; de Crespigny, *Generals*, pp. 241–250.

13. de Crespigny, *Generals*, ch. 4. On northerners' difficulties in river combat, see pp. 434–437.

14. Ibid., ch. 5–6. On the Daoist state in Sichuan, its defeat by Cao Cao, and its role in Wei politics, see Kleeman, *Great Perfection*, pp. 65–81; Goodman, *Ts'ao P'i*, ch. 4.

15. de Crespigny, *Generals*, ch. 7.

16. For a useful summary, see Holzman, *Poetry and Politics*, ch. 1, esp. pp. 7–18. For a more detailed examination, see Goodman, *Ts'ao P'i*, pp. 45–55.

17. de Crespigny, *Generals*, pp. 482–485.

18. Tang, *Wei Jin Nanbeichao shi luncong*, pp. 3–29; de Crespigny, *Generals*, pp. 493–513.

19. Miyazaki, *Kyūhin kanjinhō*; Miyakawa, *Rikuchō shi kenkyū: seiji shakai*, pp. 263–338; Tang, "Jiupin zhongzeng," in *Wei Jin Nanbeichao shi luncong*; Holzman, "Les débuts"; Grafflin, "Reinventing China"; Declercq, *Writing Against the State*, pp. 134–151; and Holcombe, *In the Shadow*, pp. 78–84.

20. Qian, *Spirit and Self*, pp. 29–36; Kroll, "Portraits," pp. 17–24. This translates "Edicts on Seeking the Worthy," in which the passages appear.

21. Tang, "Voices," pp. 116–132.

22. Shyrock, tr., *Study of Human Abilities*, pp. 95, 98, 99, 120, 132. See Qian, *Spirit and Self*, pp. 34, 67–68, 113–117, 155–156; Spiro, *Contemplating*, pp. 71–74; Mou, *Caixing yu xuanli*, pp. 43–66.

23. Qian, *Spirit and Self*, pp. 20–24, 44–47.

24. Liu Shao even employed the technical term *ji* "seed, pivot." See *Human Abilities*, pp. 130, 136–137. On *ji* in earlier traditions, see Lewis, *Sanctioned Violence*, pp. 117, 119–121, 291 n. 82.

25. Qian, *Spirit and Self*, pp. 34–35.

26. Ch. 1, nn. 21, 22.

27. *San guo zhi*, quoted in Spiro, *Contemplating*, pp. 73–74. Other memorials to and decrees from Cao Rui are translated in Fang, *Chronicle of the Three Kingdoms*, pp. 314–316, 533–538, 562; Tang, "Voices," pp. 140–145. These show Cao Rui's hostility to the "superficial and elegant [*fu hua*]," which was linked with cliques. See Tang, *Wei Jin Nanbeichao shi*, pp. 94–99.

28. Holcombe, *In the Shadow*, pp. 4–5, 79–80.

29. Declercq, *Writing*, pp. 120, 123–124, 175–178; Tang, "Voices," pp. 173–174; Holzman, *Poetry and Politics*, pp. 9–25, 34, 48, 51–53, 61, 88; Holzman, *La vie et la pensée*, pp. 28–30, 39–40, 42–43, 46–51.

30. Tang, *Wei Jin Nanbeichao shi*, pp. 118–126. One critical essay written after 290 is translated and discussed in Declercq, *Writing*, ch. 4.

31. Declercq, *Writing*, pp. 148–151, 172–174.

32. Ibid., pp. 171–174, 178, 220–224. Declercq describes Huangfu Mi, who declined to take an examination, and Xiahou Zhan, who failed to advance after a good hereditary appointment, took an examination, and wound up demoted and reduced in local rank.

33. Grafflin, "Reinventing China," pp. 150–154.

34. See, for example, Johnson, *The Medieval Chinese Oligarchy*, p. 19: "But no subject is more important for understanding the dynamics of Chinese society than the system of official recruitment. The reason is obvious: unlike England or France, where a man could rise to a position of high social status through a career in law, medicine, commerce, the Church, or the military, in China there was only one significant occupational hierarchy: the civil service. There was no alternative open to the man who wished to raise his social status."

35. Balazs, "Nihilistic Revolt or Mystical Escapism." See also Wu, *The Poetics of Decadence*, ch. 1–2; Xu, *Balanced Discourses*, p. xvii; Holcombe, *In the Shadow*, pp. 34–42, 87–93, 127–129; Tang, "Voices," p. 11—on the ideas of Miyazaki Ichisada, pp. 140–145, which show that the idea that such practices were frivolous and decadent existed in the third century. Even positive formulations, such as Yü Ying-shih's description of the "discovery of the individual," treat it as a matter of personal interests or moral character. See "Individualism." On the construction of the "individualism" of the period through using established literary tropes, see Rouzer, *Articulated Ladies*, ch. 3, esp. pp. 78–85; Diény, "Lecture de Wang Can (177–217)."

36. Holcombe, *In the Shadow*, pp. 42–56; Tanigawa, *Medieval Chinese Society*, pp. 87–126; Johnson, *Medieval Chinese Oligarchy*, pp. 114–116.

37. Shyrock, tr., *Human Abilities*, pp. 113–116, 126–127. On links between the *Study of Human Abilities* and the Nine Rank system, see Tang Yongtong, "*Du Ren wu zhi,*" in *Wei Jin xuan xue lun gao*, pp. 3–22; Tang Yiming, "Voices," pp. 154–156; Spiro, *Contemplating*, pp. 70–74; Qian, *Spirit and Self*, pp. 33–36.

38. Tang, *Wei Jin Nanbeichao shi*, pp. 289–297. This link between *qing yi* and *qing tan* is discussed in English in Balazs, "Nihilistic Revolt," pp. 227–232; Tang, "Voices," pp. 116–140; Qian, *Spirit and Self*, pp. 20–42.

39. Qian, *Spirit and Self*, pp. 3–8.

40. Mather, tr., *New Account*, p. 258.

41. Qian, *Spirit and Self*, pp. 3–4, 44–60. On the Wei-Jin elite as a "competitive community," see Rouzer, *Articulated Ladies*, ch. 3. An example of a competitive recitation is in Spiro, *Contemplating*, p. 109.

42. Mather, tr., *New Account*, p. 458.

43. On "cultivated tolerance," see Mather, tr., *New Account*, pp. 179–195; Rouzer, *Articulated Ladies*, pp. 101–110. In another anecdote, a man's ability to remain calm when forced to change clothing in the presence of women shows that he would "make a good rebel." See Mather, tr., *New Account*, p. 459.

44. Mather, tr., *New Account*, p. 190. On the centrality to the *New Account* of the rivalry between Xie An and Huan Wen, see Spiro, *Contemplating*, pp. 104–114. See also Diény, *Portrait anecdotique*.

45. On the unreliability of these accounts, see Holzman, *Poetry and Politics*, pp. 13–14. For an account of leading figures, see Tang, "Voices," pp. 144–159.

46. Berkowitz, *Patterns*, ch. 4, esp. pp. 128–130.

47. This genre emerged in the Han, but most surviving examples date from later. See Declercq, *Writing Against the State*.

48. Spiro, *Contemplating the Ancients*, esp. pp. 75–86; Tang, "Voices," pp. 160–173; Holzman, *Poetry and Politics*; Holzman, *La vie et la pensée*; Holzman, "Les Sept Sages."

49. On evolving Jin policies toward the literati and great families, see Declercq, *Writing*, pp. 123–132. For the revival of pure conversation and Dark Studies, see Tang, "Voices," pp. 174–192; Declercq, *Writing*, pp. 261–262, 277, 299–306. On the poetry of the period, see Lai Chiu-mi, "River and Ocean."

50. Graff, *Medieval Chinese Warfare*, pp. 44–47; Declercq, *Writing Against the State*, pp. 129–131.

51. Mao, "Evolution," pp. 90–93; Graff, *Medieval Chinese Warfare*, pp. 76–79. For exhaustive treatments of leading families, see Miscevic, "A Study of the Great Clans"; and Bielenstein, "The Six Dynasties: Vols. 1 and 2."

52. On the northern elite at its highest levels in relation to the Wei court, see Dien, "Elite Lineages."

3. Military Dynasticism

1. Crowell, "Government Land Policies and Systems," ch. 4; Tang, "Clients," pp. 114–115; Tang, *Wei Jin Nanbeichao shi luncong*, pp. 37–43; Wang, *Wei Jin Nanbeichao*, pp. 41–43, 123–130; de Crespigny, *Generals*, pp. 287, 313–318, 322, 325, 327, 335, 339, 389, 473–475.

2. Graff, *Medieval Chinese Warfare*, p. 39.

3. Chen Yinke, "'Tao hua yuan ji' pang zheng"; Wang, *Wei Jin Nanbeichao*, pp. 38–39, 320–321, 326, 331, 462–463; Holcombe, *In the Shadow*, pp. 42–49, 56–57; Tanigawa, *Medieval Chinese Society*, pp. 102–110; Kwong, *Tao Qian*, ch. 3; Graff, *Medieval Chinese Warfare*, pp. 55–56, 58, 61, 63, 66, 81, 85; Kawakatsu, *Rikuchō kizokusei shakai*, pp. 120–127; Miyakawa, *Rikuchō shi kenkyū: seiji shakai*, pp. 437–471.

4. Tang, *Wei Jin Nanbeichao shi luncong*, pp. 3–29; Wang, *Wei Jin Nanbeichao*, pp. 99–109; de Crespigny, *Generals*, pp. 463–524; Kawakatsu, *Rikuchō kizokusei shakai*, pp. 157–164.

5. *Jin shu*, quoted in Tang, *Wei Jin Nanbeichao shi luncong*, p. 41.

6. *San guo zhi*, "Wu zhi," and *Baopuzi wai pian*, quoted in Tang, *Wei Jin Nanbeichao shi luncong*, p. 25. See also Tang, "Clients," pp. 114–117.

7. Yang, "Evolution of the Status of 'Dependents,'" pp. 143–155.

8. Tang, "Clients," pp. 117–118.

9. De Crespigny, *Northern Frontier,* pp. 407–416.

10. Dien, "Study of Early Chinese Armor," pp. 37–38; Dien, *Six Dynasties Civilization,* ch. 6; Graff, *Medieval Chinese Warfare,* p. 41–42.

11. Goodrich, "Riding Astride," pp. 288, 293–294, 295, 297, 299–300, 304, plates 3, 8–10. Tomb figurines with clearly structured saddles date from A.D. 186–219.

12. Dien, "Stirrup," pp. 33–35, 37; Graff, *Medieval Chinese Warfare,* pp. 42–43.

13. Graff, *Medieval Chinese Warfare,* pp. 41–42.

14. Ibid., pp. 43–44.

15. Ibid., pp. 79–80; Holcombe, *In the Shadow,* pp. 25–29; Wang, *Wei Jin Nanbeichao,* pp. 318–330; Kawakatsu, *Rikuchō kizokusei shakai,* pp. 22–28.

16. Tang, "Clients," p. 119; Graff, *Medieval Chinese Warfare,* pp. 80–81.

17. Grafflin, "Great Family," pp. 71–73; Spiro, *Contemplating,* pp. 110–121.

18. Mather, tr., *New Account,* p. 45.

19. Graff, *Medieval Chinese Warfare,* pp. 86, 122–128. See also Wang, *Wei Jin Nanbeichao,* pp. 332–338.

20. *Jin shu,* quoted in Wang, *Wei Jin Nanbeichao,* p. 341 n. 13.

21. Mather, tr., *New Account,* p. 139. "Given Wen's current prestige, it seems he will achieve great things, but as I see it he will certainly achieve nothing. Why? The Jin ruling house is in decline, and Wen completely controls the state. The ministers of Jin are not necessarily in agreement with him, so for Wen to attain his ambitions is not desired by most of them. They will certainly betray and obstruct him, so as to ruin his enterprise." See Wang, *Wei Jin Nanbeichao,* p. 338.

22. Mao, "The Evolution in the Nature of the Medieval Genteel Families," pp. 92–95; Holcombe, *In the Shadow,* pp. 56–58; Mather, tr., *New Account,* p. 304.

23. Mather, tr., *New Account,* pp. 57, 58, 304, 410–411.

24. Apart from the anecdote at the end of Chapter 2, his admiration for Xie An is also demonstrated in Mather, tr., *New Account,* pp. 237, 261. His admiration for ritual scholarship appears on p. 61.

25. Spiro, *Contemplating,* pp. 117–119.

26. Tang, "Clients," pp. 120–122.

27. Crowell, "Northern Emigres"; On Huan Wen's residence determination, see pp. 191–193.

28. Graff, *Medieval Chinese Warfare,* pp. 84–85; Wang, *Wei Jin Nanbeichao,* pp. 279, 356–357.

29. Yen, *Family Instructions,* pp. 129–130. On contempt for military service

among old families of the southern dynasties, see Wang, *Wei Jin Nanbeichao*, p. 405.

30. Wang, *Wei Jin Nanbeichao*, p. 277. A stimulating, speculative account of the motives for the anti-military program in the *New Account* is Kawakatsu, *Rikuchō kizokusei shakai*, pp. 327–347.

31. Graff, *Medieval Chinese Warfare*, pp. 82–83.

32. Ibid., pp. 86–87; Wang, *Wei Jin Nanbeichao*, pp. 360–364. On the religious background, see Miyakawa, "Local Cults around Mount Lu."

33. Graff, *Medieval Chinese Warfare*, pp. 87–88, 90–92; Wang, *Wei Jin Nanbeichao*, pp. 391–395, 404–410; pp. 405–407 lists commanders who rose from humble background during the southern dynasties. Miyakawa, *Rikuchō shi kenkyū: seiji shakai*, pp. 394–395.

34. Spiro, *Contemplating*, pp. 124–126; Graff, *Medieval Chinese Warfare*, p. 88; Wang, *Wei Jin Nanbeichao*, pp. 404–418; Tang, *Wei Jin Nanbeichao shi luncong xu bian*, pp. 93–123; Miyakawa, *Rikuchō shi kenkyū: seiji shakai*, pp. 384–398.

35. There are no discussions in English. See Kawakatsu, *Rikuchō kizokusei shakai*, pp. 349–405. There is a good discussion of the level and forms of trade in Han, *Nanbeichao jingji shi tan*, pp. 154–179.

36. Wang, *Wei Jin Nanbeichao*, pp. 410–411.

37. Again, there are no discussions in English. See Kawakatsu, *Rikuchō kizokusei shakai*, pp. 407–435; Kawakatsu, *Chūgoku no rekishi: Vol. 3*, pp. 236–242. See also Kawakatsu, "La Décadence de l'aristocratie"; Wang, *Wei Jin Nanbeichao*, pp. 479–480, 487–496.

38. Graff, *Medieval Chinese Warfare*, pp. 87–89; Wang, *Wei Jin Nanbeichao*, pp. 391–398, 441–457. There are no discussions of the changing patterns of armies in English. See Kawakatsu, *Chūgoku no rekishi*, pp. 239–240; Kawakatsu, *Rikuchō kizokusei shakai*, pp. 354–357, 380–395, 425; Miyakawa, *Rikuchō shi kenkyū: seiji shakai*, pp. 555–584. The quotation is on p. 582. On the militarization of local branches of great families, see Wang, *Wei Jin Nanbeichao*, pp. 461–464.

39. Pearce, "Who, and What, was Hou Jing?"; Graff, *Medieval Chinese Warfare*, p. 89; Wallacker, "Studies in Medieval Chinese Siegecraft." For a narrative, see Wang, *Wei Jin Nanbeichao*, pp. 446–457. For social and economic background, see Kawakatsu, *Rikuchō kizokusei shakai*, pp. 349–405, 421–427.

40. Graff, *Medieval Chinese Warfare*, pp. 89, 121–122, 125, 132–135. For a narrative, see Wang, *Wei Jin Nanbeichao*, pp. 458–461, 464–467. See also Kawakatsu, *Rikuchō kizokusei shakai*, pp. 427–432.

41. On the earliest nomad polity known to the Chinese, see Di Cosmo, *Ancient China and Its Enemies*, pp. 167–190. For later examples, see Millward, "Qing Inner Asian Empire," pp. 95–96. On the Sixteen Kingdoms period, see

Barfield, *Perilous Frontier*, pp. 97–118; Graff, *Medieval Chinese Warfare*, pp. 54–69. In non-Western languages, see Wang, *Wei Jin Nanbeichao*, pp. 234–317; Tang, *Wei Jin Nanbeichao shi luncong*, pp. 127–192; Tanigawa, *Zui Tō teikoku keisei*, pp. 25–67.

42. Schreiber, "History of the Former Yen"; Klein, "Contributions of the Fourth Century Xianbei States."

43. Graff, *Medieval Chinese Warfare*, pp. 64–66.

44. Honey, "Sinification and Legitimation."

45. Rogers, *The Chronicle of Fu Chien*. This annotated translation and critical study of Fu Jian's biography in the *Jin shu* is substantial scholarship, but not always reliable. The author examines the political re-writing of the account, but he goes so far as to argue that no battle took place, so that the rapid collapse of Fu Jian's empire remains unexplained, except by "internal tensions" which were present from the beginning. Moreover, Rogers postulates a "Tang stratum" composed in the seventh century. However, virtually all the elements of this supposed Tang stratum figure in fragments of the *Chronicle of the Sixteen Kingdoms*. Since the *Chronicle* was written before the Tang, the Tang stratum does not exist.

46. Graff, *Medieval Chinese Warfare*, pp. 55–61.

47. The difficulty of distinguishing ethnic identity in this period has been emphasized in recent years. See Pearce, Spiro, and Ebrey, "Introduction," pp. 14–20; Spiro, "Hybrid Vigor"; Pearce, "Form and Matter," pp. 151–156, 177; Wong, "Ethnicity and Identity." See also Wang, *Wei Jin Nanbeichao*, pp. 468–475, which makes the same point for the south.

48. On the Tuoba victory, see Graff, *Medieval Chinese Warfare*, pp. 69–73.

49. There are no systematic treatments in English. Brief discussions appear in Barfield, *Perilous Frontier*, pp. 118–119; Eberhard, *A History of China*, pp. 137–138. In Asian languages, see Wang, *Wei Jin Nanbeichao*, pp. 512–516; Tang, *Wei Jin Nanbeichao shi luncong*, pp. 203–227; Tanigawa, *Zui Tō teikoku keisei*, pp. 123–129; Kawakatsu, *Chūgoku no rekishi*, pp. 304–309.

50. There are no discussions in English. In Asian languages, see Kawakatsu, *Chūgoku no rekishi*, pp. 309–312; Tanigawa, *Zui Tō teikoku keisei*, pp. 129–134, 188–212; Yan, *Zhongguo difang xingzheng*, vol. 3, pp. 691–797; Zhou, *Wei Jin Nanbeichao shi lunji*, pp. 215–238.

51. Brief discussions in English are Barfield, *Dangerous Frontier*, pp. 124–125; Graff, *Medieval Chinese Warfare*, pp. 97–99. On linking the leading families of the Xianbei and the Chinese, see Dien, "Elite Lineages"; and his "Introduction," pp. 22–23. In Asian languages see Wang, *Wei Jin Nanbeichao*, pp. 536–556; Tang, *Wei Jin Nanbeichao shi luncong xu bian*, pp. 132–154; Tanigawa, *Zui Tō teikoku keisei*, pp. 138–160.

52. Jenner, *Memories of Loyang*, p. 86; Tang, *Wei Jin Nanbeichao luncong*, pp. 414–426.

53. Graff, *Medieval Chinese Warfare*, pp. 98–106; Jenner, *Memories*, pp. 38–102; Wang, *Wei Jin Nanbeichao*, pp. 563–591; Tanigawa, *Zui Tō teikoku keisei*, pp. 177–217. On the Yuwen regime and its military forces, see Pearce, "The Yü-wen Regime." There are no comparable studies of the eastern state.

54. Dien, "Role of the Military."

55. Graff, *Medieval Chinese Warfare*, p. 108. Graff's discussion derives from Japanese scholarship summarized in Tanigawa, *Zui Tō teikoku keisei*, pp. 219–257. Granting Xianbei surnames to incorporate Han Chinese and other non-Xianbei peoples is discussed in Dien, "The Bestowal of Surnames."

56. The Chinese and Japanese secondary literature is summarized in Graff, *Medieval Chinese Warfare*, pp. 108–111. See also Wang, *Wei Jin Nanbeichao shi*, pp. 612–622.

4. Urban Transformation

1. Birrell, *Popular Songs and Ballads*, p. 154. For other poems mentioning cities, see pp. 132, 134, 136–137, 142, 157, 159–160, 162–163, 166–167, 168.

2. Waley, *Translations from the Chinese*, pp. 37–48; Watson, *Chinese Lyricism*, pp. 15–32 (omitting six poems). For studies, see Cai, *Matrix*, ch. 3; Diény, *Les dix-neufs poèmes anciens*, pp. 161–187. Diény also translates the poems into French.

3. See also Owen, *Mi-lou*, pp. 19–24.

4. Diény, *Les dix-neufs poèmes*, pp. 30–31.

5. Watson, *Chinese Lyricism*, pp. 24–25.

6. Cai, *Matrix*, pp. 62–72.

7. Lewis, *Construction of Space*, pp. 240–243. For archaeological evidence of cities in the different regions, see Dien, *Six Dynasties Civilization*, ch. 2.

8. Chang, "Description of Landscape"; Chang, *Six Dynasties Poetry*, ch. 2–3; Holzman, *Landscape Appreciation*, esp. ch. 4–5; Owen, *Readings*, pp. 277–286.

9. Xiao, *Wen xuan*, vol. 1, pp. 373–375. The translation is based on Knechtges, *Wen Xuan*, vol. 1, pp. 373–374.

10. Xiao, *Wen xuan*, vol. 1, pp. 385, 387, 389, 393, 395, 397, 399–401, 403, 405–421, 423, 425.

11. Ibid., vol. 1, pp. 429–433, 456–465. The limited, barbaric natures of the capitals of Shu and Wu are reiterated on pp. 471–475.

12. Ibid., vol. 1, pp. 467–469.

13. Balazs, *Le Traité économique*, p. 267; Xiao, *Wen xuan*, pp. 429–431, introductory note. More detailed is Miyakawa, *Rikuchō shi kenkyū: seiji shakai*, pp. 537–546.

14. Yen, tr., *Family Instructions*, pp. 18–19. On the Northern Qi city of Ye, see Zhu, "The Capital City Ye," pp. 111–114.

15. *Bei shi*, ch. 8, p. 302.

16. Thorp and Vinograd, *Chinese Art and Culture*, pp. 152–154; Steinhardt, *Chinese Imperial City Planning*, pp. 80–82; Jenner, *Memories*, pp. 40–42.

17. Needham and Menzies, *Science and Civilisation*, Vol. 6, Part III: *Agro-Industries and Forestry*, pp. 549–565. Xie Lingyun speaks of forest on the mountains of Guiji several decades later. See Westbrook, "Landscape Description," p. 302. For lists of the types of trees, see pp. 257–258.

18. The interlinked development of mountain forest, villa, and garden is the theme of Ōmuro, *Enrin toshi* and its companion volume, *Tōgen no musō*. There are no treatments in English.

19. Berkowitz, *Patterns*, pp. 238–241. Analogies between the condition of the traditional hermit and primitive men are noted by Xie Lingyun's commentary to his "Rhapsody on Dwelling in the Mountains." See Westbrook, "Landscape Description," p. 197; Lewis, *Sanctioned Violence*, pp. 167–174. For Confucius's remark, see *Analects*, p. 91. On animals as companions, see also Mather, tr., *New Account*, p. 60.

20. For intellectual background and a complete, annotated translation, see Westbrook, "Landscape Description," ch. 3–4.

21. Westbrook, "Landscape Description," p. 186. These equivalences, and the superiority of the mountain to the garden, are stated by Xie. See Westbrook, pp. 196–198, 278. A chapter of the *New Account* is also devoted largely to living in mountains as a mode of social activity. See Mather, pp. 331–339; also pp. 115, 288.

22. Westbrook, "Landscape Description," pp. 239–244, 270, 307–309. On landscaping hillsides and streams, see pp. 253–255, 287–297.

23. Ibid., pp. 270–286, 304, 312–316. See also Mather, "Landscape Buddhism."

24. Zhongchang Tong's discussion is translated in Ebrey, "Economic and Social History," p. 624; Balazs, "Political Philosophy and Social Crisis," pp. 215–216; and Hightower, "*Fu* of T'ao Ch'ien," pp. 217–218. For Xie Lingyun's discussion of Zhongchang Tong, see Westbrook, "Landscape Description," pp. 199–200.

25. Wilhelm, "Shih Ch'ung and his Chin-ku-yüan." The preface to the series is translated on p. 326, and in Mather, tr., *New Account*, pp. 264–265. On the depiction of Shi Chong in *New Account*, see Rouzer, *Articulated Ladies*, pp. 105–110. On links to the more celebrated "Preface on the Orchid Tower," and a translation of that preface, see Mather, tr., *New Account*, pp. 321–322. On the preface, its different versions, and its translations, see Bischoff, *Songs of the Orchis Tower*, pp. 25–50.

26. Spiro, *Contemplating*, pp. 104–119; Berkowitz, *Patterns*, p. 143; Tang, "Voices," pp. 238–248, 252–256; Diény, *Portrait anecdotique d'un gentilhomme chinois, Xie An*.

27. This garden is mentioned in Mather, tr., *New Account,* pp. 60, 194. For other references in this work to gardens, urban hermitages, and stands of trees or bamboos planted around homes, see pp. 205, 235, 388, 398, 426, 455, 456.

28. Jansen, *Höfische Öffentlichkeit,* pp. 25–26, 56–58, 66–70, 78–83. On Shen Yue's suburban estate, see Mather, *The Poet Shen Yüeh (441–513),* ch. 8. For Xie Tiao's "Rhapsody on Visiting a Private Garden," see Chang, *Six Dynasties Poetry,* pp. 113–115. For Yu Xin's poem, see Watson, *Chinese Rhyme-Prose,* pp. 103–109. In addition to these gardens, the historical records also refer to an imperial Pleasure Wandering Garden, a Fragrant Forest Garden, a Fragrant Herb Garden, a New Forest Garden built under the Qi, and another dozen named gardens built in various cities under the Liang.

29. Mather, tr., *New Account,* p. 398.

30. On Dai Kui and Dai Yong's art in relation to Buddhism and a depiction of the Seven Worthies, see Rhie, *Early Buddhist Art:* Vol. 2, pp. 94–98, 203–206.

31. Bush and Shih, *Early Chinese Texts,* pp. 21–22, 36–38, 337–338; Delahaye, *Les premières peintures,* pp. 76–84.

32. Wang, *Shaping the Lotus Sutra,* pp. 77, 407 n. 24.

33. Jenner, *Memories,* p. 173; Yang, *Record,* pp. 58–59.

34. Han, *External Forms and Internal Visions,* pp. 76–80 has collected and paraphrased relevant passages. On the garden competition of the imperial clan, their wives, and their affines at Longevity Hill, see Jenner, *Memories,* pp. 241–244; Yang, *Record,* pp. 191–196.

35. Jenner, *Memories,* p. 189; Yang, *Record,* p. 92.

36. Ho, "Portraying the Family," pp. 478–479, 490, 492–493.

37. Ho, "Loyang. A.D. 495–534." On the evolution of capital design between the Han and the Wei, emphasizing Buddhist temples, see Yang, "Changes in Urban Architecture," pp. 27–28. On the Tuoba Wei's adaptation of Han ritual structures at Luoyang, see Xiong, "Ritual Architecture."

38. Tsukamoto, *History,* pp. 135, 180; Rhie, *Early Buddhist Art,* Vol. 1, p. 107. On the career of Fotudeng, see Ch'en, *Buddhism,* pp. 79–80; Rhie, Vol. 2, pp. 245–253; Wright, "Fo-t'u-teng: A Biography." For records of temples associated with him, see Rhie, Vol. 2, pp. 251–252.

39. Rhie, Vol. 2, pp. 16, 18, 252–253, 304, 310, 363, 404. On miraculous images in the south, see Rhie, Vol. 2, pp. 41–59, 83–176; Shinohara, "Quanding's Biography of Zhiyi," pp. 154–218. On the relation of Daoan and Huiyuan to image worship, see Ch'en, *Buddhism,* pp. 100–101, 106–108; Zürcher, *Buddhist Conquest,* pp. 194–195, 212, 219–229; Tsukamoto, *History,* pp. 753–756, 844–869.

40. See Caswell, *Written and Unwritten,* ch. 1; Soper, "Imperial Cave-Chapels of the Northern Dynasties"; Soper, *Literary Evidence,* pp. 123–139.

41. On the *Lotus Sutra*'s influence on Chinese Buddhist art and architecture, see Wang, *Shaping.* On the prevalence of the image from the *Lotus Sutra,* see

pp. 3–11. On southern pagodas, see Rhie, Vol. 2, pp. 67–69; Soper, "South Chinese Influence." On early pagodas in the north, as well as the first Yongning Temple, see Caswell, *Written and Unwritten,* pp. 17, 19, 32, 33; Rhie, Vol. 1, pp. 61–64; Vol. 2, p. 301; Lai, "Society and the Sacred," pp. 240–242.

42. Jenner, *Memories,* pp. 141–142; Yang, *Record,* pp. 5–6. For Bodhidharma's remark, see Jenner, p. 151; Yang, pp. 20–21. On a foreign monk describing the city as a Buddha land, see Jenner, p. 208. On transforming China into a Buddha realm, see Sen, *Buddhism, Diplomacy, and Trade,* ch. 2. On speeches of foreign monks cited as part of this process, see pp. 79–86.

43. Lai, "Society and the Sacred," pp. 243–246, citing the statistics of Hattori Katsuhiko.

44. Ibid., pp. 231–235, 262–264.

45. Ibid., pp. 245–246.

46. Jenner, *Memories,* p. 193; Yang, *Record,* pp. 98–99.

47. Jenner, *Memories,* pp. 171, 240–241; Yang, *Record,* pp. 55–56, 189–190. For an account of these and other tales from the book, including stories of ghosts and fox spirits as well as statues, see Lai, "Society and the Sacred," pp. 246–261. For stories of wonder-working statues and stupas in south China, as well as accounts of image worship by monks and lay people, see Rhie, Vol. 2, pp. 26–54, 64–96, 112–115, 137–143, 147–153. On images and their powers, see Kieschnick, *The Impact of Buddhism,* pp. 52–80.

48. Jenner, *Memories,* p. 165; Yang, *Record,* pp. 45–46.

49. Jenner, *Memories,* p. 208; Yang, *Record,* pp. 126–127.

50. Jenner, *Memories,* pp. 147–151; Yang, *Record,* pp. 13–20. The figures given indicate a height of 296 meters, rivaling the Eiffel Tower. More plausible figures of 145 meters or 118 meters appear in other texts.

51. Jenner, *Memories,* pp. 151–163; Yang, *Record,* pp. 21–41.

52. In addition to the Buddha's Birthday and the feast day for washing statues, another major Buddhist holiday that entailed mass public gatherings was the Ghost Festival celebrated on the fifteenth day of the seventh lunar month. See Teiser, *The Ghost Festival in Medieval China.* On its observance in the Northern and Southern Dynasties, see pp. 48–58.

53. The most detailed accounts of the Yungang caves and inscriptions are Soper, *Literary Evidence,* pp. 123–139; Soper, "Imperial Cave-Chapels"; and Caswell, *Written and Unwritten.* On the related Longmen caves, which were close to Luoyang, see Caswell, pp. 33–38, and the entries listed in his index. Emphasis on securing a better rebirth for kin also dominates ideas about the uses of the *Lotus Sutra* and transformation texts as reflected in medieval Chinese tales and poetry. See Wang, *Shaping,* pp. xiv–xvi, xxi–xxii. On evidence from steles, see Wong, *Chinese Steles,* ch. 4–10. On the urban origins of most steles, see pp. 73, 91, 106–107, 135, 153. On the public nature of the steles, and their relation to a broader class of patron, see, for example, p. 178.

54. Mather, tr., *New Account,* pp. 51, 55, 74, 108, 109, 112, 122, 410.

55. On adoration and charity by tens of thousands in Jiankang, see Rhie, Vol. 2, p. 71. On the miraculous statue of Xiangyang, see p. 84. For other accounts of monasteries, images, and mass worship in the south, see pp. 23–29, 34–39, 41–46, 53–57, 61–84, 88–96, 98–111, 137–140, 143–144; Zürcher, *Buddhist Conquest,* pp. 104–105, 117, 129, 147–154, 187–195, 199–202. On the *Biography of Eminent Monks* and the genre it established, see Kieschnick, *The Eminent Monk.*

56. Janousch, "The Emperor as Bodhisattva"; Janousch, "The Reform of Imperial Ritual during the Reign of Emperor Wu." See also Tsukamoto, *History,* pp. 389–403.

57. The only systematic study in English of land policies from Han through Tang is Crowell, "Government Land Policies," which, like the standard Chinese studies, omits northern China between the Jin and the Northern Wei.

58. Grafflin, "Reinventing China," p. 163.

59. Jenner, *Memories,* pp. 19–37, 103–126. On Buddhist buildings in Pingcheng, see Rhie, Vol. 2, pp. 300–302. Pingcheng is the subject of a Japanese monograph, now translated into Chinese, of which the last three chapters are devoted to its economic character. See Maeda, *Heijō no rekishi chirigaku kenkyū.* The economies of Tuoba Wei capitals is also discussed in Han, *Nanbeichao jingji,* part 2, ch. 4. Finally, Miyakawa, *Rikuchō shi kenkyū: seiji shakai,* ch. 8 surveys the capitals of the period.

60. Liu, "Jiankang and the Commerical Empire," which is based on Liu, *Liuchao de chengshi yu shehui.* On the ruin of the great familes, see Kawakatsu, *Rikuchō kizoku shakai,* part 3, ch. 3.

5. Rural Life

1. Shih, *A Preliminary Survey of the Book Ch'i Min Yao Shu.* The same author also produced the best Chinese edition of the work. See also Needham and Bray, *Science and Civilisation:* Vol. 6, *Part II: Agriculture. Essential Methods* is introduced on pp. 55–59. References to individual tools, plants, and techniques are scattered throughout the book.

2. Shih, *Preliminary Study,* p. 2. Part of the same passage and an additional section is translated in Bray, *Agriculture,* p. 56.

3. Three hundred Han *mu* was about thirty-four acres, and Tang *mu* about fifty. Northern Wei *mu* are thought to have been closer to the Tang unit, but somewhere in between the two.

4. Crowell, "Government Land Policies," pp. 303–308. On the small size of Chinese farms as compared to those in the West, see also Bray, *Agriculture,* pp. 429–432.

5. Bray, *Agriculture,* pp. 96–97.

6. Ibid., p. 190; Crowell, "Government Land Policies," pp. 298–299.

7. Bray, *Agriculture,* pp. 221–228, 231–240; Shih, *Preliminary Survey,* pp. 40–41, 48.

8. Bray, *Agriculture,* pp. 288, 329–330, 343–345. A longer version appears in Shih, *Preliminary Survey,* pp. 42–43.

9. Bray, *Agriculture,* pp. 247–248, 498; Shih, *Preliminary Survey,* pp. 43–44.

10. Bray, *Agriculture,* pp. 254–256, 263, 270, 272, 276–277, 308, 443–446.

11. Ibid., pp. 279–281, 285–286, 314, 318.

12. Ibid., pp. 291–294; Shih, *Preliminary Survey,* pp. 44–46.

13. Bray, *Agriculture,* pp. 429–432, 464; Shih, *Preliminary Survey,* pp. 52–53.

14. Bray, *Agriculture,* pp. 378–402; Shih, *Preliminary Survey,* pp. 53–54.

15. Shih, *Preliminary Survey,* pp. 23–27, 49–63; Bray, *Agriculture,* pp. 510–552.

16. Bray, *Agriculture,* pp. 477–510; Bray, *The Rice Economies.* On other major cereals in the early period, see Bray, *Agriculture,* pp. 423, 429–430, 441–443, 446–448, 472, 474.

17. Bray, *Agriculture,* pp. 495, 497–498, 504–505.

18. Bray, *Agriculture,* pp. 587–615 sketches the history of rural China in terms of the impact of rice. Although this exaggerates the size of estates in early imperial China, their resemblance to European estates, and the degree of labor substitution undertaken by landlords, it provides insights into the impact of rice cultivation on later rural society.

19. Gernet, *Buddhism,* pp. 142–152; Ch'en, *Chinese Transformation,* pp. 151–158.

20. Tuan, *China,* pp. 90–91. On Chinese tea processing and its peasant basis, see Needham, Daniels, and Menzies, *Agro-Industries and Forestry,* pp. 477–478. There is a disputed Han reference to "boiling tea," but the question of nomenclature remains unresolved. See Kieschnick, *The Impact of Buddhism,* pp. 262–265. The same book describes the spread of tea culture, and its relation to Buddhism, on pp. 265–275.

21. Jenner, *Memories,* p. 215; Wang, *Record,* pp. 141–142.

22. Mather, tr., *New Account,* pp. 72–73, 407, 422–423, 481. Other anecdotes contrast north and south in terms of topography, pronunciation, scholarship, and political acumen. See pp. 65, 77, 78, 105, 260, 408, 417.

23. Mather, tr., *New Account,* p. 473. Pp. 407–408 tells how Wang Dao was mocked because his only skill was his ability to speak the Wu (southern) dialect. For another anecdote of his linguistic endeavors, see p. 86. On the importance of dialectical variations, see Mather, "Note on the Dialects of Lo-yang and Nanking." The classic discussion is Chen, "Dong Jin Nanchao zhi Wu yu."

24. Yen, *Family Instructions,* p. 19.

25. Ibid., p. 189.

26. Chen, "Cong shi shi lun *Qie yun,*" and "Dong Jin Nanchao zhi Wu yu."

27. Tang, "Menfa de xingcheng ji qi shuailuo," and *Wei Jin Nanbeichao Sui Tang shi san lun*, pp. 159–178; Mao, "Evolution," pp. 100–103. This contrast is sketched in Ebrey, *Aristocratic Families*, pp. 24–27.

28. *Song shu* and *Nan shi*, quoted in Mao, "Evolution," p. 102. I have followed the *Song shu*.

29. Ebrey, *Aristocratic Families*, pp. 22, 126 n. 25.

30. *Wei shu* 47, p. 1062; 48, p. 1089; 68, p. 1520.

31. For other descriptions of such situations, see *Wei shu* 110, p. 2855; *Jin shu* 127, p. 2170.

32. *Wei shu* 71, pp. 1571–1572.

33. *Taiping guangji*, ch. 247, p. 511. For an anecdote celebrating a northern family because "whenever there was some delicacy, until everyone had gathered they would not eat" and "even distant kin shared a common pot," see *Wei shu* 58, p. 1302.

34. *Song shu* 82, p. 2097. For other examples of divided families and hostility between kin, see ch. 59, p. 1609; ch. 89, p. 2229.

35. Tang, "Clients," and Yang, "Evolution of the Status of 'Dependents.'"

36. On the military contrast between north and south, see Tang, "Menfa de xingcheng," pp. 7–10. On the de-militarization of "genteel" families, see Mao, "Evolution," pp. 92–95.

37. *Wei shu* 33, pp. 773–774.

38. Ebrey, *Aristocratic Families*, pp. 52–53, 63–64.

39. *Wei shu*, quoted in Ebrey, *Aristocratic Families*, p. 57.

40. Ebrey, *Aristocratic Families*, pp. 55–61, 64–65.

41. Ibid., pp. 64–83.

42. Ibid., pp. 55, 83–86.

43. *Xin Tang shu* 199, p. 5679; quoted in Mao, "Evolution," p. 101.

44. The only detailed discussion in English is Crowell, "Government Land Policies," pp. 151–171.

45. Ibid., pp. 183–216.

46. On Southern dynasties land policies, see ibid., pp. 235–273.

47. The only detailed treatment is Sakuma, *Gi Shin Nanbokuchō suirishi*. This has a seven-page English summary at the back.

48. This follows Ch'en, *Buddhism*, pp. 154–158; Gernet, *Buddhism*, pp. 100–107, 111–112, 127–128.

49. *Wei shu* 114, p. 3037, quoted in Gernet, *Buddhism*, p. 100.

50. Gernet, *Buddhism*, pp. 98–100, 103, 112–126.

51. In addition to the discussion in Crowell, see also Xiong, *Emperor Yang*, pp. 180–182. For the institution in the Tang, see Xiong, "The Land-tenure System of Tang China."

52. Tao's writings on farm life are discussed in Kwong, *Tao Qian*, ch. 7. A more critical assessment, based on examination of textual variants, is Tian, *Tao*

Yuanming and Manuscript Culture, ch. 3. The complete writings are translated in A. R. Davis, tr., *T'ao Yüan-ming,* 2 vols.

53. A few contemporaries such as Xie Lingyun also wrote about village life, but largely in the voice of sympathetic officials rather than fellow farmers. See Holzman, "Xie Lingyun et les paysans."

54. On Tao as recluse, see Berkowitz, *Patterns,* pp. 205–226; Kwong, *Tao Qian,* part I; Chang, *Six Dynasties Poetry,* pp. 16–37. For a skeptical treatment, see Tian, *Tao Yuanming and Manuscript Culture,* ch. 3.

55. Davis, *T'ao Yüan-ming,* vol. 1, p. 58. See also p. 46 poem 2: "I always fear the coming of frost or hail, when my crops will be scattered like the weeds"; pp. 77, 85, 90. I have modified Davis's translations in accordance with my reading of the Zhonghua edition of Tao's collected poems.

56. Davis, *T'ao Yüan-ming,* vol. 1, p. 46 poem 3. This adapts lines from a Han poem by Yang Yun (d. 56 B.C.), thus representing more the result of reading than of experience. See Tian, *Tao Yuanming,* p. 248 n. 25.

57. Davis, *T'ao Yüan-ming,* vol. 1, p. 46 poem 3. On the length of the working day, see also p. 24 poem 3, p. 93.

58. Ibid., vol. 1, p. 58 poem 8, p. 132. On the toil and dangers of farming, see also pp. 93, 94.

59. Kwong, *Tao Qian,* pp. 143–144. On Zhong Rong's views of Tao Qian's verse and his attitude to Tao's being a "farmer" poet, see Yeh and Walls, "Theory, Standards, and Practice," p. 44; Xiao, *Wen xuan,* vol. 1, pp. 40–41.

60. Davis, *T'ao Yüan-ming,* vol. 1, p. 46 poem 2.

61. Ibid., vol. 1, p. 47 poem 5, p. 64 poems 1 and 2, pp. 80, 94, 106, p. 132 poem 8.

62. Ibid., vol. 1, p. 12 poems 1 and 2, p. 14 poem 2, p. 15 poem 4, pp. 49, 57, 60, 63, p. 64 poem 2, pp. 65, 88, 95–102 (poems 1–20), 106–107, 108–110, 114, p. 154 poem 1.

63. Ibid., vol. 1, pp. 67–68 poem 1.

6. China and the Outer World

1. Barfield, *Perilous Frontier,* ch. 2–3; Holcombe, *Genesis of East Asia,* pp. 109, 119–133.

2. Barfield, *Perilous Frontier,* ch. 2–3; Holcombe, *Genesis of East Asia,* pp. 109, 119–133.

3. Barfield, *Perilous Frontier,* pp. 96–99.

4. Honey, "Sinification and Legitimation," ch. 4–5; Barfield, *Perilous Frontier,* pp. 99, 101–103; Graff, *Medieval Chinese Warfare,* pp. 56–63.

5. Schreiber, "History of the Former Yen"; Barfield, *Perilous Frontier,* pp. 106–114.

6. Barfield, *Perilous Frontier,* pp. 111–112; Perdue, *China Marches West.*

7. *Wei shu* 35, pp. 817–818, quoted in Barfield, *Perilous Frontier,* p. 122. Barfield attributes this speech to "a military man" refuting a Chinese courtier, but it is actually made by the leading Chinese scholar Cui Hao, who was later executed for casting aspersions on the early Tuoba rulers in his history.

8. Barfield, *Perilous Frontier,* pp. 131–150; Molè, *Tü-yü-hun;* Holcombe, *Genesis,* pp. 114–115; Yu, "History of the Relationships," ch. 4–9. The struggle between the Wei and Rouran is summarized on pp. 303–307. See also Miller, *Accounts of Western Nations.*

9. *Zizhi tong jian,* quoted in Holcombe, *Genesis,* p. 23. See also pp. 38–52 on China as a "civilization" marked by a set of texts and rituals that could be adopted by others.

10. A useful, if sometimes eccentric, discussion is Mair, "The North(west)ern Peoples and the Recurrent Origins of the 'Chinese' State."

11. Holcombe, *Genesis,* pp. 56–60. Wang, *Ambassadors from the Islands of Immortals,* ch. 2; Barnes, *China, Korea, and Japan,* pp. 241–245. On Himiko, see Piggott, *Emergence of Japanese Kingship,* ch. 1.

12. Holcombe, *Genesis,* pp. 165–170; Yu, "Han Foreign Relations," pp. 446–451; Barnes, *China, Korea, and Japan,* ch. 13.

13. Holcombe, *Genesis,* pp. 173–175.

14. Ibid., pp. 176–178. On Japanese recruitment of Chinese people as diplomats to China, see Wang, *Ambassadors,* ch. 9.

15. Wang, *Ambassadors,* pp. 17–19, 28–29, 221–222; Holcombe, *Genesis,* pp. 190–191.

16. Holcombe, *Genesis,* pp. 186–193.

17. Piggott, *Emergence,* ch. 3, 6; Holcombe, *Genesis,* pp. 201–206. On the refraction of Chinese ideas through acculturation in Japan, see Pollack, *The Fracture of Meaning.*

18. Holcombe, *Genesis,* pp. 194–196, 206–214.

19. Traced in Holcombe, *Genesis,* ch. 6; Yu, "Han Foreign Relations," pp. 451–457.

20. The idea of a cultural sphere defined by using Chinese graphs is discussed in Holcombe, *Genesis,* pp. 60–77, 192–197.

21. The best documented city-state is Kucha, as described in Liu, *Kutscha und seine Beziehungen zu China.* For a briefer treatment, along with discussions of Karashahr, see Rhie, Vol. 2, pp. 578–600, 720–731.

22. Examples are Faxian (see Legge, tr., *Record of Buddhistic Kingdoms*), Song Yun (see Yang, *Record,* pp. 205–206, 215–248), Xuanzang (see *The Great Tang Dynasty Record of the Western Regions;* Wriggins, *Xuanzang;* Eckel, *To See the Buddha,* pp. 4–6, 11–21, 51–65, 131–143), and Yijing (I-ching; *A Record of Buddhist Religion;* I-ching, *Chinese Monks in India*). For a more complete list, see Tsukamoto, *History,* pp. 430–438. On Tang pilgrims, see Ch'en, *Buddhism,* pp. 233–240.

23. Liu, *Silk and Religion*, traces the use of silk in Buddhism, Christianity, and Islam, in association with its role in international trade.

24. Exotics and their uses are described in Schafer, *The Golden Peaches of Samarkand*.

25. Kieschnick, *Impact of Buddhism*, pp. 222–249.

26. Ibid., pp. 164–185; Needham and Tsien, *Science and Civilisation*, Vol. 5, Part 1: *Paper and Printing*, pp. 8–9, 45–47, 86–87, 135–136, 149–159.

27. Liu, *Ancient India and Ancient China*.

28. Ibid., pp. 88–92. Schopen's essays are collected in *Bones, Stones, and Buddhist Monks; Buddhist Monks and Business Matters;* and *Figments and Fragments of Mahāyāna Buddhism in India*.

29. Liu, *Ancient India and Ancient China*, pp. 92–99; Liu, *Silk and Religion*, p. 41; Wang, *Shaping*, pp. 4, 89, 96, 124, 125–127, 141, 144–145, 153, 278, 379. See also Qiang, "Patrons of the Earliest Dunhuang Caves," pp. 505–506.

30. Mather, tr., *New Account*, p. 462. On the evidence of Shi Chong's Buddhist faith, see Tsukamoto, *History*, pp. 177–179.

31. Liu, *Ancient India and Ancient China*, pp. 54–57.

32. Ibid., pp. 57–64.

33. Ibid., pp. 64–75; Liu, *Silk and Religion*, ch. 2. On the symbolism of the purple robe, and Buddhist debates about using silk, see Kieschnick, *Impact of Buddhism*, pp. 98–103. On trade in cotton, see Sen, *Buddhism, Diplomacy, and Trade*, p. 186.

34. Liu, *Ancient India and Ancient China*, pp. 84–85.

35. Liu, *Silk and Religion*, pp. 69–72.

36. Quoted in Sen, *Buddhism, Diplomacy, and Trade*, p. 190.

37. Sen, *Buddhism, Diplomay, and Trade*, pp. 44, 190–192; Liu, *Silk and Religion*, pp. 41–48; Kieschnick, *Impact of Buddhism*, pp. 29–52.

38. *Biographies of Eminent Monks*, quoted in Zürcher, *Buddhist Conquest*, p. 104. On Srimitra not speaking Chinese, see Mather, tr., *New Account*, p. 50. On his fame for casting spells, see Kieschnick, *Eminent Monk*, pp. 84, 94. Both these points are discussed in Tsukamoto, *History*, pp. 323–326.

39. Sen, *Buddhism, Diplomacy, and Trade*, pp. 6–12; Wang, *Shaping*, p. 125.

40. Zürcher, *Buddhist Conquest*, ch. 5; Kohn, *Laughing at the Tao*, introduction; Chen, *Buddhism*, pp. 137–144, 184–185, 191.

41. Jenner, *Memories*, p. 249; Yang, *Record*, p. 204.

42. Bokenkamp, *Ancestors and Anxiety*, pp. 40–41, 99–101.

43. Keischnick, *Eminent Monk*, pp. 87–90; Spiro, "Hybrid Vigor," pp. 144–145.

44. Sen, *Buddhism, Diplomacy, and Trade*, pp. 160–165, 169–176; Schafer, *Golden Peaches*, pp. 20–21; Rong, "Migrations and Settlements."

45. Rong, "Migrations and Settlements"; de la Vaissière, *Sogdian Traders;* de la Vaissière, *Les Sogdiens en Chine;* Part III of *Monks and Merchants*, pp. 220–

270. An excellent survey in Chinese is Rong, *Zhonggu Zhongguo yu wailai wenming*, pp. 17–180.

46. Enoki, "Nationality of the Ephtalites"; Tremblay, *Pour une histoire de la Sérinde*, pp. 183–188.

47. *Monks and Merchants*, pp. 222–223.

48. Dien, "The *'Sa-pao'* Problem Re-examined"; Rong, *Zhonggu Zhongguo yu wailai wenming*, pp. 169–180.

49. There are no good discussions in English. Probably the best accounts are Kawamoto, *Gi Shin Nanbokuchō jidai no minzoku*, pp. 413–442 and Zhou, "Nanchao jingnei gezhong ren," in *Wei Jin Nanbeichao shi lunji*, pp. 33–101.

50. *China: Dawn of a Golden Age*, pp. 11, 27–28, 212–215.

51. On the political uses of the *Rituals of Zhou* in this period, see Pearce, "Form and Matter." For its uses in Han-foreigner relations, see Kawamoto, *Gi Shin Nanbokuchō jidai no minzoku*, pp. 367–410.

52. *Monks and Merchants*, pp. 62–65, 69–71, 77–81, 90–93, 144–147, 298–299; Pearce, Spiro, and Ebrey, "Introduction," p. 15.

53. Spiro, "Hybrid Vigor."

7. Redefining Kinship

1. On the predominance throughout this period of the individual household, partible inheritance, and multiple households of greater lineages living together, see Johnson, *Medieval Chinese Oligarchy*, pp. 112–116. On three-generation households, see Ho, "Portraying the Family," pp. 463–464, 471–472; Knapp, *Selfless Children*, ch. 1.

2. On the Han development of family cemeteries, see Wu, *Wu Liang Shrine*, pp. 33–37; Wang, *Han Civilization*, pp. 210–211; Liu, Nylan, and Barbieri-Low, *Recarving China's Past*, pp. 561–577; Wu, *Monumentality*, ch. 4.

3. Kieser, "Northern Influence"; Hua, "The Eastern Jin Tombs," pp. 292–293.

4. Ho, "Portraying the Family," p. 468; Zheng, "A Preliminary Study," p. 424.

5. Xiao, *Wen xuan*, vol. 3, p. 181; Davis, tr., *T'ao Yüan-ming*, vol. 1, pp. 56–57.

6. Ch'en, *Chinese Transformation*, pp. 139–141.

7. On the *Qingming* festival, see Ebrey, "Early Stages," pp. 20–29. On its prehistory and origins, see Holzman, "Cold Food Festival."

8. Translated in Hsu, *Han Agriculture*, p. 216.

9. Knoblock and Riegel, tr., *Annals of Lü Buwei*, pp. 78–79. On bans on fire and sex at the summer solstice, see Bodde, *Festivals in Classical China*, pp. 289–316. The fire taboo is on pp. 290–291, 294–302. The sexual taboo is on p. 292.

10. Ebrey, "Early Stages," p. 21.

11. Johnson, *Oligarchy*, p. 97.

12. Ebrey, "Early Stages," pp. 29–34.

13. For Han examples, see Yen, *Family Instructions*, pp. x–xi. On Yan Zhitui, see Yen, *Family Instructions*, pp. xiv–xxxii; Dien, "Yen Chih-t'ui." On his ideas, see Yoshikawa, *Rikuchō seishin shi kenkyū*, pp. 263–302.

14. Yen, *Family Instructions*, ch. 2, 5, 8–9.

15. Ibid., p. 29. Another account of customs at parting indicates that southerners wept profusely, while northerners were lighthearted and even laughed. See p. 31. On taboos of names in the period, see also p. 95.

16. Yen, *Family Instructions*, pp. 29–30, 32.

17. Ibid., p. 137.

18. Ibid., pp. 22, 74, 92, 96, 111, 126, 128, 198.

19. Ibid., pp. 47, 57, 63, 77, 78, 193, 195–196.

20. Ibid., pp. 52–55, 61, 64.

21. Ibid., p. 2.

22. Johnson, *Oligarchy*, p. 104.

23. Mather, tr., *New Account*, pp. 64, 158–159, 186–187, 199–200, 201, 202–203, 208, 213, 227, 234, 238, 268, 297, 298–299, 344, 417.

24. Johnson, *Oligarchy*, pp. 100–101.

25. Ibid., pp. 101–102.

26. Ibid., pp. 98, 103–104, 110.

27. Ibid., p. 118. On one attempt to formalize the definition of the leading families, see Dien, "Elite Lineages."

28. Wu, "Buddhist Elements"; Wu, *Wu Liang Shrine*, pp. 134–141; Abe, *Ordinary Images*, ch. 2; Dien, "Developments in Funerary Practices," especially pp. 516, 521–523, 526–530, 534 for references to the use of the Buddha image on funerary jars. On a later tomb in what is now North Korea that incorporated Buddhist images in a similar manner, see Li, "Buddhist Images in Burials," pp. 502–505.

29. Soper, *Literary Evidence*, pp. 9–10.

30. Abe, *Ordinary Images*, pp. 110–123. On funerary texts from this time and place on banners, jars, and other objects, see Ning, "Patrons," pp. 514–517.

31. Abe, *Ordinary Images*, pp. 123–150.

32. Ibid., pp. 156–160, 162–165, 167–171.

33. Wang, *Shaping*, pp. 29–46; Abe, *Ordinary Images*, pp. 297–305.

34. Abe, *Ordinary Images*, pp. 270–295. The artistic combination of Buddhism and Daoism, specifically the use of imagery from Daoist texts to depict Buddhist heavens, is discussed in Wang, *Shaping*, pp. 154–170.

35. Ning, "Patrons," pp. 496–510, 517–518.

36. Wang, *Shaping the Lotus Sutra*, pp. 24–27.

37. Caswell, *Written and Unwritten*, pp. 36–39; Matsubara, *Chūgoku bukkyō chokoku*, plates 10–103a; Tsiang, "Disjunctures of Time, Text, and Imagery," pp. 319, 321, 323–324, 343.

38. Liu, "Art, Ritual, and Society," pp. 24–26, 32–33.

39. Wang, *Shaping the Lotus Sutra*, pp. 75–77. On the Tang caves, see Ning, *Art, Religion, and Politics in Medieval China: The Dunhuang Cave of the Zhai Family.*

40. Steinhardt, "From Koguryo to Gansu and Xinjiang." For the reverse process of tomb painting affecting Buddhist cave décor, see Fraser, *Performing the Visual,* pp. 100–102.

41. Teiser, *Ghost Festival;* Cole, *Mothers and Sons in Chinese Buddhism.*

42. Teiser, *Ghost Festival,* pp. 48–56. On the mythic background, see pp. 113–139.

43. On the centrality of the mother-son tie in the early story, see Teiser, *Ghost Festival,* pp. 130–134. On the story's evolution, see Cole, *Mothers and Sons;* Lai, "Father in Heaven, Mother in Hell." On Mulian in contemporary Daoist rituals securing the departure of kin who died an unhappy death, see Lagerwey, *Taoist Ritual,* ch. 13. For visits to the underworld loosely patterned on the story, see Ahern, *Cult of the Dead,* pp. 228–244. On the ritual plays, see Johnson, ed., *Ritual Opera, Operatic Ritual;* Johnson, "Mu-lien in Pao-chüan."

44. Ho, "Portraying the Family."

45. Ibid., pp. 472–479. On conventional tales of filial piety in the service of patriarchy, see Knapp, *Selfless Children.* The story of Guo Ju also figures on a lacquered Northern Wei coffin.

46. Ho, "Portraying the Family," pp. 479–494.

47. Several articles on female power in the Northern Wei are in Holmgren, *Marriage, Kinship and Power in Northern China.* The role of imperial women in the earlier Three Kingdoms period is examined in Cutter and Crowell, tr., *Empresses and Consorts.*

48. On Buddhist nuns, see Tsai, tr., *Lives of the Nuns.* On Daoist nuns and priestesses, see Kohn, *Monastic Life,* pp. 80–86; Cahill, *Transcendence and Divine Passion,* ch. 6; Kirkland, *Taoism,* pp. 135–142. On Tang princesses becoming Daoist nuns, see Benn, *Cavern-Mystery Transmission,* ch. 1; Cahill, *Transcendence and Passion,* pp. 216–218. On Daoist women becoming saints, see Cahill, "Smell Good and Get a Job." On aspects of their role, including founding lineages, see Despeux, "Women in Daoism," pp. 384–391.

49. Cahill, "Material Culture and the Dao"; Idema and Grant, *The Red Brush,* pp. 153–163, 189–195. There is also a huge body of Daoist verse attributed to female immortals in such revealed texts of the period as the *Zhen gao.*

50. Wong, "Women as Buddhist Art Patrons"; Liu, "Art, Ritual, and Society," pp. 34–35.

51. Tsai, tr., *Lives of the Nuns,* pp. 49–50.

52. On Miaoshan, see Dudbridge, *The Legend of Miaoshan.* On Chen Jinggu, see Berthier, *The Lady of Linshui.*

53. On the "Mysterious Woman," see Cahill, *Divine Traces,* pp. 70–75. On the revelation of Shangqing scriptures by the woman Wei Huacun, and later ex-

amples of female revelations, see Robinet, *Taoism,* pp. 115–116; Kirkland, *Taoism,* pp. 96, 136–139.

54. On the Queen Mother of the West as a divine transposition of the household matriarch, see Liu, Nylan, and Barbieri-Low, *Recarving China's Past,* p. 577.

55. Cahill, *Transcendence and Divine Passion,* pp. 32–58 on her roles in the Northern and Southern Dynasties, and ch. 2–6 on those in the Tang. On stories of Emperor Wu, see pp. 43–58; Campany, *Strange Writing,* pp. 318–321; Smith, "Ritual and the Shaping of Narrative."

56. Rouzer, *Articulated Ladies,* ch. 2.

8. Daoism and Buddhism

1. Miller, *Daoism,* ch. 1.

2. Harper, *Early Chinese Medical Literature,* pp. 112–118, 124–125; Puett, *To Become a God,* pp. 239–245; Holzman, "Immortality-Seeking"; Wu, *Wu Liang Shrine,* pp. 122–140; Loewe, *Ways to Paradise;* Robinet, *Taoism,* pp. 48–50.

3. Csikszentmihàlyi, "Traditional Taxonomies"; Lewis, *Sanctioned Violence,* pp. 98–103, 112; Lewis, *Writing and Authority,* ch. 6; Seidel, "Imperial Treasuries and Taoist Sacraments," pp. 291–323; Robinet, *Taoism,* pp. 70–74.

4. Anna Seidel and Ursula-Angelika Cedzich argued that Daoism introduced the first Chinese paradigm of salvation. See Seidel, "Early Taoist Ritual"; Seidel, "Chronicle of Taoist Studies," p. 237; Cedzich, "Ghosts and Demons, Law and Order." Peter Nickerson modified their argument, suggesting that Daoism adopted the world of the "tomb ordinance" texts, but supplemented it with new rituals of salvation. See Nickerson, "'Opening the Way'"; and "Taoism, Death, and Bureaucracy."

5. On the Queen Mother and her cult in Han literature and art, see Loewe, *Ways to Paradise,* ch. 4; Cahill, *Transcendence and Divine Passion,* pp. 11–32.

6. Kaltenmark, "Ideology of the T'ai-p'ing ching"; Tsuchiya, "Confession of Sins"; Robinet, *Taoism,* ch. 3; Hendrischke, "Early Daoist Movements," pp. 143–159.

7. In addition to the above references, see Kleeman, *Great Perfection,* pp. 66–85.

8. Goodman, *Ts'ao P'i,* ch. 4. On the Cao family's attitudes to Daoism, see also Holzman, "Immortality-Seeking," pp. 111–114; Holzman, "Ts'ao Chih and the Immortals."

9. Kleeman, *Great Perfection,* ch. 3.

10. Robinet, *Taoism,* ch. 4; Campany, *To Live as Long as Heaven and Earth,* pp. 18–97. The latter is the most detailed study in English of Ge Hong's writings. For a translation of the "Inner Chapters" dealing with immortality, see Ware, *Alchemy, Medicine, and Religion.*

11. Campany, *To Live as Long,* pp. 75–80. Ge's arguments against other

stances on immortality are on pp. 82–85. Withdrawal into the mountains and modes of self-defense there are described on pp. 60–75.

12. Harper, *Early Chinese Medical Literature*, pp. 110–147; Despeux, "Gymnastics"; Campany, *To Live as Long*, pp. 21–31.

13. On the variety of alchemical theories and procedures, see Campany, *To Live as Long*, pp. 31–47, 81–82; Akahori, "Drug Taking and Immortality"; Pregadio, "Elixirs and Alchemy"; Miller, *Daoism*, ch. 6; Strickmann, "Alchemy of T'ao Hung-ching."

14. Strickmann, "Mao Shan Revelations." On the "Highest Clarity" tradition, see Robinet, *Taoism*, ch. 5; Robinet, "Shangqing—Highest Clarity."

15. Translated in Bokenkamp, *Early Daoist Scriptures*, p. 320.

16. Analyses of a few cases are given in Bokenkamp, *Ancestors and Anxiety*, ch. 4–5. A fuller examination of Daoist healing practices is Strickmann, *Chinese Magical Medicine*, ch. 1.

17. Stein, "Religious Daoism and Popular Religion"; Kleeman, "Licentious Cults and Bloody Victuals."

18. Mather, "K'ou Ch'ien-chih and the Taoist Theocracy"; Kohn, "The Northern Celestial Masters"; Stein, "Religious Daoism and Popular Religion," pp. 62–65.

19. Zürcher, *Buddhist Conquest*, ch. 1; Ch'en, *Buddhism*, ch. 2; Tsukamoto, *History*, ch. 2; Wu, "Buddhist Elements."

20. Zürcher, *Buddhist Conquest*, ch. 3; Ch'en, *Buddhism*, ch. 3; Tsukamoto, *History*, ch. 6.

21. Zürcher, *Buddhist Conquest*, ch. 4; Ch'en, *Buddhism*, pp. 79–83, 103–112; Tsukamoto, *History*, ch. 5, 8.

22. Zürcher, *Buddhist Conquest*, pp. 104–113; Ch'en, *Buddhism*, pp. 73–77, 121–124; Ch'en, *Chinese Transformation*, pp. 65–81; Tsukamoto, *History*, pp. 331–338, 350–354.

23. Janousch, "The Emperor as Bodhisattva"; Gernet, *Buddhism*, pp. 266–267.

24. Forte, *Political Propaganda and Ideology*.

25. Ch'en, *Buddhism*, ch. 6; Ch'en, *Chinese Transformation*, pp. 81–116.

26. Lai, "Society and the Sacred." The story quoted is on pp. 252–253.

27. Ch'en, *Buddhism*, pp. 165–177; Caswell, *Written and Unwritten*, pp. 21–39; Liu, *Ancient India and Ancient China*, pp. 162–167.

28. Abe, *Ordinary Images*; Lingley, "Widows, Monks, Magistrates, and Concubines"; and Liu, "Art, Ritual, and Society."

29. Lai, "Earliest Folk Buddhist Religion in China."

30. This follows Gernet, *Buddhism*, ch. 9.

31. In addition to Gernet, *Buddhism*, pp. 259–277, see also Abe, *Ordinary Images*, pp. 208–230.

32. Zürcher, "Buddhist Influence on Early Taoism"; Abe, *Ordinary Images*,

ch. 5; Wang, *Shaping*, pp. 41–44. See also the works by Bokenkamp cited below on the Lingbao tradition.

33. Zürcher, "Prince Moonlight," p. 7; Zürcher, "Buddhist Influence," pp. 117, 123, 128.

34. Translated in Hurvitz, tr., *Scripture of the Lotus Blossom*, p. 243.

35. Wang, *Shaping*, pp. 219–237. These pages also discuss other texts and images dealing with apocalyptic scenarios.

36. Nattier, "Meanings of the Maitreya Myth," esp. pp. 30–32. See also Tokuno, "Evaluation of Indigenous Scriptures," pp. 41–42.

37. Zürcher, "Prince Moonlight." On the "Daoist" dates see pp. 21–22. See also Strickmann, *Chinese Magical Medicine*, ch. 2.

38. Nattier, *Once Upon a Future Time*. Chapter 4 focuses on China. On the leading sixth-century advocate of the doctrine, see Magnin, *La vie et l'oeuvre de Huisi*. On the early votive stupa, see Abe, *Ordinary Images*, pp. 141–145, 158–160.

39. Ledderose, "Thunder Sound Cave," pp. 240–246, 255.

40. Orzech, *Politics and Transcendent Wisdom*. On the centrality of the king, see pp. 61–74, 94–97, 99–107. On the incorporation of Buddhism into the state in esoteric Buddhism, see pp. 160–167, 170–174.

41. Hubbard, *Absolute Delusion, Perfect Buddhahood*; Lewis, "Suppression." Chapter 3 of Hubbard's book elaborates the impact of Daoism on Buddhist apocalyptic doctrines. On the Inexhaustible Treasury, see also Gernet, *Buddhism*, pp. 210–217.

42. Scharf, *Coming to Terms with Chinese Buddhism*, Introduction, esp. p. 12.

43. Robinet, *Taoism*, ch. 6; Yamada, "The Lingbao School"; Bokenkamp, "Sources of the Ling-pao Scriptures." For a strong formulation of the impact of Buddhism, see Zürcher, "Buddhist Influence." On reincarnation, see pp. 135–141.

44. Bokenkamp, *Ancestors and Anxiety*, ch. 6; Bokenkamp, "Death and Ascent."

45. Wright, "Formation of Sui Ideology"; Wright, *The Sui Dynasty*, pp. 48–52, 54–57, 64–66, 71–72, 74, 78–79, 126–138; Wright, "Sui Dynasty," pp. 57, 61–67, 75–78, 113–119; Sen, *Buddhism, Diplomacy, and Trade*, pp. 62–68, 71, 84, 87, 93–94.

46. Sterckx, *The Animal and the Daemon*, ch. 4.

47. This theme is elaborated in Wang, *Shaping*, ch. 4.

48. On the Ba and their relation to Daoism in Sichuan, see Kleeman, "Ethnic Identity and Daoist Identity," pp. 24–30; Kleeman, *Great Perfection*, pp. 25–54, 73–76, 120. On the critique of sacrifice, see Kleeman, "Licentious Cults and Bloody Victuals," pp. 197–205.

49. Kleeman, *A God's Own Tale*, pp. 1–7; Kleeman, "Mountain Deities," pp. 234–237.

50. Stein, "Religious Taoism and Popular Religion."

51. Kieschnick, *Eminent Monk*, pp. 85–86, 90, 91, 97–99, 108–109.

52. Quoted in Gernet, *Buddhism*, p. 255. This feeding of a tiger with one's own body is patterned on an earlier life of the Buddha. Other tales of monks' sacrificing themselves to feed animals, thereby protecting their fellow humans, relate how they exposed their bodies to blood-drinking insects. See Kieschnick, *Eminent Monk*, pp. 39–40. For early Chan monks who were "famous for subduing local gods and their manifestations as wild animals," see Faure, *Rhetoric of Immediacy*, pp. 99–100, 103, 109–110, 112, 258–261.

53. Sen, *Buddhism, Diplomacy, and Trade*, pp. 76–86; Kieschnick, *Eminent Monk*, pp. 105–107; Yü Chün-fang, "P'u-t'o Shan: Pilgrimage and the Creation of the Chinese Potalaka."

54. Johnson, "City-God Cults," pp. 402–409.

55. Ibid., pp. 365–388.

56. Ibid., pp. 374–377, 379–388.

57. Ibid., pp. 426–433; Miyakawa, *Rikuchō shi kenkyū: shūkyō*, pp. 392–397.

9. Writing

1. This idea, formulated by Lu Xun early in the twentieth century, has been widely accepted. See Cai, ed., *Chinese Aesthetics*.

2. Tang, *Wei Jin xuanxue lun gao*; Tang and Ren, *Wei Jin xuanxue zhong de shehui zhengzhi sixiang*, esp. pp. 16–45. In English, see Wagner, *Language, Ontology, and Political Philosophy in China*; Wagner, *Craft of a Chinese Commentator*; Ziporyn, *Penumbra Unbound*; and Qian, *Spirit and Self*, ch. 2. On Zhong Hui, see Chan, "Zhong Hui's *Laozi* Commentary."

3. Yang, *Canon of Supreme Mystery*. On *xuan*, see pp. 2–5, 429–464.

4. Holcombe, *In the Shadow*, pp. 88–92.

5. Tang, *Wei Jin xuanxue lun gao*, pp. 111–116.

6. On Wang Bi's theories of ontology and language, see Wagner, *Language, Ontology, and Political Philosophy*, ch. 1–2.

7. Wagner, *Language, Ontology, and Political Philosophy*, p. 168.

8. Ibid., ch. 3, esp. pp. 213–215.

9. Ibid., pp. 58–64, 198. The idea of Confucius as the embodiment of negativity extends the Han concept that he was a "king without attributes."

10. Holzman, *La vie et la pensée*, ch. 3. For translations, see Henricks, *Philosophy and Argumentation in Third-Century China: The Essays of Hsi K'ang*.

11. Holzman, *Poetry and Politics*, ch. 4–5, 10.

12. Spiro, *Contemplating*, ch. 6. Anecdotes about the Seven Worthies are on pp. 75–86.

13. Ziporyn, *Penumbra Unbound*, pp. 25–30.

14. Ibid., ch. 4, 9.

15. Declercq, *Writing*, pp. 124, 261–262, 277, 299–306.

16. On "Dark Studies" as background to the emergence of ideas about an autonomous aesthetic realm, see Cai, "Prologue," pp. 4–11, 13; Bush, "Essay on Painting by Wang Wei," pp. 65–69; Lin, "A Good Place Need Not be Nowhere," pp. 135–145; Huntington, "Crossing Boundaries," pp. 191, 194; Li, "*Shishuo xinyu* and Aesthetic Self-Consciousness," pp. 241, 243–249; Egan, "Nature and Higher Ideals," pp. 288–291, 294–301, 305. See also Lynn, "Wang Bi and Liu Xie's *Wenxin diaolong*."

17. Owen, *The Making of Early Classical Poetry*, ch. 1.

18. Owen, *Anthology*, pp. 240–243.

19. Ibid., pp. 237–240.

20. Connery, "Jian'an"; Chang, "Generic Transformation"; Miao, *Early Medieval Chinese Poetry*.

21. Sun, *Pearl from the Dragon's Mouth*, ch. 1–2.

22. On how both positive and negative assessments of his poetry have been shaped by judgments of his moral character, see Cai, *Matrix*, pp. 97–103.

23. Owen, *Traditional Chinese Poetry and Poetics*, esp. pp. 12–27, 34–40, 56–68, 117–121.

24. Cai, *Matrix*, pp. 103–110, 119–125.

25. Cao Zhi also wrote "old poem"-style verses in the classic personae of the abandoned woman or the lonely traveler. See Cai, *Matrix*, pp. 125–130.

26. Cai, *Matrix*, pp. 110–119. For the classic ballad in translation with commentary, see Birrell, *Popular Songs and Ballads*, pp. 169–173.

27. Cai, *Matrix*, pp. 130–145. On the banquet verse, see Owen, *Anthology*, pp. 274–283. On Cao Zhi's *you xian* poems, see Holzman, "Ts'ao Chih and the Immortals," pp. 28–51. The first and last sections of Holzman's article discuss evidence regarding Cao Zhi's attitudes, as well as those of his father and brother, to the possibility of immortality. On the *you xian* lyric in the Northern and Southern Dynasties, see Huntington, "Crossing Boundaries."

28. Holzman, *Poetry and Politics*, pp. 227–232.

29. Cai, *Matrix*, pp. 154–164. The poem is on p. 158.

30. A nearly complete translation of these poets' works is Mather, *The Age of Eternal Brilliance*. On individual poets, see also Mather, *The Poet Shen Yüeh*; and Chang, *Six Dynasties Poetry*, ch. 4.

31. Goh Meow Hui, "Wang Rong's (467–493) Poetics in the Light of the Invention of Tonal Prosody." Goh has phonetically reconstructed more than five hundred poems by the three poets to investigate their actual practice. See also Goh, "Tonal Prosody in Three Poems by Wang Rong."

32. Quoted in Goh, "Tonal Prosody in Three Poems," p. 60. See also Li, "Between 'Literary Mind' and 'Carving Dragons,'" p. 220.

33. Chang, *Six Dynasties Poetry*, pp. 117–120.

34. Mair and Mei, "Sanskrit Origins."

35. Marney, *Liang Chien-wen Ti*; Wu, *Poetics of Decadence*, ch. 2; Birrell, tr., *New Songs*, Introduction.

36. Wu, *Poetics of Decadence*, pp. 41–46. On pp. 47–55, Wu examines how Xiao Gang's poem "A Beautiful Woman" is completely different from the earlier poem of the same name by Cao Zhi, which was a re-working of the Luofu story discussed earlier.

37. For a translation of this fragment, see Owen, *Readings*, pp. 57–72.

38. Owen, *Readings*, pp. 68–69. That literature is the highest task in regulating a state was disputed by his brother Cao Zhi, who mourned that his literary eminence was no replacement for a political career. See "Letter to Yang Dezu," in Wong, *Early Chinese Literary Criticism*, pp. 29–30. The disagreement probably reflects the fact that the one was a ruler who could take a political role for granted, while the other was an exile. In a letter to Wang Lang, Cao Pi also treated literary attainments as second to "establishing virtue." See Cutter, "To the Manner Born?" pp. 62–63.

39. Cutter, "To the Manner Born?" pp. 56–60.

40. Owen, *Readings*, pp. 73–181.

41. Ibid., pp. 130–131.

42. Sun, *Pearl from the Dragon's Mouth*, pp. 66–69.

43. Owen, *Readings*, pp. 89–90.

44. Sun, *Pearl from the Dragon's Mouth*, pp. 70–85. The passage by Liu Xie is quoted on p. 72.

45. Owen, *Readings*, pp. 98–99.

46. Sun, *Pearl*, pp. 73–75.

47. The introduction to Zhong Rong's work is translated in Wong, *Early Chinese Literary Criticism*, pp. 89–114.

48. Sun, *Pearl*, pp. 84–85. On descriptive language in the poetry of the period, see Chang, *Six Dynasties Poetry*, pp. 62–73, 89–102.

49. Sun, *Pearl*, pp. 86–87.

50. On the anomalous status of the work in the Chinese tradition, see Owen, *Readings*, pp. 183–186. On Buddhist influence, see Mair, "Buddhism in *The Literary Mind and Ornate Rhetoric*."

51. Owen, *Readings*, pp. 202–204. For translations of the chapters mentioned, see pp. 186–194, 201–218, 239–245, 277–286. On Liu Xie's elaborations of the ideas of earlier writers, see Sun, *Pearl*, pp. 69, 75–76, 78–81, 84. For studies of the chapter "Spirit Thought," see Egan, "Poet, Mind, and World"; Lin, "Liu Xie on Imagination"; Cai, "The Making of a Critical System," pp. 51–53; Li, "Between 'Literary Mind' and 'Carving Dragons,'" pp. 212–217.

52. Translated in Owen, *Readings*, pp. 194–201.

53. Lewis, *Writing and Authority*, pp. 325–332.

54. Chang, "Liu Xie's Idea of Canonicity." The phrases cited appear on p. 18. That Liu Xie never discussed how literature could rectify human relations and bring people into accord with the spirits is also noted in Cai, "Making of a Critical System," p. 54.

55. The role of anthologies in re-defining literature and authorship in early imperial China is discussed in Lewis, *Writing and Authority*, pp. 172–192.

56. Knechtges, "Culling the Weeds and Selecting Prime Blossoms."

57. On anthologies compiled during the Northern and Southern Dynasties, see Owen, *Making of Early Chinese Classical Poetry*, pp. 28–31, 313–318.

58. While Xun Xu (d. A.D. 289) used a "four-divisions" bibliographic system, his fourth category neither included all *belles lettres* nor excluded other types of writings. Only in the Liang is there clear evidence of a category reserved for *belles lettres*. See Knechtges, "Culling the Weeds," pp. 215–217.

59. Birrell, *New Songs*, pp. 341–342. The preface is translated on pp. 339–343.

60. On the preface as a coded discussion of the position of the courtier, and the anthology as a work compiled in that light, see Rouzer, *Articulated Ladies*, pp. 129–137.

61. Mather, tr., *New Account*, pp. 364–365; Yen, *Family Instructions*, pp. 198–201. Even the celebrated calligrapher Wang Xizhi expressed contempt for mere writing. See *New Account*, p. 63.

62. Asselin, "A Significant Season."

63. Nylan, "Calligraphy, the Sacred Text," pp. 46–52.

64. On the idea that calligraphy was an extension of the writer's body, see Billeter, *Chinese Art of Writing*, ch. 6–7; Hay, "Human Body as a Microcosmic Source." On the rising importance of cursive script, see Prosser, "Moral Characters," ch. 5. For the quotation from Zhao Yi, see pp. 159–160.

65. Harrist, "Replication and Deception," pp. 33–34. The mutual borrowing from the critical vocabulary of different arts is also discussed in Egan, "Nature and Higher Ideals."

66. Harrist, "Replication and Deception," pp. 35–39. The quotation is on p. 39.

67. On calligraphy transmitting the spirit of the calligrapher, see Egan, "Nature and Higher Ideals," pp. 277–291. For intertwined evaluations of the calligraphy and character of Wang Xizhi, Wang Xianzhi, and others, see Mather, tr., *New Account*, pp. 192, 230, 231, 235, 261, 269, 315, 321, 364–365, 365–366. On how Wang Xizhi's calligraphy was linked to character, at the expense of a more accurate example preserved in a hand tracing that survived in Japan, see Wang, "Taming of the Shrew: Wang Hsi-chih [Xizhi] (303–361)."

68. On Tao Hongjing as a calligraphy expert, see Harrist, "Replication and

Deception," pp. 40–48. On calligraphy in early Daoism, see Ledderose, "Some Daoist Elements." On the influence of Yang Xi's script and its transcription into clerical graphs, see pp. 257, 269.

69. Knechtges, "Culling the Weeds," pp. 215–216; Ng and Wang, *Mirroring the Past*, pp. 99–100. On reflections on history as a form of literature, see pp. 99, 103.

70. Ng and Wang, *Mirroring the Past*, ch. 3. On writing about the Han, see pp. 90–98. On writing about dynasties and their legitimacy, see pp. 80–90. On Chen Shou, see also Cutter and Crowell, *Empresses and Consorts*, pp. 61–81.

71. On *Forest of Conversations*, see Lee, "*Yü-lin and Kuo-tzu.*" On later texts in the tradition of *New Account*, see Qian, *Spirit and Self*, Part 3. On the dispute over the generic classification of *New Account*, see *Spirit and Self*, ch. 3.

72. Campany, *Strange Writing*.

73. On these texts, see Campany, *Strange Writing*, ch. 1, 3; Lewis, *Construction of Space*, ch. 5. On using anomalies to fix boundaries that define the normal, see Campany, *Strange Writing*, ch. 6.

74. Campany, *Strange Writing*, pp. 146–149, translates Gan Bao's description of his work as a supplement to history. See also Mather, tr., *New Account*, p. 409, where Liu Tan describes Gan Bao as a historian of the ghostly world.

75. Campany, *Strange Writing*, pp. 169–173, 199–201.

76. Ibid., pp. 280–294 on the perspective of esoteric masters, pp. 294–306 on the Daoist perspective, pp. 318–321 on the Emperor Wu cycle, and pp. 321–334 on the Buddhist perspective.

77. Campany, *Strange Writing*, pp. 343–394.

Conclusion

1. Graff, *Medieval Chinese Warfare*, pp. 129–135; Wright, *Sui Dynasty*, ch. 4. On Yang Guang and his relations to the south, see Xiong, *Emperor Yang*, pp. 12–20.

2. On institutions and foreign relations under the Sui, see Xiong, *Emperor Yang*, ch. 6, 9, 10. See also Wright, "Formation of Sui Ideology."

3. Wright, "Sui Dynasty," pp. 81–93; Wright, *Sui Dynasty*, pp. 91–107. The abolition of the Nine Ranks and the system of recommendation is discussed on pp. 98–103.

4. Xiong, *Emperor Yang*, pp. 123–126. On Emperor Wen's relic distribution, see Sen, *Buddhism, Diplomacy, and Trade*, pp. 62–64.

5. Wright, "Sui Dynasty," pp. 78–81; Wright, *Sui Dynasty*, pp. 84–88; Xiong, *Sui-T'ang Chang'an*, ch. 2; Xiong, *Emperor Yang*, pp. 75–76, 82–87, 157–158.

6. Xiong, *Emperor Yang*, pp. 75–84.

7. On the canals, see Xiong, *Emperor Yang*, pp. 86–93; Wright, *Sui Dynasty*,

pp. 177–181. On the granaries, see Xiong, *Emperor Yang*, pp. 175–180. On the role of this canal in later Chinese history, see Van Slyke, *Yangtze*, ch. 6; Tregear, *Geography of China*, pp. 78–80; Chi, *Key Economic Areas*, pp. 113–121.

8. Owen, *Mi-lou*, esp. the preface. On this structure in late imperial fiction, see Li, *Fictions of Enlightenment*, pp. 149, 167, 204 n. 98.

9. Xiong, *Emperor Yang*, ch. 10.

10. On the fall of the Sui, see Wright, *Sui Dynasty*, ch. 9; Graff, *Medieval Chinese Warfare*, ch. 7. On the historical treatment of Emperor Yang, see Wright, "Sui Yang-ti." For a reassessment of his character and career, see Xiong, *Emperor Yang*.

11. Xiong, *Emperor Yang*, pp. 218–220.

12. Ibid., pp. 64–66, 71, 116–120, 232–233.

BIBLIOGRAPHY

Abe, Stanley. *Ordinary Images.* Chicago: University of Chicago Press, 2002.

Ahern, Emily. *The Cult of the Dead in a Chinese Village.* Stanford: Stanford University Press, 1973.

Akahori, Akira. "Drug Taking and Immortality." In *Taoist Meditation and Longevity Techniques.* Ed. Livia Kohn. Ann Arbor: University of Michigan, Center for Chinese Studies, 1989.

Analects of Confucius, The. Tr. Simon Leys. New York: Norton, 1997.

Asselin, Mark Laurent. "'A Significant Season': Literature in a Time of Endings: Cài Yōng and a Few Contemporaries." Ph.D. diss., University of Washington, 1997.

Backus, Charles. *The Nan-chao Kingdom and T'ang China's Southwestern Frontier.* Cambridge: Cambridge University Press, 1981.

Balazs, Etienne. "Nihilistic Revolt or Mystical Escapism: Currents of Thought in China During the Third Century A.D." In *Chinese Civilization and Bureaucracy: Variations on a Theme.* Ed. Arthur F. Wright. Tr. H. M. Wright. New Haven: Yale University, 1964.

———. "Political Philosophy and Social Crisis at the End of the Han Dynasty." In *Chinese Civilization and Bureaucracy: Variations on a Theme.* Ed. Arthur F. Wright. Tr. H. M. Wright. New Haven: Yale University Press, 1964.

———. *Le Traité économique du "Souei-chou."* Leiden: E. J. Brill, 1953.

———. "Two Songs by Ts'ao Ts'ao." In *Chinese Civilization and Bureaucracy: Variations on a Theme.* Ed. Arthur F. Wright. Tr. H. M. Wright. New Haven: Yale University Press, 1964.

Baptandier, Brigitte. *The Lady of Linshui: A Chinese Female Cult.* Tr. Kristin Ingrid Fryklund. Stanford: Stanford University Press, 2008.

Barfield, Thomas F. *The Perilous Frontier: Nomadic Empires and China.* Oxford: Basil Blackwell, 1989.

Barnes, Gina. *China, Korea, and Japan: The Rise of Civilization in East Asia.* London: Thames and Hudson, 1993.

Benn, Charles D. *The Cavern-Mystery Transmission: A Taoist Ordination Rite of A.D. 711.* Honolulu: University of Hawai'i Press, 1991.

Berkowitz, Alan J. *Patterns of Disengagement: The Practice and Portrayal of Reclusion in Early Medieval China.* Stanford: Stanford University Press, 2000.

Bielenstein, Hans. "The Six Dynasties: Vol. 1." *Bulletin of the Museum of Far Eastern Antiquities* 68 (1996): 5–324.

———. "The Six Dynasties: Vol. 2." *Bulletin of the Museum of Far Eastern Antiquities* 69 (1997): 5–246.

———. "Wang Mang, the Restoration of the Han Dynasty, and Later Han." In *Cambridge History of Ancient China,* Vol. 1: *The Ch'in and Han Empires.* Ed. Michael Loewe. Cambridge: Cambridge University Press, 1986.

Billeter, Jean François. *The Chinese Art of Writing.* New York: Rizzoli, 1990.

Birrell, Anne, tr. *New Songs from a Jade Terrace.* London: George Allen and Unwin, 1982.

———. *Popular Songs and Ballads of Han China.* London: Unwin Hyman, 1988.

Bischoff, Friedrich Alexander. *The Songs of the Orchis Tower.* Wiesbaden: Otto Harrassowitz, 1985.

Blackmore, Michael. "The Rise of Nan-chao in Yunnan." *Journal of South-east Asian History* 1 (1960): 47–61.

Bodde, Derk. *Festivals in Classical China: New Year and Other Annual Observances During the Han Dynasty, 206 B.C.–A.D. 220.* Princeton: Princeton University Press, 1975.

Bokenkamp, Stephen R. *Ancestors and Anxiety: The Birth of Rebirth in China.* Berkeley: University of California Press, 2007.

———. "Death and Ascent in Ling-pao Taoism." *Taoist Resources* 1:2 (1989): 1–20.

———. *Early Daoist Scriptures.* Berkeley: University of California Press, 1997.

———. "Sources of the Ling-pao Scriptures." In *Special Issue: Tantric and Taoist Studies in Honour of R. A. Stein,* Vol. 2. Ed. Michel Strickmann. *Mélanges chinoises et bouddhiques* 21 (1983): 434–486.

———. "Stages of Transcendence: The *Bhūmi* Concept in Taoist Scripture." In *Chinese Buddhist Apocrypha.* Ed. Robert E. Buswell, Jr. Honolulu: University of Hawai'i Press, 1990.

Boulton, Nancy Elizabeth. "Early Chinese Buddhist Travel Records as a Literary Genre." Ph.D. diss., Georgetown University, 1982.

Bray, Francesca. *The Rice Economies: Technology and Development in Asian Societies.* London: Basil Blackwell, 1986.

Buchanan, Keith. *The Transformation of the Chinese Earth.* London: G. Bell and Sons, 1970.

Bush, Susan. "The Essay on Painting by Wang Wei (415–453) in Context." In *Chinese Aesthetics: The Ordering of Literature, the Arts, and the Universe in the Six Dynasties.* Ed. Zong-qi Cai. Honolulu: University of Hawai'i Press, 2004.

Bush, Susan, and Hsio-yen Shih, eds. *Early Chinese Texts on Painting.* Cambridge: Harvard University Press, 1985.

Cahill, Suzanne. *Divine Traces of the Daoist Sisterhood.* Magdalena, New Mexico: Three Pines Press, 2006.

———. "Material Culture and the Dao: Textiles, Boats, and Zithers in the Poetry of Xu Xuanji (844–868)." In *Daoist Identity: History, Lineage, and Ritual.* Ed. Livia Kohn and Harold D. Roth. Honolulu: University of Hawai'i Press, 2002.

———. "Smell Good and Get a Job: How Daoist Women Saints were Verified and Legitimatized during the Tang Dynasty (618–907)." In *Presence and Presentation: Women in the Chinese Literati Tradition.* Ed. Sherry J. Mou. London: MacMillan, 1999.

———. *Transcendence and Divine Passion: The Queen Mother of the West in Medieval China.* Stanford: Stanford University Press, 1993.

Cai, Zong-qi, ed. *Chinese Aesthetics: The Ordering of Literature, the Arts, and the Universe in the Six Dynasties.* Honolulu: University of Hawai'i Press, 2004.

———. "The Making of a Critical System: Concepts of Literature in *Wenxin diaolong* and Earlier Texts." In *A Chinese Literary Mind: Culture, Creativity, and Rhetoric in Wenxin Diaolong.* Ed. Zong-qi Cai. Stanford: Stanford University Press, 2001.

———. *The Matrix of Lyrical Transformation: Poetic Modes and Self-Presentation in Early Chinese Pentasyllabic Poetry.* Ann Arbor: University of Michigan, Center for Chinese Studies, 1996.

Campany, Robert Ford. *Strange Writing: Anomaly Accounts in Early Medieval China.* Albany: State University of New York Press, 1996.

———. *To Live as Long as Heaven and Earth: A Translation and Study of Ge Hong's Traditions of Divine Transcendents.* Berkeley: University of California Press, 2002.

Caswell, James O. *Written and Unwritten: A New History of the Buddhist Caves at Yungang.* Vancouver: University of British Columbia Press, 1988.

Cedzich, Ursula-Angelika. "Ghosts and Demons, Law and Order: Grave Quelling Texts and Early Daoist Liturgy." *Taoist Resources* 4:2 (1993): 34–35.

Chang, Kang-i Sun. "Description of Landscape in Early Six Dynasties Poetry." In *The Vitality of the Lyric Voice: Shih Poetry from the Late Han to the T'ang.* Ed. Shuen-fu Lin and Stephen Owen. Princeton NJ: Princeton University Press, 1986.

———. "Liu Xie's Idea of Canonicity." In *A Chinese Literary Mind: Culture, Creativity, and Rhetoric in Wenxin Diaolong.* Ed. Zong-qi Cai. Stanford: Stanford University Press, 2001.

———. *Six Dynasties Poetry.* Princeton: Princeton University Press, 1986.

Chang, Sung-sheng Yvonne. "Generic Transformation from 'Yuefu' to 'Gushi':

Poetry of Cao Cao, Cao Pi, and Cao Zhi." Ph.D. diss., Stanford University, 1985.

Chen, Chi-yun. "A Confucian Magnate's Idea of Political Violence: Hsün Shuang's (A.D. 128–190) Interpretation of the Book of Changes." *T'oung Pao* 54:1–3 (1968): 73–115.

———. *Hsün Yüeh: The Life and Reflections of an Early Medieval Confucian.* Cambridge: Cambridge University Press, 1975.

Ch'en, Kenneth K. S. *Buddhism in China: A Historical Survey.* Princeton: Princeton University Press, 1964.

———. *The Chinese Transformation of Buddhism.* Princeton: Princeton University Press, 1973.

Chen, Shih-hsiang. *Biography of Ku K'ai-chih.* Chinese Dynastic Histories Translations No. 2. Berkeley: University of California Press, 1953.

Chen, Yinke. "Cong shi shi lun *Qie yun.*" In *Chen Yinke Xiansheng lunwen ji.* 2 vols. Taipei: San Ren Xing, 1974.

———. "Dong Jin Nanchao Wu yu." In *Chen Yinke Xiansheng lunwen ji.* 2 vols. Taipei: San Ren Xing, 1974.

———. "'Tao hua yuan ji' pang zheng." In *Chen Yinke Xiansheng lunwen ji.* 2 vols. Taipei: San Ren Xing, 1974.

Chi, Ch'ao-ting. *Key Economic Areas in Chinese History as Revealed in the Development of Public Works for Water-Control.* London: George Allen and Unwin, 1936.

China: Dawn of a Golden Age, 200–750 A.D. Exhibition catalogue for the Metropolitan Museum of Art, edited by James C. Y. Wyatt. New Haven: Yale University Press, 2004.

Clunas, Craig. *Fruitful Sites: Garden Culture in Ming Dynasty China.* Durham: Duke University Press, 1996.

Cole, Alan. *Mothers and Sons in Chinese Buddhism.* Stanford: Stanford University Press, 1998.

Connery, Christopher Leigh. "Jian'an Poetic Discourse." Ph.D. diss., Princeton University, 1991.

Cook, Constance A., and John S. Major, eds. *Defining Chu: Image and Reality in Ancient China.* Honolulu: University of Hawai'i Press, 1999.

Crowell, William G. "Government Land Policies and Systems in Early Imperial China." Ph.D. diss., University of Washington, 1979.

———. "Northern Emigres and the Problems of Census Registration." In *State and Society in Early Medieval China.* Ed. Albert E. Dien. Stanford: Stanford University Press, 1990.

Csikszentmihàlyi, Mark. "Traditional Taxonomies and Revealed Texts in the Han." In *Daoist Identity: History, Lineage, and Ritual.* Ed. Livia Kohn and Harold D. Roth. Honolulu: University of Hawai'i Press, 2002.

Cutter, Robert Joe. "Cao Zhi (192–232) and his Poetry." Ph.D. diss., University of Washington, 1983.

———. "To the Manner Born? Nature and Nurture in Early Medieval Chinese Literary Thought." In *Culture and Power in the Reconstitution of the Chinese Realm, 200–600.* Ed. Scott Pearce, Audrey Spiro, and Patricia Ebrey. Cambridge: Harvard University Press, 2001.

Cutter, Robert Joe, and William Gordon Crowell, tr. *Empresses and Consorts: Selections from Chen Shou's Records of the Three States with Pei Songzhi's Commentary.* Honolulu: University of Hawai'i Press, 1999.

Davis, A. R., tr. *T'ao Yüan-ming.* 2 vols. Cambridge: Cambridge University Press, 1983.

Declercq, Dominik. *Writing Against the State: Political Rhetorics in Third and Fourth Century China.* Leiden: E. J. Brill, 1998.

de Crespigny, Rafe, tr. *Emperor Huan and Emperor Ling: Being the Chronicle of Later Han for the Years 157 to 189 A.D. as Recorded in Chapters 54 to 59 of the Zizhi tongjian of Sima Guang.* Canberra: Australian National University Press, 1989.

———. *Generals of the South: The Foundation and Early History of the Three Kingdoms State of Wu.* Canberra: Australian National University Press, 1990.

———, tr. *To Establish Peace: Being the Chronicle of Later Han for the Years 189 to 220 A.D. as Recorded in Chapters 59 to 69 of the Zizhi tongjian of Sima Guang.* Canberra: Australian National University Press, 1997.

Delahaye, Hubert. *Les Premières peintures de paysage en Chine: aspects religieux.* Paris: École Française d'Extrême-Orient, 1981.

de la Vaissière, Étienne. *Les Sogdiens en Chine.* Paris: École Française d'Extrême Orient, 2005.

———. *Sogdian Traders: A History.* Tr. James Ward. Leiden: E. J. Brill, 2005.

Despeux, Catherine. "Gymnastics: The Ancient Tradition." In *Taoist Meditation and Longevity Techniques.* Ed. Livia Kohn. Ann Arbor: University of Michigan, Center for Chinese Studies, 1989.

———. "Women in Daoism." In *Daoism Handbook.* Ed. Livia Kohn. Leiden: E. J. Brill, 2000.

Di Cosmo, Nicola. *Ancient China and Its Enemies: The Rise of Nomadic Power in East Asian History.* Cambridge: Cambridge University Press, 2002.

Dien, Albert E. "The Bestowal of Surnames under the Western Wei-Northern Chou: A Case of Counter-Acculturation." *T'oung Pao* 63 (1977): 137–177.

———. "Developments in Funerary Practices in the Six Dynasties Period: The *Duisuguan* or 'Figured Jar.'" In *Between Han and Tang: Cultural and Artistic Interaction in a Transformative Period.* Ed. Wu Hung. Beijing: Wenwu, 2001.

———. "Elite Lineages and the T'o-pa Accommodation: A Study of the Edict of 495." *Journal of the Economic and Social History of the Orient* 19:1 (1976): 61–88.

———. "Introduction." In *State and Society in Early Medieval China.* Ed. Albert E. Dien. Stanford: Stanford University Press, 1990.

———. "A New Look at the Xianbei and Their Impact on Chinese Culture." In *Ancient Mortuary Traditions of China: Papers on Chinese Ceramic Funerary Sculptures*. Ed. George Kuwayama. Los Angeles: Los Angeles County Museum of Art, 1991.

———. "The Role of the Military in the Western Wei/Northern Chou State." In *State and Society in Early Medieval China*. Ed. Albert E. Dien. Stanford: Stanford University Press, 1990.

———. "The 'Sa-pao' Problem Re-examined." *Journal of the American Oriental Society* 82 (1962): 335–346.

———. "The Stirrup and Its Effect on Chinese Military History." *Ars Orientalis* 16 (1986): 33–56.

———. "A Study of Early Chinese Armor." *Artibus Asiae* 43 (1982): 5–66.

———. "Yen Chih-t'ui (531–591+): A Buddho-Confucian." In *Confucian Personalities*. Ed. Arthur F. Wright and Denis Twitchett. Stanford: Stanford University Press, 1962.

Diény, Jean-Pierre. *Les dix-neufs poèmes anciens*. Paris: Presses Universitaires de France, 1963.

———. "Lecture de Wang Can (177–217)." *T'oung Pao* 73 (1987): 286–312.

———. *Portrait anecdotique d'un gentilhomme chinois, Xie An (320–385) d'après "Shishuo xinyu."* Paris: Collège de France, Institut des Hautes Études Chinoises, 1993.

———. "Le saint ne rêve pas: De Zhuangzi à Michel Jouvet." *Études chinoises* 20:1–2 (Printemps-Automne 2001): 127–200.

Dudbridge, Glen. *The Legend of Miaoshan*. Rev. ed. Oxford: Oxford University Press, 2004.

———. *The Tale of Li Wa: Study and Critical Edition of a Chinese Story from the Ninth Century*. Oxford: Ithaca Press, 1983.

Eberhard, Wolfram. *A History of China*. Rev., enl. ed. Berkeley: University of California Press, 1971.

———. *Das Toba-Reich Nordchinas: Eine soziologische Untersuchung*. Leiden: E. J. Brill, 1949.

Ebrey, Patricia B. *The Aristocratic Families of Early Imperial China: A Case Study of the Po-ling Ts'ui Family*. Cambridge: Cambridge University Press, 1978.

———. "The Early States in the Development of Descent Group Organization." In *Kinship Organization in Late Imperial China*. Ed. Patricia Buckley Ebrey and James L. Watson. Berkeley: University of California Press, 1986.

———. "The Economic and Social History of Later Han." In *Cambridge History of Ancient China*, Vol. 1: *The Ch'in and Han Empires*. Ed. Michael Loewe. Cambridge: Cambridge University Press, 1986.

———. "Toward a Better Understanding of the Later Han Upper Class." In *State and Society in Early Medieval China*. Ed. Albert E. Dien. Stanford: Stanford University Press, 1990.

Eckel, Malcom David. *To See the Buddha: A Philosopher's Quest for the Meaning of Emptiness*. Princeton: Princeton University Press, 1992.

Egan, Ronald. "Nature and Higher Ideals in Texts on Calligraphy, Music, and Painting." In *Chinese Aesthetics: The Ordering of Literature, the Arts, and the Universe in the Six Dynasties*. Ed. Zong-qi Cai. Honolulu: University of Hawai'i Press, 2004.

———. "Poet, Mind, and World: A Reconsideration of the 'Shensi' Chapter of *Wenxin diaolong*." In *A Chinese Literary Mind: Culture, Creativity, and Rhetoric in Wenxin Diaolong*. Ed. Zong-qi Cai. Stanford: Stanford University Press, 2001.

Enoki, Kazuo. "On the Nationality of the Ephtalites." *Memoirs of the Research Department of the Toyo Bunko* 18 (1959): 1–58.

Fang, Achilles, tr. *The Chronicle of the Three Kingdoms (220–265): Chapters 69–78 from the Tzu chih t'ung chien*. Cambridge: Harvard University Press, 1952.

Faure, Bernard. *The Rhetoric of Immediacy: A Cultural Critique of Chan/Zen Buddhism*. Princeton: Princeton University Press, 1991.

Forte, Antonino. *Political Propaganda and Ideology in China at the End of the Seventh Century*. Naples: Istituto Universitario Orientale, 1976.

Frankel, Hans H. "Cai Yan and the Poems Attributed to Her." *Chinese Literature: Essays, Articles, Reviews* 5 (1983): 133–156.

Frodsham, J. D. *The Murmuring Stream: The Life and Works of the Chinese Nature Poet Hsieh Ling-yün (385–433), Duke of K'ang-lo*. 2 vols. Kuala Lumpur: University of Malaya, 1967.

Gernet, Jacques. *Buddhism in Chinese Society: An Economic History from the Fifth to the Tenth Centuries*. Tr. Franciscus Verellen. New York: Columbia University Press, 1995.

Goh, Meow Hui. "Tonal Prosody in Three Poems by Wang Rong." *Journal of the American Oriental Society* 124:1 (2004): 59–68.

———. "Wang Rong's (467–493) Poetics in the Light of the Invention of Tonal Prosody." Ph.D. diss., University of Wisconsin, 2004.

Goodman, Howard L. *Ts'ao P'i Transcendent: The Political Culture of Dynasty-Founding in China at the End of the Han*. Seattle: Scripta Serica, 1998.

Goodrich, Chauncey S. "Riding Astride and the Saddle in Ancient China." *Harvard Journal of Asiatic Studies* 44:2 (December 1984): 279–306.

Graff, David A. *Medieval Chinese Warfare, 300–900*. London: Routledge, 2002.

Grafflin, Dennis. "The Great Family in Medieval South China." *Harvard Journal of Asiatic Studies* 41:1 (June 1981): 65–74.

———. "Reinventing China: Pseudobureaucracy in the Early Southern Dynasties." In *State and Society in Early Medieval China*. Ed. Albert E. Dien. Stanford: Stanford University Press, 1990.

Graham, William T., Jr. *'The Lament for the South,': Yü Hsin's 'Ai Chiang-nan fu.'* Cambridge: Cambridge University Press, 1980.

Great Tang Dynasty Record of the Western Regions, The. Tr. Li Rongxi. Berkeley: Numata Center for Buddhist Translation and Research, 1996.

Greatrex, Roger. *The Bowu zhi: An Annotated Translation.* Stockholm: Orientaliska Studier, 1987.

Guo, Moruo, ed. *Cao Cao lun ji.* Beijing: Sanlian, 1964.

Han, Guopan. *Nanbeichao jingji shi tan.* Shanghai: Shanghai Renmin, 1963.

Han, Pao-the. *External Forms and Internal Visions: The Story of Chinese Landscape Design.* Taipei: Youth Cultural Enterprises, 1992.

Harley, J. B., and David Woodward, eds. *The History of Cartography,* Vol. 2: Book 2: *Cartography in the Traditional East and Southeast Asian Societies.* Chicago: University of Chicago Press, 1995.

Harper, Donald. *Early Chinese Medical Literature: The Mawangdui Medical Manuscripts.* London: Kegan Paul, 1998.

Harrist, "Replication and Deception in Calligraphy of the Six Dynasties Period." In *Chinese Aesthetics: The Ordering of Literature, the Arts, and the Universe in the Six Dynasties.* Ed. Zong-qi Cai. Honolulu: University of Hawai'i Press, 2004.

Hawes, Colin S. C. *The Social Circulation of Poetry in the Mid-Northern Song: Emotional Energy and Literati Self-Cultivation.* Albany: State University of New York Press, 2005.

Hay, John. "The Human Body as a Microcosmic Source of Macrocosmic Value in Calligraphy." In *Theories of the Arts in China.* Ed. Susan Bush and Christian Murck. Princeton: Princeton University Press, 1983.

Hendrischke, Barbara. "Early Daoist Movements." In *Daoism Handbook.* Ed. Livia Kohn. Leiden: E. J. Brill, 2000.

Henricks, Robert G., tr. *Philosophy and Argumentation in Third-Century China: The Essays of Hsi K'ang.* Princeton: Princeton University Press, 1983.

Hightower, James Robert. "The *Fu* of T'ao Ch'ien." *Harvard Journal of Asiatic Studies* 17 (1954): 169–230. Rpt. in *Studies in Chinese Literature.* Ed. John L. Bishop. Cambridge: Harvard University Press, 1966.

Ho, Judy Chunghwa. "Portraying the Family in the Metropolitan and Frontier Regions during the Transition between Han and Tang." In *Between Han and Tang: Cultural and Artistic Interaction in a Transformative Period.* Ed. Wu Hung. Beijing: Wenwu, 2001.

Ho, Ping-ti. "Loyang. A.D. 495–534." *Harvard Journal of Asiatic Studies* 26 (1966): 52–101.

Holcombe, Charles. *The Genesis of East Asia, 221 B.C.–A.D. 907.* Honolulu: University of Hawai'i Press, 2001.

———. *In the Shadow of the Han: Literati Thought and Society at the Beginning of the Southern Dynasties.* Honolulu: University of Hawai'i Press, 1994.

Holmgren, Jennifer. *Marriage, Kinship and Power in Northern China*. Aldershot: Ashgate, Variorum Collected Studies Series, 1995.

Holzman, Donald. "The Cold Food Festival in Early Medieval China." *Harvard Journal of Asiatic Studies* 46:1 (1986): 51–79. Rpt. in *Immortals, Festivals and Poetry in Medieval China*. Aldershot: Ashgate, Variorum Collected Studies Series, 1998.

———. "Les débuts du système medieval de choix et de classment des fonctionnaires: Les neuf catégories et l'Impartial et Juste." *Mélanges Publiés par l'Institut des Hautes Études Chinoises*, Vol. 1. Paris: University of Paris, 1957.

———. "Immortality-Seeking in Early Chinese Poetry." In *The Power of Culture: Studies in Chinese Cultural History*. Ed. W. J. Peterson, A. H. Plaks, and Y.-s. Yü. Hong Kong: Chinese University, 1994. Rpt. in *Immortals, Festivals and Poetry in Medieval China*. Aldershot: Ashgate, Variorum Collected Studies Series, 1998.

———. *Landscape Appreciation in Ancient and Early Medieval China: The Birth of Landscape Poetry*. Xinzhu, Taiwan: National Tsing Hua University, 1996. Rpt. in *Chinese Literature in Transition from Antiquity to the Middle Ages*. Aldershot: Ashgate, Variorium Collected Studies Series, 1998.

———. "La poésie de Ji Kang." *Journal Asiatique* 248: 1/2, 3/4 (1980): 107–177, 323–378. Rpt. in *Immortals, Festivals and Poetry in Medieval China*. Aldershot: Ashgate, Variorum Collected Studies Series, 1998.

———. *Poetry and Politics: The Life and Works of Juan Chi (A.D. 210–263)*. Cambridge: Cambridge University Press, 1976.

———. "Les premiers vers pentasyllabiques datés dans la poésie Chinoise." In *Mélanges de sinologies offerts à Monsieur Paul Demiéville*. Paris: Presses Universitaires de France, 1974. Rpt. in *Chinese Literature in Transition from Antiquity to the Middle Ages*. Aldershot: Ashgate, Variorum Collected Studies Series, 1998.

———. "Les Sept Sages de la Forêt des Bambous et la société de leur temps." *T'oung Pao* 46 (1956): 317–416.

———. "Ts'ao Chih and the Immortals." *Asia Major, Third Series* 1:1 (1988): 15–57. Rpt. in *Immortals, Festivals and Poetry in Medieval China*. Aldershot: Ashgate, Variorum Collected Studies Series, 1998.

———. *La vie et la pensée de Hi K'ang (223–262 Ap. J.-C.)*. Leiden: E. J. Brill, 1957.

———. "Xie Lingyun et les paysans de Yongjia." In *Hommage à Kwong Hing Foon: Études d'histoire culturelle de la Chine*. Ed. J.-P. Diény. Paris: Institut des Hautes Études Chinoises, 1995. Rpt. in *Immortals, Festivals and Poetry in Medieval China*. Aldershot: Ashgate, Variorum Collected Studies Series, 1998.

Honey, David B. "Sinification and Legitimation: Liu Yüan, Shi Le, and the

Founding of Han and Chao." Ph.D. diss., University of California at Berkeley, 1988.

———. "Sinification as Statecraft in Conquest Dynasties of China: Two Early Medieval Case Studies." *Journal of Asian History* 30:2 (1996): 115–151.

Hou, Naihui. *Shi qin yu you jing: Tang da wenren de yuanlin shenghuo*. Taipei: Dongda Tushu, 1991.

———. *Tang Song shiqi de gongyuan wenhua*. Taipei: Dongda Tushu, 1997.

Hsu, Cho-yun. *Han Agriculture: The Formation of Early Chinese Agrarian Economy (206 B.C.–A.D. 220)*. Seattle: University of Washington Press, 1980.

Hua, Guorong. "The Eastern Jin Tombs of the Wang, Xie, and Gao Families near Nanjing." In *Between Han and Tang: Visual and Material Culture in a Transformative Period*. Ed. Wu Hung. Beijing: Wenwu, 2003.

Hubbard, Jamie. *Absolute Delusion, Perfect Buddhahood: The Rise and Fall of a Chinese Heresy*. Honolulu: University of Hawai'i Press, 2001.

Huntington, Rania. "Crossing Boundaries: Transcendents and Aesthetics in the Six Dynasties." In *Chinese Aesthetics: The Ordering of Literature, the Arts, and the Universe in the Six Dynasties*. Ed. Zong-qi Cai. Honolulu: University of Hawai'i, 2004.

Hurvitz, Leon, tr. *Scripture of the Lotus Blossom of the Fine Dharma*. New York: Columbia University Press, 1976.

I-ching. *Chinese Monks in India: Biographies of Eminent Monks Who Went to the Western World in Search of the Law during the Great Tang Dynasty*. Tr. Latika Lahiri. Delhi: Motilal Banarsidas, 1986.

I-ching. *A Record of the Buddhist Religion as Practised in India and the Malay Archipelago*. Tr. Takakusu Junjirō. Reprint ed. Dehli: Munshiram Manoharlal, 1966.

Janousch, Andreas. "The Emperor as Bodhisattva: The Bodhisattva Ordination and Ritual Assemblies of Emperor Wu of the Liang Dynasty." In *State and Court Ritual in China*. Ed. Joseph P. McDermott. Cambridge: Cambridge University Press, 1999.

———. "The Reform of Imperial Ritual during the Reign of Emperor Wu of the Liang Dynasty (502–549)." Ph.D. diss., Cambridge University, 1998.

Jansen, Thomas. *Höfische Öffentlichkeit im frühmittelalterlichen China: debatten im Salon des Prinzen Xiao Ziliang*. Freiburg im Breisgau: Rombach, 2000.

Jenner, W. F. J. *Memories of Loyang: Yang Hsüan-chih and the Lost Capital (493–534)*. Oxford: Clarendon, 1981.

Johnson, David G. "The City-God Cults of T'ang and Sung China." *Harvard Journal of Asiatic Studies* 45 (1985): 363–457.

———. *The Medieval Chinese Oligarchy*. Boulder: Westview, 1977.

———. "Mu-lien in Pao-chüan: The Performance Context and Religious Meaning of the *Yu-ming Pao-ch'uan*. In *Ritual and Scripture in Chinese Popular*

Religion: Five Studies. Ed. David Johnson. Berkeley: Publications of the
Chinese Popular Culture Project, 1995.

———, ed. *Ritual Opera, Operatic Ritual: "Mu-lien Rescues his Mother" in
Chinese Popular Culture.* Berkeley: Publications of the Chinese Popular
Culture Project, 1989.

Johnson, Wallace. *The T'ang Code,* Vol. I: *General Principles.* Princeton: Princeton University Press, 1979.

———. *The T'ang Code,* Vol. II: *Specific Articles.* Princeton: Princeton University Press, 1997.

Kaga, Eiji. *Chūgoku koten kaishaku shi: Gi Kin hen.* Tokyo: Keisō Shobō, 1964.

Kaltenmark, Max. "The Ideology of the T'ai-p'ing ching." In *Facets of Taoism.*
Ed. Holmes Welch and Anna Seidel. New Haven: Yale University Press,
1979.

Kawakatsu, Yoshio. "L'Aristocratie et la société féodale au début des Six Dynasties." *Zinbun* 17 (1981): 107–160.

———. *Chūgoku no rekishi:* Vol. 4: *Gi Kin Nanbokuchō.* Tokyo: Kodansha, 1974.

———. "La Décadence de l'aristocratie chinoise sous les Dynasties du Sud."
Acta Asiatica 21 (1971): 13–38.

———. *Rikuchō kizokusei shakai no kenkyū.* Tokyo: Iwanami, 1982.

Kawamoto, Yoshiaki. *Gi Shin Nanbokuchō jidai no minzoku mondai.* Tokyo:
Kyuko Shoin, 1998.

Kieschnick, John. *The Eminent Monk: Buddhist Ideals in Medieval Chinese Ha-
giography.* Honolulu: University of Hawai'i Press, 1997.

———. *The Impact of Buddhism on Chinese Material Culture.* Princeton:
Princeton University Press, 2003.

Kieser, Annette. "Northern Influence in Tombs in Southern China after 317
CE?—A Reevalution." In *Between Han and Tang: Cultural and Artistic Interaction in a Transformative Period.* Ed. Wu Hung. Beijing: Wenwu, 2001.

Kirkland, Russell. *Taoism: The Enduring Tradition.* New York: Routledge,
2004.

Kleeman, Terry F. "Ethnic Identity and Daoist Identity in Traditional China." In
Daoist Identity: History, Lineage, and Ritual. Ed. Livia Kohn and Harold
D. Roth. Honolulu: University of Hawai'i Press, 2002.

———. *A God's Own Tale: The Book of Transformations of Wenchang, the Divine Lord of Zitong.* Albany: State University of New York Press, 1994.

———. *Great Perfection: Religion and Ethnicity in a Chinese Millennial Kingdom.* Honolulu: University of Hawai'i Press, 1998.

———. "Licentious Cults and Bloody Victuals: Sacrifice, Reciprocity, and Violence in Traditional China." *Asia Major, Third Series* 7:1 (1994): 185–211.

———. "Mountain Deities in China: The Domestication of the Mountain God
and the Subjugation of the Margins." *Journal of the American Oriental Society* 114 (Jan.–June 1994): 226–238.

Klein, Kenneth Douglas. "The Contributions of the Fourth Century Xianbei

States to the Reunification of the Chinese Empire." Ph.D. diss., University of California at Los Angeles, 1980.

Knapp, Keith N. *Selfless Offspring: Filial Children and Social Order in Medieval China*. Honolulu: University of Hawai'i Press, 2005.

Knechtges, David N. "Culling the Weeds and Selecting Fine Blossoms: The Anthology in Early Medieval China." In *Culture and Power in the Reconstitution of the Chinese Realm, 200–600*. Ed. Scott Pearce, Audrey Spiro, and Patricia Ebrey. Cambridge: Harvard University Press, 2001.

———, tr. *Wen xuan, or Selections of Refined Literature*. Vol. 1. Princeton: Princeton University Press, 1982.

Knoblock, John, and Jeffrey Riegel, tr. *The Annals of Lü Buwei: A Complete Translation and Study*. Stanford: Stanford University Press, 2000.

Kohn, Livia. *Laughing at the Tao: Debates among Buddhists and Taoists in Medieval China*. Princeton: Princeton University Press, 1995.

———. *Monastic Life in Medieval Daoism: A Cross-Cultural Perspective*. Honolulu: University of Hawai'i Press, 2003.

———. "The Northern Celestial Masters." In *Daoism Handbook*. Ed. Livia Kohn. Leiden: E. J. Brill, 2000.

Kroll, Paul. "Portraits of Ts'ao Ts'ao: Literary Studies on the Man and the Myth." Ph.D. diss., University of Michigan, 1976.

———. "Verses from on High: The Ascent of T'ai Shan." In *The Vitality of the Lyric Voice: Shih Poetry from the Late Han to the T'ang*. Ed. Shuen-fu Lin and Stephen Owen. Princeton: Princeton University Press, 1986.

Kwong, Charles Yim-tze. *Tao Qian and the Chinese Poetic Tradition: The Quest for Cultural Identity*. Ann Arbor: University of Michigan, Center for Chinese Studies, 1994.

Lagerwey, John. *Taoist Ritual in Chinese Society and History*. New York: MacMillan, 1987.

Lai, Chiu-mi. "River and Ocean: The Third Century Verse of Pan Yue and Lu Ji." Ph.D. diss., University of Washington, 1990.

Lai, Sufen Sophia. "Father in Heaven, Mother in Hell: Gender Politics in the Creation and Transformation of Mulian's Mother." In *Presence and Presentation: Women in the Chinese Literati Tradition*. Ed. Sherry J. Mou. London: MacMillan, 1999.

Lai, Whalen. "The Earliest Folk Buddhist Religion in China: *T'i-wei Po-li Ching* and Its Historical Significance." In *Buddhist and Taoist Practice in Medieval Chinese Society: Buddhist and Taoist Studies II*. Ed. David W. Chappell. Honolulu: University of Hawai'i Press, 1987.

———. "Society and the Sacred in the Secular City: Temple Legends of the *Lo-yang Ch'ieh-lan-chi*." In *State and Society in Early Medieval China*. Ed. Albert E. Dien. Stanford: Stanford University Press, 1990.

Lawton, Thomas, ed. *New Perspectives on Chu Culture During the Eastern Zhou Period*. Washington, DC: Smithsonian Institution, 1991.

Leban, Carl. "Ts'ao Ts'ao and the Rise of Wei: The Early Years." Ph.D. diss., Columbia University, 1971.

Ledderose, Lothar. "Some Taoist Elements in the Calligraphy of the Six Dynasties." *T'oung Pao* 70 (1984): 246–278.

———. "Thunder Sound Cave." In *Between Han and Tang: Visual and Material Culture in a Transformative Period*. Ed. Wu Hung. Beijing: Wenwu, 2003.

Lee, Lily Hsiao Hung. "Yü-lin and Ku-tzu: Two Predecessors of Shi-shuo hsin-yü." In *A Festschrift in Honour of Professor Jao Tsung-I on the Occasion of His Seventy-Fifth Birthday*. Hong Kong: Chinese University of Hong Kong, Institute of Chinese Studies, 1993.

Legge, James, tr. *A Record of Buddhistic Kingdoms: Being an Account by the Chinese Monk Fa-Hien of his Travels in India and Ceylon (A.D. 399–414) in Search of the Buddhist Books of Discipline*. New York: Dover, 1965.

Lewis, Mark Edward. *The Construction of Space in Early China*. Albany: State University of New York Press, 2006.

———. *Early Chinese Empires: Qin and Han*. In History of Imperial China, ed. Timothy Brook. Cambridge: Harvard University Press, 2006.

———. *Sanctioned Violence in Early China*. Albany: State University of New York Press, 1990.

———. "The Suppression of the Three Stages Sect: Apocrypha as a Political Issue." In *Chinese Buddhist Apocrypha*. Ed. Robert E. Buswell, Jr. Honolulu: University of Hawai'i Press, 1990.

———. *Writing and Authority in Early China*. Albany: State University of New York Press, 1999.

Li Bo ji jiao zhu [Collected Poems of Li Bo]. Shanghai: Guji, 1980.

Li, Qiancheng. *Fictions of Enlightenment: Journey to the West, Tower of Myriad Mirrors, and Dream of the Red Chamber*. Honolulu: University of Hawai'i Press, 2004.

Li, Qingquan. "Buddhist Images in Burials: The Murals from Changchuan Tomb No. 1." In *Between Han and Tang: Visual and Material Culture in a Transformative Period*. Ed. Wu Hung. Beijing: Wenwu, 2003.

Li, Wai-yee. "Between 'Literary Mind' and 'Carving Dragons': Order and Excess in *Wenxin diaolong*." In *A Chinese Literary Mind: Culture, Creativity, and Rhetoric in Wenxin Diaolong*. Ed. Zong-qi Cai. Stanford: Stanford University Press, 2001.

———. "*Shishuo xinyu* and the Emergence of Aesthetic Self-Consciousness in the Chinese Tradition." In *Chinese Aesthetics: The Ordering of Literature, the Arts, and the Universe in the Six Dynasties*. Ed. Zong-qi Cai. Honolulu: University of Hawai'i Press, 2004.

Li, Xueqin. *Eastern Zhou and Qin Civilizations*. Tr. K. C. Chang. New Haven: Yale University Press, 1985.

Lin, Shuen-fu. "A Good Place Need Not Be a Nowhere: The Garden and Utopian Thought in the Six Dynasties." In *Chinese Aesthetics: The Ordering of*

Literature, the Arts, and the Universe in the Six Dynasties. Ed. Zong-qi Cai. Honolulu: University of Hawai'i Press, 2004.

———. "Liu Xie on Imagination." In *A Chinese Literary Mind: Culture, Creativity, and Rhetoric in Wenxin Diaolong.* Ed. Zong-qi Cai. Stanford: Stanford University Press, 2001.

Lin, Wen-yüeh. "The Decline and Revival of *Feng-ku* (Wind and Bone): On the Changing Poetic Styles from the Chien'an Era through the High T'ang Period." In *The Vitality of the Lyric Voice: Shih Poetry from the Late Han to the T'ang.* Ed. Shuen-fu Lin and Stephen Owen. Princeton: Princeton University Press, 1986.

Lingley, Kate. "Widows, Monks, Magistrates, and Concubines: Social Dimensions of Sixth-Century Buddhist Art Patronage." Ph.D. diss., University of Chicago, 2004.

Liu, Mau-tsai. *Kutscha und seine Beziehungen zu China vom 2. Jh. bis zum 6. Jh. n. Chr.* 2 vols. Wiesbaden: O. Harrassowitz, 1969.

Liu, Shufen. "Art, Ritual, and Society: Buddhist Practice in Rural China during the Northern Dynasties." *Asia Major,* third series, 8:1 (1995): 19–47.

———. "Jiankang and the Commercial Empire of the Southern Dynasties." In *Culture and Power in the Reconstitution of the Chinese Realm, 200–600.* Ed. Scott Pearce, Audrey Spiro, and Patricia Ebrey. Cambridge: Harvard University Press, 2001.

———. *Liuchao de chengshi yu shehui.* Taipei: Xuesheng, 1992.

Liu, Xinru. *Ancient India and Ancient China: Trade and Religious Exchanges, AD 1–600.* Delhi: Oxford University Press, 1988.

———. *Silk and Religion: An Exploration of Material Life and the Thought of People, AD 600–1200.* Delhi: Oxford University Press, 1996.

Loewe, Michael. *Ways to Paradise: The Chinese Quest for Immortality.* London: George Allen and Unwin, 1979.

Lü, Qianju. "Liang Jin Liu Chao de shixue." In *Zhongguo shixue shi lunwen xuanji.* Vol. 1. Ed. Du Weiyun and Huang Jinxing. Taipei: Huashi, 1976.

Lynn, Richard John. "Wang Bi and Liu Xie's *Wenxin diaolong*: Terms and Concepts, Influence and Affiliations." In *A Chinese Literary Mind: Culture, Creativity and Rhetoric in Wenxin Diaolong.* Ed. Zong-qi Cai. Stanford: Stanford University Press, 2001.

Maeda, Masana. *Heijō no rekishi chirigaku kenkyū.* Tokyo: Kazema Shobō, 1979.

Magnin, Paul. *La vie et l'oeuvre de Huisi (515–577): Les origins de la secte bouddhique chinoise du Tiantai.* Paris: Adrien-Maisonneuve, 1979.

Mair, Victor H. "Buddhism in *The Literary Mind and Ornate Rhetoric*." In *A Chinese Literary Mind: Culture, Creativity and Rhetoric in Wenxin Diaolong.* Ed. Zong-qi Cai. Stanford: Stanford University Press, 2001.

———. *T'ang Transformation Texts: A Study of the Buddhist Contribution to the Rise of Vernacular Fiction and Drama in China.* Cambridge: Harvard University Press, 1989.

———, tr. *Tun-huang Popular Narratives.* Cambridge: Cambridge University Press, 1983.

———. "Xie He's 'Six Laws' of Painting and their Indian Parallels." In *Chinese Aesthetics: The Ordering of Literature, the Arts and the Universe in the Six Dynasties.* Ed. Zong-Qi Cai. Honolulu: University of Hawai'i Press, 2004.

Mair, Victor, and Tsu-lin Mei. "The Sanskrit Origins of Recent Style Prosody." *Harvard Journal of Asiatic Studies* 51:2 (December 1991): 375–470.

Makeham, John. *Transmitters and Creators: Chinese Commentators and Commentaries on the Analects.* Cambridge: Harvard University Press, 2003.

Mao, Han-kuang. "The Evolution in the Nature of the Medieval Genteel Families." In *State and Society in Early Medieval China.* Ed. Albert E. Dien. Stanford: Stanford University Press, 1990.

Marney, John. *Chiang Yen.* Boston: Twayne, 1981.

———. *Liang Chien-wen Ti.* Boston: Twayne, 1976.

Martin, François. "Les joutes poétiques dans la Chine médiévale." *Extrême Orient, Extrême Occident* 20 (1998): 87–109.

Mather, Richard B. *The Age of Eternal Brilliance: Three Lyric Poets of the Yung-ming Era (483–493).* 2 vols. Leiden: E. J. Brill, 2003.

———. "K'ou Ch'ien-chih and the Taoist Theocracy at the Northern Wei Court, 425–451." In *Facets of Taoism.* Ed. Holmes Welch and Anna Seidel. New Haven: Yale University Press, 1979.

———. "The Landscape Buddhism of the Fifth-Century Poet Hsieh Ling-yun." *Journal of Asian Studies* 18 (1958–1959): 67–79.

———, tr. *A New Account of Tales of the World by Liu I-ch'ing with Commentary by Liu Chün.* Minneapolis: University of Minnesota Press, 1976.

———. "A Note on the Dialects of Lo-yang and Nanking during the Southern Dynasties." In *Wen-lin.* Ed. Chow Tse-chung. Madison: University of Wisconsin Press, 1968.

———. *The Poet Shen Yüeh (441–513): The Reticent Marquis.* Princeton: Princeton University Press, 1988.

Matsubara, Saburō. *Chūgoku bukkyō chokoku shi kenkyū.* Tokyo: Yoshikawa Kōbunkan, 1966.

Mazumdar, Sucheta. *Sugar and Society in China: Peasants, Technology, and the World Market.* Cambridge: Harvard University Press, 1998.

McCausland, Shane. *First Masterpiece of Chinese Painting: The Admonitions Scroll.* New York: George Braziller, 2003.

McKnight, Brian E. *The Quality of Mercy: Amnesties and Traditional Chinese Justice.* Honolulu: University of Hawai'i Press, 1981.

Miao, Ronald C. *Early Medieval Chinese Poetry: The Life and Verses of Wang Ts'an (A.D. 177–217).* Wiesbaden: Franz Steiner, 1982.

Michaud, Paul. "The Yellow Turbans." *Monumenta Serica* 17 (1958): 47–127.

Miller, James. *Taoism: A Short Introduction.* Oxford: One World, 2003.

Miller, Roy Andrew. *Accounts of Western Nations in the History of the Northern Chou Dynasty.* Chinese Dynastic Histories Translations No. 6. Berkeley: University of California Press, 1959.

Millward, James A. "Qing Inner Asian Empire and the Return of the Torghuts." In *New Qing Imperial History: The Making of Inner Asian Empires at Qing Chengde.* Ed. James A. Millward, Ruth W. Dunnell, Mark C. Elliott, and Philippe Forêt. London: RoutledgeCurzon, 2004.

Miscevic, Dusanka D. "A Study of the Great Clans of Early Medieval China." *Bulletin of the Museum of Far Eastern Antiquities* 65 (1993): 5–256.

Miyakawa, Hisayuki. "Local Cults around Mount Lu at the Time of Sun En's Rebellion." In *Facets of Taoism: Essays in Chinese Religion.* Ed. Holmes Welch and Anna Seidel. New Haven: Yale University Press, 1979.

———. *Rikuchō shi kenkyū: seiji shakai hen.* Kyoto: Heirakuji, 1964.

———. *Rikuchō shi kenkyū: shūkyō hen.* Kyoto: Heirakuji, 1964.

Miyazaki, Ichisada. *Kyūhin kanjinhō no kenkyū: kakyo zenshi.* Kyoto: Tōyōshi Kenkyūkai, 1956.

Molè, Gabriella. *The T'ü-yü-hun from the Northern Wei to the Time of the Five Dynasties.* Rome: Istituto Italiano per il Medio ed Estremo Oriente, 1970.

Monks and Merchants: Silk Road Treasures from Northwest China, Gansu and Ningxia, 4th–7th Century. Exhibition catalogue for the Asia Society Museum, edited by Annette L. Juliano and Judith A. Lerner. New York: Harry N. Abrams, 2001.

Morino, Shigeo. *Rikuchō shi no kenkyū: shūdan no bungaku to kojin no bungaku.* Tokyo: Daiichi Gakush, 1976.

Mou, Zongsan. *Caixing yu xuanli.* Taipei: Xuesheng, 1978.

Nattier, Jan. "The Meanings of the Maitreya Myth." In *Maitreya: The Future Buddha.* Cambridge: Cambridge University Press, 1988.

———. *Once Upon a Future Time: Studies in a Buddhist Prophecy of Decline.* Berkeley: Asian Humanities Press, 1991.

Needham, Joseph, and Francesca Bray. *Science and Civilisation in China:* Vol. 6: *Biology and Biological Technology, Part II: Agriculture.* Cambridge: Cambridge University Press, 1984.

Needham, Joseph, Christian Daniels, and Nicholas K. Menzies. *Science and Civilisation in China,* Vol. 6: *Biology and Biological Technology, Part III: Agro-Industries and Forestry.* Cambridge: Cambridge University Press, 1996.

Needham, Joseph, Gwei-djen Lu, and Hsing-tsung Huang. *Science and Civilisation in China:* Vol. 6: *Biology and Biological Technology, Part I: Botany.* Cambridge: Cambridge University Press, 1986.

Needham, Joseph, and Ling Wang. *Science and Civilisation in China,* Vol. 3: *Mathematics and the Sciences of the Heavens and the Earth.* Cambridge: Cambridge University Press, 1970.

Ng, On-cho, and Q. Edward Wang. *Mirroring the Past: The Writing and Use of History in Imperial China*. Honolulu: University of Hawai'i Press, 2005.

Nickerson, Peter. "'Opening the Way': Exorcism, Travel, and Soteriology in Early Daoist Mortuary Practice and Its Antecedents." In *Daoist Identity: History, Lineage, and Ritual*. Ed. Livia Kohn and Harold D. Roth. Honolulu: University of Hawai'i Press, 2002.

———. "Taoism, Death, and Bureaucracy in Early Medieval China." Ph.D. diss., University of California, 1996.

Ning, Qiang. *Art, Religion, and Politics in Medieval China: The Dunhuang Cave of the Zhai Family*. Honolulu: University of Hawai'i Press, 2004.

———. "Patrons of the Earliest Dunhuang Caves: A Historical Investigation." In *Between Han and Tang: Religious Art and Archaeology in a Transformative Period*. Ed. Wu Hung. Beijing: Wenwu, 2000.

Nylan, Michael. "Calligraphy, the Sacred Text and Test of Culture." In *Character and Context in Chinese Calligraphy*. Ed. Cary F. Liu, Dora C. Y. Ching, Judith G. Smith. Princeton: The Art Museum, Princeton University, 1999.

Ōmuro, Mikio. *Enrin toshi: chūsei Chūgoku no sekaizō*. Tokyo: Sanseido, 1985.

———. *Tōgen no musō: kodai Chūgoku no han gekijō toshi*. Tokyo: Sanseido, 1984.

Orzech, Charles D. *Politics and Transcendent Wisdom: The Scripture for Humane Kings in the Creation of Chinese Buddhism*. University Park: Pennsylvania State University Press, 1998.

Owen, Stephen, ed. and tr. *An Anthology of Chinese Literature: Beginnings to 1911*. New York: Norton, 1996.

———. *The Great Age of Chinese Poetry: The High T'ang*. New Haven: Yale University Press, 1981.

———. *The Making of Early Chinese Classical Poetry*. Cambridge: Harvard University Press, 2006.

———. *Mi-lou: Poetry and the Labyrinth of Desire*. Cambridge: Harvard University Press, 1989.

———. *Readings in Chinese Literary Thought*. Cambridge: Harvard University Press, 1992.

———. *Remembrances: The Experience of the Past in Chinese Literature*. Cambridge: Harvard University Press, 1986.

———. *Traditonal Chinese Poetry and Poetics: Omen of the World*. Madison: University of Wisconsin Press, 1985.

Pan, Tianshou. *Gu Kaizhi*. Shanghai: Shanghai Renmin, 1958.

Pearce, Scott. "Form and Matter: Archaizing Reform in Sixth-Century China." In *Culture and Power in the Reconstitution of the Chinese Realm, 200–600*. Ed. Scott Pearce, Audrey Spiro, and Patricia Ebrey. Cambridge: Harvard University Press, 2001.

———. "Who, and What, Was Hou Jing?" *Early Medieval China* 6 (2000): 1–31.

———. "The Yü-wen Regime in Sixth Century China." Ph.D. diss., Princeton University, 1987.

Pearce, Scott, Audrey Spiro, and Patricia Ebrey. "Introduction." In *Culture and Power in the Reconstitution of the Chinese Realm*. Ed. Scott Pearce, Audrey Spiro, and Patricia Ebrey. Cambridge: Harvard University Press, 2001.

Perdue, Peter C. *China Marches West: The Qing Conquest of Central Eurasia*. Cambridge: Harvard University Press, 2005.

Piggott, Joan R. *The Emergence of Japanese Kingship*. Stanford: Stanford University Press, 1997.

Pollack, David. *The Fracture of Meaning: Japan's Synthesis of China from the Eighth through the Eighteenth Centuries*. Princeton: Princeton University Press, 1986.

Pregadio, Fabrizio. "Elixirs and Alchemy." In *Daoism Handbook*. Ed. Livia Kohn. Leiden: E. J. Brill, 2000.

Prosser, Adriana G. "Moral Characters: Calligraphy and Bureaucracy in Han China (206 B.C.E.–C.E. 220)." Ph.D. diss., Columbia University, 1995.

Puett, Michael J. *To Become a God: Cosmology, Sacrifice, and Self-Divinization in Early China*. Cambridge: Harvard University Press, 2002.

Pulleyblank, E. G. *The Background of the Rebellion of An Lu-shan*. London: Oxford University Press, 1955.

Qian, Nanxiu. *Spirit and Self in Medieval China: The Shih-shuo hsin-yü and Its Legacy*. Honolulu: University of Hawai'i Press, 2001.

Reischauer, Edwin O., tr. *Ennin's Diary: The Records of a Pilgrimage to China in Search of the Law*. New York: Ronald Press, 1955.

———. *Ennin's Travels in T'ang China*. New York: Ronald Press, 1955.

Rhie, Marilyn Martin. *Early Buddhist Art of China and Central Asia*. 2 vols. Leiden: E. J. Brill, 1999–2002.

Robinet, Isabelle. "Shangqing—Highest Clarity." In *Daoism Handbook*. Ed. Livia Kohn. Leiden: E. J. Brill, 2000.

———. *Taoism: Growth of a Religion*. Tr. Phyllis Brooks. Stanford: Stanford University Press, 1997.

Rogers, Michael C. *The Chronicle of Fu Chien: A Case of Exemplar History*. Chinese Dynastic Histories Translation No. 10. Berkeley: University of California Press, 1968.

Rong, Xinjiang. "The Migrations and Settlements of the Sogdians in the Northern Dynasties, Sui and Tang." *China Archaeology and Art Digest* 4:1 (December 2000): 117–163.

———. *Zhonggu Zhongguo yu wailai wenming*. Beijing: Sanlian, 2001.

Rouzer, Paul. *Articulated Ladies: Gender and the Male Community in Early Chinese Literature*. Cambridge: Harvard University Press, 2001.

Sage, Steven F. *Ancient Sichuan and the Unification of China*. Albany: State University of New York Press, 1992.

Sakuma, Kichiya. *Gi Shin Nanbokuchō suirishi kenkyū*. Tokyo: Kaimei, 1980.

Schafer, Edward H. *The Golden Peaches of Samarkand: A Study of T'ang Exotics.* Berkeley: University of California Press, 1963.

———. *The Vermilion Bird: T'ang Images of the South.* Berkeley: University of California Press, 1967.

Scharf, Robert H. *Coming to Terms with Chinese Buddhism: A Reading of the Treasure Store Treatise.* Honolulu: University of Hawai'i Press, 2002.

Schopen, Gregory. *Bones, Stones, and Buddhist Monks: Collected Papers on the Archaeology, Epigraphy, and Texts of Monastic Buddhism in India.* Honolulu: University of Hawai'i Press, 1997.

———. *Buddhist Monks and Business Matters: Still More Papers on Monastic Buddhism in India.* Honolulu: University of Hawai'i Press, 2004.

———. *Figments and Fragments of Mahāyāna Buddhism in India: More Collected Papers.* Honolulu: University of Hawai'i Press, 2005.

Schreiber, Gerhard. "The History of the Former Yen Dynasty." *Monumenta Serica* 15 (1956): 1–141.

Seidel, Anna K. "Chronicle of Taoist Studies in the West, 1950–1990." *Cahiers d'Extrême-Asie* 5 (1990): 223–347.

———. "Early Taoist Ritual." *Cahiers d'Extrême-Asie* 4 (1988): 199–204.

———. "Imperial Treasures and Taoist Sacraments: Taoist Roots in the Apocrypha." In *Tantric and Taoist Studies* 2. Ed. Michel Strickmann. Brussels: Institut Belge des Hautes Etudes Chinoises, 1983.

Sen, Tansen. *Buddhism, Diplomacy, and Trade: The Realignment of Sino-Indian Relations, 600–1400.* Honolulu: University of Hawai'i Press, 2003.

Shih, Sheng-han. *A Preliminary Survey of the Book* Ch'i Min Yao Shu: *An Agricultural Encyclopedia of the 6th Century.* Peking: Science Press, 1974.

Shinohara, Koichi, "Quanding's Biography of Zhiyi, the Fourth Chinese Patriarch of the Tiantai Tradition." In *Speaking of Monks: Religious Biography in India and China.* Ed. Phyllis Granoff and Koichi Shinohara. Oakville, Ontario: Mosaic Press, 1992.

Shyrock, J. K., tr. *The Study of Human Abilities: The* Jen wu chih *of Liu Shao.* New Haven: American Oriental Society, 1937.

Skinner, G. William. "Cities and the Hierarchy of Local Systems." In *The City in Late Imperial China.* Ed. G. William Skinner. Stanford: Stanford University Press, 1977.

———. "Marketing and Social Structures in Rural China." 3 parts. *Journal of Asian Studies* 24:1 (1964): 3–44; 24:2 (1964): 195–228; 24:3 (1965): 363–399.

———. "Regional Urbanization in Nineteenth-Century China." In *The City in Late Imperial China.* Ed. G. William Skinner. Stanford: Stanford University Press, 1977.

Smith, Thomas Eric. "Ritual and the Shaping of Narrative: The Legend of the Han Emperor Wu." Ph.D. diss., University of Michigan, 1992.

Somers, Robert M. "Time, Space and Structure in the Consolidation of the T'ang Dynasty (A.D. 617–700)." In *State and Society in Early Medieval China*. Ed. Albert E. Dien. Stanford: Stanford University Press, 1990.

Soper, Alexander C. "Imperial Cave-Chapels of the Northern Dynasties: Donors, Beneficiaries, Dates." *Artibus Asiae* 28 (1966): 241–270.

———. *Literary Evidence for Early Buddhist Art in China*. Ascona: Artibus Asiae, 1959.

———. "South Chinese Influence on Buddhist Art of the Six Dynasties." *Bulletin of the Museum of Far Eastern Antiquities* 32 (1960): 47–112.

Spiro, Audrey. *Contemplating the Ancients: Aesthetic and Social Issues in Early Chinese Portraiture*. Berkeley: University of California Press, 1990.

———. "Hybrid Vigor: Memory, Mimesis, and the Matching of Meanings in Fifth-Century Buddhist Sculpture." In *Culture and Power in the Reconstitution of the Chinese Realm, 200–600*. Ed. Scott Pearce, Audrey Spiro, and Patricia Ebrey. Cambridge: Harvard University Press, 2001.

———. "New Light on Gu Kaizhi: Windows on the Soul." *Journal of Chinese Religions* 16:1 (Fall 1988): 1–16.

Stein, Rolf A. "Religious Daoism and Popular Religion from the Second to Seventh Centuries." *Facets of Taoism*. Ed. Holmes Welch and Anna Seidel. New Haven: Yale University Press, 1979.

———. "Remarques sur les mouvements de taoïsme politico-religieux au IIe siècle ap. J.C." *T'oung Pao* 50 (1963): 1–78.

Steinhardt, Nancy S. *Chinese Imperial City Planning*. Honolulu: University of Hawai'i Press, 1990.

———. "From Koguryŏ to Gansu and Xinjiang: Funerary and Worship Space in North Asia 4th–7th Centuries." In *Between Han and Tang: Cultural and Artistic Interaction in a Transformative Period*. Ed. Wu Hung. Beijing: Wenwu, 2001.

Sterckx, Roel. *The Animal and the Daemon in Early China*. Albany: State University of New York Press, 2002.

Strassberg, Richard E. *Inscribed Landscapes: Travel Writing from Imperial China*. Berkeley: University of California Press, 1994.

Strickmann, Michel. "On the Alchemy of T'ao Hung-ching." In *Facets of Taoism: Essays in Chinese Religion*. Ed. Holmes Welch and Anna Seidel. New Haven: Yale University Press, 1979.

———. *Chinese Magical Medicine*. Ed. Bernard Faure. Stanford: Stanford University Press, 2002.

———. "The Mao Shan Revelations: Taoism and the Aristocracy." *T'oung Pao* 63 (1977): 1–64.

———. *Le Taoïsme du Mao chan: chronique d'une revelation*. Paris: Collège de France, Mémoires de l'Institut des Hautes Études Chinoises, Vol. 17, 1981.

Sullivan, Michael. *The Arts of China*. 3rd ed. Berkeley: University of California Press, 1984.

———. *The Birth of Landscape Painting in China*. Berkeley: University of California Press, 1961.

Sun, Cecile Chu-chin. *Pearl from the Dragon's Mouth: Evocations of Feeling and Scene in Chinese Poetry*. Ann Arbor: University of Michigan, Center for Chinese Studies, 1995.

Takeda, Akira. *Sō Sō: sono kōdō to bungaku*. Tokyo: Hyōron Shakai, 1973.

Tang, Yiming. "The Voices of Wei-Jin Scholars: A Study of 'Qingtan.'" Ph.D. diss., Columbia University, 1991.

Tang, Yongtong. *Wei Jin xuanxue lun gao*. Rpt. in *Tang Yongtong quan ji*. Shijiazhuang: Hebei Renmin, 2000.

Tang, Zhangru. "Clients and Bound Retainers in the Six Dynasties Period." In *State and Society in Early Medieval China*. Ed. Albert E. Dien. Stanford: Stanford University Press, 1990.

———. "Menfa de xingcheng ji qi shuailuo." *Wuhan Daxue Renwen Kexue Xuebao* 8 (1959): 1–24.

———. *Wei Jin Nanbeichao shi luncong*. Beijing: Sanlian, 1955.

———. *Wei Jin Nanbeichao shi luncong xu bian*. Beijing: Sanlian, 1959.

———. *Wei Jin Nanbeichao Sui Tang shi san lun*. Wuhan: Wuhan Daxue, 1992.

Tanigawa, Michio. *Medieval Chinese Society and the Local "Community."* Tr. and intr. Joshua A. Fogel. Berkeley: University of California Press, 1985.

———. *Zui Tō teikoku keisei shi ron*. Tokyo: Chikuma Shobo, 1971.

Teiser, Stephen F. *The Ghost Festival in Medieval China*. Princeton: Princeton University Press, 1988.

———. *The Scripture of the Ten Kings of Hell and the Making of Purgatory in Medieval Chinese Buddhism*. Honolulu: University of Hawai'i Press, 1994.

Thorp, Robert L., and Richard Ellis Vinograd. *Chinese Art and Culture*. New York: Harry N. Abrams, 2001.

Tian, Xiaofei. *Tao Yuanming and Manuscript Culture: The Record of a Dusty Table*. Seattle: University of Washington Press, 2005.

Tokuno, Kyoko. "The Evaluation of Indigenous Scriptures in Chinese Buddhist Bibliographical Catalogues." In *Chinese Buddhist Apocrypha*. Ed. Robert E. Buswell, Jr. Honolulu: University of Hawai'i Press, 1990.

Tregear, T. R. *A Geography of China*. Chicago: Aldine, 1965.

Tremblay, Xavier. *Pour une histoire de la Sérinde: Le Manichéisme parmi les peuples et religions d'Asie Centrale d'après les sources primaires*. Vienna: Verlag der Österreichischen Akademie der Wissenschaften, 2001.

Tsai, Kathryn Ann, tr. *Lives of the Nuns: Biographies of Chinese Buddhist Nuns from the Fourth to Sixth Centuries*. Honolulu: University of Hawai'i Press, 1994.

Tsiang, Katherine R. "Disjunctures of Time, Text, and Imagery in Reconstructions of the Guyang Cave at Longmen." In *Between Han and Tang: Religious Art and Archaeology in a Transformative Period*. Ed. Wu Hung. Beijing: Wenwu, 2000.

Tsuchiya, Masaaki. "Confessions of Sins and Awareness of Self in the *Taiping jing*." In *Daoist Identity: History, Lineage, and Ritual*. Ed. Livia Kohn and Harold D. Roth. Honolulu: University of Hawai'i Press, 2002.

Tsukamoto, Zenryū. *A History of Early Chinese Buddhism: From Its Introduction to the Death of Hui-yüan*. 2 vols. Tr. Leon Hurvitz. Tokyo: Kodansha International, 1985.

Tuan, Yi-fu. *China*. Chicago: Aldine, 1969.

Twitchett, D. C. "The Composition of the T'ang Ruling Class: New Evidence from Tunhuang." In *Perspectives on the T'ang*. Ed. Arthur F. Wright and Denis Twitchett. New Haven: Yale University Press, 1973.

———. *Financial Administration under the T'ang Dynasty*. Cambridge: Cambridge University Press, 1970.

———. "Monasteries and China's Economy in Medieval Times." *Bulletin of the School of Oriental and African Studies* 19:3 (1957): 526–549.

Van Slyke, Lyman P. *Yangtze: Nature, History, and the River*. Reading: Addison-Wesley, 1988.

Vervoorn, Aat. *Men of the Cliffs and Caves: The Development of the Chinese Eremetic Tradition to the End of the Han Dynasty*. Hong Kong: Chinese University, 1990.

von den Steinen, Diether. "Poems of Ts'ao Ts'ao." *Monumenta Serica* 4 (1939–1940): 135–181.

von Glahn, Richard. *The Sinister Way: The Divine and the Demonic in Chinese Religious Culture*. Berkeley: University of California Press, 2004.

Wagner, Rudolph G. *The Craft of a Chinese Commentator: Wang Bi on the Laozi*. Albany: State University of New York Press, 2000.

———. *Language, Ontology, and Political Philosophy in China: Wang Bi's Scholarly Exporation of the Dark (Xuanxue)*. Albany: State University of New York Press, 2003.

Waley, Arthur. *Translations from the Chinese*. New York: A. A. Knopf, 1941.

Wallacker, Benjamin E. "Studies in Medieval Chinese Siegecraft: The Siege of Chien-k'ang." *Journal of Asian History* 5:1 (1971): 35–54.

Wang, Eugene. *Shaping the Lotus Sutra: Buddhist Visual Culture in Medieval China*. Seattle: University of Washington Press, 2005.

———. "The Taming of the Shrew: Wang Hsi-chih [Xizhi] (303–361) and Calligraphic Gentrification in the Seventh Century." In *Character and Context in Chinese Calligraphy*. Ed. Cary F. Liu, Dora C. Y. Ching, and Judith G. Smith. Princeton: The Art Museum, Princeton University, 1999.

Wang, Ling. *Tea and Chinese Culture*. San Francisco: Long River, 2005.

Wang, Siu-kit, tr. *Early Chinese Literary Criticism*. Hong Kong: Joint Publishing, 1983.

Wang, Zhenping. *Ambassadors from the Islands of Immortals: China-Japan Relations in the Han-Tang Period*. Honolulu: University of Hawai'i Press, 2005.

Wang, Zhongluo. *Cao Cao*. Shanghai: Renmin, 1956.

———. *Wei Jin Nanbeichao shi*. 2 vols. 2nd ed., rev. and expanded. Shanghai: Shanghai Renmin, 1979.

Wang, Zongshu. *Han Civilization*. Tr. K. C. Chang et al. New Haven: Yale University Press, 1982.

Ware, J. R. *Alchemy, Medicine, and Religion in the China of* A.D. *320: The Nei P'ien of Ke Hung*. Cambridge: Massachusetts Institute of Technology Press, 1981.

Watson, Burton. *Chinese Lyricism: Shih Poetry from the Second to the Twelfth Century*. New York: Columbia University Press, 1971.

———. *Chinese Rhyme-Prose: Poems in the Fu Form from the Han and Six Dynasties*. New York: Columbia University Press, 1971.

Wechsler, Howard J. *Offerings of Jade and Silk: Ritual and Symbol in the Legitimation of the T'ang Dynasty*. New Haven: Yale University Press, 1985.

Wei, Jiazan, ed., *Suzhou lidai yuanlin lu*. Beijing: Yanshan, 1992.

Westbrook, Francis. "Landscape Description in the Lyric Poetry and 'Fuh on Dwelling in the Mountains' of Shieh Ling-yunn." Ph.D. diss., Yale University, 1972.

Wiens, Herold. *China's March into the Tropics*. Washington, DC: Office of Naval Research, U.S. Navy, 1952.

Wilhelm, Hellmut. "Shih Ch'ung and his Chin-ku-yüan." *Monumenta Serica* 18 (1959): 314–327.

Wong, Dorothy C. *Chinese Steles: Pre-Buddhist and Buddhist Use of a Symbolic Form*. Honolulu: University of Hawai'i Press, 2004.

———. "Ethnicity and Identity: Northern Nomads as Buddhist Art Patrons during the Period of Northern and Southern Dynasties." In *Political Frontiers, Ethnic Boundaries, and Human Geographies in Chinese History*. Ed. Nicola Di Cosmo and Don J. Wyatt. London: RoutledgeCurzon, 2003.

———. "Women as Buddhist Art Patrons during the Northern and Southern Dynasties." In *Between Han and Tang: Religious Art and Archaeology in a Transformative Period*. Ed. Wu Hung. Beijing: Wenwu, 2000.

Wriggins, Sally Hovey. *Xuanzang: A Buddhist Pilgrim on the Silk Road*. Boulder: Westview, 1996.

Wright, Arthur F. "The Formation of Sui Ideology, 581–604." In *Chinese Thought and Institutions*. Ed. John K. Fairbank. Chicago: University of Chicago Press, 1957.

———. "Fo-t'u-teng: A Biography." *Harvard Journal of Asiatic Studies* 11 (1948): 322–370.

———. "The Sui Dynasty (581–617)." In *The Cambridge History of China*, Vol. 4: *Sui and T'ang China, 589–906, Part I*. Ed. Denis Twitchett and John K. Fairbank. Cambridge: Cambridge University Press, 1979.

———. *The Sui Dynasty: The Unification of China*, A.D. *581–617*. New York: Alfred A. Knopf, 1978.

————. "Sui Yang-ti: Personality and Stereotype." In *The Confucian Persuasion*. Ed. Arthur F. Wright. Stanford: Stanford University Press, 1960.

Wu, Fusheng. *The Poetics of Decadence: Chinese Poetry of the Southern Dynasties and Late Tang Period*. Albany: State University of New York Press, 1998.

Wu, Gongzheng. *Liu chao yuan lin*. Nanjing: Nanjing Chubanshe, 1992.

Wu, Hung. "Buddhist Elements in Early Chinese Art." *Artibus Asiae* 47:3–4 (1986): 263–316.

————. *Monumentality in Early Chinese Art and Architecture*. Stanford: Stanford University Press, 1995.

————. *The Wu Liang Shrine: The Ideology of Early Chinese Pictorial Art*. Stanford: Stanford University Press, 1989.

Xiao, Chi. *The Chinese Garden as Lyric Enclave: A Generic Study of the Story of the Stone*. Ann Arbor: University of Michigan, Center for Chinese Studies, 2001.

Xiao, Tong. *Wen xuan or Selections of Refined Literature*, Vols. 1–3. Tr. David R. Knechtges. Princeton: Princeton University Press, 1982–1996.

Xiong, Victor Cunrui. *Emperor Yang of the Sui: His Life, Times, and Legacy*. Albany: State University of New York Press, 2006.

————. "*Ji*-Entertainers in Tang Chang'an." In *Presence and Presentation: Women in the Chinese Literati Tradition*. Ed. Sherry J. Mou. London: MacMillan, 1999.

————. "The Land-tenure System of Tang China: A Study of the Equal-field System and the Turfan Documents." *T'oung Pao* 85 (1999): 328–390.

————. "Ritual Architecture under the Northern Wei." In *Between Han and Tang: Visual and Material Culture in a Transformative Period*. Ed. Wu Hung. Beijing: Wenwu, 2003.

————. *Sui-Tang Chang'an*. Ann Arbor: University of Michigan, Center for Chinese Studies, 2000.

Xu, Gan. *Balanced Discourses*. Tr. John Makeham. Intr. John Makeham and Dang Shengyuan. New Haven: Yale University Press, 2002.

Yamada, Toshiaki. "The Lingbao School." In *Daoism Handbook*. Ed. Livia Kohn. Leiden: E. J. Brill, 2000.

Yan, Gengwang. *Zhongguo difang xingzheng zhidu shi*, Vol. 3. Nangang: Zhongyang Yanjiuyuan Lishi Yuyan Yanjiusuo, 1963.

Yan, Zhitui. *See* Yen Chih-t'ui.

Yang, C. K. *Religion in Chinese Society: A Study of Contemporary Social Functions of Religion and Some of Their Historical Factors*. Berkeley: University of California Press, 1961.

Yang, Chung-i. "Evolution of the Status of 'Dependents.'" In *Chinese Social History: Translations of Selected Studies*. Ed. E-tu Zen Sun and John De Francis. New York: Octagon Books, 1972.

Yang, Hong. "Changes in Urban Architecture, Interior Design, and Lifestyles between the Han and Tang Dynasties." In *Between Han and Tang: Visual and Material Culture in a Transformative Period*. Ed. Wu Hung. Beijing: Wenwu, 2003.

Yang, Hsiung [Xiong]. *The Canon of Supreme Mystery*. Tr. Michael Nylan. Albany: State University of New York Press, 1993.

Yang, Hsüan-chih. *A Record of the Buddhist Monasteries in Lo-yang*. Tr. Wang Yi-t'ung. Princeton: Princeton University Press, 1984.

Yang, Lien-sheng. "Great Families of the Eastern Han." In *Chinese Social History: Translations of Selected Studies*. Ed. E-tu Zen Sun and John De Francis. New York: Octagon Books, 1972.

———. "Notes on the Economic History of the Chin Dynasty." *Harvard Journal of Asiatic Studies* 9 (1945–1947): 107–185. Rpt. in *Studies in Chinese Institutional History*. Cambridge: Harvard University Press, 1961.

Yang, Xiaoshan. *Metamorphosis of the Private Sphere: Gardens and Objects in Tang-Song Poetry*. Cambridge: Harvard University Press, 2003.

Yeh, Chia-ying and Jan W. Walls. "Theory, Standards, and Practice of Criticizing Poetry in Chung Hung's *Shih-p'in*." In *Studies in Chinese Poetry and Poetics*. Vol. 1. Ed. Ronald C. Miao. San Francisco: Chinese Materials Center, 1978.

Yen, Chih-t'ui. *Family Instructions for the Yen Clan*. Tr. Teng Ssu-yü. Leiden: E. J. Brill, 1968.

Yoshikawa, Tadao. *Rikuchō seishin shi kenkyū*. Kyoto: Doshosha. 1984.

Yü, Chün-fang. "P'u-t'o Shan: Pilgrimage and the Creation of the Chinese Potalaka." In *Pilgrims and Sacred Sites in China*. Berkeley: University of California Press, 1992.

Yu, Taishan. "A History of the Relationships between the Western and Eastern Han, Wei, Jin, Northern and Southern Dynasties and the Western Regions." *Sino-Platonic Papers* 131, March, 2004.

Yü, Ying-shih. "Han Foreign Relations." In *Cambridge History of Ancient China*, Vol. 1: *The Ch'in and Han Empires*. Ed. Michael Loewe. Cambridge: Cambridge University Press, 1986.

———. "Individualism and the Neo-Taoist Movement in Wei-Chin China." In *Individualism and Holism: Studies in Confucian and Taoist Values*. Ed. Donald Munro. Ann Arbor: University of Michigan, Center for Chinese Studies, 1985.

Zheng, Yan. "A Preliminary Study of Wei-Jin Tombs with Murals in the Hexi Region." In *Between Han and Tang: Cultural and Artistic Interaction in a Transformative Period*. Ed. Wu Hung. Beijing: Wenwu, 2001.

Zhou, Yiliang. *Wei Jin Nanbeichao shi lunji*. Beijing: Beijing Daxue, 1997.

Zhu, Yanshi. "The Capital City Ye of the Eastern Wei and the Northern Qi." In *Between Han and Tang: Visual and Material Culture in a Transformative Period*. Ed. Wu Hung. Beijing: Wenwu, 2003.

Ziporyn, Brook. *The Penumbra Unbound: The Neo-Taoist Philosophy of Guo Xiang*. Albany: State University of New York Press, 2003.

Zürcher, Erik. *The Buddhist Conquest of China*. 2 vols. Leiden: E. J. Brill, 1959.

———. "Buddhist Influence on Early Taoism: A Survey of Scriptural Evidence." *T'oung Pao* 66 (1980): 84–147.

———. "Prince Moonlight: Messianism and Eschatology in Early Medieval Chinese Buddhism." *Toung Pao* 68 (1982): 1–75.

ACKNOWLEDGMENTS

I would like to express my appreciation to all the scholars whose research I have drawn upon in writing this history of the Northern and Southern Dynasties. Their names can be found in the notes and bibliography. I also wish to acknowledge my debt to Timothy Brook, general editor of the History of Imperial China, for support and many helpful conversations; to Kathleen McDermott of Harvard University Press for conceiving and sponsoring the series; and to Susan Wallace Boehmer, also at the Press, for numerous suggestions on how to improve this book. I further owe a great deal to Albert Dien, who read the entire manuscript and offered many criticisms and comments, and whose *Six Dynasties Civilization* provided invaluable assistance in learning about the material culture of the period and the range of images available. Finally, I would like to thank my wife, Kristin Ingrid Fryklund, for all her work in preparing and proofreading the manuscript. Any remaining errors and, unless otherwise noted, all translations are my own.

INDEX

Against Cursive Script, 242

Agriculture, 118–127; agricultural colonies, 55, 57, 135–137, 138–139; barley, 122, 123, 124; beans, 124; and Buddhism, 16–17, 121, 126, 138–139, 158; crop rotation, 124–125; and Daoism, 16–17, 121; *Essential Methods of the Common People (Qi min yao shu)*, 116, 118–125, 174; fertilizer use, 124; fruits, 101, 116, 120, 124, 125; ginger, 123; grain storage, 125; harrowing techniques, 121; irrigation, 10, 13, 14, 119, 136, 137; market farming, 120, 125; millet, 7, 11, 122, 124, 125, 127, 138, 139; milling mechanization, 126; in north China, 7, 10–11, 16, 55, 56–58, 78–79, 114, 116, 119, 120–121, 124, 125, 135–137, 138–139; plows, 121; rice cultivation, 5, 14, 116, 120, 121, 122–124, 125–126, 127; and samgha households, 138–139, 207; seeds, 122–124; and slavery, 116, 120, 135; sorghum, 7, 11; in south China, 7, 10, 12, 13–14, 16, 56, 57, 116, 119, 121, 122–123, 124, 125, 126, 137–138; sugar, 158; tea, 126, 127, 158; vegetables, 7, 124, 125; wheat, 7, 11, 122, 123, 124, 125. *See also* Peasants

Amu Darya river, 164

Animal husbandry, 114, 119, 127, 138, 139

An Lushan rebellion, 182

Appearance of Southern Grasses and Trees, The (Nan fang cao mu zhuang), 21

Ban Gu, 89, 91, 235

Baoji, 15

Ba people, 217

Bei Jian River, 15

Beijing, 256, 257

Bian Mountain, 220

Big Dipper, 185

Biographies of Eminent Monks (Gao seng zhuan), 112–113, 218, 245

Biography of Mu, Son of Heaven (Mu tianzi zhuan), 194, 246

Bodhgaya, 161

Bodhidharma, 108, 163

Bodhisattva Guanshiyin Scripture, 193

Boling, 132–133

Book of the Jin, 68

Book of the Han, 18

Book of the Liang Dynasty, 112

Book of the [Northern] Wei, 245

Book of the Song Dynasty, 245

Book of the Southern Qi, 245

Book of the Sui, 116, 238–239, 245

Book of the Wei (Wei shu), 105, 138, 167

Brahmanic faith, 161

Broad Records of the Taiping Reign Period (Taiping guangji), 131

Buddhism, 4, 204–220; afterlife/rebirth in, 170, 178, 184, 186–189, 206–207, 209–210, 212, 214–215, 216; and agriculture, 16–17, 121, 126, 138–139, 158; Amitabha, 205–206, 210; animals and topography in, 216–217; arrival in China, 3, 25, 196, 204–205; bodhisattvas, 158, 163, 199, 206–207, 210, 213, 215, 219; Chan (Zen) school, 108; charitable contributions, 117, 158, 159, 188, 207, 214, 215; devotion to images in, 104, 108, 109–110, 112–113, 116–117, 160, 205, 207, 208–210, 213, 215;

Buddhism (continued)

divinities in, 208, 212; Dunhuang caves, 101, 184, 187; five moral precepts, 210–211; foreign monks, 162, 163; future Buddha Maitreya, 158, 163, 186–187, 188, 213; The Great Event, 159; in Han dynasty, 4, 162, 184, 205, 210, 215; Heaven-Man Teaching, 210–211; hermits in, 23; and India, 24–25, 156–157, 159; Inexhaustible Treasury, 214; karma, 214, 215; and kinship, 5, 178, 183–189, 196; and landownership, 138–139; lay piety, 158–159, 161; and literary theory, 236–237; local cults rejected by, 216–217, 218–219, 220; and Longmen caves, 112, 209–210; Lotus Sutra, 105, 212–213; magic in, 163–164, 247; meditation in, 187, 210; merit cloisters, 173; millenarianism in, 212–214; and miracle tales, 109; monasticism in, 16–17, 25, 96, 109, 115, 116, 118, 126, 138–139, 152, 156–157, 159, 160, 161, 162, 163, 173, 184, 188–189, 205, 207–208, 210, 211–212, 213–214, 215, 216, 218–219, 231; Mulian, 188–189; in north China, 144, 204–206, 207–212; past Buddhas, 185; Prince Moonlight, 213; Pure Land school, 205–206, 210, 215; and Queen Mother of the West, 199; relationship to Daoism, 16–17, 187, 212–216; relics, 161–162, 163, 249, 250; rituals, 158, 160, 170, 184, 210, 215; sacred texts, 105, 158, 159, 166, 193, 205, 212, 213, 214, 215; Sakyamuni, 168, 185, 207; and samgha households, 138–139, 207, 211; Sect of the Three Stages, 214; seven treasures, 159–160, 162; and social elites, 108, 110, 111, 112, 204–205, 210; in south China, 16–17, 23–24, 71, 144, 205, 206; state sponsorship, 5, 205, 206–208, 215–216, 248, 249; stupas, 158, 161, 184, 185–187, 213, 215–216; Sumedha, 168–169; and tea drinking, 126; temples, 5, 16, 24, 86, 101, 102–113, 114, 158–159, 161, 188, 196, 208, 215, 249, 252; Three Evil Paths, 188; Three Treasures in, 188; and trade, 156–162, 164, 196, 204, 205; travels of monks, 152, 156–157, 162; Tushita Heaven, 186–187; Vulture Peak, 212–213, 216–217; and women, 110, 192–193; and Yungang caves, 104–105, 112, 207, 209–210

Bukong, 214

Byzantine empire, 160–161, 166

Cai Shun, 168

Cai Yong, 241–242

Calligraphy, 20, 98, 100, 179, 241–244; copies and forgeries, 242–244

Canon of Change (Yi jing), 40, 48, 185, 186, 197, 202, 221, 222, 223, 224

Canon of Great Peace (Taiping jing), 197

Canon of Mountains and Seas (Shan hai jing), 246

Canon of Odes (Shi jing), 236, 238

Canon of the Way and Its Power, 199, 205, 221, 222, 223

Cao Cao, 33–37, 58, 59, 78, 92, 200; cold-food cult banned by, 174; military and agricultural colonies established by, 54–55, 57; and Nine-Rank system, 38–39, 40, 41; as poet, 227, 228

Cao Pi, 227, 228; Authoritative Judgments (Dian lun), 232–233; as Emperor Wen of Wei, 19–20, 36; poetry anthology compiled by, 238; The Qualities of the Gentleman, 40–41

Cao Rui, 36, 41

Cao Shuang, 36, 48–49

Cao Wei state. See Wei, kingdom of (Three Kingdoms period)

Cao Zhi, 19–20, 41; "Mulberry on the Bank," 228; as poet, 195, 227–228, 231–232; "Rhapsody on the Goddess of the Luo River," 195

Central Asia, 144, 168, 185, 250, 256; and Buddhism, 3, 156–157, 164, 196, 204, 205, 231; trade with China, 3, 160, 164, 196, 204, 205

Ceylon, 160

Chang'an, 69, 78–79, 92, 168, 205, 248, 255; and Dong Zhuo, 33; as Han capital, 6, 15, 25, 35, 252; as Han Zhao capital, 74; and Huan Wen, 65; as Jin capital, 51; as Northern Zhou capital, 251; as Sui capital, 164, 251; as Western Wei capital, 84, 133

Changqiu Temple, 109–110

Changsha, 15

Character evaluation, 38–44, 53, 180–181, 235; and calligraphy, 241, 242, 243; and pure conversation, 45–49, 222

Chen Baxian, 73

Chen dynasty: collapse of, 73, 85, 249, 252; establishment of, 73; the military in, 70, 73

Chen Jinggu, 193

Chen Shou: Records of the Three Kingdoms, 245

Chengdu, 64, 90, 91

Chengdu plain, 11
Cheng-Han state, 64
Cheng Pu, 57
Chi Chao, 214–215
Chiang Qu: *Record of the States South of Mount Hua (Huayang guo zhi)*, 21, 245
Chile tribes, 148, 149
Chinese culture: and countryside excursions, 19, 22, 23, 100; expansion and diversification of, 2, 3, 18–21, 26–27; and gardens, 23, 26, 86, 94, 95, 96, 98–102, 120, 196; in Jiangnan region, 6, 20–21, 24, 25–27; and mountains, 23–24; music, 20, 52, 224, 231; in north China, 2, 7, 25, 100–102; regional cultures, 17–22, 23–24, 25–27; relationship to urban life, 86, 94; and rural villas, 94, 95, 96–98; and social elites, 2, 3, 5, 19–20, 22–23, 26–27, 31, 41, 44–51, 52–53, 67, 71, 86, 89–90, 94, 96, 98, 100, 102, 108, 120, 180–181, 205, 229–232; and Sogdians, 166; in south China, 2, 6, 7, 19–27, 35, 94–96, 98–100, 118, 258. *See also* Calligraphy; Literature
Chronicle of the Sixteen Kingdoms (Shiliu guo chunqin), 217
Chu Pou, 65
City god cults, 219–220
Civil society vs. Chinese state, 45
Classic of the Way and Its Power (Dao de jing), 48
Cold Food Festival, 171, 174–175
Commentary to the Classic of Waterways (Shui jing zhu), 21, 171–172
Confucianism, 86, 156, 176, 238, 245; *Analects*, 223; Confucius on eremitism, 95; and great families, 28, 30–31, 53; in Han dynasty, 28, 30–31, 222, 224; virtue of filiality in, 31, 39, 43, 168; Wang Bi on, 223–224
Country estates. *See* Rural villas
Cui Hao, 204

Dai Yong, 99
Danyang, 256
Daoan, 104
Daoism, 4, 96, 167, 168, 197–204, 225; afterlife/rebirth in, 197, 200–201, 203, 212, 214, 215; and agriculture, 16–17, 121; and alchemy, 201–202; and anomaly accounts, 246–247; blood sacrifices rejected by, 203, 204, 217, 218, 220; and calligraphy, 243–244; collective salvation in, 199, 200; diet in, 199, 201; divinities in, 197, 198–199, 203, 204–205, 212; end of time/Great Peace, 199; in Han dynasty, 4, 198–201, 215; Heaven of Great Purity, 202; Heaven of Supreme Purity, 202; hermits in, 23, 26, 95; individual immortality in, 200–201, 204; and kinship, 5, 184, 196; Laozi, 197, 199, 203, 204, 205, 223–224; Lingbao tradition, 24, 184, 214–215, 218; local cults rejected by, 216, 217–218, 220; Maoshan school/Highest Clarity (*Shangqing*) tradition, 24, 194, 202–203, 243–244; meditation in, 199, 202, 203, 204; millenarianism in, 199–200, 204, 212, 213; Mysterious Woman in, 193–194, 197; in north China, 198, 200, 203–204, 218; paradises in, 159; Perfected Men and Women, 202; and Queen Mother of the West, 168, 198–199; relationship to Buddhism, 16–17, 187, 212–216; rituals, 197, 200, 203, 215; sacred texts, 196, 197, 199, 202–203, 204, 212, 218, 222, 223, 224, 235, 243–244; self-perfection in, 224; in Sichuan, 13, 35, 64, 199–200, 217; Six Heavens, 203; and social elites, 202–203, 204, 212; in south China, 16–17, 23–24, 199–200, 202–203, 204, 218; state sponsorship, 5, 199–200, 203, 204, 248, 249; Three Worms, 201; transformation of human bodies and longevity, 197; wandering sages, 211; in Warring States period, 196, 197; Way of the Heavenly Masters, 199–200, 202, 203–204, 217; and women, 192, 193–194
Dark Studies, 48–49, 50, 205, 221–225, 245; and binary oppositions, 221; and literary theory, 233, 235, 237; and nothingness (*wu*), 222, 223, 224–225; and spontaneity, 221, 224, 225
Daxingcheng: as Sui capital, 251–252, 253–254, 258; as Tang capital, 252
Declarations of the Perfected (Zhen gao), 244
Dengxian, 167, 190
Di Renjie, 211
Di tribe, 76, 79
Dong Fangshuo, 246–247
Dong Zhuo, 32–33
Dongso'n culture, 155
Dongting Lake, 12, 15
Duan Chengshi, 161–162
Dujiangyan project, 10, 11
Dunhuang, 164, 166, 173, 205, 211–212; caves at, 101, 184, 187; tombs at, 189–190

Eastern Jin dynasty, 62–70; Buddhism in, 205, 206; collapse of, 69–70; establishment of, 25–26, 51–52, 62–63, 64–65, 100, 137, 202; Jiankang as capital, 25–26, 51–52, 63, 64, 69, 96, 100, 127, 153; Wang family, 172
Eastern Wei dynasty, 84, 85, 92, 133
Economic conditions: currency policies, 117; household economy, 127–128; in north China, 113–116; in south China, 71, 113, 116–117, 129, 255–256, 258. See also Trade
Equal-field system (jun tian), 120, 133–134, 139–140, 248
Eremitism, 118, 140–141, 211, 222; hermits, 22–23, 49, 95–96, 201; among social elites, 22–23, 45, 49–50, 53, 67, 98, 183
Erzhu Rong, 83, 109, 111
Essential Methods of the Common People (Qi min yao shu), 116, 118–125, 174
Examination of Ancient Histories, 245

Family Instructions of the Yan Clan, The, 176–180, 241
Fan Ye, 245
Faxian, 24–25, 157, 160
Fei River, 77
Fen River, 10
Fen River valley, 35
Five Classics, 237–238, 241. See also Canon of Change (Yi jing); Canon of Odes (Shi jing); Spring and Autumn Annals
Five Pecks of Grain rebellion, 199–200
Forest of Conversations (Yu lin), 245
Former Liang state, 74
Former Qin state, 67–68, 76–77, 79, 146, 148
Former Yan state, 74, 79, 138, 148
Former Zhao state, 65, 74, 145, 167
Fotudeng, 104, 108, 205
Fu Jian, 53, 67–68, 76–77, 79, 98, 148, 152, 205
Fujian province, 12, 73
Funerary practices, 31, 184–185, 215, 241; tomb art, 102, 121, 167, 168, 187, 194, 197, 198, 205, 210
Funiu Mountains, 15
Fuxi, 185, 194

Gan Bao, 201, 246
Gan River, 12, 15
Ganzu corridor, 148, 164

Gao Huan, 83–84
Gaochang, 156, 256
Gaozu, Emperor, 126–127
Gardens: and Chinese culture, 23, 26, 86, 94, 95, 96, 98–102, 120, 196; as images of paradise, 196, 212–213; in Jianking, 23, 94, 95, 98, 99, 100; in Luoyang, 101–102; and poetry, 100
Ge Hong, 218; The Master Who Embraces Simplicity (Bao Puzi), 57, 200–202
Ghost Festival, 188–189, 215
Ghost writings, 163–164
Grand Canal, 5, 7, 254–256, 257
Great Dark, The, 222
Great families: and Buddhist temples, 108; Cao family, 19–20, 33–37, 36, 38–39, 40–41, 48–49, 50, 54–55, 57, 58, 59, 78, 92, 114, 126, 135–137, 138, 145, 146, 152, 155, 159, 171–172, 174, 200, 227, 228, 232–233, 238; cemeteries of, 171–172; and collapse of Han dynasty, 28; and Confucianism, 28, 30–31, 53; Cui family, 132–133, 134; cultural activities, 3, 19–20, 24, 31, 44–51, 52–53, 67, 94, 98, 108, 205; dependent tenants/clients of, 55–59, 67, 116, 120, 135, 137; of Eastern Jin dynasty, 51–53, 64, 67, 68, 69–70; Gongsun family, 146; of Han dynasty, 3, 28, 30–31, 37, 55, 61, 94, 118, 129, 140, 170; of Jin dynasty, 42–44, 47, 51–52, 56–57, 58, 61–62, 63, 137, 172; landownership by, 3, 7, 13, 28, 30, 31, 33, 56–57, 71, 116, 117, 119–120, 135, 137–138; Ly family, 155; in north China, 13, 19, 53, 56–57, 85, 91, 129, 130, 131–135, 223; relations with military dynasts, 37, 54, 70; rural villas of, 86, 94, 95, 96–98, 100, 117, 118, 137; Sima family, 36, 41–42, 48, 49, 51, 56–57, 58, 137; in south China, 13, 14, 51–53, 63, 66–67, 70–71, 94, 96, 116, 117, 129, 130, 131–132, 134–135, 137, 166, 202–203, 206, 212, 249; in Sui dynasty, 134, 250; Sun family, 37; in Tang dynasty, 156; of Three Kingdoms period, 33, 36–37, 38–39, 40–42, 43–44, 47, 51; Wang family, 29, 172, 180; Wu family, 172; Xie family, 130, 180; Yang family, 171, 172; Zhou family of Yixing, 172, 173. See also Social elites
Great Perfection (Da Cheng), kingdom of, 200
Gu Bijiang, 98–99

Gu Kaizhi, 96; on mountain landscapes, 21–22

Guan Yu, 35–36

Guandong region, 12, 15

Guangdong province, 73, 155

Guangxi province, 73, 155

Guangzhou, 3, 117

Guangzhou region, 155

Guanyin, 193

Guanzhong region, 53, 55, 65, 84–85, 134, 148, 211; Di and Qiang tribes in, 76–77, 79; Former Qin state, 76–77, 148; in Han dynasty, 12, 217

Guiji region, 64, 69, 96, 98, 112, 116, 121

Guizhou province, 12, 151

Guo Ju, 190

Guo Tai, 46, 241

Guo Wen, 95

Guo Xiang, 221, 233; on nothingness, 224–225

Han dynasty: agriculture in, 11, 55, 58, 120, 121, 122, 123–124, 125, 135; animals and topography in, 216–217; *Book of the Han*, 18; Buddhism in, 4, 162, 184, 205, 210, 215; calligraphy in, 241–242; the capital in, 3, 4, 17, 18, 25, 31–32, 86–89, 91, 94, 95, 102, 150, 171, 239, 252; collapse of, 1, 4, 6, 12, 13, 19, 25, 28, 30, 31–37, 55–56, 135, 140, 144, 145, 155, 221, 222; Confucianism in, 28, 30–31, 222, 224; Daoism in, 4, 198–201, 215; Eastern Han dynasty, 2, 29, 31, 32, 41, 51, 56, 58, 65, 68, 87, 96, 123–124, 151, 162, 170, 171, 174, 194, 197, 198, 200, 205, 225, 252; Emperor Wu, 29, 146, 194, 197, 198, 200, 246–247; eunuchs in, 29–30, 32–33, 39, 46; genealogies in, 181, 182; Grand Academy, 18, 28; great families of, 3, 28, 30–31, 37, 55, 61, 94, 118, 129, 140, 170; Guanzhong and Guandong in, 12; Heaven and humankind in, 247; hermits in, 22–23, 49; historical writing in, 244, 245; imperial government in, 28–33; inner vs. outer court in, 29–30; kinship in, 170, 171, 174; Korea in, 151, 152; land-ownership in, 131, 135, 139; literature in, 3, 13, 17, 18–19, 21, 35, 39, 86–89, 91, 96, 141, 194, 225–228, 238, 239, 240, 244; marshal of state in, 29; military of, 3–4, 6, 31–32, 55, 56, 58, 59–61, 68; painting in, 22; peasants in, 54–55; policies regarding nomadic tribes, 3–

4, 6, 32, 51, 145, 146, 148; regional cultures in, 17–19, 21; social elites of, 3, 19, 28–31, 38, 39, 46; taxation in, 55; tomb art in, 121, 167, 187, 194, 197, 198, 205, 210; trade in, 164; Vietnam in, 155; villages in, 18, 32; Western Han dynasty, 2, 29, 171, 197, 222; Yangzi River valley in, 6; Yellow River valley in, 6, 11, 34; and Yue people, 166

Hangzhou, 15

Hangzhou Bay, 254

Han River, 12, 15, 35, 35–36, 63

Han River valley, 73, 167

Hanzhong, 35

Haoli, 197

He Yan, 49, 221, 223

He Zhiyuan, 72

Hebei, 79, 91

Hegel, G. W. F., 45

Henan, 167

Hermits, 22–23, 49, 95–96, 201

Highest Clarity (*Shangqing*) tradition of Daoism, 24, 194, 202–203, 243–244

Himiko, 151, 154

Histories of the Northern Dynasties, 92

Hongdu Academy, 241

Hongnong, 171

Hou Jing, 72, 131, 132, 155–156, 249

Hu/Ling, Dowager Empress, 110, 111, 192

Huai River, 66, 77, 254

Huai River valley, 15, 64, 73, 121, 136, 167

Hualin Garden, 98, 99, 100

Huan, Emperor, 30

Huan Tan, 222

Huan Wen, 26, 64, 65–66, 69, 200

Huan Xuan, 67, 69

Huanglao, 204–205

Huanzhong, 167

Huijiao: *Biographies of Eminent Monks*, 112–113, 218, 245

Huiyuan, 21, 23, 100, 104, 205–206

Huo Guang, 29

Imperial Academy, 241, 244–245

Imperial government: in Han dynasty, 28–33; hereditary entry-level posts, 3, 5, 28–29, 38–39, 40–41, 42–44, 62, 70, 183, 250; and human talent, 38–42, 43–44, 45–46; relationship to military power, 2, 4, 5, 33; relationship to society, 2, 4, 5, 28–31, 32, 37, 45, 49, 84; Secretariat, 70

India, 3, 160; and Buddhism, 24–25, 156–157, 159, 160, 161, 163, 164, 168–169,

India (continued)
185, 213, 231; Sanscrit literature, 231, 236–237; trade with China, 159, 160, 161, 164, 166
Irrawaddy River, 164
Islam, 158

Japan: Buddhism in, 152, 153, 154, 163; and Chinese conquest dynasties, 151; Chinese knowledge of, 3; Nara, 94; relations with China, 12, 116, 117, 151–152, 154–155, 156, 250; relations with Korea, 154; trade with south China, 116, 117, 154, 156; Yamato state, 154–155
Jia Mi, 51
Jia Sixie: Essential Methods of the Common People (Qi min yao shu), 116, 118–125
Jiang Mengying, 242
Jiangdu, 256, 258
Jiangling, 35, 100, 240, 249
Jiangnan Canal, 254
Jiangnan region, 89; Chinese culture in, 6, 20–21, 24, 25–27; social elites in, 26–27
Jiangsu region, 204, 218
Jiangxi province, 12, 73, 112, 219
Jiankang: Black Clothing Street, 20; Buddhist monasteries in, 25; Buddhist temples in, 112, 113; as Chen capital, 249; as Danyang, 249; as Eastern Jin capital, 25–26, 51–52, 63, 64, 69, 96, 100, 127, 153; economic conditions, 116; gardens in, 23, 94, 95, 98, 99, 100; after Han collapse, 15; Western Residence, 98; as Wu capital, 25, 56, 90–91, 100
Jianwen of the Liang, Emperor, 231
Jianyang, 172
Jiaozhou region, 117, 155–156
Jiayuguan, 173, 184–185, 189–190
Jie/Jie Hu, 82–83
Jie Zitui, 174, 175
Jin dynasty, 1, 159, 250; Buddhism in, 192, 205, 206; Dowager Empress Wenming, 192; Emperor Wu, 58, 61, 63; great families of, 42–44, 47, 51–52, 56–57, 58, 61–62, 63, 137, 172; Korea in, 151; land policy in, 137; literature in, 89; the military in, 38, 56–57, 58–69; poetry in, 233; policies regarding nomads in, 59, 73, 145, 146, 147; and Sima family, 56–57, 58, 61, 63; Ye in, 92. See also Eastern Jin dynasty; Western Jin dynasty
Jingkou/Yangzhou, 254
Jingming Temple, 110

Jing province, 35–36, 64
Jingzhou, 222–223
Jiuquan, 173

Kang Sengyuan, 162
Karashahr, 156
King Father of the East, 185
Kinship: ancestor worship, 173–174, 175, 189; and Buddhism, 5, 178, 183–189, 196; communal families without property division, 176; and Daoism, 5, 184, 196; family instructions, 176–181; family/lineage cemeteries, 170–175; family/lineage festivals, 170–171, 188–189; father-son relationships, 170, 188, 190; in Han dynasty, 170, 171, 174; mother-son relationships, 170, 188–190, 192; in north China, 130–131, 132–134, 147, 173, 176, 177–178, 183; nuclear family, 170, 189–190; in south China, 129, 130–131, 134, 172, 177–178; written genealogies, 3, 5, 134, 170, 176, 178, 181–183
Korean peninsula: Buddhism in, 152, 154, 163; Koguryo state, 151, 152, 154, 254, 256, 257; Paekche state, 151, 153, 154; relations with China, 117, 144, 146, 151, 152, 153–154, 156, 250, 254, 256, 257; relations with Japan, 154; Silla state, 154
Kou Qianzhi, 203–204, 218
Kroraina, 156
Kuaiji region, 23
Kucha, 156, 161, 187
Kumarijiva, 105, 161, 205
Kunlun, 198

Lake Tai, 96, 116, 220
Landownership: equal-field system, 120, 133–134, 139–140, 248; by great families, 3, 7, 13, 28, 30, 31, 33, 56–57, 116, 117, 119–120, 135, 137–138; in Han dynasty, 131, 135, 139; in north China, 56–57, 118, 131, 135–137, 138–140; in south China, 56, 57, 116, 117, 137–138; by the state, 55, 56, 57, 58, 72, 84, 114, 116, 118, 135–140
Lapis lazuli, 159, 160
Later Liang state, 74
"Later Preface to the Family Genealogy of the Yu Line of Henan," 181–182
Later Yan state, 74, 79, 138
Later Zhao state, 74, 76, 83, 92, 145–146, 205

Legalism, 222

Li Bo (Li Bai), 15–16

Li Daoyuan: *Commentary to the Classic of Streams (Shui jing zhu)*, 21, 171–172

Liang dynasty: Buddhist temples in, 112–113; collapse of, 72–73; currency policies, 117; Daoism in, 203; Emperor Wu, 23, 113, 178, 206–207, 214, 244; establishment of, 72, 117; gardens in, 100; literary anthologies in, 239–240; the military in, 70, 72–73, 155–156; poetry circles in, 71, 229–230, 231–232

Liang Gongda, 242

Liangzhou, 104, 138, 164

Liaodong, 152

Liao dynasty, 257

Liao River, 257

Ling, Emperor, 30, 32, 241

Ling/Hu, Dowager Empress, 110, 111, 192

Lingnan region, 155–156

Lis of Zhaojun, 133

Literary Mind and the Carving of Dragons (Wenxin diao long), 236–238, 245

Literature: anomaly accounts, 246–247; anthologies, 238–240; biographies of social elites, 31, 39; goddesses in, 194–195; in Han dynasty, 3, 13, 17, 18–19, 35, 39, 90, 159; histories, 244–246; and India, 157; in Jin dynasty, 89; literary theory, 230, 232–240; local histories, 21, 27; prose narrative, 244–247; in Qin dynasty, 18; relationship to human character, 41; rural and agricultural life in, 118, 140–143; and social elites, 5, 19–20; in Tang dynasty, 13, 15–16, 25, 194, 195, 217, 230, 231; textual canon, 154, 168, 237–238, 241. *See also* Dark Studies; Poetry

Liu Bei, 35–36

Liu Biao, 35

Liu Cong, 78–79

Liu Fang, 134

Liu Jin, 71

Liu Laozhi, 69

Liu Ling, 49

Liu Shao: *Study of Human Abilities (Ren wu zhi)*, 39–40, 45–46, 222

Liu Xie, 230, 233, 234; *Literary Mind and the Carving of Dragons (Wenxin diao long)*, 236–238, 245

Liu Yao, 74

Liu Yiqing, 46; *New Account of the Tales of the World*, 19–20, 22, 66–67, 68, 98, 180–181, 241, 243, 245

Liu Yizong, 243

Liu Yu, 26, 69–70

Liu Yuan, 51, 145, 167

Liu Zongyuan, 175

Liu Song dynasty, 244–245; currency policies in, 117; establishment of, 69–70, 218; the military in, 69–70; princes in, 71–72

Longmen caves, 112, 209–210

Lotus Sutra, 105

Lü Bu, 33

Lu Ji, 51, 237; "Rhapsody on Literature" (*Wen fu*), 233–235

Lu Meng, 57

Lu Xiujing, 218

Lu Xun, 69

Lu Yun, 51

Luo River, 115, 252–253, 254

Luoyang, 69, 74, 92, 148, 200; Buddhist monasteries in, 115, 116, 163, 208; Buddhist temples in, 102, 104, 105, 108–112, 163, 192, 208; economic conditions, 115–116; gardens in, 101–102; as Han capital, 6, 15, 25, 33, 171, 252; and Huan Wen, 65–66; as Jin capital, 51, 61, 89; as Northern Wei capital, 81, 83, 84, 102, 105, 108–112, 115–116, 133, 149, 167, 208, 248, 252; as Sui capital, 164, 252–254, 258; Tongji Canal, 253, 254; as Wei capital, 101, 115–116

Ma Rong, 222

Man Zhangzhi, 182–183

Manchuria, 144, 148, 152

Manichaeism, 158

Manjusri, 163, 219

Man people, 166, 167

Maoshan school of Daoism, 24, 194, 202–203, 243–244

Marxism, 36

Master Green Bird, 185

Master Who Embraces Simplicity (Bao Puzi), The, 57, 200–202

Master Zhuang (Zhuangzi), 48, 205, 221, 224, 234, 243

Meiling Pass, 15

Memorial on Calligraphy, 243

Merchants, 54, 71, 116; and Buddhism, 157–162, 164, 196, 204, 205; foreigners as, 115, 164, 166; Sogdians as, 164, 166. *See also* Trade

Miaoshan, Princess, 193

Military, the: *buqu*, 58; cavalry, 59–61; of Han dynasty, 3–4, 6, 31–32, 55, 56, 58,

Military (continued)
  59–61, 68; hereditary soldiery, 2, 55, 59,
  69, 80, 248; military colonies, 55, 56,
  57, 58, 114, 131, 136, 137, 138; non-
  Chinese troops, 3–4, 59, 61, 62, 84; in
  north China, 26, 33–35, 54, 55, 56–57,
  58–61, 73–85, 131–132, 134, 135, 206,
  255–256, 258; Northern Headquarters
  Troops, 67–69, 77; relations between
  military dynasts and great families, 37,
  54, 70; in south China, 15, 20, 26, 54,
  56, 62–73, 77, 131–132, 206; in Three
  Kingdoms period, 33, 37, 38, 55, 59–61;
  Twenty-Four Armies, 84–85
Millenarianism: in Buddhism, 212–214; in
  Daoism, 199–200, 204, 212, 213
Ming dynasty, 256
Min River valley, 13, 15
Mongols, 148, 256
Monthly Ordinances of the Four Classes of
  People (Simin yueling), 123–124, 174
Moral authority, 39, 41, 43
Mountain Classic, 91
Mountains: in literature, 21, 90, 94, 95–
  96; in north China, 16, 17, 23–24; in
  painting, 22, 100; relationship to urban
  life, 94–96; in south China, 16–17, 23–
  24
Mount Heng, 100
Mount Jia, 218
Mount Jilong, 98, 100
Mount Lu, 23, 100
Mount Mao, 23
Mount Wutai, 163, 219
Mu, King, 194
Mulan, story of, 226
Murong Hui, 146–147
Murong Xianbei, 66, 74, 76, 79, 138, 146–
  149, 152
Mysterious Woman, 193–194, 197

Nagarahara, 161
Nestorian Christianity, 158
New Account of Tales of the World
  (Shishuo xinyu), 46–48, 53, 98, 112,
  127, 180–181
New Catalogue of Palace Texts, 244
New Songs from a Jade Terrace, 239–240
Nine-Rank system, 42–43, 45–46, 134,
  183, 235; and Cao Cao, 38–39, 40, 41;
  Sui abolition of, 248, 250
Nineteen Ancient Poems, 87–89
Nomads, 17, 92; animal husbandry among,
  114; Han policies regarding, 3–4, 6, 32,
  51, 145, 146, 148; Jin policies regarding,
  59, 73, 145, 146, 147; nomadic states,
  51, 66, 73–74, 77–80, 144, 145–151,
  207
North China: agriculture in, 7, 10–11, 16,
  55, 56–58, 78–79, 114, 116, 119, 120–
  121, 124, 125, 135–137, 138–139; Buddhism in, 144, 204–206, 207–212; climate in, 10, 11, 94, 124, 128–129; culture in, 2, 7, 25, 100–102; Daoism in,
  198, 200, 203–204, 218; Dark Studies
  in, 222–223; diet in, 126–127; drought
  in, 11; economic conditions in, 113–116;
  famine in, 7; great families in, 13, 19, 53,
  56–57, 85, 91, 129, 130, 131–135, 223;
  kinship in, 130–131, 132–134, 147, 173,
  176, 177–178, 183; landownership in,
  56–57, 118, 131, 135–137, 138–140;
  migration to south China from, 1–2, 6–
  7, 12, 13, 14–17, 37, 51–52, 56, 86, 94,
  125, 129, 202, 248; the military in, 26,
  33–35, 54, 55, 56–57, 58–61, 73–85,
  131–132, 134, 135, 206, 255–256, 258;
  mountains in, 16, 17, 23–24; poetry in,
  226–227; Sixteen Kingdoms, 73–74, 76–
  79; speech in, 128–129; villages in, 11,
  118; women in, 92, 127–128
Northern Headquarters Troops, 67–69, 77
Northern Liang state, 74
Northern Qi dynasty: Buddhism in, 188;
  collapse of, 85, 249; equal-field system
  in, 139, 248; establishment of, 84, 92,
  119, 167–168, 257; tomb art in, 168
Northern Wei dynasty, 91, 99, 130, 160,
  182, 190, 250; agriculture in, 121, 138–
  140; Buddhism in, 188, 192, 204, 207–
  212, 211; cold-food cult in, 174; collapse
  of, 83–84, 92, 118–119; Daoism in,
  203–204, 207; Dowager Empress Hu,
  192; Emperor Taiwu, 104; Emperor
  Xiaowen, 81, 101, 120, 139, 167; establishment of, 53, 79–81, 114–115, 148,
  150–151, 257; great families in, 132–
  133; Japan in, 151–152, 154; Luoyang
  as capital, 81, 83, 84, 102, 105, 108–
  112, 114–116, 133, 149, 167, 208, 248,
  252; Rouran people in, 149; and samgha
  households, 138
Northern Yan state, 74, 79, 138
Northern Zhou dynasty, 248, 251, 258;
  Buddhism in, 188, 215; collapse of, 248–
  249; equal-field system in, 139, 248; establishment of, 84–85, 167–168, 257;
  the military in, 249

North Star, 185
Nugua, 185, 194

Orchid Pavilion, 20

Painting of landscapes, 21–22, 23, 96, 100
Pakistan, 156
Palhai (Bohai), 94
Pan Yue, 51; "Rhapsody on Recalling Old Friends and Kin," 173
Pearls, 159, 160
Peasants, 68–69, 129, 131, 146; Cao Cao's policies regarding, 54–55, 57; and equal-field system, 120, 133–134, 139, 248; *Essential Methods of the Common People (Qi min yao shu)*, 116, 118–125, 174; in Han dynasty, 117, 135; in Qin dynasty, 135; taxation of, 55, 72, 145, 147. *See also* Agriculture
Pei Hui, 49
Pei Qi: *Forest of Conversations (Yu lin)*, 245
Pei Wei, 224–225
Pei Zhi, 130–131
People's Republic of China, 11, 36
Persia, 160–161, 164
Pingcheng, 79, 105, 114–115
Pingdeng monastery, 109
Pingyang, 79
Poetry: anthologies of, 238, 239; commemoration of sites, 25; descriptive language in, 235, 236; evocation (*xing*) in, 236; excursion rhapsodies, 89; and family cemeteries, 173; farmstead poetry, 140–143; "frontier" verse, 25; and gardens, 100; goddesses in, 194–195; Han ancient poems (*gu shi*), 225–226, 227; Han epideictic rhapsodies, 18, 19; Han Music Bureau (*yuefu*) ballads, 225–226, 227, 228, 240; Han rhapsodies recounting imperial hunts, 90, 95, 239; Han rhapsodies regarding urban life, 86–89, 91, 239; Jin epideictic rhapsodies, 233; Li Bo, 15–16; lyric verse, 19–20, 41, 89, 98, 225–232, 233–234, 239; mountains as theme in, 21, 90, 94, 95–96; *Nineteen Ancient Poems*, 87–89; palace-style poetry, 231, 240; poetry circles, 20, 26–27, 41, 49, 51, 53, 71, 94, 96, 100, 229–232; poetry of presentation, 227–228; and poet's emotions, 19, 233–234, 235, 239; relationship to political power, 19–20; and rural villas, 96; *Songs of the Orchid Tower*, 94, 98; in south China, 229–

232; in Tang dynasty, 15–16, 25, 194, 195, 217, 230, 231; tonal prosody in, 230–231; regarding urban life, 86–91
Poyang Lake, 12, 15
Print, 158
Pure conversation, 20, 21, 41, 45–49, 52, 67, 89, 94, 98, 205, 222
Pure critique movement, 30, 39, 46
Puyo state, 146, 152

Qiang tribe, 76, 79
Qiao Zhou: *Examination of Ancient Histories*, 245
Qin dynasty: and Ba people, 217; culture in, 17, 18, 150; First Emperor, 60, 197, 200; hermits in, 22; imperial system in, 150; landownership in, 135; religion in, 4; Yellow River in, 6
Qin Shihuang, 26
Qing dynasty, 148, 245, 256, 257
Qingming Festival, 171, 174–175
Qinling Mountains, 15
Queen Mother of the West, 184, 185, 194, 195, 197, 205, 210; and Buddhism, 199; and Daoism, 168, 198–199

Ran Min, 76, 146
Rankings of Poetry (*Shi pin*), 140, 142, 235
Rebellions of the Eight Princes, 51, 63, 137, 145, 147
Record of Dwelling in Famous Mountains (Ju ming shan zhi), 21, 95–96
Record of Seasonal Observances in Jing and Chu, 189
Record of the Buddhist Temples of Luoyang (Luoyang qielan ji), 12, 101–102, 105, 108, 109–111, 126–127, 163, 192, 208, 245
Record of the Remarkable Objects of the Southern Provinces (Nan zhou yi wu zhi), A, 21
Record of the States South of Mount Hua (Huayang guo zhi), 21, 245
Records of the Historian/Astrologer (Shi ji), 90
Records of the Three Kingdoms, 245
Red Cliff, battle at, 35
Red coral, 159–160
Regionalism: regional capitals, 86, 89–94; regional cultures, 17–22, 23–24, 25–27; among social elites, 25–27, 30, 31
Revolt of the Six Garrisons, 131, 133, 167–168

"Rhapsody on Literature" (*Wen fu*), 233–235

Rituals of Zhou, 86, 168, 174

Rouran people, 149

Ruan Ji, 49, 221–222, 224; *Songs of My Cares*, 229

Ruan Xian, 49

Rural villas, 86, 94, 95, 96–98, 100, 117, 118, 137

Samarkand, 164

Sassanian empire, 160

Scholars, 28–29, 178–181

Scripture for Humane Kings (Ren wang jing), 214

Seasonal Methods of the Mid-Yangzi Region (Jing Chu sui shi ji), 174

Selection of Refined Literature (Wen xuan), 239, 240

Sengduan, 193

Seven Masters of the Jian'an, 227

Seven Worthies of the Bamboo Grove, 49, 50, 222, 224, 225, 228–229

Shaanxi, 171

Shan Tao, 49

Shandong region, 32, 134, 171, 199

Shanghai delta, 14

Shaoxing province, 23

Shen Yang: *A Record of the Remarkable Objects of the Waters and Soils in the Coastal Regions (Lin hai shui tu yi wu zhi)*, 21

Shen Yue, 98, 230, 231; *Book of the Song Dynasty*, 245

Shi Chong, 96, 126, 159–160

Shi Hu, 74, 76, 146, 147

Shi Le, 74, 79, 145–146, 174, 205, 211

Shu, kingdom of (Three Kingdoms period), 13, 19, 33, 41, 137, 223

Shun, 194

Sichuan region, 12, 15–16, 32, 36, 41, 66, 70, 73, 89, 164, 249; Ba culture in, 217; Chengdu, 64, 90, 91; Daoism in, 13, 35, 64, 199–200, 217; Dujiangyan project, 10, 11; Five Pecks of Grain movement in, 199–200; Liu state, 37; state of Great Perfection (Da Cheng), 64, 200

Silk trade, 157–158, 160–161, 164, 166

Sima Biao, 245

Sima family: and Jin dynasty, 56–57, 58, 61, 63; and kingdom of Wei, 36, 41–42, 48–49

Sima Qian, 232

Sima Rui, 63

Sima Xiangru, 90; "Rhapsody on the Imperial Hunting Park," 18

Sima Yan, 58, 61, 63

Sima Yi, 42

Sixteen Kingdoms, 73–74, 76–79

Slaves, 116, 120, 135

Social elites: biographies of, 31; and Buddhism, 108, 110, 111, 112, 204–205, 210; and city god cults, 220; cultural activities of, 2, 3, 5, 19–20, 22–23, 26–27, 31, 41, 44–51, 52–53, 67, 71, 86, 89–90, 94, 96, 98, 100, 102, 108, 120, 180–181, 205, 229–232; and Daoism, 202–203, 204, 212; diet of, 126–127; emergence of, 2, 3; eremitism among, 22–23, 45, 49–50, 53, 67, 98, 183; of Han dynasty, 3, 19, 28–31, 38, 39, 46; hereditary claims to entry-level government posts by, 3, 5, 28–29, 40–41, 42–44, 45, 62, 70, 183, 250; of Jiangnan region, 26–27; and mountains, 23–24; poetry circles among, 20, 26–27, 41, 49, 51, 53, 71, 94, 96, 100, 229–232; pure conversation among, 20, 21, 41, 45–49, 52, 67, 89, 94, 98, 205, 222; and pure critique movement, 30; regionalism among, 25–27, 30, 31; relations with imperial court, 28–31, 32, 37, 45, 46, 49, 54, 69–70; tea drinking by, 126; trade in luxury goods for, 158; and written genealogies, 3, 5, 134, 170, 176, 178, 181–183. *See also* Great families

Social mobility, 28–29

Sogdians, 164, 165

Song dynasty, 45, 131, 160, 176, 250

Songs of My Cares (Ruan Ji), 229

Songs of the Orchid Tower, 94, 98

Songs of the South, 194, 228

Song Yu: "Rhapsody on the Gaotang Shrine," 194; "Rhapsody on the Goddess," 194

Song Yun, 160

Songyue pagoda, 106, 107

South China: agriculture in, 7, 10, 12, 13–14, 16, 56, 57, 116, 119, 121, 122–123, 124, 125, 126, 137–138; anomaly accounts in, 246; attitudes toward north China in, 26, 64–66, 67; Buddhism in, 16–17, 23–24, 71, 144, 205, 206; central Yangzi region, 12–13, 14–15, 35, 52, 54, 63–64, 65, 69, 70, 71–72, 121, 222–223, 240, 249; city god cults in, 219–220; climate in, 12, 13, 14, 94, 124, 125, 126, 128–129; culture in, 2, 6, 7, 19–27,

35, 94–96, 98–100, 258; Daoism in, 16–17, 23–24, 199–200, 202–203, 204, 218; Dark Studies in, 222; diet in, 126–127; economic conditions in, 71, 113, 116–117, 129, 255–256, 258; fishing in, 12; great families in, 13, 14, 51–53, 63, 66–67, 70–71, 94, 96, 116, 117, 129, 130, 131–132, 134–135, 137, 166, 202–203, 206, 212, 249; international trade in, 12; kinship in, 129, 130–131, 134, 172, 177–178; landownership in, 56, 57, 116, 117, 137–138; landscape in, 11–12; lower Yangzi region, 12–13, 14–15, 35, 37, 56, 63–64, 255, 258; migration from north China to, 1–2, 6–7, 12, 13, 14–17, 37, 51–52, 56, 86, 94, 125, 129, 202, 248; the military in, 15, 20, 26, 54, 56, 62–73, 77, 131–132, 206; mountains in, 16–17, 23–24; poetry in, 226; Sichuan, 12, 13, 15–16, 32, 35, 36; southeast coast, 12; southwest region, 12; speech in, 128–129; villages in, 11; women in, 92, 127–128; Yue people, 17, 56, 129, 166–167

Southeast Asia, 12, 13, 117, 124, 125, 144, 156, 196, 250; Vietnam, 15, 151, 155

Southern Liang state, 74

Southern Qi dynasty, 117, 130; collapse of, 249; Daoism in, 203; establishment of, 72; literary anthologies in, 239; the military in, 70; poetry circles in, 71, 229–230; Xiao Ziliang, 98, 230, 231

Southern Yan state, 74, 79, 138

Southern Yue state, 155

Spring and Autumn Annals, 244, 245

Srimitra, 162

Steles, 31, 112, 184, 187, 188, 192, 210, 211, 241

Study of Human Abilities (Ren wu zhi), 39–40, 45–46, 222

Su Jun, 64

Sui dynasty: Board of Civil Office, 250; Buddhism in, 159, 163, 188, 214, 215–216; cave paintings in, 188; collapse of, 252, 254–255, 256, 257–258; Emperor Wen, 159, 249–250, 251, 254; Emperor Yang, 250, 252, 253, 254, 255, 256–258; establishment of, 5, 6, 85, 133–134, 149, 156, 159, 163, 164, 182, 215–216, 248–250; examination system in, 250–251; festival for cleaning graves in, 175; Grand Canal in, 254–256, 257; great families in, 134, 250; and Han dynasty, 248, 250, 251; Japan in, 154; Korea in,

154; landownership in, 133–134; the military in, 255, 256, 257; non-Han peoples in, 248; policies regarding Man people, 167

Sun En, 68–69

Sun family, 37

Sun Quan, 35, 36, 56

Sun Zhuo, 26

Syama/Shanzi, 190

Syr Darya river, 164

Syria, 164

Taiping Princess, 192

Taiwan, 12

Taiwu, Emperor, 104

Taiyuan, 174

Taizhou, 219

Taizong, 150

Talents, human, 38–42, 43–44, 180–181, 235; and pure conversation, 45–46, 222; relationship to education, 40, 180

Tang dynasty, 4, 5, 12, 58, 93, 134, 173, 219, 258; An Lushan rebellion, 13; Buddhism in, 160, 161–162, 163, 188, 214, 216; cave paintings in, 188; Cold Food Festival in, 175; Daoism in, 204, 216; Empress Wu, 192, 207; equal-field system in, 139, 248; establishment of, 149, 252; examination system in, 250; festival for cleaning graves in, 175; genealogies in, 182–183; grain storage in, 125; and Han dynasty, 248; India in, 161; Japan in, 154; kinship in, 134, 182–183, 188; Korea in, 154; Lingnan in, 156; literature in, 13, 15–16, 25, 194, 195, 217, 230, 231; non-Chinese people in, 144, 149–150; non-Han peoples in, 248; tea drinking in, 126

Tanyao, 138

Tao Hongjing, 23, 203; Declarations of the Perfected (Zhen gao), 244

Tao Kan, 64

Tao Qian, 64, 243; "Peach Blossom Spring," 140; poetry of, 140–143

Tao Yuanming, 173

Taxation, 55, 67, 71, 72, 116, 135, 136, 139, 145, 147

Three Gorges region, 13

Three Kingdoms period, 1, 33–37; capitals in, 89–91; Dark Studies in, 222–223; great families of, 33, 36–37, 38–39, 40–42, 43–44, 47, 51; landownership in, 36, 41, 56–57, 135–137; the military in, 33, 37, 38, 55, 59–61. See also Shu,

Three Kingdoms period (continued)
  kingdom of; Wei, kingdom of; Wu, king-
  dom of
Tibet, 164
Tomb art, 102, 121, 167, 168, 187, 194,
  197, 198, 205, 210
Trade, 71, 113–114, 116–117, 155, 254;
  and Buddhism, 156–162, 164, 196, 204,
  205; silk trade, 157–158, 160–161, 164,
  166; and Sogdians, 164, 166. See also
  Merchants
Transmission of Master Zuo (Zuo zhuan),
  216
Transoxiana, 164
Treatise on Curiosities (Bo wu zhi), A, 21
"Tribute of Yu," 246
Trigrams, 185, 186, 202
Trung sisters rebellion, 155
Tuoba Gui, 79–81, 114, 148
Tuoba (Tabatch) tribe, 53, 144, 145, 148–
  149, 167; and Northern Wei dynasty, 53,
  79–82, 114
Turks, 149–150, 256–257
Twenty-Four Armies, 84–85
Twenty-Four Friends, 51

Urban life: Buddhist temples, 102–113;
  economic conditions, 113–117; in north
  vs. south China, 91–92; poetry regarding, 86–91; regional capitals, 86, 89–94;
  relationship to culture, 86, 94; relationship to mountains, 94–96. See also Gardens

Vietnam, 15; Jiaozhi, 155; Panyu, 155; relations with China, 151, 155; Trung sisters rebellion, 155
Villages: in Han dynasty, 18, 32; in north
  China, 11, 118; poetry about life in,
  140–143; in south China, 11

Wan Zhen: A Record of the Remarkable
  Objects of the Southern Provinces (Nan
  zhou yi wu zhi), 21
Wang Bi, 49, 221, 233; on Confucious and
  Laozi, 223–224; on necessity of single
  ruler, 223–224, 225; on nothingness
  (wu), 222, 223, 224, 225
Wang Chong, 28–29, 197, 222, 225
Wang Dao, 26, 51, 63, 64, 65, 95, 98, 127,
  130
Wang Dun, 63, 64, 66, 130
Wang Gong, 69
Wang Kai, 159–160
Wang Ming, 162

Wang Rong, 49, 230
Wang Su, 126–127
Wang Xianzhi, 20, 243
Wang Xizhi, 20, 65, 98, 98–99, 243
Wang Xuance, 161
Wang Yi, 130
Wang Yu, 130
War of Uncles and Nephews, 71
Warring States period, 2, 16, 174–175,
  194, 219; calligraphy in, 241; Daoism in,
  196, 197, 205; vs. Han dynasty, 4, 18,
  123, 150, 151; vs. Qin dynasty, 150,
  151; towers in, 105
Wei An, 98
Wei Shou: Book of the [Northern] Wei,
  245
Wei Tang, 182
Wei Wenlang, 187
Wei, kingdom of (Three Kingdoms period),
  33, 46, 47, 52, 58, 155, 159, 223, 240,
  244; and Cao family, 19–20, 36–37, 38,
  40–41, 200; policies regarding nomads,
  145, 146; relations with Wu, 36, 136,
  223; and Sima family, 36, 41–42, 48–49;
  state ownership of land in, 55, 56, 57,
  114, 135–137, 138
Wei River, 10, 254
Wenchang, 217
Wenming, Dowager Empress, 192
Wen of the Song, Emperor, 99–100
Wen of the Sui, Emperor, 159, 249–250,
  251, 254
Western Jin dynasty, 43, 74, 172, 240; col-
  lapse of, 44, 51–52, 61–63, 79, 102,
  104, 132, 137, 145, 147, 152, 156, 200,
  202; establishment of, 33, 42, 56–57,
  58–59, 137, 257
Western Liang state, 74
Western Military Command, 15
Western Wei dynasty, 84–85, 133, 249
Wie An, 64
Wine, 143
Women: attitudes toward, 176, 179; and
  Buddhism, 110, 192–193; and Daoism,
  192, 193–194; in north China vs. south
  China, 92, 127–128; roles of, 170, 189–
  190, 192–195; as shamans, 192; in Ye,
  92, 128
Writing system, 51, 155, 156
Wu Liang, 31
Wu Zhi, 19
Wu, Empress (Tang), 192, 207
Wu, kingdom of (Three Kingdoms period),
  19, 33, 51, 58, 155, 172; establishment
  of, 37, 56; Jianking as capital of, 25, 56,

90–91, 100; the military in, 56; relations with Wei, 36, 136, 223; state ownership of land in, 114

Wu of the Han, Emperor, 29, 146, 194, 197, 198, 200, 246–247

Wu of the Jin, Emperor, 58, 61, 63

Wu of the Liang, Emperor, 23, 113, 178, 206–207, 214, 244

Wuhuan, 35, 59

Wuling Pass, 15

Wuxing, 220

Xi Han: *The Appearance of Southern Grasses and Trees (Nan fang cao my zhuang)*, 21

Xi Kang, 21, 49, 50, 224, 229

Xi Kant, 221

Xiahou Hui, 46

Xiahou Xuan, 49

Xian, Emperor, 33–34

Xianbei, 79–84, 167–169; Murong, 66, 74, 76, 79, 138, 146–149, 152

Xiang Xiu, 49, 221, 224

Xiang Yu, 220

Xiang River, 12, 15

Xiangyang, 15, 35–36, 113, 240

Xiao Daocheng, 72

Xiao Gang, 100, 231–232; and *Selection of Refined Writing*, 239–240

Xiao Tong, 239

Xiao Yan, 72

Xiao Yi, 100

Xiao Ziliang, Prince, 98, 230, 231

Xiao Zixian: *Book of the Southern Qi*, 245

Xiaowen, Emperor (Jin), 192

Xiaowen, Emperor (Northern Wei), 81, 101, 120, 139, 167

Xiaowu, Emperor, 71

Xie An, 64, 65, 66, 67, 68, 98

Xie Lingyun, 46, 98; "On Dwelling in the Mountains," 95–96; poetry anthology compiled by, 238; *Record of Dwelling in Famous Mountains (Ju ming shan zhi)*, 21, 95–96

Xie Tiao, 230

Xie Wan, 65–66, 68

Xie Xuan, 67, 68

Xinjiang, 148, 156, 161, 166

Xinting, 26

Xiongnu, 73, 148, 149, 150, 156, 184; Former Zhao dynasty, 51, 65, 74, 145, 167; Later Zhao dynasty, 74, 76, 83, 92, 145–146, 205

Xiongnu Han state, 74, 145

Xiongnu Zhao state, 74, 145

Xu, 33, 135, 138

Xu Mian, 98

Xuanwu, Emperor, 163

Xuanzang, 161

Xun Can, 49

Xun Xu: *New Catalogue of Palace Texts*, 244

Xunyang, 57

Yalu River valley, 152

Yan Yanzhi, 235–236

Yan Zhitui, 68, 92, 127–128; *The Family Instructions of the Yan Clan*, 176–180, 241

Yan Zun, 222

Yang Guang, 249

Yang Jian, 85

Yang Xi, 202–203, 243–244

Yang Xiong, 90, 222, 238

Yang Xuanzhi: *Record of the Buddhist Temples of Luoyang (Luoyang qielan ji)*, 12, 101–102, 105, 108, 109–111, 126–127, 163, 192, 208, 245

Yang Yi, 202

Yang Zhen, 171

Yang of the Sui, Emperor, 250, 252, 253, 254, 255, 256–258

Yangzi River: Dujiangyan project, 10, 11; trade on, 116; tributaries of, 12

Yangzi River valley: central region, 12–13, 14–15, 35, 52, 54, 63–64, 65, 69, 70, 71–72, 121, 222–223, 240, 249; city god cults in, 219; colonization and settling of, 1–2, 6–7, 12, 14–17, 37, 56, 86, 94, 125, 129, 248; in Eastern Jin, 63; in Han dynasty, 6; lower region, 12–13, 14–15, 35, 37, 56, 63–64, 255, 258; in Sui dynasty, 5, 167, 258

Ye, 79, 91, 92–94, 146, 200; Bronze Sparrow Park in, 93; women in, 92, 128

Yellow Emperor, 193, 194

Yellow River: confluence with Luo River, 254; dikes on, 10; flooding of, 10, 11; in growing season, 10

Yellow River valley, 64–65, 89; agriculture in, 121; in Han Dynasty, 6, 11, 34, 55; in Jin dynasty, 73–74; non-Chinese in, 144; in Northern and Southern Dynasties period, 1, 4, 6–7, 51; in Northern Wei dynasty, 80, 84; in Three Kingdoms period, 1, 155

Yellow Turban rebellion, 30, 32–33, 54, 55, 135, 199

Yijing, 161

Yin and yang, 194, 222

Yin Hao, 65

Yi River, 115

Yongning Temples, 163; first, 105; second, 108, 110–112

Youngzhou province, 167

Yu, 194

Yu He: *Memorial on Calligraphy,* 243

Yu Jin, 182

Yu Shao: "Later Preface to the Family Genealogy of the Yu Line of Henan," 181–182

Yu Xin, 98

Yuan Hao, 111

Yuan Hong, 245

Yuan Shao, 33, 34

Yuan Shu, 33

Yuan dynasty, 256

Yue people, 17, 56, 129, 166–167

Yuhang, 254

Yungang caves, 104–105, 112, 207, 209–210

Yunnan province, 12, 151, 164

Yuwen Tai, 84

Yuwen tribe, 147

Zhang Daoling, 217

Zhang Heng, 89, 91

Zhang Hua: *A Treatise on Curiosities (Bo wu zhi),* 21

Zhang Lu, 35, 200, 218

Zhang Lun, 101–102

Zhang Xie, 235

Zhang Yong, 99

Zhao, Emperor, 29

Zhao Kuo, 123

Zhao Yi: *Against Cursive Script,* 242

Zhejiang, 219

Zhen Zhong, 220

Zhi Dun, 98, 205

Zhi Yu, 51

Zhong Hui, 41, 49, 221

Zhong Rong, 231–232, 233; *Rankings of Poetry (Shi pin),* 140, 142, 235

Zhongchang Tong, 96

Zhou Fu, 66

Zhou Yi, 26, 64

Zhou Yu, 57

Zhou dynasty, 25, 238

Zhuang, Emperor, 111

Zhuge Liang, 25–26

Zitong, 217

Zong Bing, 99–100

Zoroastrianism, 158, 166

Zuo Si, 51; "Three Capitals," 89–91